DOLMENS IN DENMARK

Architecture and Function

DOLMENS IN DENMARK
Architecture and Function

Palle Eriksen & Niels H. Andersen
with a contribution by Chris Scarre

RINGKØBING-SKJERN MUSEUM
ARKÆOLOGI VESTJYLLAND
MOESGAARD MUSEUM

JUTLAND ARCHAEOLOGICAL SOCIETY

DOLMENS IN DENMARK
Architecture and function

Layout: Louise Hilmar

Cover: Louise Hilmar
Cover illustration: Poskær Stenhus. Photo: Thomas Nykrog
Translation: Anne Bloch & David Earle Robinson, HSLS, Ebeltoft
Printed by: Narayana Press, Gylling
Bound by: Buchbinderei S.R. Büge
Paper: 135g Galerie Art Volume
Originally published as *Stendysser – Arkitektur og funktion*, 2014

Jutland Archaeological Society Publications vol. 95
ISBN 978-87-93423-07-7

Published by Jutland Archaelogical Society
in association with
Moesgaard Museum, Ringkøbing-Skjern Museum and Arkæologi Vestjylland
Distribution:
Aarhus University Press

MIX
Paper from responsible sources
FSC® C010651

Contents

Preface

On the edge of Mols Bjerge, just by the road between Agri and Knebel, stands Poskær Stenhus, Denmark's best known and most renowned dolmen. In 1995, we worked at Poskær Stenhus for a couple of days, surveying, recording and describing the monument as part of a project on dolmens in the Mols area. Reliable up-to-date ground plans and survey data are of course essential to any detailed study of dolmens. Precise ground plans are, however, rarely available for Danish dolmens and it is usually necessary to do the job yourself. Poskær Stenhus was no exception in this respect, as the most recent survey had been carried out more than a century earlier. Surveying and recording are not tedious tasks. On the contrary, they are enjoyable and productive activities which enable one to focus one's attention on a monument, "get under its skin" so to say, and really become acquainted with it. At the same time there is also the opportunity to speculate about and study any quirks and peculiarities. At Poskær Stenhus there were several notable aspects we discussed as we worked.

The idea for this book comes from those days spent at Poskær Stenhus in 1995. Back then we had no idea our work there would represent the first in a long series of site visits to, and surveys of, Danish dolmens, but a project "Dolmens without mounds – our oldest architecture" gradually began to take form.

Since then we have, when time permitted, embarked on several "dolmen tours" in Denmark. The Danish stock of scheduled dolmens numbers around 1800 monuments. Of these, less than 100 are well known to the general public, and these 100 members of the "old guard" appear time and again in national guides and on websites. Even so, they, and the other 1700 or so Danish dolmens, have largely been ignored in a research context. Perhaps this is because we Danes are so in awe of the dolmens and passage graves of Ireland and Brittany that we have undervalued our own representatives in misplaced modesty relative to these foreign monuments. Scheduled Danish dolmens actually hold an enormous potential, both with respect to public interest and research. A potential that lies virtually unexploited because studies carried out on dolmens to date have traditionally been based on early surveys, accounts and descriptions held in the archives of the National Museum of Denmark, with no inclusion of critical site visits and modern field survey data. This general inadequacy or lack of research arises from the fact that dolmens have not aroused the passion and interest of archaeologists to the same degree as the larger and more architecturally complex passage graves, which are rendered even more attractive by their rich content of flint axes, pottery etc. As for an appraisal of the general perception of the original appearance of dolmens, the results are really quite disheartening: Were their stone chambers originally covered by mounds, or were they – like so many of these monuments today – completely exposed with fully visible capstones? It is actually astonishing that we do not know – or are unsure about – the appearance of our earliest stone monuments in the Neolithic. One of the major aims here is to rectify this situation.

The main theme and subject of this book is "dolmens without mounds", because we believe dolmens did not originally have a mound that was intended to cover the stone chamber. The primary aim of our project – and therefore also of this book – was to investigate, illuminate and document the origin of dolmens, their original appearance and their possible step-wise transformation from simple stone cists placed, as at Barkær on Djursland, in elongate structures with or without a covering mound, to more complex dolmen chambers standing in isolation or in long or round barrows. This unambiguous architectonic objective means that many aspects relating to dolmens are only dealt with in passing or are not touched upon at all here: For example, the location of dolmens in the Neolithic landscape and their relationship to the large causewayed enclosures with their system ditches, as seen at Sarup, contemporary settlements and human sacrifices and other offerings.

The popular perception of a dolmen is of a monument with large conspicuous stones, standing fully exposed on top of a mound. This conception of the appearance of dolmens has become incorporated into Danish consciousness and is further reinforced by the iconic status of these monuments as being something particularly Danish; an aspect that is dealt with in the next chapter, *The Danish dolmen*. This is followed by a presentation of the relevant methods and research history, after which the Neolithic society that built the dolmens is described. Fourteen dolmens, one Scanian and 13 Danish, are then picked out as being of particular interest and rich in information with respect to the original appearance of these monuments. The 14 dolmens are described and analysed in a series of case studies. This is preceded by a more general appraisal of the architectural antecedents of these monuments, where wood was the building material employed, i.e. plank-built coffins within elongate enclosures, as first identified at the site of Barkær on the Djursland peninsula – hence the term Barkaer-structure (note the anglicised spelling of this general term). This is a structure like an unchambered long barrow, but it may contain wooden chambers and it may not have a mound. Plank coffins developed into stone cists, referred to here as dolmen cists, and these can also be found in Barkaer-structures. In some cases, dolmen cists were incorporated into long dolmens possessing a substantial amount of mound material. These latter monuments may also contain dolmen chambers of the earliest type, which developed from dolmen cists. From here, the link is made to the Gunderslevholm dolmen, another dolmen chamber of the earliest type that is not enclosed within a mound and stands fully exposed.

Although dolmens were built in Denmark in the early part of the Neolithic, in a period known as the Funnel Beaker culture, they are in no way an exclusively Danish phenomenon, as these structures are found all over the world. However, the earliest dolmens – such as the Danish examples – only occur in western and northwestern Europe. Professor Chris Scarre, of the University of Durham, England, gives an account of these in the chapter *Dolmens without mounds in Britain, France and Ireland.*

In an exemplary and thought-provoking way, this account puts Danish dolmens into perspective. In his analysis, Chris Scarre comments upon the fact that the impressive capstones were often exposed in prehistory, too. This perspective is further developed in a chapter on the capstones evident on Danish scheduled dolmens.

Although prominent and often scheduled dolmens form the basis of the present analysis, one must not forget the many damaged, destroyed and repeatedly ploughed-over dolmen sites. These may hold substantial and significant evidence relating to the earliest phases of these monuments and provide a wealth of finds and other information when subjected to modern archaeological excavation techniques. Examples of this are presented in the chapter *Dolmens without mounds in the Sarup area*, which reports and examines the results of three investigations, each involving the remains of several demolished dolmens and their relative development and context.

Before we pull together the various strands of evidence and present our conclusions, the chapter *The living and the dead* takes a critical look at the widespread perception – also held by some archaeologists – of dolmens as burial monuments for single individuals, chieftains perhaps. We arrive at a very different and far from unequivocal conclusion, as it is difficult to comprehend why, more than 5000 years ago, Neolithic people invested such enormous efforts and resources in the construction of dolmens. We are only now beginning to understand both the appearance and use of dolmens, and the mentality of the people and the society that created these impressive monuments which still fascinate us today and will continue to do so far into the future.

Acknowledgements

A number of institutions and individuals have helped to make this book possible in many respects: From excavations and investigations in the Sarup area (1), study trips (2), surveys and recording of the individual monuments and writing of the manuscript (3), production of the drawings (4), the layout and printing of the book (5) and the translation of the English edition (6). Many thanks are therefore due to Beckett-Fonden (3), Dronning Margrethe II's Arkæologiske Fond (2, 3), Farumgaard-Fonden (3), Flemming Elvin-Jensen (6), Gurli og Knud Pedersens Fond (6), Harboefonden (4), Jutland Archaeological Society (4, 5, 6), The Agency for Culture and Palaces (1, 3, 4, 5), Moesgaard Museum (1, 3), New Carlsberg Foundation (5), Rieck-Andersens Familiefond (6), Ringkøbing-Skjern Museum (3), The Danish Council of Museums (3) and VKRs Familiefond (1, 6).

Similarly, a large number of people and institutions have been asked for advice or assistance in various other ways and have willingly and patiently responded or loaned out material free of charge. Many landowners have kindly and interestedly allowed us access, time and again, to their property, regardless of whether the dolmen we were interested in stood far out in the middle of a field, deep in a forest or in a garden, or whether, as at Sarup, we would excavate there for many years. They are all due our heartfelt thanks.

1. The Danish dolmen

A dolmen, often perched on top of a mound, is one of the most iconic and oft-used symbols of Danishness. Time and again, in cartoons and the like focussing on the special quirks and peculiarities of Denmark and the Danish character, we see the dolmen's characteristic appearance and profile: Three or four large stones supporting an even larger stone – the capstone.

Dolmens are also a popular motif sculpturally, as they are physically simple, but nevertheless rather droll and interesting, and an impressive effect is created simply by placing one large stone on top of three smaller ones, regardless of whether or not any deeper significance is involved. These new, modern dolmens are, as a rule, of modest size in relation to the genuine article from the Neolithic. On the other hand, large numbers of them are found scattered across the country and new examples are continually being added.

It is rather surprising that these more than 5000-year-old monuments have become a Danish national icon on a par with the Danish flag, Dannebrog, and the Little Mermaid – incidentally also seated on a dolmen – because Neolithic dolmens are not something specifically and exclusively Danish. Large numbers are also found in Germany, Poland, France, Spain, Portugal, England, Wales and Ireland. Dolmens also occur outside Europe, for example in Jordan, Indonesia, Korea and India.[1] Some of these have, in all seriousness, been constructed as burial monuments in modern times.

Dolmens are actually a global phenomenon, so why has the Danish dolmen become something special, and when did this happen?

National Romanticism

Very precise answers can be given to the above questions. To do this we have to go back two centuries, to the first decades of the 19th century, when Danish national sentiment, identity and love of the fatherland became aroused as a consequence of the restless pan-European political and spiritual currents of the time. Specifically in Denmark, this burgeoning nationalism was well-nourished by the humiliation of the English Wars, when the Danish fleet was lost following the bombardment of Copenhagen in 1807. Then Denmark was forced to hand over Norway to Sweden in 1814 after, as extra salt rubbed into the wound, having to endure state bankruptcy in 1813.

Poems such as Adam Oehlenschläger's *Guldhornene* – The Golden Horns, from 1803, and N.F.S. Grundtvig's *Gunderslev Skov* – Gunderslev Wood, from 1808, conjured up a vision of faded, musty, moss-covered prehistory and celebrated it in glorifying phrases, almost with awe and veneration, so the hard-pressed Danes could block out the painful present. The spiritual inspiration came from Germany, borne to Copenhagen in 1802 by the natural philosopher Henrik Steffens, who had become acquainted with German Romanticism and natural philosophy in Jena. The zeitgeist was all about romantic, sensitive souls pondering, wondering and dreaming about a long-lost time and wishing themselves back there. As Ancient Rome and Greece had been reborn in the Renaissance, Nordic prehistory was now rediscovered and revitalised, clad in a new guise. N.F.S. Grundtvig's three books on Nordic mythology from 1808-11 were also typical of the time and were crucial to the growing interest in a Nordic past.[2] People felt a direct connection to the mighty warriors and noble shield-maidens of the sagas and Eddic poems who, in their time, had performed heroic deeds of great valour.

Artists were rather slow in discovering and catching on to this new trend. Probably because they were still being sent to Rome to paint and study under southern skies among the ancient classical buildings, and the fact that the obligatory Scandinavian historical painting lay over them like a thick, heavy blanket.

The person primarily responsible for turning the minds and motifs of Danish painters was N.L. Høyen, Denmark's first art historian. At that time, most Danish artists were trained at the Royal Danish Academy of Fine Arts in Copenhagen. In addition to toiling away at their drawing, painting and modelling, they also attended edifying lectures on European art history. These had previously concentrated on Classical Antiquity, the Renaissance and the Baroque, but in N.L. Høyen's lectures, during the late 1830s, attention became exclusively focussed on portraying Denmark and the Danes in their broadest sense: landscape, historical monuments, daily life and people.

The artists who were active in the first half of the 18th century, later referred to as the painters of the Golden Age, enthusiastically took up the challenge, with major consequences for Danish landscape painting. These changes were perhaps already in the air, but now they were adopted consistently with fresh eyes and new brushes, notably by painters such as P.C. Skovgaard, Dankvart Dreyer and J.Th. Lundbye. The Golden Age painters sought their motifs across Denmark – J.Th. Lundbye looked predominantly to his beloved western Zealand – and they enthusiastically portrayed the burial mounds and dolmens scattered across the landscape.[3] In the process, they helped build up an historical awareness in the Danish national consciousness and soul. "To paint dearest Denmark" was J.Th. Lundbye's primary goal, and it was this artist's drawings and paintings, by virtue of their originality and freshness, that proved particularly central to national romantic perception in Denmark.

Historic monuments and buildings, such as castles, strongholds, churches, burial mounds and, not least, dolmens, played a special role in the paintings of romantic nationalism. Their very location in the landscape, often idealised by artists, constituted a demonstration of the Danes' affinity with an ancient right and title to the land and was, at the same time, also a reminder of a glorious past.

A prehistoric burial mound at Raklev on Refsnæs

The best-known of the Golden Age artists' paintings of dolmens – and justifiably so – is J.Th. Lundbye's *En gravhøj fra oldtiden ved Raklev på Refsnæs* – A Prehistoric Burial Mound at Raklev on Refsnæs, painted in 1839 (fig. 1.1). It is now on display in the Thorvaldsen Museum, in the same room as his *Landskab ved Arresø* – Landscape at Arresø, from 1838, a major work in Danish art. The painting of Arresø also features a megalithic tomb – albeit very badly damaged – in the foreground, but this does not have the same dominant role as the Raklev dolmen on the painting from Refsnæs. Raklev is now virtually a suburb of Kalundborg, but back then it was a separate village. The dolmen still stands there today, just east of the church on the opposite side of the road, and easily recognisable from the characteristic shape of its capstone (see fig. 19.2a). But the landscape around it has changed completely since J.Th. Lundbye's time. There is no longer an open view out across Kalundborg Fjord, as the monument is now screened by trees, bushes and buildings. Moreover, it may be that the landscape in 1839 was perhaps not quite as J.Th. Lundbye painted it. He may well have rearranged it when he converted his sketches into the finished painting at his home in Copenhagen.

In order fully to understand the painting, and J.Th. Lundbye's inspired composition and arrangement, it is useful to go a further 30 years back in time. In 1807, the Romantic German painter Caspar David Friedrich had produced his fascinating and

Fig. 1.1. "En gravhøj fra oldtiden ved Raklev på Refsnæs" *by Johan Thomas Lundbye, 1839.*

Fig. 1.2. "Hünengrab im Schnee" *by Caspar David Friedrich, 1807.*

intriguing painting *Hünengrab im Schnee* – Dolmen in Snow, one of the first paintings – perhaps even the very first – in which a dolmen forms the central motif (fig. 1.2). The dolmen stands elevated on the central axis of the painting in a bitterly cold, snow-clad, wooded landscape. Three large oak trees intertwine their network of branches and twigs and encompass the megalithic tomb in a complex, enthralling decorative web.

On the face of it, this is a simple, objective depiction of a dolmen in a wood in winter. Nevertheless, the picture – like all good art – exerts a strange compelling effect, because on closer examination it is found to be so much more than a simple depiction of an ancient monument among some trees. The two oak trees in the foreground, with their severed branches and lopped off crowns, signal a greater but amputated past, when the harmless dolmen was an elevated shrine that was not locked away in a cold, mystified, desolate world.

A Norwegian, J.C. Dahl, was responsible for introducing German Romantic landscape painting to the Danish art scene. After frequenting the Royal Danish Academy of Fine Arts in Copenhagen, J.C. Dahl went to live in Dresden in 1818. At that time, the city was the centre of German Romanticism, and landscape painting, which occupied J.C. Dahl totally and absolutely, was much more in focus and far more developed here than in the Danish capital further north. Moreover, Dresden was where Caspar David Friedrich lived and worked, and his paintings – including *Hünengrab im Schnee* – greatly influenced J.C. Dahl.

In Dresden in the late 1820s, J.C. Dahl created some paintings featuring Danish dolmens that are very closely related to Caspar David Friedrich's *Hünengrab*. In one enormous work, more than 2 m in length, *Vinterlandskab ved Vordingborg* – Winter Landscape near Vordingborg, from 1829, the influence of Friedrich's painting is clearly evident (fig. 1.3). The same cold winter landscape with the picturesque, rather stunted oak trees, one of which has long since been felled and taken away – sic transit gloria mundi – that obscure and shut-in the dolmen. A new feature relative to Caspar David Friedrich's painting is that the dolmen has been shifted to the left, away from the central axis, out of the wood and into the open countryside. This makes room to portray the landscape, populated in a slightly clichéd way with a hunter and his dog and a couple of solitary cottages.[4]

With his painting *En gravhøj fra oldtiden ved Raklev på Refsnæs*, J.Th. Lundbye abandons Caspar David Friedrich and J.C. Dahl's oak-tree screen around the dolmen and replaces icy winter with warm, temperate summer. He emphasises the dolmen's

Fig. 1.3. "Vinterlandskab ved Vordingborg" *by Johan Christian Dahl, 1829.*

Fig. 1.4. *On J.F. Willumsen's monument to Viggo Hørup, erected in 1908 in Rosenborg Castle Gardens in Copenhagen, one of the reliefs on the base features a dolmen.*

Fig. 1.5. *A monument was erected in Haderslev Dampark in 1927 in memory of the town's Danish-oriented soldiers who fell in German service during the First World War. The dolmen on top of the monument underlines their links with Denmark.*

monumentality by moving it closer to the observer and, in silhouette, allows it to dominate the picture completely. The dolmen is demystified, but new signals are introduced instead. The setting is open Danish agricultural land, sloping down towards the sea and the fjord, both characteristic elements of the Danish landscape, with its deep time horizon reflected by the ancient monument.

Fig. 1.6. *A dolmen was erected in 1920 on the top of a large burial mound at Vejrum, just next to the main road between Holstebro and Struer, to celebrate Danish reunification. The man responsible was local schoolteacher Chr.E. Rauff.*

The painting became incredibly popular and it is found today in the form of innumerable copies, reproductions and imitations. From then on, a dolmen standing on top of a burial mound, seen in profile against the sky with the capstone starkly outlined, became the standard image of the Danish dolmen, and has since been depicted in this way time and again.

Dolmens become national treasures

J.Th. Lundbye preferred most of all to draw, and his drawings were more known during his lifetime than his paintings. These works, some illustrating dolmens, became widely distributed among the population, not least when they appeared in almanacs, a kind of contemporary pocket diary containing edifying reading matter. Moreover, J.J.A. Worsaae's popular book on Danish prehistory *Danmarks Oldtid oplyst ved Oldsager og Gravhøie* from 1843 was illustrated with J.Th. Lundbye's drawings, including the title page.

J.Th. Lundbye was not alone in painting and drawing dolmens, and "dolmen-mania" intensified over time as the fatherland became increasingly hard pressed, notably after the loss of Schleswig-Holstein to Germany in 1864. An interplay between an atmosphere of defeat and patriotic fervour, democratisation following the adoption of the Danish Constitution in 1849, burgeoning political awareness and education of the peasantry, folk high-schools, the cooperative movement and so on, required symbols that unified and forged an identity, thereby demonstrating Denmark's ancient entitlement and links with prehistory – the country's very "raison

Fig. 1.7. "Gravhøj" *by Maja Lisa Engelhardt, 2001.*

d'être". Dolmens of all kinds were well-suited to this purpose. There is a dolmen on the Danish poet Holger Drachmann's grave on Grenen at Skagen – he died in 1908. A dolmen is also depicted, together with a ploughman, on the base of J.F. Willumsen's monument to the Danish politician Viggo Hørup, erected in 1908 in Rosenborg Castle Gardens in Copenhagen (fig. 1.4). As part of celebrations of the reunification of Denmark in 1920, several memorial dolmens were erected around the country, including examples at Brundby on the island of Samsø, at Ringkøbing and on a burial mound at Vejrum, south of Struer (fig. 1.6).[5]

When the people of Haderslev wished to commemorate the Danish-oriented men who fell in German military service during the First World War, their names were inscribed on a large plinth topped by an impressive memorial dolmen. The monument was erected in Haderslev Dampark in 1927 (fig. 1.5).[6] On Bornholm, a memorial dolmen to the island's fallen sons during the Second Schleswig War of 1864 was erected in Almindingen in 1938.

In comparison, around 370 memorial stones were erected between 1945 and 1955 to celebrate the liberation of Denmark after the Second World War, but only a few of these took the form of dolmens.[7] This declining trend – fewer and fewer dolmens in public spaces – has continued ever since. On the other hand, innumerable decorative dolmens have been erected in Denmark, standing in their hundreds in private gardens across the country. One of the oldest, probably from around 1860, stands in the garden of Ørnslund on Samsø.[8]

Dolmens are today an integral symbol of Danishness, helped along over the years by illustrations in school history books, on bank notes, on stamps and on souvenirs, providing a reference for newspaper illustrators and cartoonists. Today, many adults' efforts to draw and paint dolmens would be judged as kitsch, as the original gravity and significance of portraying our oldest monuments has been forgotten. But all is not lost. Dolmens can, as Maja Lisa Engelhardt's images, with their inherent mystery clearly demonstrate, still inspire new and intriguing art that one never tires of looking at and reflecting upon (fig. 1.7).[9]

2. With or without a mound

As mentioned in the preface, the seed for this book was sown on the edge of Mols Bjerge, between Agri and Knebel, at the dolmen Poskær Stenhus (fig. 2.1 and photos on pages 6 and 20).[1] Its dolmen chamber consists of five large stones, on which rests a mighty capstone weighing rather more than 16 tonnes.[2] The chamber, which has an area of 5 m^2, has a hexagonal ground plan when the opening to the passage is included. The latter is marked outside the chamber by two stones, one on each side. The chamber forms part of a round dolmen, as 23 large kerbstones are arranged around it, forming a circle with a diameter of 15.5 m. Originally there were 24 kerbstones, but one was removed in the mid-19th century before the dolmen was scheduled in 1860.

Poskær Stenhus' renown is due to several factors, not least the impressive size of its stones, several as tall as a man and some even higher, which reinforces the monumentality and experience value of this dolmen and gives it a striking and imposing appearance. This is further augmented, viewed from the Agri side, by the monument's location in a rolling, hilly Golden Age landscape.

One of the remarkable features of Poskær Stenhus is the low level of the internal surface between the kerbstones and the chamber, where there is so little fill that all the dolmen's stones are freely exposed and stand tall. This is remarkable because many other well-preserved dolmens have a large amount of so-called mound material between their kerbstones and chamber (fig. 2.2). This fill may even form a slight dome shape, extending from the upper part of the kerbstones to the top of the chamber orthostats and the lower surface of the capstone. A round dolmen of this type, with a large amount of mound fill and a chamber corresponding to that of Poskær Stenhus, lies only a couple of kilometres away at Grovlegård, between Agri and Vrinners. Even though these two dolmens were built at the same time and are further related in that their capstones constitute two halves of one and the same stone, they are nevertheless very different.[3] Why is this?

The widely accepted explanation was, until recently, summarised on an information board at Poskær Stenhus, and can also be found in many books and on numerous websites dealing with dolmens (fig. 2.3). The board stated that the dolmen originally had a mound, the surface of which extended from the top of the kerbstones and up to the capstone, which was perhaps completely concealed. But stones and earth were subsequently dug away and removed, after which natural erosion reduced and levelled out the mound fill, giving the dolmen its present appearance, with a very low internal surface and exposed stones. Dolmens like Poskær Stenhus, with very little mound material, are referred to here as dolmens without mounds or open dolmens, while those with abundant mound material are termed dolmens with mounds. In 1995, this explanation, termed here the "dolmens with mounds theory" or "erosion

Fig. 2.1. *The interior of the round dolmen Poskær Stenhus has so little mound material that a large proportion of the stones is visible. Seen from outside, the appearance of the kerbstones was once even more monumental and impressive, but in 1943 earth was laid up against them to prevent them from toppling over.*

Fig. 2.2. *The long dolmen in Halskov Vænge on Falster is a good example of a dolmen with a large amount of mound fill. One half of the monument was restored in 1976. Note the stacked slabs that, as dry-walling, fill out the gaps between the large stones.*

theory", was widely and generally accepted by most archaeologists (fig. 2.4). In the previous year, a scheduled round dolmen at Tustrup, northern Djursland, with a low, flat interior very like that of Poskær Stenhus, had been filled up with soil to show visitors what a proper Danish dolmen originally looked like.

When we began our survey of Poskær Stenhus in 1995, we had no particular opinion about the monument's low internal surface. But gradually the questions emerged.

What happened to the missing mound material? How could the entrance have been kept clear if there had been a mound of this type? If the mound was intended to cover the capstone, why were such massive, monumental capstones, which would be difficult to conceal, chosen for so many dolmens?

Only 4 km from Poskær Stenhus, just north of Strands, stands another dolmen with a similar chamber. It is called Stenhus and it has a unique location in the landscape: Stenhus stands on the top of a small, round, steep-sided hill, and it is very difficult to imagine that this dolmen has ever been covered by a mound. Was it possible that these two dolmens – Poskær Stenhus and Stenhus at Strands – had much the same appearance in the Neolithic as they do today? The erosion theory was perhaps not so robust after all and could be challenged, and clearly not all dolmens could be made to fit with the theory's stages of destruction and decay.

A new awareness of some dolmens without mounds as relatively undamaged monuments shows that the very diverse appearance of dolmens today is not simply a consequence of better or poorer preservation. It could also be due to the fact that these monument actually differed in appearance from the time when they were built and used, after which they were perhaps altered and adapted before finally being abandoned.

The erosion theory has a further weakness in that it is unable to explain why there are so many apparently eroded dolmens in contrast to the slightly later passage graves, the mounds of which are so often intact. We would expect these passage graves to have been exposed to the same degree of degradation as the earlier dolmens.

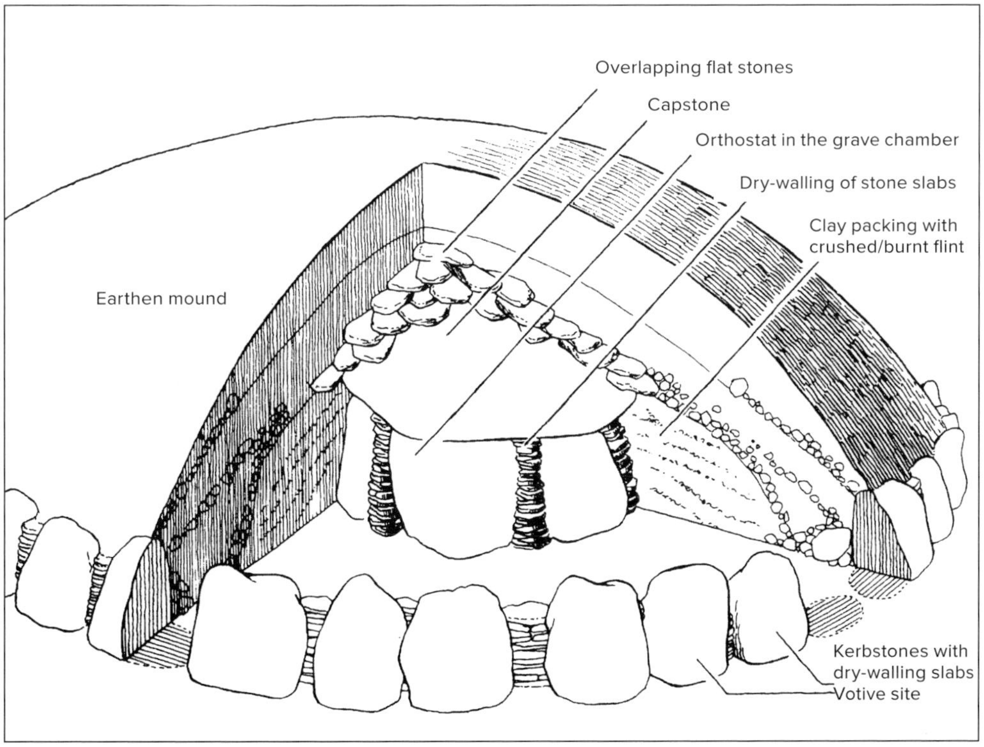

Fig. 2.3. *For many years, an information board stood at Poskær Stenhus with this drawing accompanied by the text: "Reconstruction of the original appearance of the round dolmen before destruction of the dry-walling between the kerbstones and removal of the earthen mound, which perhaps enclosed the entire grave chamber. The grave chamber was therefore not as it appears today – open and accessible, but was very probably only opened for new burials and during offerings to the deceased and to the gods."*

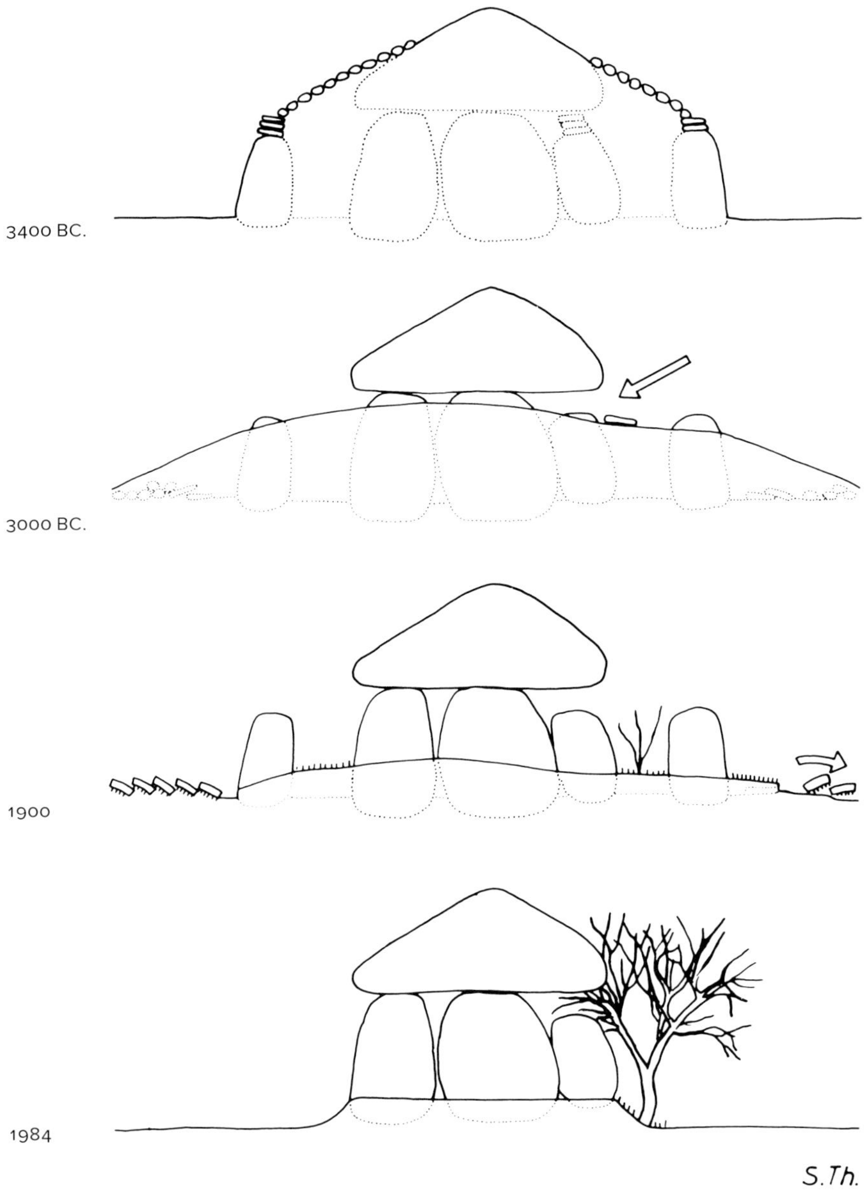

Fig. 2.4. *The erosion theory illustrated by four sections through the same dolmen monument. Uppermost, the newly constructed monument in the Neolithic with the capstone almost completely hidden within the mound. Over the subsequent millennia, wind and weather erode the mound material, which moves steadily outwards and then, after ploughing and removal of the kerbstones, only the chamber remains.*

Viewed in the light of the dolmens without mounds theory, many otherwise inexplicable pieces of evidence fall into place. The theory also explains why dolmen chambers have almost always been visible, while those of the passage graves lie well concealed within their associated mound. Only destruction and erosion can expose the stones of the passage graves to the light of day, as demonstrated by the scheduled examples of these monuments on Samsø.[4]

Before we continue down the exciting new paths that the dolmens without mounds theory opens up for us, it would be interesting to take a closer look at the status of research into the original appearance of Danish dolmens.

Guide to dolmens

As yet there are no guide books or websites in Danish that focus exclusively on dolmens. The best known dolmens are mentioned in general ancient monuments guides such as *Fortidsminder i Danmark* by Henning Dehn-Nielsen, *Vejviser til Danmarks Oldtid* by Ingrid Falktoft Andersen, *Danmarks Oldtid* by Karsten Kjer Michaelsen and, of course, the very first in this genre *Med Arkæologen Danmark rundt*, in the early series of *Politikens håndbøger.* Many less well-known dolmens that are also absolutely worth seeing, including several mentioned in this book, are not featured in these guides.

On the internet there is the Danish Agency for Culture and Palace's website *Fund og Fortidsminder* – Sites and Monuments, which lists all recorded dolmens and shows their map locations. Sites and Monuments is based on the Danish National Museum's more than two centuries of recording and excavation activities. The database can be searched by map, place name, municipality, scheduled and unscheduled monuments etc. It contains information on almost 170,000 localities, of which 33,000 are scheduled ancient monuments. Under the heading *Undersøgelseshistorie* – Research history – there is a description of each individual monument from the district field surveys, which began in 1874 and have continued up the present day. In some fortunate cases, early drawings are reproduced.

Each ancient monument – including dolmens – has its own record number, referred to in this book is as its *F&F* – i.e. Sites and Monuments – number. The number for Poskær Stenhus is 140507-15, where the first six digits represent the site number (*stednummer*), which identifies the relevant (pre-1971) county, district and parish. The number for Poskær Stenhus reveals that the dolmen lies in Randers county (14), Mols district (05) and Knebel parish (07). The final number (15), after the hyphen, is the monument's number in the parish, referred to as the parish record number (*sognebeskrivelsesnummer*). Precise locations for the individual dolmens are not given here, but at the first mention of a dolmen in the text, a broad reference is made to its location. Help is though at hand in the book's site index, which includes the *F&F* numbers for all the mentioned scheduled Danish ancient monuments and thereby provides access to their precise locations.

It would be useful to be able to search by site number in the Sites and Monuments database, but this is not possible in the public access version. However, if the *F&F* number – for example that for Poskær Stenhus – is entered into Google – possibly accompanied by *Lokalitet* – Locality, one of the first links to be shown will be "Paaskjær Stenhus – Lokalitet", from where a single click leads directly to information on the dolmen held in Sites and Monuments. Should this not function, it is possible to try the more laborious: www.kulturarv.dk/fundogfortidsminder/Lokalitet/140507-15.

It is then possible to find the site reference and other information on an individual dolmen by entering its *F&F* number.

The long dolmen Tingstedet on Ærø, as shown in the Danish Sites and Monuments database. From this view it is possible to click further and obtain information on the monument's research history or see pictures.

3. Research history

Even though there are three times as many surviving dolmens as passage graves in Denmark, by far the greatest number of archaeological investigations undertaken over the years have been of the latter. This is largely due to the considerable numbers of artefacts that are to be found in passage graves, whereas the finds in the much smaller dolmen chambers are generally more modest. Moreover, the architecturally more complex passage graves have tempted and attracted archaeologists and other excavators to a much greater degree. This disparity in the intensity of investigations of dolmens and passage graves has continued into recent decades and even up to the present day, when archaeological investigations of scheduled megalithic tombs are carried out almost exclusively in connection with restoration work. The passage graves, with their large chambers, long passages and special architecture, have a much greater and more urgent requirement for repairs and maintenance than the simpler dolmens.[1]

In investigations of both dolmens and passage graves, focus has previously been directed specifically towards chambers and passages. The complete excavation of a passage grave at Mejls near Varde in 1901 by G.V. Blom of the Danish National Museum was an isolated phenomenon, performed long before the attention of archaeologists became directed towards the *whole* monument.[2] In the 1930s, the Dutch archaeologist Albert van Giffen also began to investigate the mounds associated with these monuments, and it was in his excavations that the first excavated sections through a passage-grave mound were recorded.[3] Sections are vertical surfaces, i.e. "trench sides", in archaeological excavations and positioned appropriately they can reveal the layers formed during and after the construction of the mound and enable study of its phases and numerous other details and relations. This was obviously a very informative and productive development and it represented a huge scientific step forward. Today, sectioning is standard procedure in any investigation of a dolmen or passage grave.

After the Second World War, a new generation of archaeologists emerged in Denmark who similarly introduced a holistic approach to the investigation of ancient monuments, including the use of excavated sections. Investigations also became more painstaking, and consequently more time consuming, as they involved the recording of pits, stone traces, postholes and other structural features exposed on the excavated surfaces. The rapid excavations of early times were definitely passé. In 1935, Therkel Mathiassen of the Danish National Museum spent only eight days in the Ringkøbing area investigating the Ølstrup complex's three long dolmens, with a total of four dolmen chambers, as well as two inhumation graves and a small round barrow from Single Grave times.[4] In the early 1960s, two long barrows covered by saltmarsh peat deposits – Abterp at Bredbro in South Jutland – containing a total of four small passage grave chambers – were investigated and restored by Olfert Voss of the Danish National Museum (fig. 3.1). The investigation, including restoration of

Fig. 3.1. *The two long dolmens at Abterp were covered by saltmarsh and peat deposits. The excavation in progress in 1962.*

the two long dolmens, extended over more than six months in total.[5] Today, excavation and recording techniques have become ever more refined: An investigation by one of the present authors, Niels H. Andersen, Moesgaard Museum, of a demolished passage grave at Damsbo on southwestern Funen in 2006-2008 lasted a total of 20 months. The increased time expenditure reflects the fact that archaeologists have become more careful and meticulous in their work, gathering greater amounts of data. Systematic, targeted investigations and post-excavation analyses provide more and more information on the sites and structures that are examined.

How then, over the years, have Danish archaeologists imagined the original appearance of dolmens in the Neolithic? The main trends in this respect are evident from various published overviews of Danish prehistory.

The first of its kind was J.J.A. Worsaae's *Danmarks Oldtid oplyst ved Oldsager og Gravhøie* from 1843: "A large number of these [dolmen] chambers have previously been excavated and investigated, probably mostly by people who hope to find great treasures in them. They therefore very often stand open, but at first they were undoubtedly covered with earth, though only such that a part of the capstone was visible. Of this kind, not even a few survive."[6]

The next overview, *Vor Oldtid* by Sophus Müller, was published 50 or so years later in 1897 – a book of 714 pages. J.J.A. Worsaae's work had only 124, and the almost 600-page difference reflects the massive developments that had taken place in archaeology in the intervening years, and not least in research into dolmens, passage graves and barrows. Moreover, since 1872, archaeologists from the Danish National Museum had travelled around the country, recording ancient monuments in all the country's parishes, an endeavour that was first completed in 1934. This great recording campaign is known as the *herredsrejser* – district surveys.[7] The documentary record that resulted from these district surveys is popularly referred to as the *sognebeskrivelse* – parish record, and today constitutes the nucleus of the archaeological database *Fund og Fortidsminder* – Sites and Monuments (www.fundogfortidsminder.dk). Sophus Müller himself was one of the most diligent and skilled of these "recorders" and had well-developed observational skills. In 1897 he wrote: "The dolmen [dolmen chamber] was always surrounded by a mound of earth and stone, which served to strengthen the construction and secure it against external disturbance … It is, however, characteristic of all the four-, five- and six-sided chambers, which are our sole concern here, that the capstone is not earth-covered; often the earthen mound does not even reach the top of the orthostats, but allows them to protrude by 1-2' [31-63 cm]. That the earth has not been dug away in later times, and that it was originally the intention for the capstone to be freely exposed and visible, is clearly apparent alone from the latter's form. It is namely most commonly a very high, thick, domed stone, much more massive than is necessary simply to cover the grave – the placing of such a boulder high up on top of other stones must have been seen as an endeavour in honour of the deceased and there was no sense in immediately covering completely it with earth … Sometimes, however, chambers of this type do occur completely concealed by a mound; but it has almost always been possible to demonstrate that most of this mound was added in a later period, in the Bronze Age …"[8]

A third overview was written by Hans Kjær, a curator at the Danish National Museum, who had undertaken numerous excavations and was also an experienced recorder. His book *Vor Oldtids Mindesmærker* was published in 1925 and in this he writes: "If a chamber of this kind stands quite open, the orthostats will only be able to withstand the pressure from the capstone for a time. They will collapse outwards. A counter pressure has to be established, and this was accomplished by laying a broad packing of head-sized stones and earth up around the sides of the chamber, forming a small, flat mound around the chamber, as a rule though such that the mound only covered the actual chamber, leaving the capstone, or most of it, exposed and visible, like a monument. … These chambers are, with their often massive capstone, notably when they have come to stand exposed over the course of time, our most monumental of ancient monuments."[9] Like Sophus Müller, Hans Kjær believed that if the capstone is completely earth-covered, this is because a barrow had been built on top of it, but otherwise he does not express himself as clearly as his predecessor.

In 1938, Johannes Brøndsted, in his great work *Danmarks Oldtid*, stated the following about dolmen chambers and their associated mounds: "Even though the dolmen, by virtue of its origin as a stone-fenced earth grave, is sometimes subterranean, covered by flat ground or a modest mound, it is the rule, and more so the larger the dolmen chamber, that the massive, domed capstone was exposed and widely visible. ... Given that the origin of the dolmen chamber is from the earth grave, it seems very likely that the chamber of the round dolmen was often completely covered by the earthen mound, but on the other hand it must be assumed that the large, massive chambers, often the height of a man inside, which are often crowned by a high, domed capstone, were partially exposed, such that the surrounding earthen mound ... extended some way up the capstone ... Not infrequently, the long dolmen's sometimes very considerable earthen mound covered the chamber completely, or concealed it such that now, where the removed chamber had stood, there is a deep hole in the top of the earthen mound. Often though, the earthen mound is quite low or completely absent."[10] It seems that Johannes Brøndsted holds rather an equivocal view, covering the entire spectrum from dolmen chambers with no surrounding mound whatever, to completely mound-covered monuments. He explains the earth-covered chambers as being the result of a development from subterranean earth graves to stone-set dolmen chambers placed on the soil surface. It is, however, important that Johannes Brøndsted recognises the existence of long dolmens without any mound material whatsoever, and that the capstones over the large dolmen chambers were exposed and widely visible.

Four years later, in 1942, P.V. Glob's *Danske Oldtidsminder* was published. Glob was clearly in no doubt as to the original appearance of dolmens with a polygonal chamber (see chapter 5). After a photo of Poskær Stenhus, where the free-standing kerbstones and the capstone are seen in silhouette against the sky, he writes: "These later and more complicated grave structures often lie exposed, merely concealed by an earthen mound around their foot. Together with the surrounding kerbstones, which can stand as high as a man, the chamber forms an architectonic entity of great beauty when the monument has stood untouched since prehistory. This effect was to a great degree deliberate."[11] This is the same view that Sophus Müller expressed almost 50 years earlier. P.V. Glob, like Sophus Müller and Hans Kjær before him, was well acquainted with Denmark's ancient monuments through countless official site visits carried out for the Danish National Museum in connection with the scheduling of ancient monuments. These were prompted by the passing of a new nature protection act in 1937, whereby all Denmark's unscheduled but interesting and, in landscape terms, valuable ancient monuments were scheduled at a stroke. However, at the same time, the National Museum's archaeologists were given the task of revisiting all the country's parishes in order to determine which monuments fell into this particular category. This was an enormous task which, it was estimated, would take 20 years; it was completed in 1957.[12]

Whereas archaeologists mainly saw the kerbstones around the monument as a purely practical measure, intended to retain the packing and mound and delimit the dolmen relative to its surroundings, there was much more scope for an imaginative interpretation when writers of fiction took the floor. Martin A. Hansen was, as

Fig. 3.2. *Martin A. Hansen's* Orm og Tyr *was illustrated with woodcuts by Sven Havsteen-Mikkelsen. The Vielsted dolmen is shown here.*

a native of Zealand, very familiar with dolmens and in his book *Orm og Tyr* from 1952, he let his imagination run riot: "The Vilsted dolmen lies in central Zealand, at the northwestern end of the lake Gyrstinge Sø, by boggy terrain, a desolate place at dusk on a winter's day, when the last lapwing flock of the year alights like an apparition over the bog, and the corn bunting in the tree over the dolmen once more bemoans its desperate lot. This is one of the country's most beautiful round dolmens. About the low mound stands a garland of massive stones, nineteen in all ... The stones form a circle, a ring around the low mound, hence the name round dolmen. They were the fence around the temple, the sacred ground. It does not seem that a fence like this could shepherd either animals or people. One must understand that in antiquity this fence was just as dangerous as a high-voltage cable. If anyone approached too close at the wrong moment. People could die as a result ... The deterrent power lay in the fence stones, and only with the aid of magical rites could someone enter the temple, where the deity lived in the great capstone, the sacred." (fig. 3.2 and photo on page 38).[13]

With Sophus Müller and P.V. Glob's observations, Martin A. Hansen's pithy description and Poul Kjærum's investigations of the two Tustrup dolmens on northern Djursland in the 1950s (see chapters 16 and 17), which were not earth-covered in antiquity, one would have thought that it was generally accepted in archaeological circles that dolmens could also originally, in the Neolithic, have had the appearance of exposed structures.

But in 1984, Sven Thorsen of the then National Agency for the Protection of Nature, Monuments and Sites, who was engaged in the restoration and maintenance of megalithic tombs, presented his view of the degradation of the mounds by erosion (see fig. 2.4): "The function of the mound was to cover the chamber, and the kerbstones were intended to hold the mound together." There then follows a description of the process of decay as the dry-walling and the kerbstones collapse, and part of the mound fill slips outwards. Finally, the conclusion is reached that: "The long dolmens must originally have almost had the form of a house. The kerbstones and dry-walling formed the walls, and the mound fill formed a roof-like mound that enclosed the entire chamber. In certain instances, it can be further documented that the surface of the mound was covered by a layer of stones, so the entire structure appeared as a mighty house-shaped block of stone. Round dolmens must similarly have resembled round stone houses. – The houses of the dead!"[14]

In the 1980s and subsequently, the erosion theory had several adherents among prominent Danish archaeologists.[15] In a figure caption for a photo of Poskær Stenhus, Jørgen Jensen wrote in 1988: "But the dolmen chambers of the Neolithic were not exposed, they were covered with earth."[16] As a logical consequence of all this, the aforementioned mound-less Tustrup round dolmen was, in 1994, given new dry-walling, filled up with earth and fitted with a capstone in order to show the appearance of a proper Danish dolmen in the Neolithic (figs. 3.3 and 3.4).[17]

A shift had apparently taken place in the general perception of the original appearance of dolmens. Forgotten were Sophus Müller and P.V. Glob's arguments in favour of open dolmens, at least with regard to the later examples of these monuments. So when the present authors wrote an article in *Skalk* in 1996 on "Dysser uden høje" – Dolmens

Fig. 3.3. *Following the investigation in 1956, the round dolmen at Tustrup was restored by toppled kerbstones being righted, but otherwise it appeared as it had prior to the excavation. On each side of the outwardly-toppled kerbstone, which could not be righted due to a furrow carved in it, there is a missing kerbstone.*

Fig. 3.4. *In 1994, the appearance of the Tustrup round dolmen was completely altered in order to show how – according to its restorer – it had originally appeared in the Neolithic.*

without mounds, we stood more or less in opposition to all Danish archaeologists who, at that time, held an opinion about dolmens – with the exception of a small handful, including Harald Andersen, the editor of *Skalk*. Andersen, a former recorder and a great dolmen expert who had known both P.V. Glob and Martin A. Hansen, could not understand archaeologists who were opponents of the theory about dolmens without mounds. He made reference to several open dolmens on Zealand, including the Gunderslevholm dolmen and to Martin A. Hansen's description in *Orm og Tyr*.

The dolmens without mounds theory was further elaborated in Palle Eriksen's book on Poskær Stenhus in 1999 and consequently won support from archaeologists such as Jørgen Jensen, in the Neolithic volume of his major work *Danmarks Oldtid* from 2001, and in Nina Nielsen's article from 2003 on the free-standing Ormslev dolmen west of Aarhus.[18] One of the present authors, Niels H. Andersen, has, in research investigations of demolished dolmen sites in the Sarup area in southwestern Funen carried out since 1984, also made several observations, which show that some of the dolmens investigated could not have had mounds (see chapter 20). Moreover, we have, on several occasions, commented in print on the reconstruction of the round dolmen at Tustrup and recommended that it be returned to the form it had prior to 1994.[19] Despite all this, adherents of the dolmens with mounds theory expressed views as late as 2009 and 2013 that both the Gunderslevholm dolmen (see chapter 11) and the round dolmen at Tustrup (see chapter 17) were originally covered by mounds such that perhaps only the upper part of the capstones was visible.[20]

4. Dolmens and the people of the Neolithic

Until around 4000 BC, people in Denmark lived predominantly by hunting and fishing. Archaeologists refer to the time of these hunters as the Mesolithic. The period is divided up into a number of sub-periods and cultures, the latest of which is known as the Ertebølle culture (5200-3900 BC), named after a large kitchen midden by the Limfjord. During the Ertebølle culture, the land was covered by primeval forest, which had developed over the millennia since the last ice age.

Mesolithic people lived in small groups in settlements near open water by marine fjords, sounds and coves or by freshwater lakes and rivers, where there were good opportunities for hunting and fishing. The population grew in Ertebølle times, judging from the appearance of more and larger settlements that culminated in the often substantial and impressive kitchen middens, consisting primarily of oyster shells. Here, by by these great refuse heaps, it can be imagined how the otherwise scattered groups from a large area gathered together in summer. But these gatherings apparently did not lead to the construction of large buildings or burial monuments. In ones or twos, or sometimes more, the dead were buried on the settlements in simple grave pits with no traces of a burial structure, barrow or suchlike. The best known burial places in Denmark and Sweden from this time are at Vedbæk and Nivå on Zealand and Skateholm in Scania.[1]

Beginning around 3900 BC, the economy gradually changed from being hunting- and fishing-based to a foundation comprising arable agriculture and animal husbandry. This new period is known as the Neolithic, from the Greek words *neo* for new and *lithos* for stone. In Denmark, the Neolithic is divided up into the Early Neolithic (3900-3400 BC), Middle Neolithic (3400-2400 BC) and Late Neolithic (2400-1700 BC). The Early and Middle Neolithic periods are of particular interest here, because this is when great stone tombs, megalithic monuments, were constructed by the people of the Funnel Beaker culture: First dolmens, beginning around 3500 BC, and later passage graves, from around 3200 BC. The Funnel Beaker culture was distributed across at large part of northern Europe, encompassing the Netherlands, northern Germany, Poland, Denmark and the southernmost parts of Sweden and Norway. The culture has its name from the characteristic pottery vessels of the time, which have a funnel-like, out-turned neck.

After the demise of the Funnel Beaker culture in 2800 BC, large stone structures continued to be built during the succeeding Single Grave culture (2800-2400 BC) and Late Neolithic, but these now took the form of stone cists. Compared with the great megalithic tombs of the Funnel Beaker culture, they are something quite different; the stones used are smaller and resemble large flagstones. These stone cists are not considered as actual megalithic structures in Denmark, whereas in France, the largest megalithic chambers – including La Roche aux Fées and Bagneux – were built during a time corresponding to the Late Neolithic in Denmark.

With the gradual introduction of a farming economy around 3900 BC, critical technological, economic, societal and religious changes took place during the subsequent couple of centuries. Polished stone axes, for felling trees and roughing-out timbers such as those used to build houses, together with quernstones, for grinding grain into flour, and pottery vessels, for the storage of foodstuffs, were the most conspicuous of the new artefacts. Although pottery vessels were manufactured in Late Ertebølle times, there were virtually only a couple of standard forms, and these were rarely ornamented. In the Neolithic, and especially towards the end of the Early Neolithic, pots were produced in a wide range of different forms and were often richly decorated with various patterns. Moreover, even a small area such as that covered by present-day Denmark had great regional differences in shape and ornamentation, though these were still subject to the common conventions of the Nordic Funnel Beaker culture.

While these technological advances are easy to trace, even from the earliest part of the Early Neolithic, the situation is quite different with respect to other changes in society. It is as if the farming economy first became properly established after a few hundred years. This is when the first well-built houses appeared, fields were ploughed with a so-called ard, and long trapezoid or rectangular enclosed structures were built, together with long barrows, as part of a cult focussing on ancestors and the dead. Whereas the Mesolithic population lived in small scattered groups that were obliged to move around in pursuit of resources, the situation in the Neolithic was quite different. Thanks to more stable food sources – domestic animals and cereals and other cultivated plants – people in the Neolithic were able to live together in large numbers in one place all year round. For this to be possible, and for it to function, it required a new – relative to that of the Mesolithic – social order to enforce and regulate aspects such as the right of use to land, animals and houses, communality regarding the cultivation of the fields, life together in general and the religious world of ideas.

Experience and understanding of the cosmos – the inexplicable but nevertheless fundamental – we must presume, both as an entity or a term, was not detached from daily life, but woven into and determinative for all aspects of life, also after death. By keeping on good terms with the cosmic powers – "the deities" resident in the water, the earth and the celestial bodies of the air – through votive offerings in pottery vessels, thousands of amber beads, magnificent axes, often several together, oxen and even humans, people secured the continued fertility of plants and animals and, with that, the well-being, prosperity and health of the community. This fertility cult appears to have been closely bound up with death and the worship of ancestors, and dolmens are one of its visible consequences today.

In this book, we present a view of dolmens, not as burial places in an ordinary sense, but more as places where people "deposited" and kept body parts, reliquaries almost, from deceased individuals who we can presume were important to their community, or perhaps could be expected to attain this status. The ancestor cult, and the myths associated with it, were an assurance or guarantee of society's existence and they legitimised the social order and underlined its validity, as well as its links with the land. At the end of the book (chapter 21), an overview is given of what dolmen studies have contributed to our picture of Neolithic society and our knowledge relating to the aims and intentions associate with the construction and use of these monuments.

5. Typology and chronology

Dolmens and megaliths

The Danish word for dolmen, *dysse*, comes from the Old Norse dys, which simply means "stone heap". *Dysse* did, however, also see early linguistic use in reference to dolmens in the sense understood here: i.e. a large stone resting on top of some smaller stones, thereby forming a chamber, often surrounded by a rectangle or a circle of kerbstones. In 1808, the Danish Royal Commission for the Collection and Preservation of Antiquities – more commonly known as the Antiquities Commission – sent out a questionnaire from Copenhagen to the country's clergymen. The commission, the modest predecessor to the Danish National Museum, was set up in 1807. Clergymen were asked to provide information on the occurrence in their respective parishes of ancient monuments such as *kæmpegrave* – giants' graves *hedenske altre* – pagan altars and *tingsteder* – thingsteads, the contemporary Danish terms, respectively, for passage graves, dolmens and long dolmens (fig. 5.1). In their responses – the clerical reports – the clergymen employed both the term *hedensk alter* – pagan alter – and that which later replaced it, *steen dys* or simply dys (fig. 5.2).[1] Nowadays, and in this book, the word *dysse* – dolmen – is used in reference to both the dolmen chamber, including structures standing in isolation, and the kerbstones forming a circular or elongate, rectangular structure around the dolmen.

Dolmens and passage graves are also referred to as megalithic tombs, megalithic monuments or sometimes simply megaliths. The word *megalith* means "large stone" and comes from the Greek words *mega* for large and *lithos* for stone. The term "megalithic tomb" is actually rather unfortunate (see chapter 21), because these structures are not graves or tombs in a traditional sense, but the term is in such general use, and is such an integral part of archaeological language, that it will also be used here.

The large stones used to construct the Danish dolmens were all brought here by ice movements, primarily during the last ice age. In the Neolithic, they lay freely exposed, so the dolmen builders could readily select the most suitable examples.

The dolmen chambers

In its simplest form, a dolmen consists of four large stones – *the orthostats*, arranged to form an elongate, rectangular space – *the chamber*, which is covered by a large stone – *the capstone*. The stones were carefully chosen so that each had a flat side facing in towards the chamber (fig. 5.3a).

If all the orthostats are flat, flag-like stones, with parallel front and back sides, and are less than half a metre thick, then the structure is referred to not as a dolmen chamber, but a dolmen cist. We use this term, rather than the simpler stone cist,

Fig. 5.1. *Dolmen at Eskildstrup, southeast of Ringsted, drawn and described in 1756 by Søren Abildgaard, who wrote the following above his drawing: "On the road from Ringsted to Hømb Mølle this pagan altar can be seen on Hømb Mark, on which the upper stone is all of 15½ Alen in circumference, this same stone rests on 3 other upright stones." This dolmen, which even in Abildgaard's time lacked a couple of orthostats, is scheduled.*

in order to emphasise the connection with, and difference from, dolmen chambers, which are constructed of thicker and more irregular boulders.

The orthostats, which lean slightly inwards towards the chamber in order to take the weight of the capstone, were carefully adjusted, by being let into the ground to various degrees, so their tops were on a level. Measured from the ground surface, this meant they were of equal height. Even though the orthostats were positioned close together, there are often gaps between them, especially in the slightly later and larger dolmen chambers. These gaps were frequently filled, from the bottom of the chamber to on a level with the surrounding mound or packing around the chamber, with dry-walling, comprised of stacked horizontal flagstones, usually red sandstone, but unlike modern masonry these were not bound together with mortar. Ordinary field stones were also used for dry-walling. The *floor* of the dolmen chamber was predominantly made of more or less carefully laid stones/flagstones, crushed/burnt flint, or a combination of these materials.

The dolmen chambers are classified into four groups, types I-IV, according to their form in plan.

Type I. The dolmen chamber as described immediately above. This is narrow, rectangular, sometimes slightly trapezoid and is, with its straight, tall orthostats, completely closed when the capstone is in place (fig. 5.3a). Each side often consists of a single stone, laid on its "long" side. The sides of the chamber can, however, also consist of two and, in rare cases, even three stones. The chamber is usually around 1.8 m in length, 0.6-1 m in width and with an internal height of 1 m, but there are both larger and smaller, as well as higher and lower, examples.[2]

Type II. Dolmen chambers of type II differ from those of type I solely by having a shorter stone – an *entrance stone* – at one end, so that a generally 40-80 cm opening into the chamber is formed when the capstone is in position (fig. 5.3b). In some cases, instead of an entrance stone, there is a lower *threshold stone* in the form of a broad flagstone, often of worked, shaped sandstone, set on edge so that it only protrudes a little above the floor level in the chamber. This means that it was possible to enter the chamber without, as in the case of the type I dolmens, having to lift off the capstone. In the cases where a type II chamber is enclosed in a mound, the upper surface of which is on level with the top of the chamber's orthostats, the problem of entering the chamber may be solved – as in the chamber of the Capeshøj long dolmen – by the construction of a stone-lined *entrance shaft*.[3] In both type I and type II chambers, the ends are often formed of large flagstones.

Type III. Dolmen chambers of types I and II, with a narrow elongate form and relatively low interior, are closely related. In type III – *the expanded dolmen* – the chamber's elongate form was retained, but the proportions were altered, so both

Fig. 5.2. *Several clergymen augmented their responses to the Antiquities Commission with drawings of ancient monuments. Here is a long dolmen at Sønder Jernløse, south of Holbæk, drawn in 1807 by Jørgen Reingaard. It was not until the following year that he took over the post of clergyman after his father.*

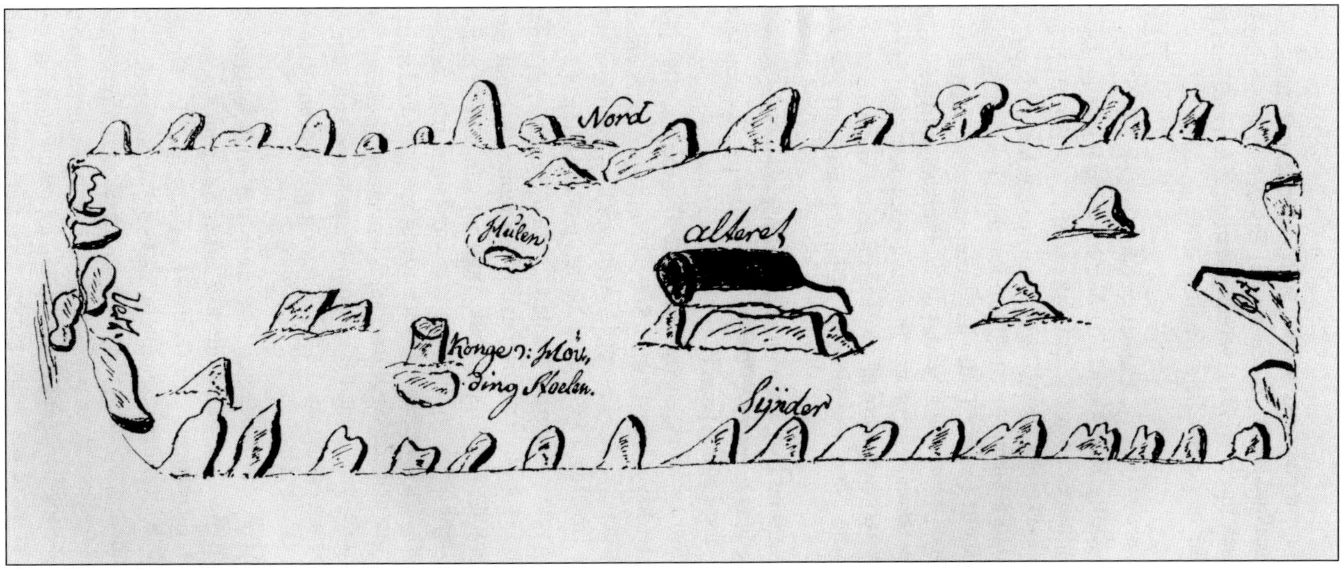

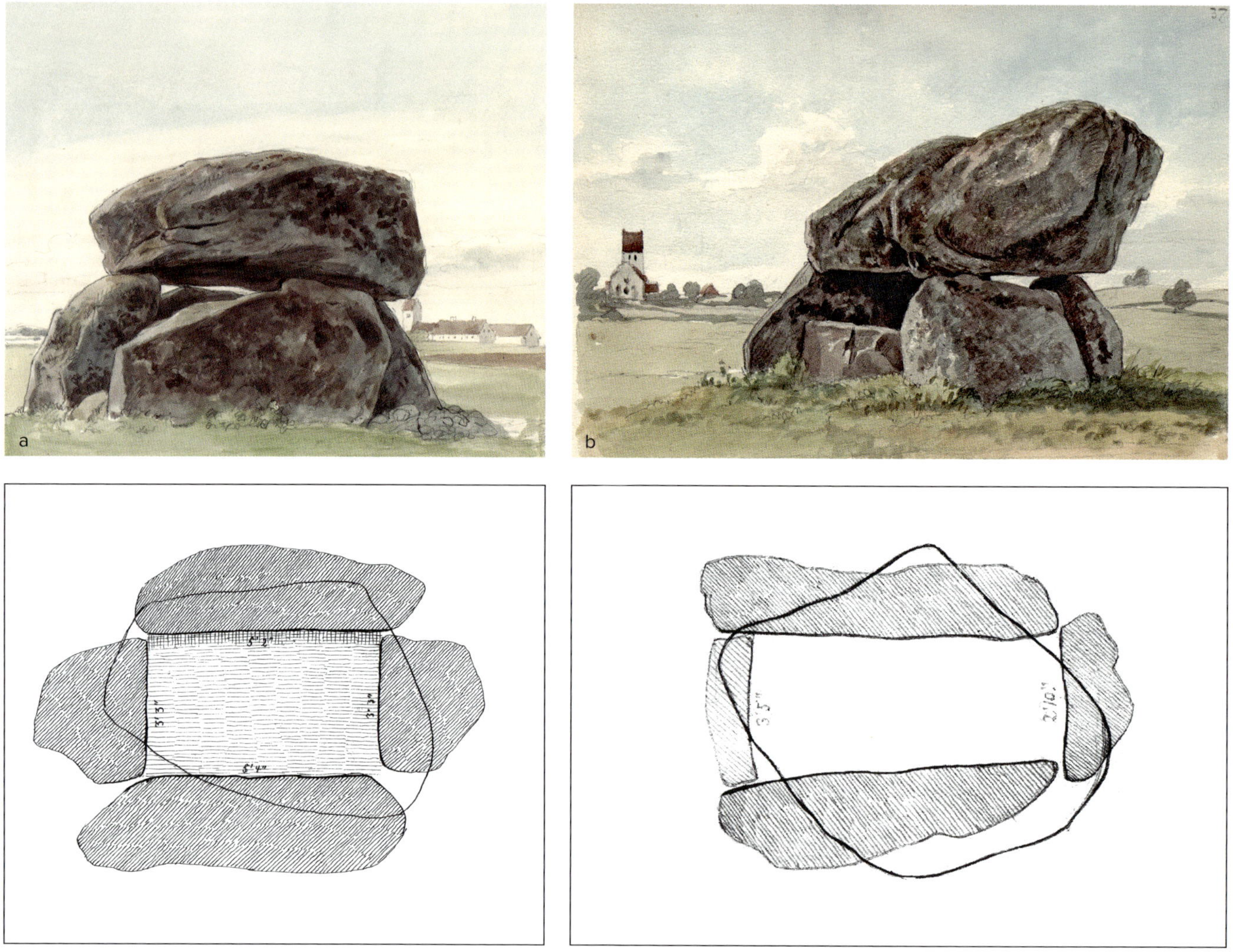

Fig. 5.3. *Dolmen chambers of early type. a: type I, Reerslev at Ruds Vedby, north of Slagelse. b: type II, Vollerup on Møn, in the background Fanefjord church. Drawn by A.P. Madsen 1889 (a) and 1880 (b).*

the floor area and the height were increased (fig. 5.4a). The larger floor area was achieved by angling one or both of the long sides outwards and often by allowing the orthostats in the chamber's short side to slope sharply inwards. The increased height in these expanded dolmens was achieved by exploiting the full height of the orthostats by standing them on end, i.e. on their short sides. In general, a larger number of orthostats was also employed in these expanded dolmen chambers, at least two in each side, while the norm was only one in the early type II dolmens. The expanded type III dolmens have, like the type II dolmens, an opening – an entrance – at one end. In front of the entrance there may be a minor demarcation in the form of a small passage composed of one pair – more rarely two pairs – of passage stones. The qualification "may be" is important, because expanded dolmens are also found without passage stones, while a couple of passage stones may well be present in type II dolmens.

Type IV. The expanded type III dolmen chambers are, as such, polygonal in form, but the term *polygonal dolmen* – type IV – is only used in reference to chambers where the ground plan is not elongate, but pentagonal to octagonal, or rhomboid in form (fig. 5.4b). As a rule, polygonal dolmens have an opening and a more or less short passage, demarcated by a set of passage stones, as seen at Poskær Stenhus. A few polygonal dolmen chambers are very large and rounded in outline, like the long dolmen Troldkirken, west of Aalborg in Himmerland, and Hylledysse, near Roskilde (fig. 5.5). Some of these large chambers were encountered during investigations of demolished dolmens in southwest Funen (see chapter 20), for example at Vartov and Damsbo, but none of the four large dolmen chambers at these sites show traces of passage stones. The polygonal type IV dolmens have many features in common with the expanded type III dolmens and it is true of both types that the passage never extends out to the foot of the mound – if the latter is present. The passage does, however, reach the exterior in a completely different type of structure, with a completely different construction, namely a passage grave.

Passage graves. Even though passage graves, in chronological terms, follow on directly after, or are possibly coeval with, the latest dolmens, the polygonal examples, there are also crucial differences between type IV dolmens and the much larger and generally higher and longish passage graves. These differences relate in particular to the passages (fig. 5.6b). Firstly, the passage graves, which are rectangular/elon-

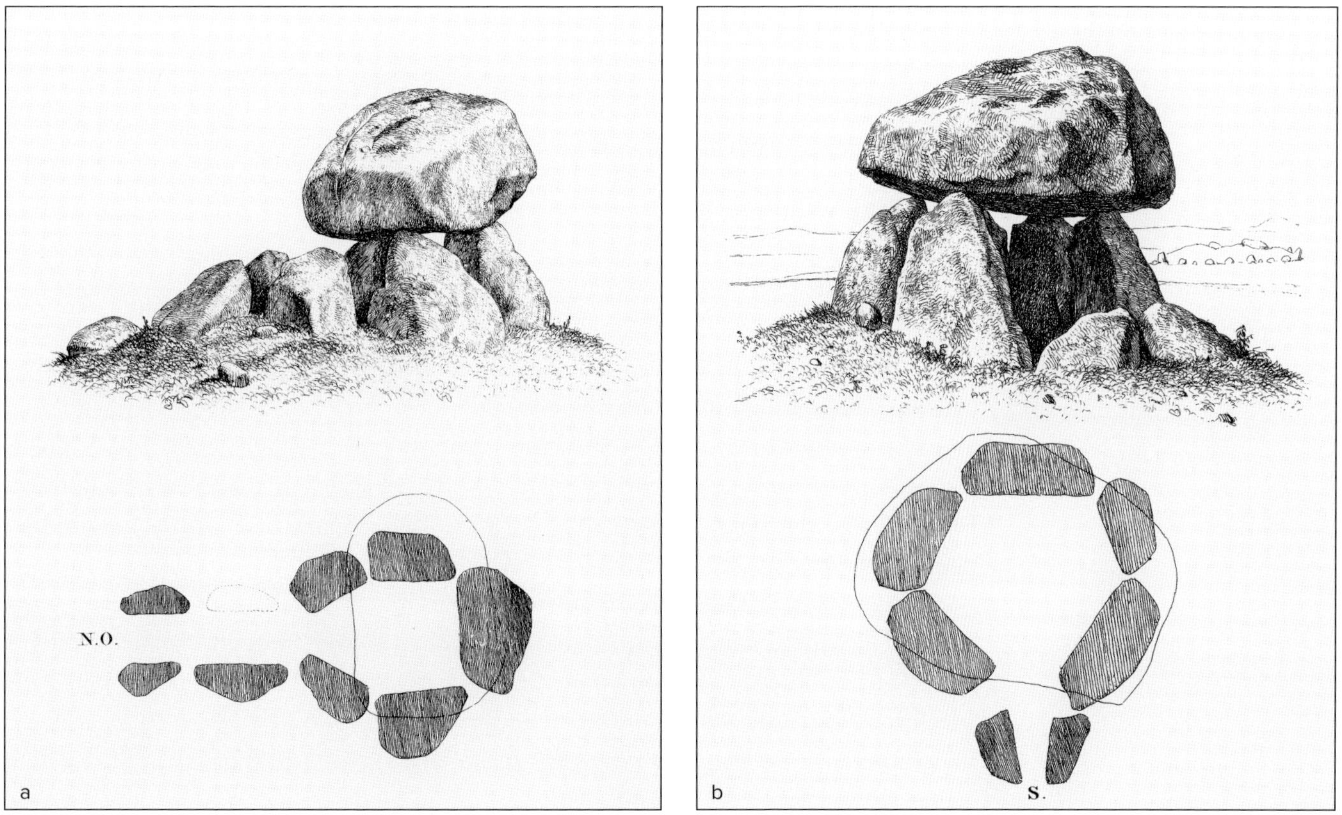

Fig. 5.4. *Dolmen chambers of later type. a: type III, Bregninge on Lolland. b: type IV, Mejekirke, south of Nødager on Djursland. Drawn by A.P. Madsen before 1868.*

Fig. 5.5. *The Troldkirken, Hylledysse and Vartov dolmens all have extremely large chambers of polygonal form. The ground plan of the Troldkirken dolmen is even larger than shown, as it is not drawn at floor level. The plan of the Vartov dolmen shows traces of missing stones in the subsoil.*

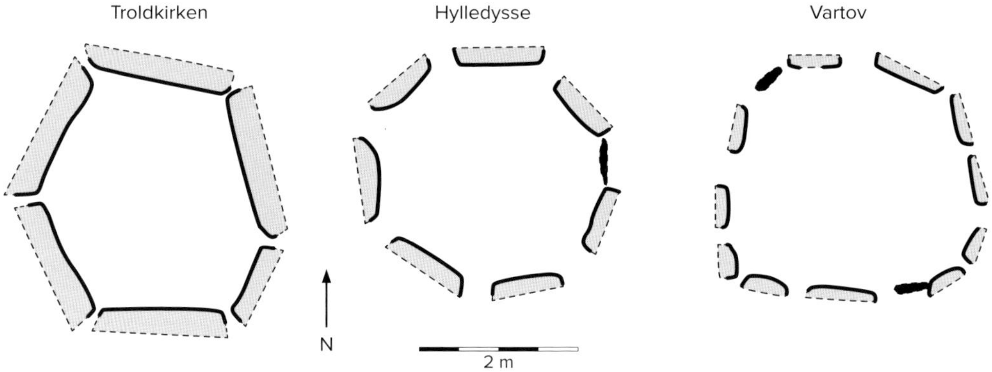

Fig. 5.6. *Ground plans of two forms of passage grave, one with a rounded chamber, where the passage abuts a short side (a), and the other with an elongate chamber, where the passage abuts a long side (b). Passage graves with rounded chambers were previously referred to as great dolmens. The small passage grave is the Brejninggård dolmen at Spjald near Ringkøbing, the large one is the Hulbjerg passage grave in southern Langeland.*

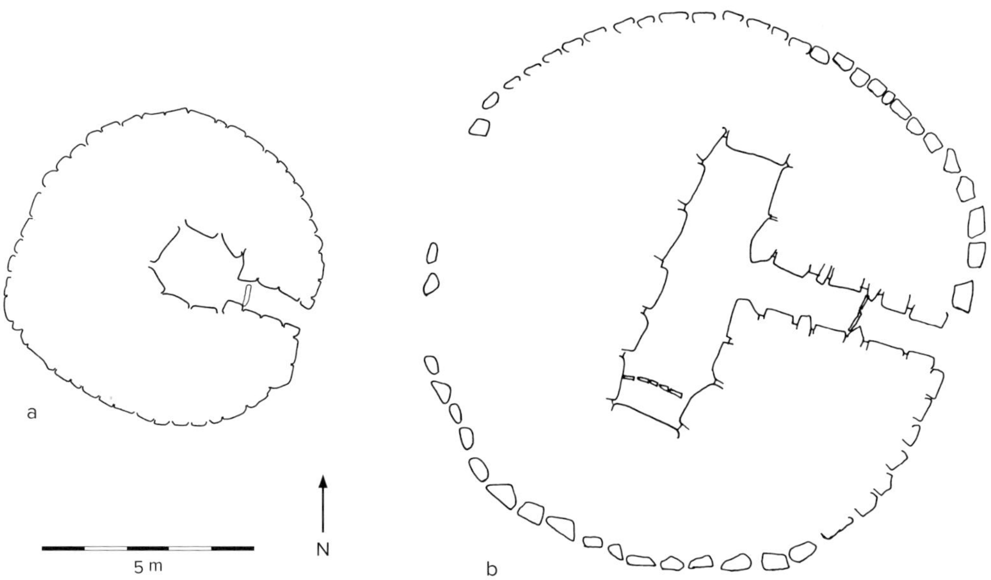

gate-oval in ground plan, always have a passage that runs at right angles, or approximately at right angles, to the longitudinal axis of the chamber, whereas in dolmens with a passage, the latter normally lies in continuation of this axis. Secondly, the passage in a passage grave always extends all the way out to, and is incorporated into, the mound foot, which is most commonly demarcated by kerbstones. Thirdly, the passage of a passage grave is covered with capstones, unlike that of a dolmen. Fourthly, the chambers and passages of passage graves are, as a rule, covered by mound material,

"Great dolmens". One type of passage grave has a more rounded ground plan, where the passage, due to the form of the chamber, cannot abut one of the chamber's "long" sides – simply because none of the sides is longer than the others. This type is referred to by the rather unfortunate term "great dolmens", even though these, like the actual passage graves, have a passage that extends all the way out to the foot of the mound (fig. 5.6a). Another group of monuments that can be assigned to the

same category are the chambers with a so-called pear-shaped ground plan, where the passage abuts the "pointed" end of the chamber, running out to the foot of the mound. Like passage graves, the great dolmens and the pear-shaped dolmens were also covered by a mound. Consequently, these structures are not dolmens according to our terminology, but small or round passage graves. So when we speak of dolmens, we mean dolmens of types I-IV.[4] Whereas when we speak of passage graves, we mean the long chambers, as has traditionally been the norm, and also, as something "new", the round chambers that have until now been perceived as dolmens, but have always had a passage that extended out to the mound foot.

It is tempting to see a chronological development: closed dolmens (type I) – open dolmens (type II) – expanded dolmens (type III) – polygonal dolmens (type IV) – round passage graves – long passage graves. This sequence can be argued for typologically, as has been done above, but is also supported by the finds encountered in the investigated chambers. These include pottery vessels, flint axes and other artefacts that may be coeval with the construction of the chambers (fig. 5.7). Whether the first two types are coeval, or whether type II is later, being derived from type I, it has not as yet been possible to determine on the basis of the artefacts found in these monuments.

Fig. 5.7. *Artefacts that may be found in dolmen chambers and which can date from the earliest time of the structure. a: Lugged flask, 18 cm tall. b: Collared flask, 15 cm tall. c: Thin-butted polished stone axe, 12.5 cm long. d: Amber beads. e: Flint blades, 9-10 cm long. a, b and e are from a demolished dolmen that once stood on Tåstrup Mark in Harlev parish, west of Aarhus. c is from a demolished dolmen at Tolstrup in Næsborg parish near Løgstør. d is a stray find from the Løgstør area.*

Mound or packing

Dark stripes resulting from ploughing with an ard, and postholes in the subsoil – the pale material beneath the Neolithic topsoil – show that dolmens were frequently built on previously cultivated fields or settlements, and even directly on the former sites of houses. It can often be seen in archaeological excavations how the topsoil was removed before the stones were erected. In very rare instances, like at Harreby in South Jutland, the chambers were buried to such a degree that not even their capstones were visible.[5] But here we will concentrate on dolmens "above ground" and their relationship to the possible mounds of material that may have covered them.

Archaeologists have generally had rather an unsophisticated view of dolmen mounds and a similar level of understanding of their structure. The function of the mounds has generally been seen as purely structural, with their purpose being solely to support and conceal the chamber. Externally, the mound fill was held in place by the kerbstones. In instances where there was not much fill between the dolmen chamber and the kerbstones, this absence was explained in terms of the stones and earth simply having been removed and/or eroded away.

But closer examination of the records resulting from archaeological investigations of the earth and stone layers running up to the dolmen chambers permits the identification of at least five kinds of mound fill: packing layers, cult layers, fill layers, natural layers and other deposits.

The purpose of *packing layers* was to support and stabilise the large stones of the chamber and the passage.

Cult layers, which include stone pavements of one or more courses, soil layers, burnt flint and the like, were deposited in conjunction with isolated or repeated actions related to cult activities at the dolmen.

As for *fill layers*, which consist of actual mound material in a traditional sense – stone, earth, turf and crushed flint, the intention must have been to make the mound higher, but they could also have had properties relating to the monument's construction, such as directing away water.

Natural layers are products of natural sedimentation, blown sand deposits, formation of vegetation/turf horizons and so on.

Further to these are *other deposits*, which can be anything from layers formed in the Neolithic as a result of digging the holes to take the large stones, to deposits from more recent times resulting for example from people digging in search of the large stones.

In the following, we will confine ourselves to using the old and well-established term "mound", well aware that in several cases this is simply a packing or cult layer, in turn possibly overlain by a fill layer, the surface of which is today covered by a natural layer. With the term *dolmens without mounds* or *open dolmens*, we mean dolmens that have no or only very little mound material or fill, such that at least half a metre of the chamber's orthostats is visible above the surface of the mound.

Round and long dolmens

Of the 33,000 scheduled ancient monuments in Denmark, around 2400 are dolmens and passage graves.[6] It is estimated that there are some 600 scheduled passage graves, while the remaining 1800 scheduled megalithic tombs are mostly dolmens. Many structures are, however, so badly damaged that they cannot be securely identified as one or the other, and the term "dolmen" is also used in reference to the round chambers, which we believe should more correctly be termed passage graves. But for the moment let us say that the estimated number of actual scheduled dolmens is 1500.

Dolmens, and here we mean the entire monument structure, including any kerbstones present, occur in three forms: *free-standing dolmen chambers*, *round dolmens* and *long dolmens* (fig. 5.8).

Many dolmen chambers that today are free-standing were originally encapsulated within round or long dolmens. This is apparent partly from early descriptions, partly from the remains of a more or less demolished mound. But, as we will see in chapters 15 and 20, there are also free-standing dolmens that have never been enclosed within a mound, let alone been surrounded by kerbstones.

The chambers of round and long dolmens are, as their names suggest, surrounded by respectively round or rectangular enclosures made up of closely-spaced kerbstones. The gaps between the kerbstones may be filled with dry-walling (fig. 5.9), which in some cases perhaps, as in the Tustrup dolmen, could have reached the top of the kerbstones. Parallel with the kerbstones of the long dolmens, or concentric with those of the round dolmens, there may have been an outer frame or circle formed of free-standing stones – *standing stones* – placed a certain distance apart (fig. 5.10).[7] Instead of kerbstones, a mound demarcation could have been formed by smaller stones, stacked in a couple of courses to form a low wall, or planks of heavy timber or stakes and posts.[8]

Four times as many long dolmens as round dolmens are preserved, something that has been explained in terms of long dolmens being generally more difficult to demolish than round dolmens, because the former are more often surrounded by larger kerbstones than the latter.[9] But this is more likely due to the fact that long dolmens were also more numerous than round dolmens back in the Neolithic.

Round dolmens normally only contain a single chamber, though a few do have two, for example that at Holløse near Næstved. Most round dolmens have diameter of 7-15 m. Poskær Stenhus, with its diameter of 15.5 m, is one of the largest round dolmens in Denmark.[10]

More than half of the long dolmens have only a single chamber, but long dolmens with two or three chambers are not unusual, and some even have as many as four chambers, for example Tokkekøb Hegn in northern Zealand. The Danish record is five chambers and is held by the scheduled long dolmen Ellested in southeastern Funen.[11] Close to the Ellested long dolmen, at Lindeskov, stands one of Denmark's best preserved long dolmens. It is 158 m in length – not 168 m, as is commonly stated. It is surpassed in length by a few other monuments, of which Odins Alter in

Fig. 5.8. *a: The long dolmen Kong Humbles Grav on Langeland, drawn by A.P. Madsen in 1887. b: The round dolmen Mølsødyssen, east of Slagelse, drawn by Erik Schiødte in 1877. c: Free-standing dolmen chamber at Bregninge on Lolland, drawn by A.P. Madsen before 1868.*

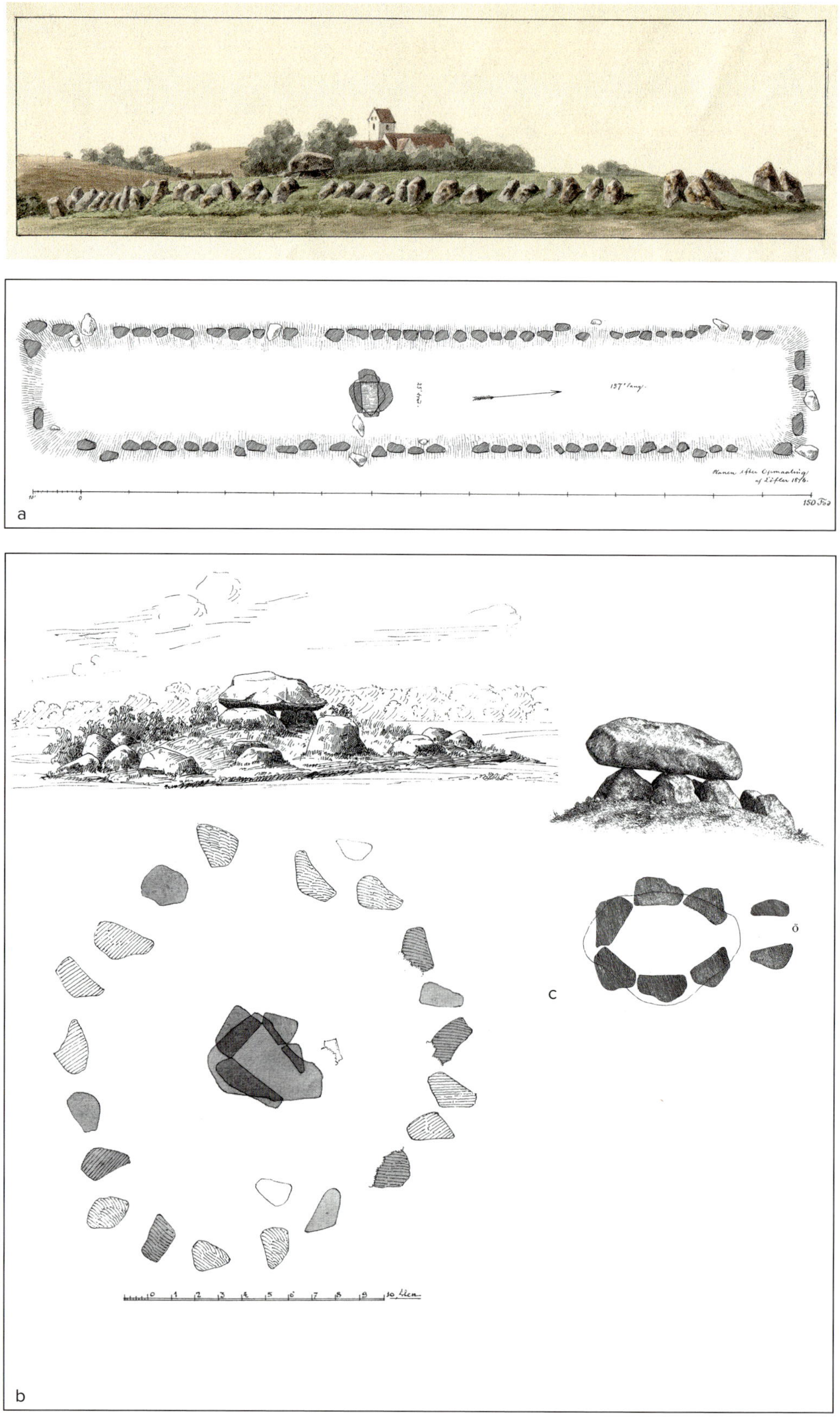

Fig. 5.9. *The gaps between the kerbstones of the dolmens were as a rule closed with dry-walling made of stacked flagstones. The upper part of the dry-walling collapsed long ago, but the original lower parts are preserved, like here at the Capeshøj long dolmen on Tåsinge.*

Trinderup Krat near Hobro and the Tastum long dolmen near Skive, with lengths of respectively 180 and 184 m, are considered to be the longest (fig. 5.11). Long dolmens are, however, normally 10-50 m long and 6-10 m wide. The largest kerbstones may be placed in the gables, with the very largest, as much as 3 m in height, in the middle and thereby reminiscent of a house gable (fig. 5.12).

It should be noted that, in the case of long and round dolmens, these measurements are taken from the outside of in situ kerbstones. As for the dolmen chambers, the internal dimensions at floor level are always given or, if the chamber has not been excavated, at the present-day surface.

In long dolmens with chambers of types I and II, these most often stand on the central axis of the monument and with the same longitudinal orientation. The chamber can also lie across the monument and a few are even oriented diagonally relative to the dolmens axis. The reason for this very varied orientation is unknown.

Of the estimated 1500 surviving dolmens, the majority lie in eastern Denmark, especially Zealand, eastern Lolland, Møn, Langeland and southern Funen, in eastern South Jutland and on Djursland (fig. 5.13). They are sparsest in western and central Jutland, even though these areas came under cultivation later and have not been as

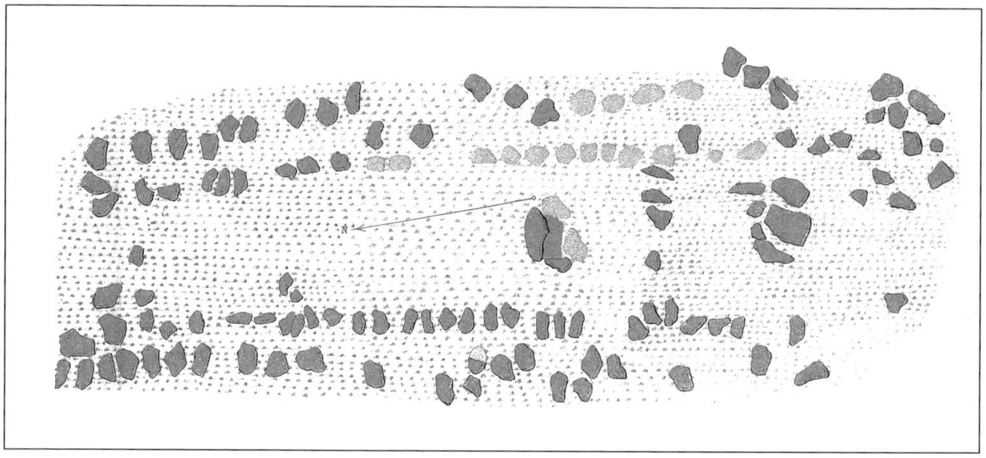

Fig. 5.10. *The long dolmen Brudager at Gudme in southern Funen, with its extra rows of large stones outside the kerbstones, must have been an impressive sight before it was destroyed by the stones being removed, blown up or toppled. As is clear from this drawing, its destruction was already well advanced in 1878. The area containing the stones is 57 m long.*

intensively exploited for arable agriculture as the rest of the country. The scarcity of megalithic tombs in these areas can be attributed to the geological conditions. There are simply fewer large stones here because these areas lay beyond the main ice limit during the last ice age. The ice incorporated moraine material that included large boulders from the Scandinavian bedrock of Norway and Sweden.

Three kinds of monument – three epochs

A detailed chronology has been compiled for the Early and Middle Neolithic, incorporating several phases and regional variations, based on studies carried out over the last 70 years into developments in the form and ornamentation of pottery vessels. As the pottery underwent frequent changes during these periods – both in its form and in its symbol-laden ornamentation – a pottery vessel, or even a fragment, can often be identified to a particular pottery style, which can then be dated to within 50 years. While archaeologists more or less agree in dividing the Middle Neolithic Funnel Beaker culture (3400-2800 BC) into six main periods (MN Ia, Ib, II, III, IV and V), there is great controversy with respect to the Early Neolithic. Similarly, it is still debated whether the Fuchsberg phase, defined in 1978, should be placed at the end of the Early Neolithic (EN) or the beginning of the Middle Neolithic (MN).[12]

As pottery is often found during investigations of dolmens and passage graves, and as it may, in several instances, originate from the first period of use of these monuments and can be used to date them, it is important to be able to establish its age reliably. Pottery dating is, however, sometimes difficult, both stylistically and critically in terms of the archaeological record.

Due to this uncertainty, we employ a chronology here that takes its point of departure in the actual structures, and which has the advantage that it is relatively easy to assign a given monument to a given period or epoch. Radiocarbon dates show that dolmens should be dated, roughly speaking, to a couple of centuries around 3350 BC and passage graves to a century around 3200 BC. For the sake of clarity, the division between dolmens and passage graves is fixed here at 3250 BC. In the time immediately preceding the dolmen epoch, during three centuries around 3600 BC, elongate enclosures were built that often later became transformed into long barrows. These structures were first discovered at the locality of Barkær on Djursland and are named after this site. The "Barkaer-structure epoch" is accordingly the first monumental epoch. This results in the following very schematic chronology and typology, which we consider to be both useful and easy to understand.

The Barkaer-structure epoch, 3600 ± 150 BC. The term Barkaer-structure refers to a rectangular or elongate, trapezoid area enclosed by either a fence or a ditch, and with or without a mound, within which there is often a wooden plank-built cist or a dolmen cist made of large stone flags. No definite round dolmens have as yet been identified. The Barkær complex itself is dealt with in more detail in chapter 9. The Barkaer-structure epoch is in the later part of the Early Neolithic (EN).

Dolmen epoch, 3350 ± 100 BC. The early Dolmen epoch saw the construction of rectangular dolmen chambers of types I and II, while in the late Dolmen epoch dolmen chambers of type III (expanded dolmens) and type IV (polygonal dolmens)

Fig. 5.11. *With a length of 184 m, the Tastum long dolmen is easy to pick out from the air. This aerial photo was taken on 25th June 2008 as part of Holstebro Museum's project "An aerial view of the past – Aerial archaeology in Denmark".*

were built. All four types, built of rectangular stone blocks, can be found in round or long barrows, surrounded by kerbstones and corresponding to round and long dolmens. Instead of kerbstones, the mound foot may have been marked with posts, stakes or a ditch. The earliest dolmens, with dolmen chambers of types I and II, were built late in the Early Neolithic, while the later dolmens with dolmen chambers of types III and IV were built during the Fuchsberg phase and at the beginning of the Middle Neolithic in MN Ia. It is possible that polygonal dolmens were also constructed in MN Ib.

Passage-grave epoch, 3200 ± 50 BC. Passage graves encompass both the traditional, and generally larger, passage graves with longish chambers and a passage abutting one of the long sides, and the generally somewhat smaller passage graves with round or slightly elongate chambers, where the passage abuts one of the short sides of the chamber. Passage graves are found in both round and long barrows. Passage graves were built at the beginning of the Middle Neolithic, in MN Ia and MN Ib. The smaller, rounded passage graves were constructed during both periods, while the larger, longish passage graves were only built during the latter of the two.

It could actually be considered whether the Dolmen and Passage-grave epochs should be perceived as one single culturally cohesive period – a megalithic epoch.[13] That is, not merely an artificial time interval, but a period which people at the time could have recognised as something special: "Back in the time when our ancestors built the great stone graves." The construction of megalithic tombs ceased at the end

Fig. 5.12. *In 1889 A.P. Madsen drew the long dolmen at Busemarke on Møn. Like many other long dolmens, it has particularly tall kerbstones at its gables. If the capstone had not been removed, it would have been possible to see that a dolmen chamber was located in the middle of the long dolmen.*

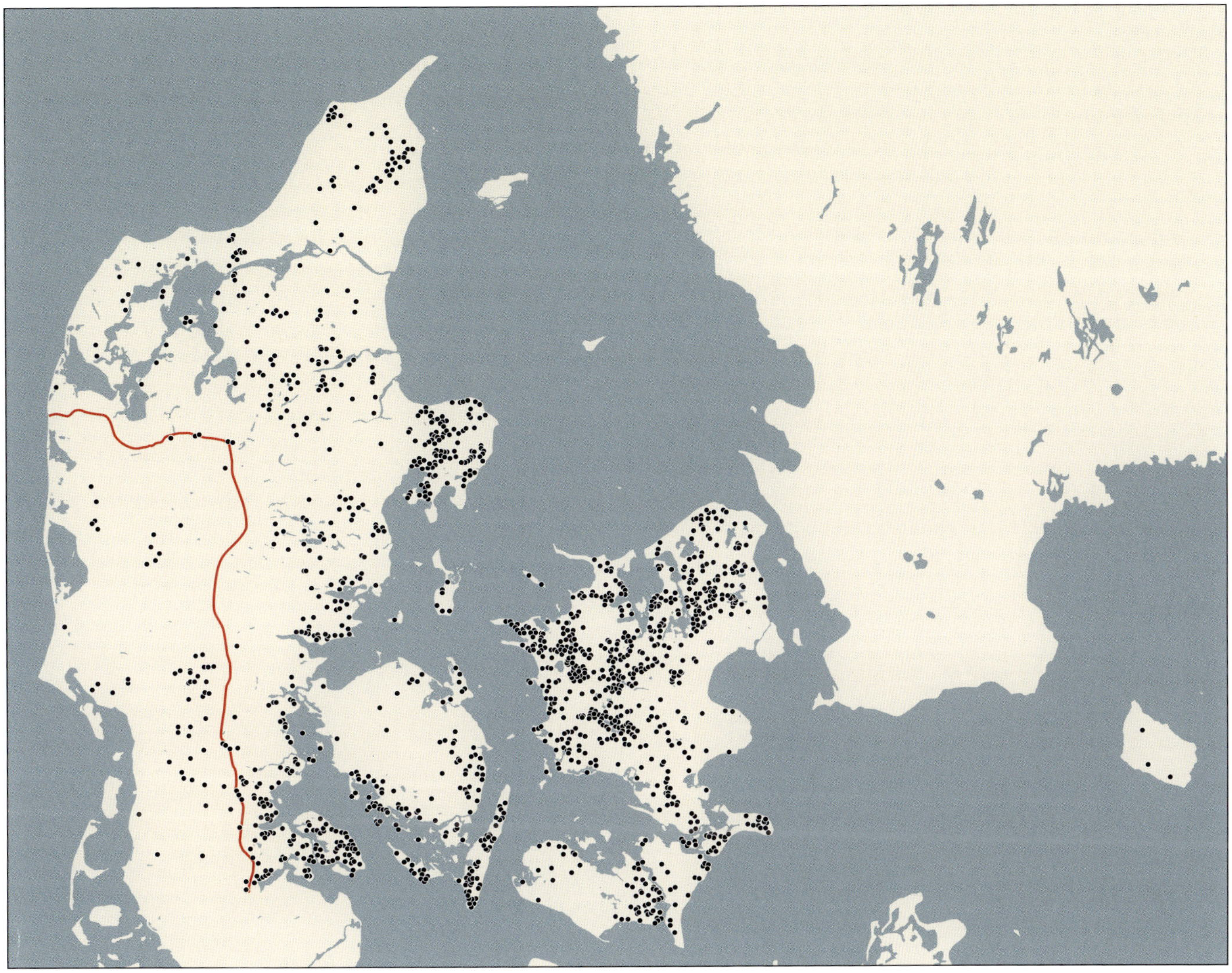

of MN Ib, but these monuments continued to be well used, with quantities of pottery being placed in them in MN II. Later, in MN III-V, they also saw deposition of burnt flint axes and chisels.

Fig. 5.13 *The distribution of dolmens in Denmark is partly dependent on the occurrence of large stones brought here by the ice during the last glaciation. Beyond the main ice limit, marked on the map in red, there were consequently much fewer stones suitable for building dolmens.*

Concurrent with the cessation of megalith construction, many other major changes took place during the final part of the Funnel Beaker culture. People gathered together in fewer but larger settlements and abandoned the construction of the large, communal causewayed enclosures. There is a great deal to suggest that these changes coincided with the emergence of a fully developed farming economy and concomitant changes in the structure and rites of Neolithic society.[14] A new era had begun.

The great stones

The great stones that were used to build the dolmens came from Norway and Sweden. These stones – mostly granite and gneiss – are broken-off pieces of the bedrock and, together with soil, they were carried here by the ice. When the ice melted and finally receded, about 15,000 years ago, it left huge quantities of stones of many different sizes. For the first many millennia, these lay freely exposed on the surface. But with time, as the climate became warmer and trees migrated in, they became hidden in dense primeval forest.

It was first 5000-6000 years ago, when Neolithic farmers began to make clearings in the forest, that these stones again became visible. Some clearances were perhaps undertaken in order to gain access to specific chosen examples, because these stones were not seen as a hindrance, but as attractive building materials for the new monuments that we now call dolmens; our earliest form of architecture in stone.

Not all stones were suitable, because in order for them to be used to construct grave chambers, they had to have at least one flat side. It was important for the inside of the chamber to have smooth, straight walls and roof comprised, respectively, of orthostats and a capstone. There is nothing to suggest that the dolmen builders were able to cleave the great stones, unless they already had existing planes of weakness.

When the site for a dolmen had been decided upon, the stones had then to be transported there. They could come from quite a distance away, at least 2 km, like the 16 tonne capstone used for Poskær Stenhus. The easiest way of transporting a large stone was to load it on to a wooden sled and pull it with ropes over branches and trunks laid out on the ground.

When a dolmen was to be constructed, the dolmen builders probably selected the largest and most impressive stones first. But when the time came to build the next

dolmen in the vicinity of the first, there may have been a lack or a shortage of really big stones. This is evident at Poskær Stenhus, where the capstone and kerbstones are massive compared to examples half the size used to build the dolmen Sognefogedens Dysse, a mere 400 m to the west.

In some cases, the construction site was prepared by removing the topsoil. First the chamber was built by putting its wall stones – the orthostats – in place. As the tops of these had to be at the same height, some of them were set into in larger or smaller pits, so their tops were on a level. All the stones were positioned so that a flat surface faced in towards the chamber and care was taken to ensure that they were jammed securely against each other and leaned inwards so they were able to take the weight of the often very large and heavy capstone. When the capstone was put in place (see box 5 in chapter 19) "It was actually not Frederik VII who ..." in chapter 19 – the entire construction was self-locking.

An important and essential role in the monument's durability was played by the packing of stones and crushed flint that surrounded the orthostats and held them in place so they did not topple over. This packing against the orthostats could be as much as 70-80 cm high and must have been assembled before the capstone was put in place. The chamber must have been braced internally with timbers, which were easy to remove after the capstone had been added. Subsequently, the chamber was given its finishing touches: The upper gaps between the orthostats and the capstone were filled with dry-walling – predominantly made up of stone flags – and the floor was laid, as a rule with small stones. The entrance was often, but not always, marked with one or two sets of passage stones.

The finished chamber now stood exposed and surrounded by a low shield-like bank, which counteracted the outward force of the orthostats. The chamber may well have been very dark if the dry-walling in the gaps between the orthostats extended all the way up to the lower surface of the capstone, so the only light entering the chamber came through the entrance to the dolmen.

The most demanding part of constructing a dolmen was transporting the stones to the construction site. From a modern rational point of view, the actual construction of the chamber, and the laying on of the capstone, could not have required the efforts of more than five to ten men. The Neolithic mentality was, however, quite different. The building of a dolmen, where the stones had to be brought to the site, the dolmen chamber constructed and the capstone laid in place, probably involved and attracted hundreds of men, women and children, as part of the contemporaneous social universe. Just as in the case of modern dolmen construction a century ago in Indonesia, where such an event was a feast with enormous prestige involved.

References: Eriksen 2002. Cleavage of stones: Eriksen 1999, pp. 58-67.

During the hauling of an 8 tonne stone in Nias in 1914, the workers take a break for the photographer. There is no doubting the motivation of those hauling or who is in charge: two important factors in ensuring a successful outcome.

6. Dolmens with mounds

Many Danish long and round dolmens have mound material within the kerbstones. The surface of this fill extends from the top of the kerbstones, either flat or sloping, up to the middle of the monument, often to the underside of the chamber's capstone or even part way up its sides. Adherents of the erosion theory believe that this was how all dolmens looked before destruction and decay began to take their toll – even suggesting that the capstone may well have been fully concealed.[1] At the root of this is the idea that dolmens were built in one continuous process.

But have these dolmens with mound material always looked like this? Is it conceivable that the fill is a result of one or more building phases later in the Neolithic and that these monuments could originally have had a completely different appearance? It is generally known from excavations that some long dolmens – such as that at Troelstrup (see chapter 9) – have been extended in length one or more times, and that round dolmens – like the one at Tårup (see below) – could also have been made larger and higher. These alterations, whereby dolmens were extended and expanded, can generally be revealed by archaeological investigation.

In the following, an account is given of seven published investigations of dolmens – six long dolmens and one round dolmen – each containing a large amount of mound material, where the structure of the mound was exposed and documented by excavated sections.

Grøfte

At Grøfte near Sorø, three scheduled long dolmens stand close together. Two were scheduled in 1894, while the third stood in a cultivated field and was first scheduled following an investigation in 1946-47.[2] The investigation, carried out by Harald Andersen of the Danish National Museum, revealed that within the c. 85 m long and 9 m wide long dolmen, which had been surrounded by kerbstones, were two concealed chambers positioned on the longitudinal axis of the monument and only 5 m apart, centre to centre. The two chambers, A and B, were of similar form in that each was narrow, rectangular and constructed of six stones of equal height, one at each short side and two at each long side, i.e. they were of type I. Their internal measurements were 1.7 x 0.8 m and they were only 80-90 cm high. Over each chamber lay a single capstone, which was unusual in being only 25-60 cm in thickness and thereby more like a large stone slab or flagstone. The thinner of the two capstones, that over chamber B, was only 20-25 cm thick and of red sandstone. Around the upper part of the chambers were stacks of smaller stones (fig. 6.1). Both chambers had thin stone slabs at their ends, a feature seen in many other dolmens. The sides of chamber A were, however, also constructed of stone flags and it is, consequently, a dolmen cist rather

Fig. 6.1. *Chamber B in the Grøfte long dolmen was well packed around with stones before it was covered by a mound in the Neolithic. Here are three views from the excavation. Note the flat capstone.*

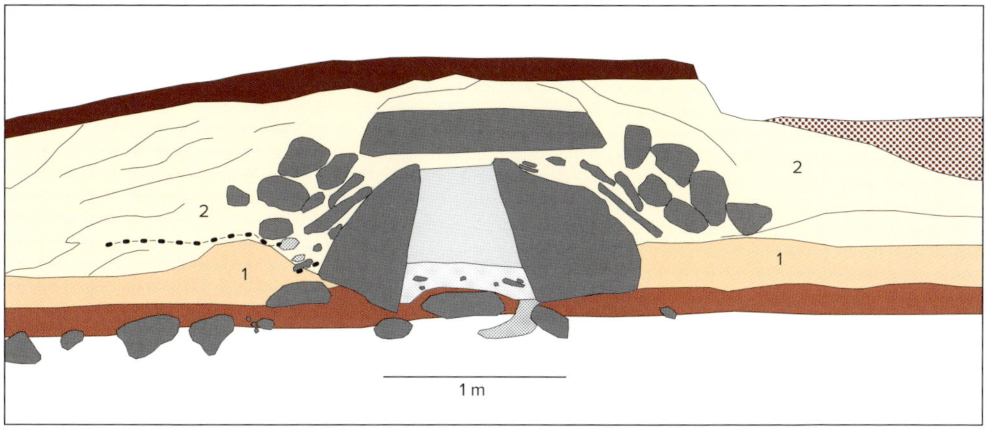

Fig. 6.2. *The section through the Grøfte long dolmen clearly shows two layers around chamber B. Lowermost, layer 1 on the Neolithic topsoil, followed by the stone packing around the chamber, then layer 2, which is overlain by the modern plough soil.*

than a dolmen chamber, and will be referred to as such in the following. Chamber B, on the other hand, is a proper dolmen chamber with irregularly shaped stones making up its sides.

A transverse section through the mound by chamber B reveals its structure here (fig. 6.2). The orthostats were partly sunk into the Neolithic topsoil. Lowermost, directly over the topsoil, the chamber was surrounded by layer 1, which was up to 40 cm thick and generally very sandy with a striped appearance. On this layer, and in some places in the lower part of the overlying layer, were charcoal fragments of various sizes – evidence of a fierce fire here. Over the burnt layer, and from the top of layer 1, stones had been stacked up around the chamber. These were encapsulated within layer 2, which was up to 1 m thick when the upper soil layer was included. The stratigraphy by the dolmen cist (A) was more or less the same, though not as distinct.

In addition to the dolmen cist and chamber, which stood close together in the middle of one half of the NW-SE-oriented monument, a small stone pavement was found in the middle of the long dolmen, which was very reasonably interpreted as a possible inhumation grave. In the Neolithic, this structure, C, was encapsulated within a mound of at least 40 m in length, which rested on a layer of larger stones, placed on the surface of the Neolithic soil. This stone pavement extended almost all the way to the later dolmen chamber and can clearly be seen in the background of the excavation photographs (fig. 6.1). The inhumation grave, the 40 m long stone pavement and the covering mound were perceived by Klaus Ebbesen, who published the investigation, as coeval phenomena, despite the fact that – judging from the section – the inhumation grave lies much higher than the stone pavement.[3] Instead, the sequence must have been the stone pavement first and then the inhumation grave.

The investigation showed that the long dolmen had a complicated construction history. The earliest structure was the 40 m long stone pavement (phase 1), which was then covered by a 40 m long mound (phase 2). Outside this mound, but in continuation of it, the dolmen cist and dolmen chamber were constructed and a low packing or mound was established around them (layer 1, phase 3). A large fire was then lit next to the cist and the chamber (phase 4), before stones were stacked up around them so they were securely sealed (phase 5). At the same time, both the chamber and cist and the now 85 m-long mound were covered with a thick layer of earth (layer 2, phase 6). We do not know when, during the course of all this, the mound was extended to 85 m long and the kerbstones were erected, but this could have been as early as phase 3.

The six phases into which we, on the basis of Klaus Ebbesen's presentation, have rather cavalierly divided the long dolmen's construction history, need not necessarily all have been proper phases, separated by long intervening periods. Some of them could have been merely punctuated by brief pauses in the building work or activities.

Both the dolmen cist and the dolmen chamber contained scattered human skeletal material and artefacts: Two lugged flasks and a flint halberd were found in the dolmen cist and a lugged flask in the dolmen chamber. In the possible inhumation grave were a flint blade and the remains of a funnel beaker. The three collared vessels were ornamented in Virum style, which is dated to the end of the Early Neolithic; a date that may well also apply to the dolmen cist and the dolmen chamber.[4] Chapter 21 includes a discussion of the interpretation of the bones and artefacts from Grøfte as a possible burial.

Pæregård

In the 1950s and 60s, Hakon Berg of Langeland Museum carried out a large number of investigations of scheduled dolmens and passage graves on the island of Langeland. Of these, the two long dolmens of Pæregård and Ormstrup deserve special mention.

The Pæregård long dolmen, which was investigated in 1951, was 36 m long and 8 m wide and had three chambers.[5] Two of the chambers had the same form, and this was possibly also the case for the third, which was less well preserved: A broad stone in the short side, two side stones in each long side that narrowed slightly towards the opening, marked by a threshold stone, outside which were a pair of passage stones. The capstones were not preserved (fig. 6.3).

The two well-preserved chambers, which were oriented across the mound's longitudinal axis, were of approximately equal size: 2-2.25 m long, 1-1.25 m wide and 1-1.6 m high. The associated passages were 1.25-1.5 m long, 50-75 cm wide and 1-1.1 m high. The floor of the passages lay 50 cm above that of the chambers. Neither passage extended out to the kerbstones, so access to the chambers could only have been gained from the mound surface, through narrow entrance shafts.

A transverse section through the middle of the mound was recorded very schematically (fig. 6.3 lower). The surface of the mound in the middle of the monument was on a level with the top of the kerbstones, and sloped evenly outwards, so the tops of the kerbstones were exposed both internally and externally. As can be seen from the section drawing and a photograph, the mound fill consisted of three layers: At the base, a stone layer of three courses, covered by a layer of sand which, in turn, was

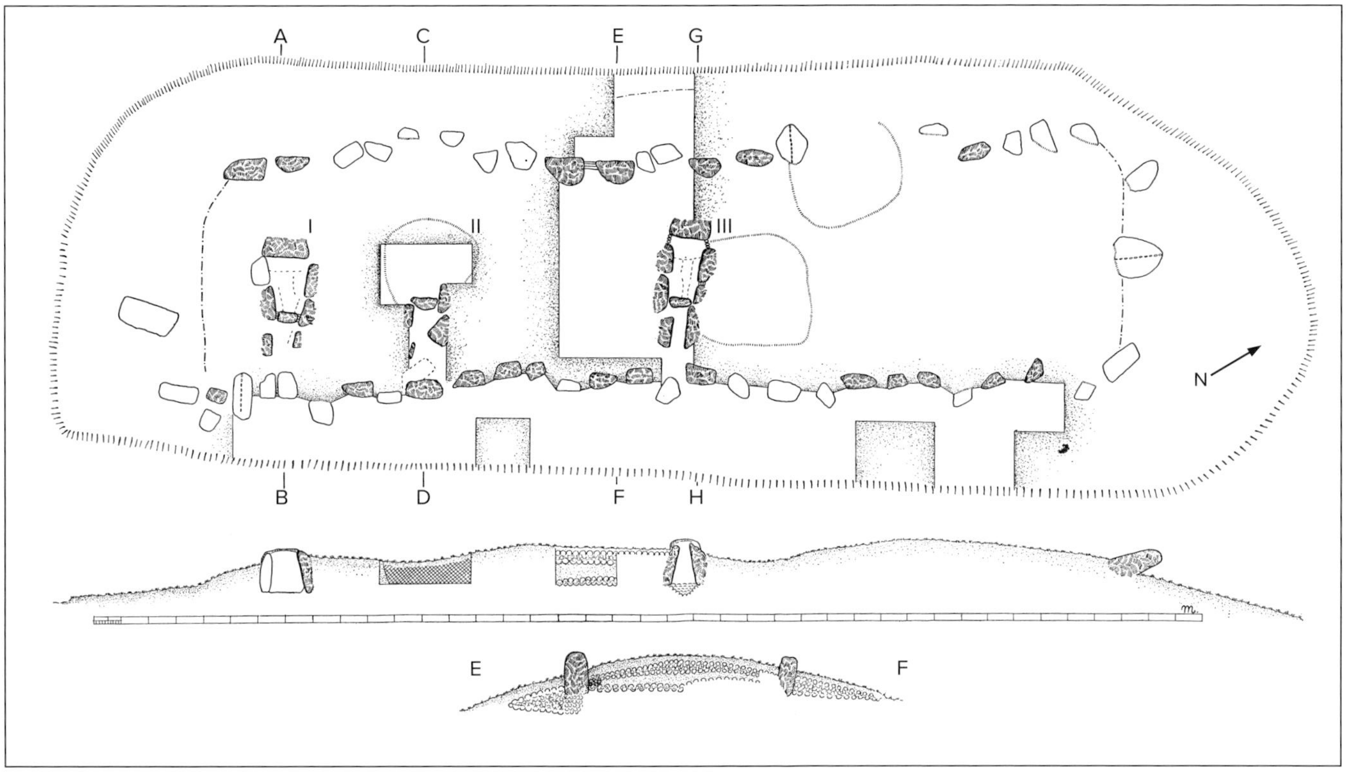

Fig. 6.3. *Plan of the Pæregård long dolmen, together with a longitudinal and transverse section. The sections clearly show the three layers of mound fill: i.e. two layers of stones separated by a layer of sand.*

overlain by a further stone layer of up to at least three courses that lay directly below the surface turf (fig. 6.4). On both long sides outside the kerbstones were "pavements" in the form of layers of stones, the presence of which could have one or more explanations: packing, cultic activities and slippage of material from the mound.

Judging from the three layers evident in the section – two stone layers separated by a sand layer – there may well have been three construction phases. A longitudinal section shows how the layers related to the well-preserved chamber in the middle of the mound (fig. 6.3 middle). The lowermost stone layer lay deep within the mound and presumably only extended a little way up the chambers' capstones, though this cannot be determined. It was followed by the sand layer and over this the upper stone layer, the surface of which was almost on a level with the tops of the orthostats in the chamber.

There was also a lower stone layer in the long dolmen at Grøfte, and it is tempting to see the lower layer in the Pæregård dolmen as its earliest phase, when the chamber and stone pavement could have stood exposed. Or perhaps the stone pavement is older than the chamber.

On the basis of a quantity of potsherds found in front of the kerbstones, Hakon Berg assigned the Pæregård long dolmen to MN Ib (c. 3200 BC) – on the face of it a surprisingly late date for a dolmen chamber, as this is a period normally earmarked for passage graves. If the chambers had had a further set of passage stones abutting the kerbstones, these structures would clearly have been seen as passage graves.

Fig. 6.4. *Large quantities of stone were incorporated into the mound fill of the Pæregård long dolmen. The lower stone layer can be seen exposed in the foreground. In the middle of the picture is dolmen chamber III.*

The slightly trapezoid form of the chambers and opening in one of their short sides apparently assigns them typologically to type II, but the fact that the orthostats stood on end so the chambers were relatively high – 1.5-1.6 m – suggests that they could be later.

Ormstrup

Another long dolmen on the island of Langeland, Ormstrup, was investigated by Hakon Berg in 1957.[6] This monument, the ends of which were missing, was 20 m long and 7.5 m wide. It had a transverse dolmen chamber of type II, which was rectangular, 2.2 m long, 1.2 m wide, 1.3 m high and covered by a capstone. It was built of three stones, one at one end and one at each side. The other end took the form of an opening, opposite which were a couple of passage stones that abutted the inner surface of the kerbstones. The dolmen stands – very unusually – on a small hill, which contributes considerably to its monumentality. This effect was reinforced in the Neolithic by the topsoil being dug away in an up to 7 m wide belt around the monument (see photo on page 56).

No fewer than five transverse sections were recorded and these showed that the interior of the mound consisted of a massive stone packing covered with grass turf and soil (fig. 6.5), but also that this packing did not extend all the way out to the kerbstones. We can therefore imagine two mound phases: An early phase with stone packing, chamber and kerbstones and a space along the inside of the kerbstones – as in the Tårup dolmen, described below – and a later phase, when the inside of the long dolmen was completely filled up with grass turves and earth.[7]

The earliest finds from the chamber were potsherds from MN I and MN Ib. There were several pots from MN I along the south side of the monument, where they could have been placed as votive offerings.

Following the investigation, the Ormstrup long dolmen was restored by Hakon Berg who, albeit with some reservation, believed that the surface of the mound had sloped upwards from the top of the kerbstones to a flat top, above which the chamber's capstone protruded.

Capeshøj

Capeshøj, on the island of Tåsinge, is a 36 m long and 7 m wide long dolmen with a dolmen chamber. When the investigation commenced in 1976, the long dolmen was concealed beneath a large ploughed-down barrow from the Early Bronze Age. When the excavation ended in 1979, the Bronze Age barrow had been dug away and the long dolmen, in a restored state, again stood free (fig. 6.6).[8] The investigation was led by one of the authors, Palle Eriksen, on behalf of Fyns Stiftsmuseum. The overlying Bronze Age barrow was found to have protected the long dolmen well. Some kerb-

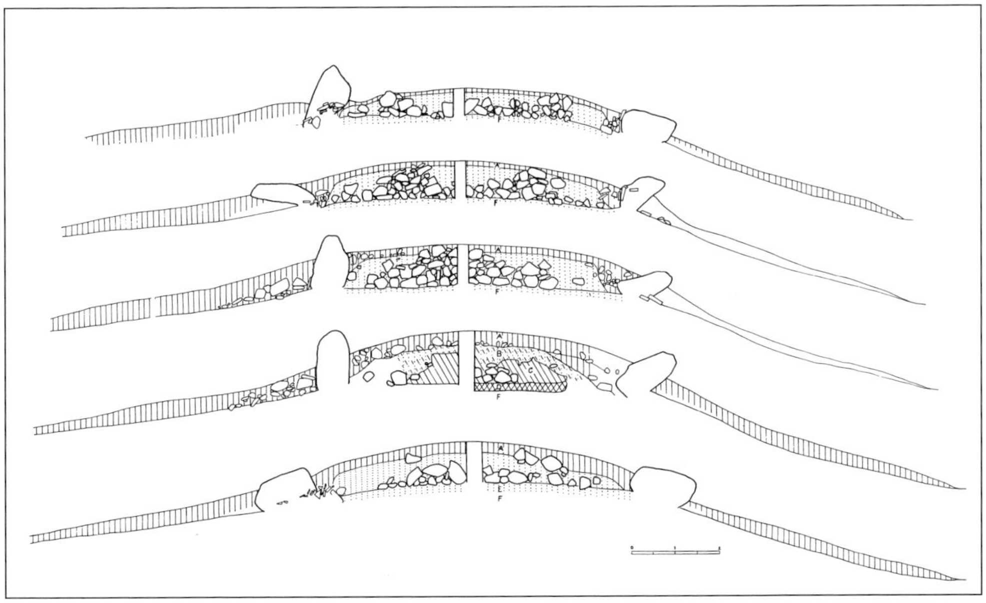

Fig. 6.5. *During the investigation of the Ormstrup long dolmen in 1957, the entire mound was excavated. The five transverse sections generally show two layers: first a stone core with a very uneven surface, followed by an almost stone-free layer.*

Fig. 6.6. *The Capeshøj long dolmen was covered by a large barrow in the Early Bronze Age. It was first in connection with an excavation in the 1970s that the long dolmen again reappeared. It is seen here from the north, surrounded by a circle of small kerbstones belonging to the Bronze Age barrow.*

stones were removed in the period 1952-68, so that only 43 remained of the original 56. The capstone had been removed much earlier, probably around 1900.

The narrow, rectangular chamber lay along the longitudinal axis, approximately in the middle of the long dolmen. Each side consisted of a single large stone. At one end was a threshold stone, which left a 70 cm high opening into the 1.9 m long, 70 cm wide and 1.3 m high chamber (fig. 6.7). In front of the threshold stone was an entrance pit, the sides of which consisted of stacked flagstones. The chamber was of type II.

During the excavation, a 1.5 m wide trench was cut through the middle of the mound, rather more than 6 m from the chamber. From the resulting section, it could be seen that the fill of the long dolmen included large quantities of stone, surrounded by clayey sand (fig. 6.8). It was not possible to observe any system or pattern in the placing of the stones in the relatively narrow trench, apart from the fact that the largest stones lay lowermost and, consequently, directly on the original vegetation surface. At the time this was explained in terms of this being the physically most convenient solution for the dolmen builders. It was clear that the mound comprised two kinds of fill, one near the base, containing large quantities of stone, and another above this, which was almost stone-free. In Capeshøj – as was the case in the Ormstrup long dolmen – there appears to have been an earth- and stone-free belt along the inside of the kerbstones. If the section's testimony is stretched a little, the inner side of this belt – in towards the mound – could well have sloped evenly upwards and been clad with stones.

The section also shows the status of the long dolmen when, two millennia after its construction, it became encapsulated within a large barrow in the Early Bronze Age. Some of the kerbstones, especially those at the gables of the long dolmen, had toppled completely outwards and others leaned heavily, the upper parts of the dry-walling had slipped outwards and the earth and stone fill from inside the long dolmen had followed suit. A new turf layer had formed over the dilapidated long dolmen, which was then sealed by the grass-turf fill of the Bronze Age barrow. But prior to this, the Bronze Age barrow-builders had pushed over those of the long dolmen's kerbstones that would otherwise protrude above the surface of their barrow.

The section through the middle of the mound provides a unique opportunity to reconstruct the original surface of the long dolmen, because it appears that modern

Fig. 6.7. *The chamber of the Capeshøj long dolmen is of type II, i.e. with an entrance at one end, over a threshold stone.*

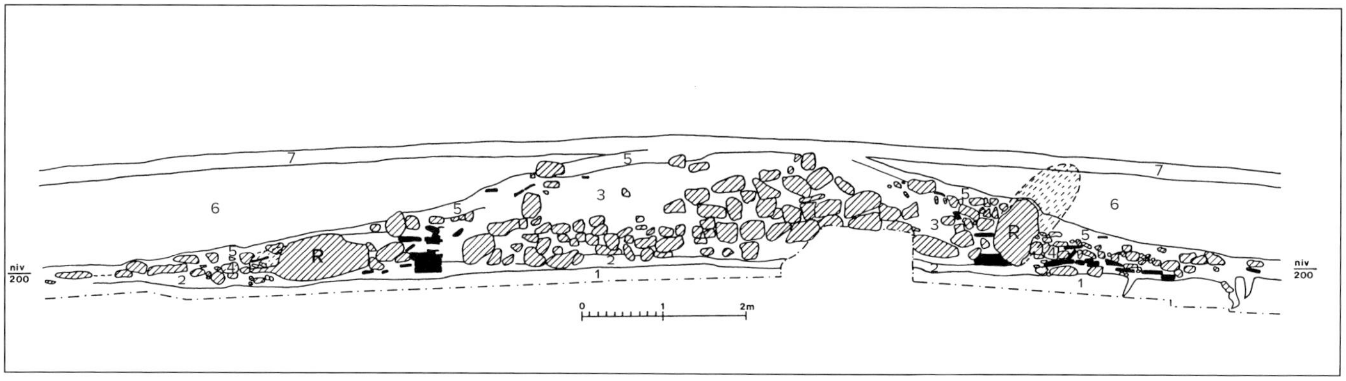

Fig. 6.8. *The transverse section through Capeshøj shows that the long dolmen's overgrown surface, layer 5, has lain undisturbed since the Bronze Age. 1: Subsoil. 2: Topsoil on which the long dolmen was built. 3: Mound fill of the long dolmen. 4: Slippage from 3. 5: Topsoil on which the Bronze Age barrow was built. 6: Fill of the Bronze Age barrow, originally grass turf. 7: Modern topsoil. R: Kerbstone. Red sandstone slabs belonging to the dry-walling are marked in black.*

ploughing had not levelled the top of the monument significantly. If the kerbstones are righted, the collapsed dry-walling is re-established and the slipped-out fill replaced, a flat surface is obtained that possibly slopes slightly up towards the middle of the monument. Judging from the section by the chamber, the slippage here has been considerable, and if this material is replaced, the capstone could not have been fully exposed (fig. 6.9). It is, however, possible that the lowermost part of this layer was not the result of slippage, but was deposited here in connection with the rituals performed at the long dolmen.

Asnæs Forskov

In 1986, Anne Birgitte Gebauer of Kalundborg Museum investigated a long dolmen that stood on the edge of the coastal slope on the Asnæs peninsula, south of Kalundborg.[9] The reason was that parts of the monument had already collapsed into the sea and the part closest to the coastal slope would soon follow suit. The north-south-oriented long dolmen had therefore only one surviving gable (fig. 6.10). Its length in 1986 was slightly more than 23 m, its width was 7 m and its height 1.4 m. An investigation was carried out of the 10 m part of the monument closest to the coastal slope. The long dolmen had originally been surrounded by closely-spaced kerbstones, of which 23 were preserved. The largest kerbstones were situated in the gable. The long dolmen must be presumed to have had at least one stone-built chamber, which could have either stood in the part of the monument that had fallen into the sea prior to the investigation, or was still hidden in the uninvestigated part. A grave of Konens Høj type was, however, discovered – in the form of a wooden cist surrounded by stones. The grave had the same orientation as the long dolmen, but lay displaced relative to its central axis. No traces were found of a mound over the grave and the excavator believes that both the stratigraphy and the asymmetric position of the grave relative to the mound indicate that the long dolmen was added later in the area to the north of the grave.

As usual, the gaps between the kerbstones were closed with dry-walling. The material that had collapsed and slipped out from the dilapidated long dolmen

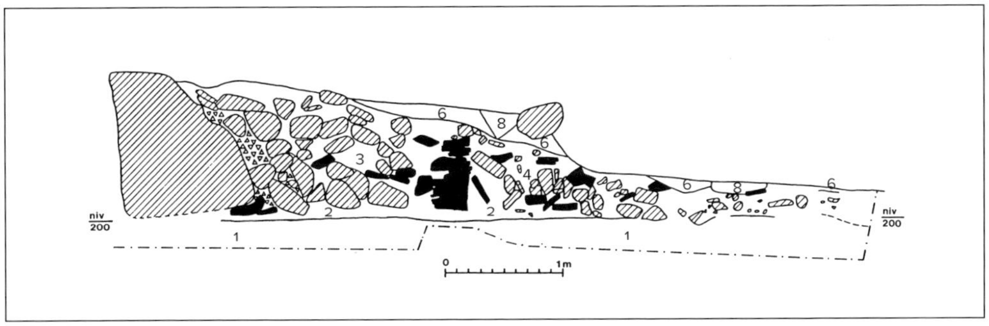

Fig. 6.9. *Around dolmen chambers there is often a solid packing containing large quantities of stones, as seen here at Capeshøj. This section, seen from the north, is cut at right angles to the chamber's western orthostat. The dry-walling, shown in black, is preserved almost in its full height. All the stone slabs are marked in black. The packing around the chamber often includes crushed flint, marked here with small triangles. Otherwise the description is the same as for figure 6.8.*

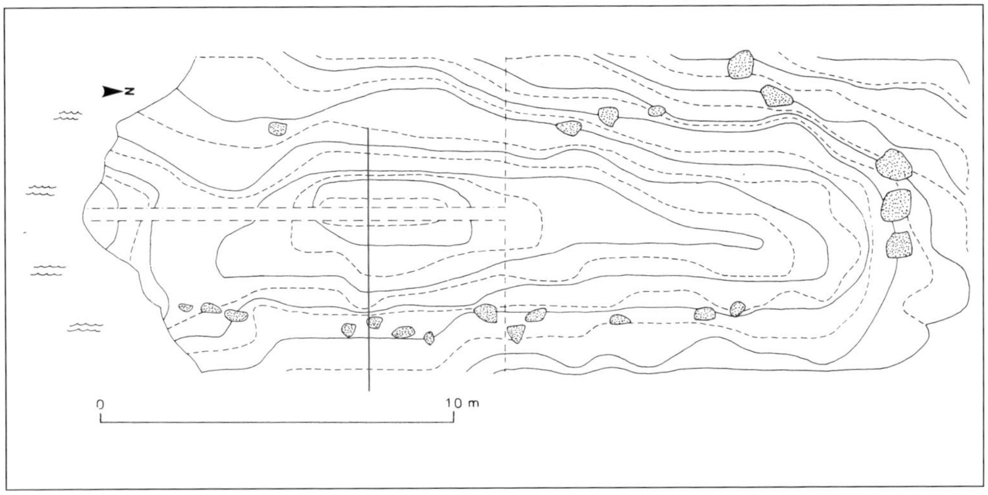

Fig. 6.10. *Plan of the long dolmen in Asnæs Forskov, the left half of which was investigated in 1986. The red line marks the position of the reproduced section.*

included such large quantities of flagstones that the excavator suggests that the dry-walling had extended to the top of the kerbstones.

At the time of the investigation, the surface of the long dolmen was almost horizontal, though slightly domed. Longitudinal and transverse sections revealed that, lowermost, it had an inner core of stones covered with earth, and uppermost a surface covering consisting primarily of two layers of smaller stones, including flagstones (fig. 6.11). The intervening layer, the soil layer between the two stone layers, deserves more detailed description: It is very similar to the subsoil at the site, largely uncontaminated, slightly sandy, greyish-yellow clay, but containing charcoal particles. This layer also had areas with larger quantities of charcoal, crushed flint and clayey gravel. These deposits perhaps reflect the fact that the associated surface has had its own time and its own activities. From this it follows that the mound fill of the long dolmen, which also includes the massive stone layer below and the fine stone pavement above the aforementioned soil layer with charcoal, accumulated in several stages.

The long dolmen in Asnæs Forskov is later than the Konens Høj grave, but its construction cannot be dated more precisely than to no later than the beginning of the Middle Neolithic. The reason it is, nevertheless, included here is due partly to

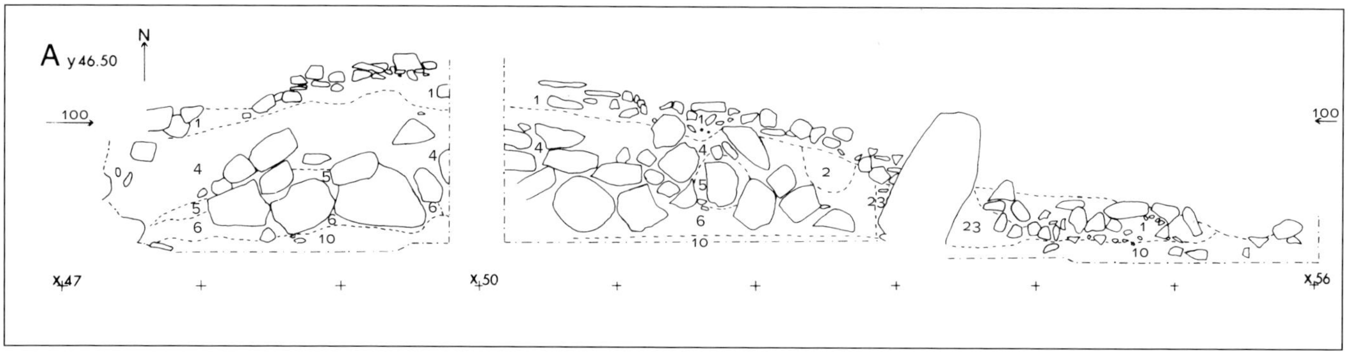

Fig. 6.11. *The section through the Asnæs Forskov long dolmen shows three layers. At the base, and earliest, is a layer of large stones, followed by a stone-free zone. Uppermost, and latest, is a layer of stone slabs and smaller stones that constituted the final surface of the long dolmen.*

its well-preserved mound, which perhaps had three phases, and partly because its final appearance can apparently be very reliably reconstructed. The long dolmen was surrounded by kerbstones, the gaps between which were closed all the way to the top with dry-walling. The surface of the mound was flat or slightly domed and covered with smaller stones and flagstones.

Skelde

In 1990-91, Per Ethelberg of Haderslev Museum undertook an investigation of a large ploughed-down barrow at Skelde on the Broager Land peninsula.[10] The barrow proved to comprise three mound phases: A long dolmen that, in the Early Bronze Age, was almost completely covered by a round barrow which, in turn, was extended later in that same period (fig. 6.12). Due to the overlying Bronze Age barrow, the long dolmen was not only exceptionally well-preserved, but had also survived in virtually its full height. Following the investigation, the long dolmen, which has one chamber, was restored and scheduled.

According to the excavator, construction of the long dolmen proceeded as follows: First the dolmen chamber was erected, after which it was surrounded by a rectangular, 24 m long and 7.5 m wide stone pavement. A total of 52 kerbstones were then erected on top of the stone pavement, enclosing an area of 21 x 4.5 m. There were particularly tall kerbstones at the long dolmen's four corners. After the kerbstones had been erected, further infilling of the interior of the long dolmen took place with head-sized and larger stones, covered with a grey-black mixture of soil and clay. Very probably only the uppermost parts of the kerbstones and capstone were visible – though the cornerstones must have been more prominent. Within the kerbstones, the mound was flat, but outside them its sides sloped downwards.

The chamber, which lay along the longitudinal axis of the mound, was of the narrow, rectangular kind with orthostats of equal height; two at each side and one at each end (figs. 6.13 and 9.12). The capstone must have been removed long ago, perhaps already in antiquity. The chamber, which internally was 2 m long, 50-60 cm wide and 70 cm high, was built of stone slabs, i.e. stones with parallel sides and of relatively modest thickness, no more than half a metre. In our terminology this is therefore a dolmen cist, and as a type it is probably earlier than the earliest dolmen chambers. The chamber was found to contain a collared flask and a lugged flask.

The construction history of the Skelde long dolmen contains several phases or stages: dolmen cist – stone pavement – kerbstones – further stones in the interior – and finally a grey-black soil-clay mixture on top. The final layer could perhaps represent a turf layer on which the Bronze Age barrow was built, in which case the long dolmen had, for a time, a stone-covered surface like the other long dolmens mentioned in this chapter.

The fact that there are at least two distinct phases, separated by a longer period, is also demonstrated by pollen samples taken from the fill of the Skelde long dolmen. The pollen data show a clear difference between the vegetation and its exploitation represented in the soil layer on which the long dolmen was built and that in the mound fill of the monument. Pollen analysis revealed that the soil on which the dolmen was

Fig. 6.12. *On this aerial photo of the Skelde long dolmen under excavation, the monument is apparent as an elongate, rectangular stone pavement, with the chamber to the left. The two arcs of stones each belong to a separate Bronze Age barrow, built one over the other, and over the long dolmen.*

Fig. 6.13. *After the excavation, the Skelde long dolmen was restored and scheduled. Given its not very thick stones, the structure is classified as a dolmen cist – the forerunner of actual dolmen chambers made of thicker stones.*

built in the Early Neolithic lay in an area where birch woodland had been burnt, while the mound fill was taken from clearances in hazel woodland. Scrub woodland dominated by hazel has, to date, not been found associated with Early Neolithic structures. So it is very likely that the soil for the dolmen was added later, probably at the transition to the Middle Neolithic, when hazel woodland expanded as a consequence of slash and burn agriculture and woodland management, i.e. coppicing.[11]

Tårup

During the construction of the motorway between Vejle and Fredericia, a previously unknown round dolmen discovered at Tårup was excavated in 1992, as it would be adversely affected by the construction works. The round dolmen was found to be well preserved because it had been covered by a large barrow with a diameter of 60 m in the Early Bronze Age. The investigation was led by Lone Hvass of Vejle Museum, and another participant was Mads Kähler Holst, who also published the findings.[12] When the investigation was complete, the stones of the round dolmen were moved and the chamber re-erected at the newly-built motorway service station at Skærup Øst, east of the motorway. A copy of the great Bronze Age barrow was also built beside it. The round dolmen, which was surrounded by kerbstones, had a diameter of 10 m (fig. 6.14). The chamber lay roughly in the middle of the mound. It was built of two stones at each side and one broader stone at one end. At the other end, to the south, was a threshold stone. Here, too, was the entrance, a 50 x 50 cm opening into the chamber when the capstone was in place. There were no passage stones. The chamber, which had internal dimensions of 2.2 x 1.3 m, and a height of 1.2 m, had lost its capstone, presumably as a consequence of a secondary burial in the Late Neolithic. No artefacts were found originating from the earliest use of the chamber, so it must be dated typologically. It is of type III, an expanded dolmen, corresponding to the southern Funen Klokkehøj dolmen, which is dated to the Fuchsberg phase.[13]

During the investigation, attention was focussed on finding possible traces, which could reveal whether the chamber had, for a time, been free-standing. It was not, however, possible to demonstrate this unequivocally, but according to Mads Kähler Holst it appears likely this was the case. In addition to this hypothetical free-standing phase there were two clearly demonstrable phases, 1 and 2, in the round dolmen's construction history.

Phase 1 was evident both in plan and in section as remains of a stone wall of up to four courses in height that had delimited a mound with a diameter of 6.5-7 m around the chamber (fig. 6.14 yellow). According to the excavators, outside this stone wall was a 1-1.5 m wide stone- and earth-free belt, screened outwardly by a circle of kerbstones. There was no dry-walling between the kerbstones.

In *phase 2*, the free area between the phase 1 mound and the circle of kerbstones was filled up with sand and covered with stones that were preserved in up to five courses (fig. 6.14 red). This stone layer probably covered the entire mound, giving it the appearance of a cairn, with the upper part of the capstone possibly visible. Outside the kerbstones were traces of an up to 2 m wide stone pavement that may have encircled the entire monument.

Mounds with many phases

Described above are six long dolmens and a round dolmen that were all well-furnished with mound material and had stone-covered surfaces which, in their final phases, extended from the top of the kerbstones to the lower surface of the capstone

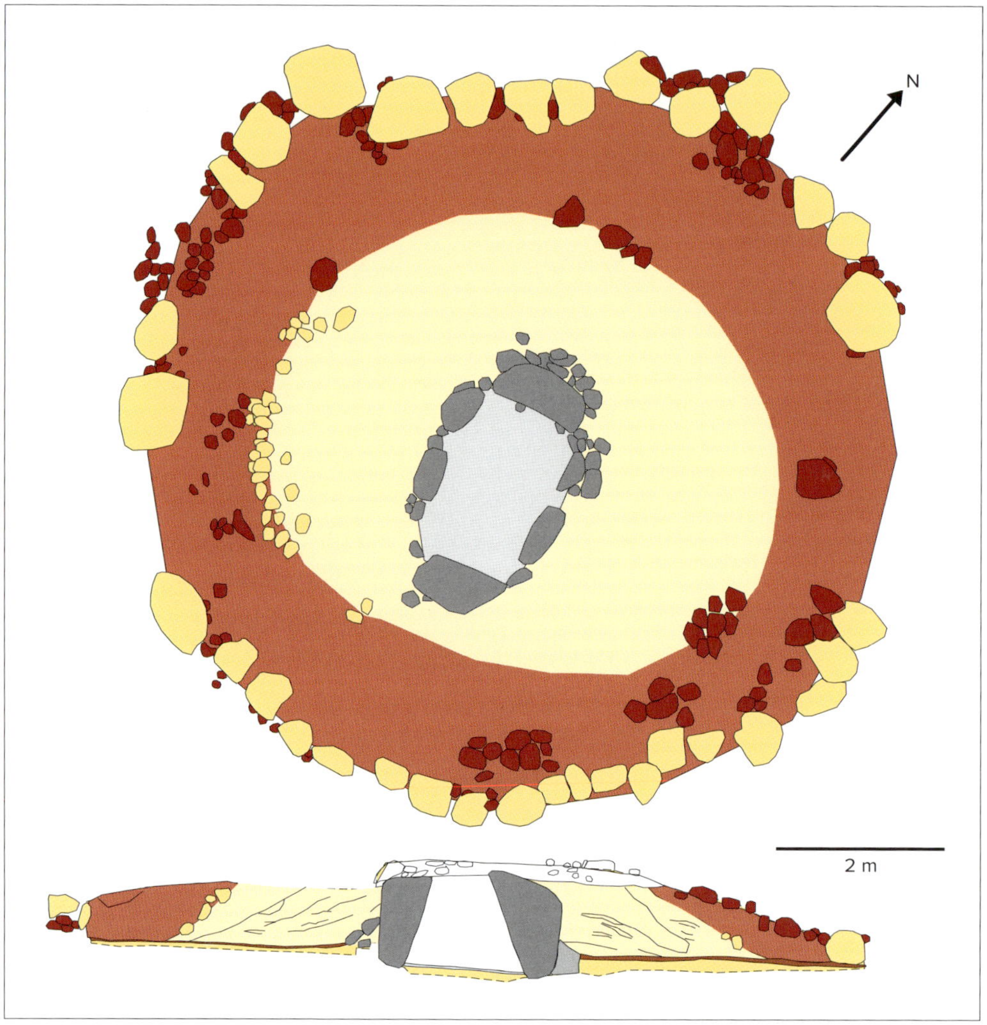

Fig. 6.14. *Plan of and section through the Tårup round dolmen, showing the two main phases of the monument's construction history, as proposed by the excavators. Earliest – phase 1, shown in yellow – is a small stone-clad mound around the chamber and a circle of kerbstones. Between the mound and the kerbstones is a stone- and earth-free belt. Latest – phase 2, shown in red – is the filling up of the stone- and earth-free belt with a layer of soil that also covered the sides of the earlier mound. The surface of this mound was also clad with a layer of stones. Very earliest – phase 0, and not documented in the excavation – could have been the chamber itself, which may have been free-standing, without a mound and kerbstones.*

on the chamber. The surfaces of these mounds were horizontal or sloped slightly up towards the middle. In all these dolmens it is clear that their final appearance was the result of a construction sequence that included at least two, and often more, phases, i.e. they are *multi-period mounds*. If the use of any one of these dolmens had, for some reason or other, ceased at an early stage in this sequence, the monument could today have been a dolmen without a mound.

A long dolmen at Strids Mølle, beautifully situated by the river Suså, northwest of Næstved, was excavated in 2005 by Svend Hansen of the Danish Agency for Culture and Palaces (at that time the Danish Heritage Agency). This demonstrated the presence of a compact mound structure around the chamber, which was of type I. This feature was interpreted as showing that the *entire* long dolmen mound had consisted of stones laid at the same time as the construction of the chamber.[14]

However, sections through long dolmens that include the actual chamber are, as such, not representative of the mound composition and construction as a whole, because the chambers, with their massive stones, require special supportive and drainage structures in the surrounding mounds. This is the case for example at both Grøfte (fig. 6.1) and Capeshøj, where a dense concentration of stones is seen in the section running up to the chamber (fig. 6.9).[15]

In the long dolmens where the mound surface is on a level with the top of the chamber's capstone, it is interesting to see how the problem of gaining access to the chamber has been solved. In two of the investigated dolmens – Pæregård and Capeshøj – access to the dolmen chamber was made possible by the construction of an entrance shaft. Whether shafts of this kind are a primary or a secondary feature has yet to be resolved. If either of these two dolmens has had a mound-free stage, the entrance shafts could well be a later addition.

7. Tricky open dolmens

There are many open dolmens around Denmark that have no, or almost no, mound material between the chamber and the kerbstones. Some of these have split, broken or even missing stones, and together with holes and irregularities in the surface, they bear witness to human disruption and disturbance in modern times, and to the fact that the mound fill could well have been removed as a consequence.

But there are also numerous undisrupted open dolmens that have all, or almost all, their stones intact and in place and also level inner surfaces with no indication whatsoever of digging or other human activity. The Sites and Monuments database and other records (see chapter 8) state that some of these dolmens have been restored. Formerly – in the 1930s and 1940s – this meant that they had been rendered neat and attractive. A number of dolmens were restored at that time by conservator Julius Raklev of the Danish National Museum: Leaning kerbstones were righted and missing stones were sometimes replaced, fallen capstones were restored to their original positions, holes in the surface were filled in and mound fill presumed to have slipped downwards and outwards was "put back in place". Posterity has not passed kind judgement on these restorations, the aim of which was to enhance the appearance of the monuments so they appeared as it was believed they did in prehistory.[1] The restoration work involved extensive interventions into these dolmens and was also undertaken without prior scientific investigation.

As a consequence, we cannot exclude the possibility that mound fill has also been removed in the case of these "neat" open dolmens. In the following, accounts and assessments are given of three *very* open dolmens: one in Korsør Skov and one in Vinskoven, both in western Zealand, and one at Rønde on Djursland, eastern Jutland.

The long dolmen in Korsør Skov

The guide *Vore Fortidsminder* (see chapter 8) contains a very intriguing account, relative to open dolmens, of a dolmen in Korsør Skov: "Long dolmen without earthen mound. Chamber of 3 orthostats and 1 capstone and surrounded by kerbstones." (fig. 7.1). The same forest also contains a magnificent example of a dolmen without a mound: a 40 m long and 7 m wide long dolmen, oriented approximately east-west and with a large number of kerbstones, the tallest of which stand at its gables. Its only chamber lies oriented on the long dolmen's long axis, 13-15 m from the western end. There is no mound fill whatsoever, so the narrow, elongate chamber is free-standing and very conspicuous. It has a stone at each side and one of matching height at the east gable, while there is no stone at the west gable. As it appears today, the chamber is therefore of type II. It is closed from above by a capstone, half of which is, however, missing (fig. 7.2). Even so, as it stands in the forest the long dolmen is a striking monu-

Fig. 7.1. *The long dolmen in Korsør occupies an idyllic setting, surrounded by tall, ancient beech trees.*

ment, with all its kerbstones upright. On a plan produced by A.P. Madsen in 1890, 48 kerbstones are drawn in and it appears that a further 18 are missing. At the site today, however, there are 62 kerbstones and only around nine are missing.[2]

The dolmen in Korsør Skov was scheduled by its owner, Korsør Town Council, in 1890, and of the kerbstones, the scheduling declaration states: "A good many of them have lain fallen, but have been re-erected in their original positions." As for the chamber, this is said to have previously been in a state of collapse with half of the capstone lying some distance away.[3] The archive also contains a letter from Korsør Forskønnelsesselskab. The society wrote to the National Museum of Denmark on 28th June 1917, following its annual general meeting, asking permission for a stone mason to remove the blast hole "that at some time has been drilled in connection with the dynamiting" of the capstone. Permission appears either not to have been given or exercised, as the blast hole is still visible today (fig. 7.2).

So a degree of interest and enthusiasm was directed towards giving the dolmen an attractive appearance in the publicly-owned woodland, which was probably a popular picnic and walking destination for the town's citizens. It is therefore obvious to conclude that, at some time prior to 1890, the long dolmen had been extensively tidied up, with any holes and irregularities in its surface being filled and levelled out.

Even so, there is a latent suspicion that this is not a true dolmen without a mound. The scheduling declaration states that: "The earthen fill within the kerbstones is very low." But as this applies to the situation in 1890, the long dolmen could well have had a different appearance prior to this – as testified to by the toppled kerbstones and the cloven capstone.

The clerical reports of the early 19th century (see chapter 8) include a description from 1809 of the excavation of a dolmen chamber in Corsøer Bøgeskov: "… there was on top of the high bank a pagan burial with large and heavy victory stones or *bauta* stones. I ordered an excavation to gain access. The grave had large, heavy stones on both sides and on top a large stone which covered the grave. At the eastern side I could, with great difficulty, gain access to the grave, which was hollow like a cellar …"[4]

The pagan burial referred to is the actual dolmen chamber, and the "victory stones" or bauta stones, as they are termed, must be the kerbstones. All in all, this is consistent with "our" long dolmen, which stands high in the terrain. But the information given by the excavator, customs officer Jacob Machesen, that he entered the chamber via an opening in the eastern side does not fit with the situation today, where the chamber is closed to the east and has a convenient opening to the west. The chamber had though collapsed, and could well have been altered later during the restoration carried out by the good citizens of Korsør, who may similarly have added further kerbstones.[5]

That caution should be exercised when dealing with information on old excavations provided by laymen is clearly evident from customs officer Machesen's account of finding "a human skeleton" in the chamber. According to Machesen, this skeleton was of an individual who, when alive, had been 5½ alen tall – i.e. 3.5 m!

Fig. 7.2. *Part of the capstone over the chamber of the Korsør Skov long dolmen is missing. A drilled blast hole is obvious in its cloven surface.*

The long dolmen in Korsør Skov may originally have been an open monument, but given the possibility that it once had mound fill, and in the light of the tidying and restoration work carried out in recent times, we must for the time being dismiss it as a true open dolmen.

The long dolmen in Vinskoven

Another open dolmen is a long dolmen located in Vinskoven, 6 km south of Mørkøv in western Zealand. In *Vore Fortidsminder* it is described as an "Exceptionally fine and impressive long dolmen, somewhat restored by the owner; there is no earthen mound but a large chamber of 3 orthostats, threshold stone and 1 large capstone; the kerbstones are large and handsome." The long dolmen, which occupies an idyllic setting next to a half-timbered house directly by the road running through Vinskoven, is almost 40 m long and 8.5 m wide (fig. 7.3). Nearly all its kerbstones are in place and number 66 in total. Roughly in the middle of the monument, and oriented across its longitudinal axis, stands a dolmen chamber with a capstone. This is rectangular in form and apparently of the earlier type II, with three orthostats and a threshold stone (fig. 7.4).

Fig. 7.3. *The long dolmen in Vinskoven stands next to the road running through the forest.*

Fig. 7.4. *The dolmen chamber in the Vinskoven long dolmen could very well have been restored, as the long dolmen has been "tidied up", with toppled kerbstones being re-erected and aligned. This probably took place during the second half of the 19th century.*

In 1891, Master of the Royal Hunt Carl Treschow, Torbenfeldt, bequeathed the dolmen for scheduling, though on the condition that he retained the right to a large stone that lay beside the chamber. It was presumed at the time that this stone represented the remains of a second chamber. It is also known that several of the kerbstones were re-erected, probably on the order of Treschow. The large stone was taken away in 1900 and has since stood by the manor chapel, Frydendal church, at Torbenfeldt. The original plan was to place it by the manor house, but it was considered imprudent to transport such a heavy stone over the bridge crossing the moat. A contemporary photograph shows how long levers were used to raise the stone on to a heavy cart in order to carry it away from the long dolmen (fig. 7.5).

If one did not know that the long dolmen in Vinskoven had been restored, one could very easily be fooled. On the face of it, the monument appears rather undisturbed; there are not many missing kerbstones and of those remaining, few show signs of being cleaved with explosives. On closer examination, however, it turns out that some of the kerbstones, especially those at the corners, stand rather oddly and a kerbstone is missing in one place because, at the time the stones were re-erected, a tree grew there. The chamber too seems a little strange, and the orthostat at the gable has features resembling cleavage marks. Moreover, the monument is very trim and almost *too* neat and well maintained. The traces of the second chamber have been completely obliterated. At other dolmens with cloven chamber stones, larger or smaller fragments of stone usually remain. A flat stone on the soil surface perhaps marks the position of the demolished chamber.

Fig. 7.5. *In 1900, a large stone was removed from the long dolmen in Vinskoven and transported to the nearby manor of Torbenfeldt, where it was placed by the chapel. The stone may well have been a capstone from a demolished dolmen chamber, so this monument originally had two chambers.*

As in the case of the long dolmen in Korsør Skov, we are again fortunate in having a clerical report, this time from 1808, which contains a description of the long dolmen in Vinskoven: "In Sønderskov at Viinhuset is a large long dolmen, in the middle of which is a burial that still lies quite undisturbed and the cavity of which under the large capstone between the four side stones, on which it rests, appears very deep – There are in the stone heap many large dressed stones, which permit the assumption that constructed here was a building of very considerable size …"[6]

An important piece of information given here is that, in 1808, the chamber had four orthostats, on which the capstone rested. If this is taken at face value, then all the orthostats were of the same height and the chamber was of type I, i.e. it had a different appearance to that of today. The "many large dressed stones" that are present in the "stone heap" could either be from the second chamber which was destroyed by stone masons or stones that lay within the kerbstones as a form of mound fill, corresponding to the situation evident at the Gunderslevholm dolmen (see chapter 11). The former explanation appears most likely.

In the 19th century and the first decades of the 20th century, many estate owners established large collections of antiquities.[7] The ancient monuments on manorial lands were often the focus of eager attention and selected barrows or, as in the case here in Vinskoven, dolmens were enhanced and embellished and in some cases even moved or transformed, especially when they stood close to the manor houses. For example, a round dolmen was constructed at Moesgaard near Aarhus, and a long dolmen at Marienborg on the island of Møn (fig. 7.6).

For the same reasons as given for the long dolmen in Korsør Skov, the impressive open dolmen in Vinskoven must unfortunately also be dismissed as a genuine open dolmen. This may well have been the case, but we simply cannot be certain of this.

A long dolmen and a round dolmen at Rønde

It was not only wealthy urban citizens and rural lords of the manor, or for that matter the Danish National Museum, who were responsible for the restoration and tidying up of dolmens. Ordinary farmers and smallholders, whose interest in prehistory and the fatherland had perhaps found ample nourishment during time spent at a folk high-school, also transformed and embellished monuments according to their own personal tastes. There are several examples, and a case from Jutland will be outlined here.

South of the old Aarhus-Grenå highway, between Følle and Rønde, a group of trees stands out in the middle of a field and encloses an area containing some large stones (fig. 7.7 and photo on page 74). These belong to an impressive dolmen which has no mound, but several chambers. The monument is not easy to decipher: It has the form of a long dolmen, oriented almost north-south, and has 28 kerbstones which describe a course that constitutes a semicircle to the south and which narrows towards the north. Within the circle to the south there is a single chamber, while there are three chambers in the northern part. None of these chambers is complete; they all lack their capstones, and several orthostats are also missing. Moreover, to an

Fig. 7.6. *In Kløverværnget at Marienborg Manor on the island of Møn stands an artificial "long dolmen", which was drawn by A.P. Madsen in 1880. The 14 m long structure is pointed oval in form and surrounded by kerbstones, with tall bauta-like stones at the gables. The "monument", which also has a chamber with a capstone, was built in the 1790s as a piece of prehistoric scenery in a romantic garden, on the orders of the antiquarian lord of the manor, Antoine de la Calmette. Several of the stones used in it were taken from genuine ancient monuments.*

Fig. 7.7. *From a distance, the dolmen at Rønde has a picturesque appearance. The silhouettes of the many stones show that not much mound material is present.*

archaeologist's eye, some of the chambers and the form of the long dolmen appear rather odd. It is, nevertheless, an impressive monument, with sizable free-standing stones, protruding vertically from the soil and unconcealed by mound fill. The monument has very clearly been restored; no stones lie toppled and it all appears so neat and tidy (fig. 7.8).

The explanation for the peculiar form of the kerbstone circle is to be found in the earliest description of the monument from 1894. This states that the round end is part of a round dolmen and that, to the north, this meets the narrow end of a long dolmen. The description, with accompanying sketch (fig. 7.9), is the work of J.V. Nissen, a schoolteacher in Ramten, who was an enthusiastic participant in the Danish National Museum's country-wide district surveys and was very active in surveying and recording the ancient monuments on Djursland. Djursland's dolmens held his particular interest, and thanks to his records we have a great deal of information that otherwise would have been lost. In the case of "Remains of a long dolmen and a round dolmen, Følle", he refers first to the long dolmen: "Towards the north, the dolmen is truncated and the soil is cultivated. Close by are two 4′ [1.3 m] high orthostats. Stones a, b, c and d are earthfast stones, but whether they actually belong to the long dolmen cannot be determined for certain. Similarly, there is on the whole a great lack of clarity about the remains of the long dolmen. It seems very likely that a chamber stood in the southern part of the dolmen at [the place marked] gr. but now there is not the least trace of its stones. Neither are any traces evident of the capstone and the missing orthostats in the northern chamber. With the construction of the nearby highway in 1854, this and several other dolmens in the area were plundered. There is no likelihood of grave goods being present. None of the stones shows score marks or worn surfaces. The kerbstones are 3′ to 4′ [0.9-1.3 m] high, only a few are taller."[8]

He then continues with a description of the round dolmen: "A is presumably a piece of the capstone. The chamber is ruined; but it has not been ascertained whether the grave goods are still present. The kerbstones are from 3-4′ [0.9-1.3 m] high, and as there is only a little fill between them and the chamber, they are quite free-standing."

It could not have been easy to describe the two structures. Moreover, he states that: "Both dolmens are heavily overgrown with thorns, brambles and wild roses, so several measurements were difficult to take, and others are lacking, as they could not be taken." According to the accompanying sketch, the preserved part of the long dolmen was 40′ long, corresponding to 12.5 m, while the dimensions of the round dolmen are not recorded. Later, in 1946, the round dolmen was measured as having a diameter of 11 m.[9]

Judging from schoolteacher Nissen's description and sketch, we appear to be dealing with a round dolmen with a destroyed chamber and a long dolmen with a truncated northern end and traces of two ruined chambers. The curved course of the long dolmen's west side – the earthfast stones a, b, c and d on the sketch shown in figure 7.9 – appears strange and "round-dolmen-like".

Fig. 7.8. *All the surviving stones in the Rønde dolmen, which comprises both a round and a long dolmen, have been righted. To the left, towards the tree, an uneven row of kerbstones can be seen on the eastern side of the long dolmen. The round dolmen is in the background.*

Fig. 7.9. *On his visit to the Rønde dolmen in 1894, schoolteacher J.V. Nissen drew this ground plan. To the south stands the round dolmen and to the north the disrupted long dolmen. In the round dolmen is a stone marked "A" with a number of cleavage holes. Nissen suggested that the stone represented the remains of a capstone from the demolished chamber. He wrote that the stones marked "a, b, c, d" on the west side of the long dolmen possibly do not belong to it. In the place marked "gr" inside the long dolmen there could have been a chamber. Nissen noted that "All stones very large and standing. This is the result of heavy-handed and unfortunate restoration undertaken by the owner himself."*

In the years between schoolteacher Nissen's recording work in 1894 and our visit in 2010, something must have happened at the site. In this respect there is help to be found in the archives. In 1936, the owners of the site, farmer Niels Peter Andersen and his wife Petrea Andersen, had the two monuments scheduled. On that occasion museum curator Mogens B. Mackeprang of the Danish National Museum provided new information about them in a letter to the National Museum written at Rønde Hotel. He reports that the structures were more exposed than in 1894, such that there appear to have been three chambers in the long dolmen: "According to the owner, the chambers were fully exposed in 1916-17 and many loads of earth and stone were transported away … Some of the large stones that schoolteacher Nissen mentions, including the remains of the capstones, were probably taken away during the period between his visit and the aforementioned exposure." And then Mackeprang ends his letter in a rather puzzling and thought-provoking way with the words: "a scheduling stone marker should probably be erected at the site as the farmer states that people pester him for the stones for various purposes."[10] A scheduling stone was erected two years later.

These two closely adjacent dolmens have had a strange fate. After having been subjected to stone plundering in the middle of the 19th century, the very degraded monuments were restored around 1920, when the owner "tidied up" their interior, straightened and re-erected the stones as he thought they should stand. It is an instructive chain of events. Earth and stones could well have been taken away without interfering with the large stones, instead of which the latter were actually taken care of. So the long dolmen could originally have had a quantity of mound fill, while the round dolmen may well have been an open dolmen, similar to Poskær Stenhus and the Tustrup round dolmen.

The moral of the story

Some examples have been given here of how seemingly obvious open dolmens, which appear convincing as *genuine* open dolmens, need not necessarily be so. Searches in the archives (see next chapter) can provide information on destruction and subsequent restoration work undertaken in former times.

There is therefore good reason to carry out a thorough search of the archives and older literature when we want to discover as much as possible about a monument without actually undertaking an excavation. The latter is now the preserve of professional archaeologists and, in the case of scheduled ancient monuments, there have to be very special grounds before permission can be given for these to be excavated. Excavation will often reveal whether a dolmen has one or more phases, and whether special circumstances suggest that it originally was an open dolmen. Results of such investigations of non-scheduled monuments are outlined in chapter 20.

Early descriptions of the appearance of dolmens and the details of excavations, as well as the presence of stone pavements and stone circles (see chapters 11-13) on the surface between the chamber and the kerbstones, can confirm whether monuments are authentic open dolmens.

But in many cases we do not know whether monuments that appear to be open dolmens have always been so. Appearances can be deceptive, and they can be tricky. Some of these monuments have perhaps always been open, in other cases the mound fill may have been dug away in recent times.

8. The selection process

The popular symbol of "the Danish dolmen" is of some large stones standing on a mound and supporting an even larger stone. The popular symbol of an archaeologist is someone permanently on fieldwork. Both images contain an element of truth, but they do not tell the whole story. An archaeologist on fieldwork investigates monuments or deposits that ultimately represent the best sources of information about prehistory. But this gives a very incomplete picture of an archaeologist's work, because much of it takes place behind a desk, in the library and in the archives.

Poskær Stenhus was the first dolmen that opened our eyes to the phenomenon of the genuine open dolmen, and the nearby Stenhus dolmen at Strands could perhaps fall into the same category. Then there were a number of open dolmens mentioned in the literature, or those to which helpful colleagues drew our attention: Tustrup, Ormslev near Aarhus, Tårup near Vejle, Skelde near Sønderborg, Hydeskov Fredskov on the island of Lolland, Lunden on the island of Langeland and, on Zealand, the Gunderslevholm dolmen and the dolmens in Vinskoven and Grøfte II – not to be confused with the nearby Grøfte long dolmen, not forgetting Trollasten in Scania, Sweden. The hunt for open dolmens then began in earnest. But how were we to gain an overview and obtain further information, or even identify them among Denmark's around 1500 scheduled dolmens, before we set off to seek them out across the country? The first places to look are, of course, always in the archives and in the literature.

Archives and the literature

The basic archive for ancient monuments in Denmark today is the Sites and Monuments (*Fund og Fortidsminder*) database (see box 1 on page 25) "Guide to dolmens" on page 25. But this has played a minor role in our search for dolmens without mounds, because the database back then – pre-2010 – was not as developed as it is today.

The Danish National Museum's prehistory archive is, nevertheless, an absolute goldmine of information in this respect. The drawings archive contains the sketches that were produced in connection with the district surveys (fig. 8.1). Most of these pre-date 1900, and some are from the time when the district surveys began in 1872. A number are available online in the Sites and Monuments database, but far from all of them, and some of those reproduced have been cropped or lack certain pieces of information.[1] The National Museum also has a photo archive and an archive of reports on excavations and restoration works. A special resource available at the museum is the topographic archive, in which correspondence, site visits, clerical reports, newspaper cuttings etc., referring to cases that do not have their own archive number, are archived by parish. This contains a lot of "dolmen material". Further to this is much other useful material in the archive room, also at the National Museum.[2]

Fig. 8.1. *Kongsøre Skov in Odsherred contains many scheduled ancient monuments. Best known is the long dolmen Kong Øres Grav, but there are other dolmens in the forest too. In 1874, J.B. Løffler produced this captivating drawing of one of them – the Torneløkke dolmen.*

Another goldmine is the much overlooked declaration archive, which has accompanied the administration of scheduled ancient monuments since the time of the chancellery schedulings in the early 19th century, and is therefore now located in the Monuments and Archaeological Heritage Division of the Danish Agency for Culture and Palaces. This archive relates to scheduled ancient monuments and includes for example correspondence, accounts of early site visits, title registration records and sometimes survey data and drawings for each individual monument. The Monuments and Archaeological Heritage Division also has other items relating to scheduled ancient monuments, archived under unique archive numbers, for example site visit reports, prosecutions arising from damage, exemptions etc. In the same place are also records relating to subjects such as the scheduling work prior to the act of 1937 and the notebooks used in connection with the scheduling surveys undertaken in the period 1937-57.

Local cultural-historical museums with archaeological departments and local archives may also hold relevant material.

Literature providing an overview of scheduled dolmens is scarce. The existing guides to, and overviews of, scheduled ancient monuments deal with only the best known sites and those "most worth visiting". To some degree, these guides are often based on each other and frequently the authors have not personally visited the sites, have no knowledge of the local conditions and, in particular, have not been aware of the phenomenon "open dolmens"; something for which they cannot be criticised.

In his book *Danske dysser* from 2007, Klaus Ebbesen presents the early descriptions from the parish surveys and a large number of drawings from the district surveys depicting many dolmens, both scheduled and ruined or demolished examples.[3] Similarly, much useful information and knowledge is contained in Klaus Ebbesen's works *Danmarks megalitgrave* and *Danske jættestuer* from 2008-11. The latter – despite the reference to passage graves in its title – contains a lot of information about dolmens.[4] A digital version of the catalogue, volume 2 of *Danmarks megalitgrave*, is available online at www.megalitgrave.dk. According to its author, *Danmarks megalitgrave* is "a complete catalogue of all Denmark's megalithic graves – i.e. dolmens and passage graves from the Dolmen and Passage-grave epochs – and the finds from these".[5] It is based in particular on the descriptions from the district surveys and follows the same topographic divisions and numbering system – county-district-parish – as the online Sites and Monuments database, and is very usefully augmented with references to the literature.

In fortunate cases, earlier works can contain descriptions or drawings of open dolmens, but these tend to be few and far between. Special mention should, however, be made of the Danish clerical reports submitted to Ole Worm in the 17th century and to the Danish Royal Commission for the Collection and Preservation of Antiquities in the 19th century, Erik Pontoppidan's *Den Danske Atlas* from the second half of the 18th century and the accounts of the chancellery schedulings at the beginning of the 19th century.[6]

Vore Fortidsminder

In addition to the books, records and documents mentioned above, there is also a, now largely overlooked, 50-year-old portal to an overview of the best preserved of Denmark's megaliths and other ancient monuments: the map series *Vore Fortidsminder* – Our Ancient Monuments. This was published from 1932-64 in a collaboration between the Danish national mapping agency Geodætisk Institut and the Danish National Museum.[7] It covers all of Denmark and consists of 67 beautiful maps reproduced at a scale of 1:100,000 (fig. 8.2). All scheduled ancient monuments are marked on these maps with red symbols: barrows "are marked with a dot, other prehistoric monuments (namely megalithic graves) with a cross; barrow groups are shown with a dotted ring. ... only the most important have a number and a corresponding description in the text. All the monuments that are not numbered and mentioned in the text are small and medium-sized barrows or more or less damaged dolmens and passage graves."[8]

The first sheet in the series *Vore Fortidsminder*, covering northeast Zealand, was published in 1932. That same year, Therkel Mathiasseen was appointed as curator at the National Museum and, as a consequence, "Danish archaeology gained both an experienced and a dynamic working capacity. And it needed it."[9] The latter was true of the National Museum's scientific work as much as its relationship with the public who, from 1935, were able to view a new and much-needed Stone Age exhibition. The idea for *Vore Fortidsminder* probably also came from the newly-appointed museum curator. He could thereby silence the heavy criticism that people such as author

Fig. 8.2. *The map series "Vore Fortidsminder", published from 1932-64, consists of 67 booklets with map sheets, some produced in several editions. Each book lists the scheduled ancient monuments most worth visiting and these are marked on beautiful maps at a scale of 1:100,000. All the booklets have an identical cover, showing the same dolmen.*

Fig. 8.3. *The long dolmen in Avnede Skov was drawn by Magnus Petersen in 1876.*

Johannes V. Jensen had directed at the National Museum's dull, plodding presentation of scheduled ancient monuments. Jensen pointed out that "An ABC of archaeology with information on grave types and some of the most important localities in the country would not be elementary knowledge for most, but something quite new. What is needed is simply a *guide*, a leaflet such as one is handed when one arrives in a strange place. For foreigners, the need is acute, but the country's own inhabitants could benefit from having their eyes opened to their own special historic landmarks. A map, first and foremost, is also needed with this, accompanied by an informative text in both Danish and English."[10]

The author of the text to *Vore Fortidsminder* is not credited, but Therkel Mathiassen must have had a hand in a good part of it and he also functioned as its main editor.[11] He led the scheduling surveys in 1937-57, a response to the Nature Conservation Act's article 2, and was without doubt the archaeologist with the greatest knowledge of scheduled ancient monuments in Denmark; this gives *Vore Fortidsminder* a very special quality and consistency.[12]

Vore Fortidsminder contains 4263 reference numbers. In many cases, these numbers cover two or three ancient monuments and some of them even refer to entire barrow groups, so the total number of ancient monuments included is much greater.

Megalithic graves from the Neolithic total 1061 dolmens, 319 passage graves and 34 stone cists. Further to these are a number of indeterminable megalithic graves, which are nevertheless deemed worthy of mention. The 1061 scheduled dolmens constitute only two-thirds of Denmark's complete stock of scheduled monuments of this type. Of these, 430 are on Zealand, 407 in Jutland and the remaining 224 in the rest of the country.[13] On the face of it, this distribution is intriguing, i.e. roughly equal numbers of dolmens on Zealand and in Jutland, as one often reads that dolmens are particularly numerous on Zealand. This is also true in terms of concentration, i.e. monuments per km^2, because Jutland, occupying two thirds of Denmark's total area, is four times as large as Zealand. The 1061 monuments comprise 583 long dolmens (55%), 157 round dolmens (15%), 255 dolmen chambers (24%) and 60 dolmens with no further description (6%).[14] This distribution is more or less the same for Jutland or the Danish islands on their own.

There are 29 dolmens with both a chamber/chambers and kerbstones, and where the description in *Vore Fortidsminder* mentions that there is no, or only a low/very low mound – i.e. "dolmens without mounds" – these are listed below. Descriptions of them are given in a note at the back of this book.[15] The 29 dolmens are:

1: Avnede Skov, Lolland (fig. 8.3). – 2-4: Hildesvig Skov, Lolland. – 5-8: Hamborg Skov, Lolland. – 9: Flintinge Byskov, Lolland. – 10: Priorskov, Lolland. – 11: Keldskov, Lolland. – 12: Store Møsten, northwest Zealand. – 13: Vinskoven, northwest Zealand. – 14-15: Ugerløse, northwest Zealand. – 16-17: Grønholt Hegn, northeast Zealand. – 18: Videdysse in Birkede, northeast Zealand. – 19: Valbygård, southwest Zealand. – 20. Valbygård Skov, southwest Zealand. – 21. Broby Vesterskov, southwest Zealand. – 22: Korsør Skov, southwest Zealand. – 23: Syllinge Skov, southwest Zealand. – 24: Gunderslevholm Skov, southwest Zealand. – 25: Herlufmagle, southwest Zealand. – 26: Vejlø, southwest Zealand. – 27: Magleby Skov, southeast Zealand. – 28: Strandegårds Dyrehave, southeast Zealand. – 29: Valdemars Plads in Vinterbølle Skov, southeast Zealand.

If this list is expanded with the open dolmens already mentioned, and we continue the numbering system, we then have the following:

30: Kjallesten, Lolland. – 31: Poskær Stenhus, eastern Jutland. – 32: Stenhus near Strands, eastern Jutland. – 33: Tustrup round dolmen, eastern Jutland. – 34: Tustrup passage dolmen, eastern Jutland. – 35: Hydeskov Fredskov, Lolland. – 36: Lunden, Langeland. – 37: Ormslev, eastern Jutland. – 38: Grøfte II, southwest Zealand. – 39: Tårup, southeast Jutland. – 40: Skelde, southeast Jutland. – 41: Trollasten in Scania, Sweden.

The next step, after the necessary archival studies, was to visit these 41 potentially genuine open and scheduled dolmens. This was undertaken between 1998 and 1999 (fig. 8.4). The aim of these field trips was, first and foremost, to find the dolmens without mounds that had definitely also lacked a mound in the Neolithic, and then to describe and possibly survey them.

Fig. 8.4. *On one of our dolmen trips to Zealand, Niels takes a closer look at the long dolmen on Knudshoved.*

Genuine open dolmens

The account given in chapter 7 of three very open dolmens – Korsør Skov (no. 22), Vinskoven (no. 13) and Rønde – shows that all three of these could, to some extent, have had a mound. There is no way of knowing whether they were originally genuine open dolmens, i.e. they also lacked mounds in prehistory. Without new excavations they must therefore, in the first instance, be dismissed as open dolmens.

The same also applies to a number of other monuments, especially long dolmens, where there is evidence of blasting or removal of stones and of uneven mound surfaces, where holes resulting from digging or re-erected stones are testimony to human activities in recent times, and where, as a consequence, much mound fill could well have been removed. Of the selected potential open dolmens, this situation is found to prevail at for example Ugerløse (nos. 14-15), Grønholt Hegn (nos. 16-17), Valbygård (no. 19), Valbygård Skov (no. 20), Valdemars Plads (no. 29) and Grøfte II (no. 38) (fig. 8.5).

On the other hand, there are many unsullied open dolmens – both round and long dolmens – where the chambers and kerbstones stand clearly exposed, and with little or no mound fill and few, albeit some, damaged or missing stones. Moreover, their interiors are flat and even, with no holes. Similarly, the area outside the kerbstones shows no indication that the mound fill could have moved downwards and outwards. Good examples of dolmens of this kind are Store Møsten (no. 12), the dolmens in Hamborg Skov (nos. 5-8), two of the dolmens in Hildesvig Skov (nos. 2-4) and a dolmen in Broby Vesterskov (no. 21) (fig. 8.6), and several others could also be mentioned. It may well be that these are genuine open dolmens, but this can only be securely ascertained through archaeological excavation and that lies outside the scope of the present project. The long dolmens in Avnede Skov (no. 1) (fig. 8.3), Flintinge Byskov (no. 9), Keldskov (no. 11), Magleby Skov (no. 27) and Priorskov (no. 10) are therefore taken out of consideration, as is the round dolmen at Vejlø (no. 26). Furthermore, another potential open dolmen – Strandegårds Dyrehave (no. 28) – proved to be the remains of a passage grave chamber.

All in all, only three of the potentially genuine open dolmens mentioned in *Vore Fortidsminder* survive critical appraisal. These are Syllinge Skov (no. 23), which was a new monument to us, and the Gunderslevholm dolmen (no. 24) and Videdysse (no. 18), both of which we were already aware of.

Very special conditions must be met for a monument to be approved as a genuine open dolmen. It must either have a special inner surface, perhaps with stone circles

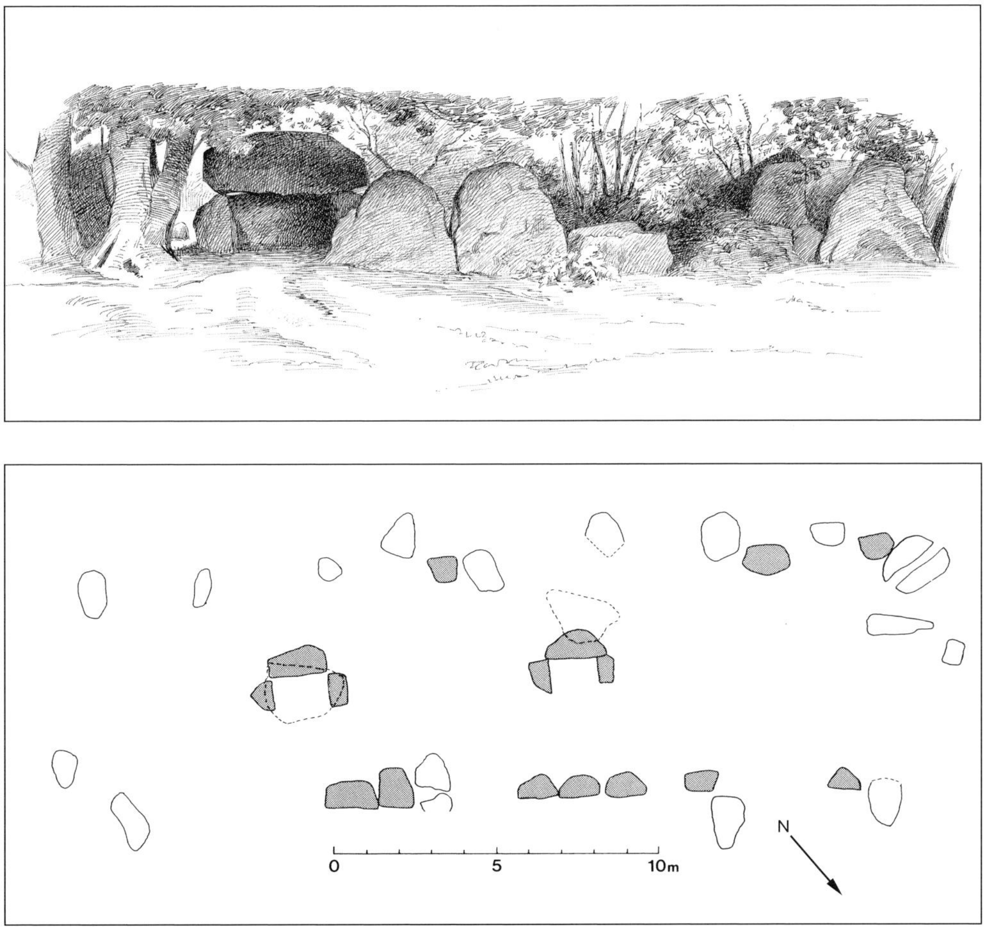

Fig. 8.5. *The long dolmen Grøfte II has no mound fill. But as it lacks several kerbstones and both chambers are missing a stone at one side, any mound fill may have been removed in connection with the monument's destruction. Drawing by G.V. Blom in 1893.*

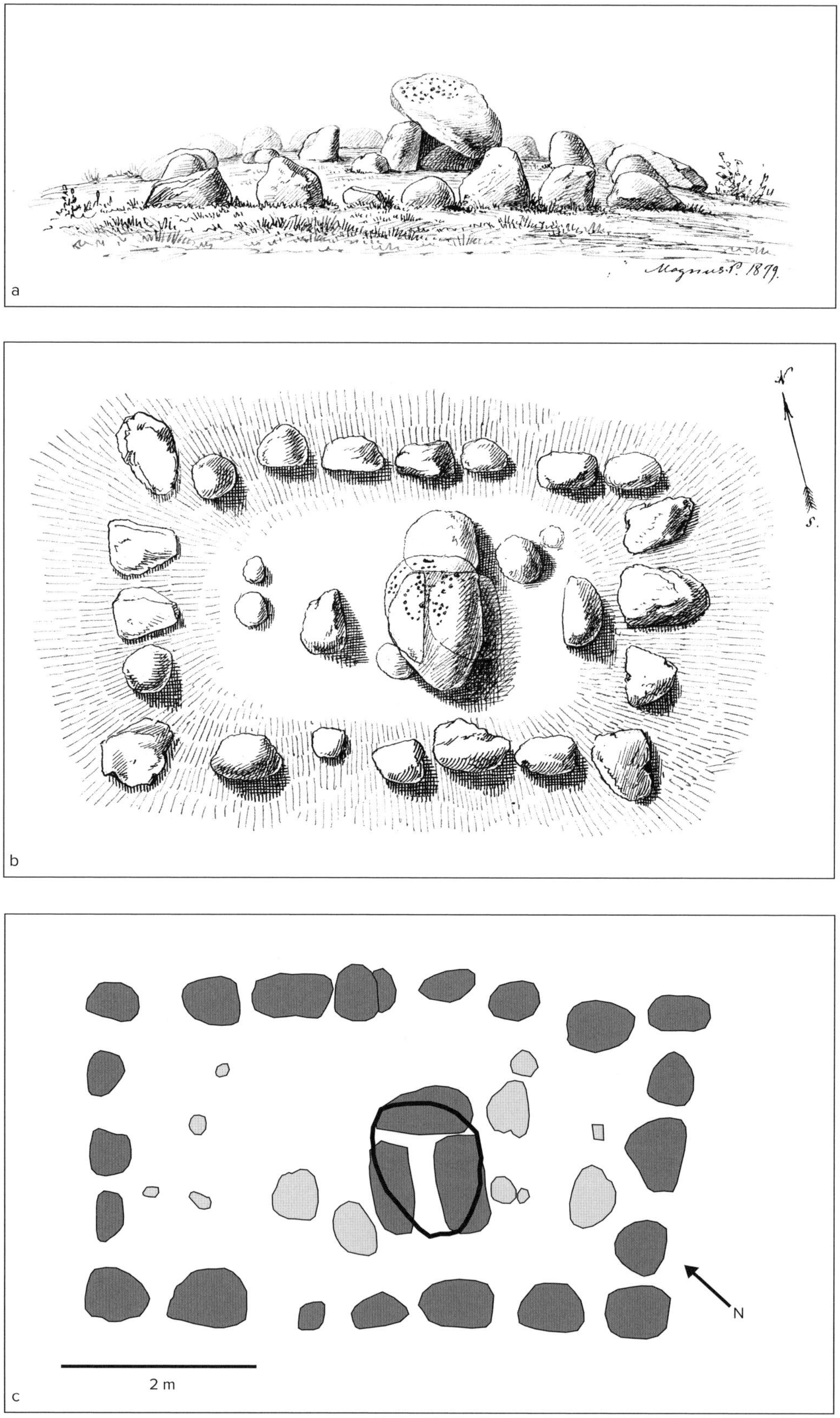

Fig. 8.6. *This long dolmen in Hamborg Skov also had no mound fill when Magnus Petersen sketched it in 1879 (a, b). Subsequently, the monument was restored by Julius Raklev of the Danish National Museum in 1947. The dolmen was resurveyed in 1999 as part of our dolmens without mounds project (c).*

or stone rows or a loose, stony interior as in the case of the Gunderslevholm dolmen, a particularly high topographic location, or features, documented by archaeological excavation, that support its interpretation as an open dolmen.

The list of genuine open scheduled dolmens is then found to include 13 Danish monuments, plus the dolmen Trollasten in the former Danish area of Scania, Sweden. The 14 dolmens are all included in this book, accompanied by illustrations, description, analysis and comments. They can be classified according to four criteria:

Long and round dolmens with stone scatterings or internal stone circles

Gunderslevholm Skov, long dolmen – chapter 11
Kjallesten, round dolmen – chapter 12
Hydeskov Fredskov, very small long dolmen – chapter 12
Syllinge Skov, very small long dolmen – chapter 12
Poskær Stenhus, round dolmen – chapter 12
Videdysse, long dolmen – chapter 13

Special topographic conditions

Stenhus, round dolmen – chapter 14

Investigated, free-standing dolmen chambers

Trollasten – chapter 15
Ormslev – chapter 15
Lunden – chapter 15

Investigated round and long dolmens

Skelde, long dolmen – chapter 6
Tårup, round dolmen – chapter 6
Tustrup, passage dolmen – chapter 16
Tustrup round dolmen – chapter 17

Further to these are archaeological investigations of *demolished dolmens* – primarily in southwest Funen – where genuine open dolmens have been demonstrated (see chapter 20).

9. From wood to stone – from fence to mound

Well-constructed, monumental long and round dolmens, with one or more stone-built chambers, did not just appear out of thin air. Their appearance and – despite all their differences – their apparently standardised form, slowly and gradually evolved and developed through a couple of centuries. The starting point was simple wooden plank-built cists, surrounded by rectangular, trapezoid or oval frames in the form of wooden fences or ditches, with no mound fill and no large stones, but often featuring a striking façade at one end. These structures, which may have been quite monumental, are termed *Barkaer-structures*. Some of them were partially or completely covered with earth, stones or grass turves and thereby converted into long barrows. Subsequently, these were either permitted to stand alone or, during the course of the Dolmen and Passage-grave epochs, were given new chambers, now built of large stones, and the associated mounds were as a rule then enclosed within kerbstones to form true long dolmens.

In this chapter, we will take a broad look at these developments and illustrate and illuminate them with some selected characteristic examples.

From wooden cists to stone chambers

In Late Ertebølle times the dead were, as already mentioned above, buried in pits in the ground – in so-called pit graves. No traces have been found of wooden coffins, mounds or other markers associated with the graves of this culture. And this situation appears not to have changed at the beginning of the Neolithic, as shown by a grave found at Dragsholm in northwest Zealand, where the person interred – a man accompanied by a pottery vessel and battle axe – is clearly from "the new era".[1]

About a century ago, however, it was realised that there was another grave form in the early part of the Neolithic, quite different from the pit graves and the dolmen chambers. This newly-discovered grave type was usually of the size of a single grave and consisted of a wooden plank cist, supported by a frame of stones or a stone pavement. These graves were often found to contain a polished thin-butted flint axe and/or a pottery vessel and/or amber beads, corresponding to the grave furnishings seen in a small number of dolmen chambers. The graves were discovered beneath a flat surface and originally, due to their simple construction and in order to distinguish them clearly from megalithic graves, they were referred to as *earth graves* or *non-megalithic graves*.[2]

The term earth grave has though largely been abandoned today, in recognition of the fact that these structures often represent more complex monuments. Due to several further finds of these plank-built graves, and improved excavation and observation techniques, these graves can now be classified into three groups. The classification is based on whether there is a rectangular, superficial (or "super-terrestrial") plank cist, whether this cist is open at one end and whether or not there is a wooden construction within the excavated pit. Graves of these three types are termed, respectively, Konens Høj, Troelstrup and Bygholm Nørremark type, named after the three localities where characteristic graves of each of the types have been found. It is worthy of note that graves of both Konens Høj and Troelstrup types were not placed in a pit cut into the subsoil, but were established on the actual soil surface. This was a quite remarkable and completely new feature relative to previous grave types.[3]

Wooden cists

Graves of Konens Høj type are of special interest here, because – as we will see – they are closely related to the earliest dolmen chambers. Konens Høj is the name of a sandy hillock near the lake of Stubbe Sø on Djursland. Here, in 1963-65, Bjørn Stürup of Kulturhistorisk Museum in Randers, now Museum Østjylland, investigated an Early Neolithic grave that proved to be more complex than expected.[4] On the base of the grave, a rectangular, cobbled surface, were bone fragments, tooth enamel, a copper spiral ring, a copper plate, a pair of amber beads and a lugged flask. Alongside the cobbled area, which measured 3.5 m in length and 80 cm in width, were two parallel rows of stones, and at each end there was a collection of stones covering a deep pit. The two pits, which had a diameter corresponding to the width of the grave base, were exceptional due to their great depth, extending 1-1.2 m below the grave base, and by being oblique in section, leaning slightly in towards the middle of the grave. In both pits, flat stones had been wedged down from each side (fig. 9.1).[5]

It is interesting to read the excavator's interpretation of the findings and proposed reconstruction of the grave: "These pits can only be understood as foundations for

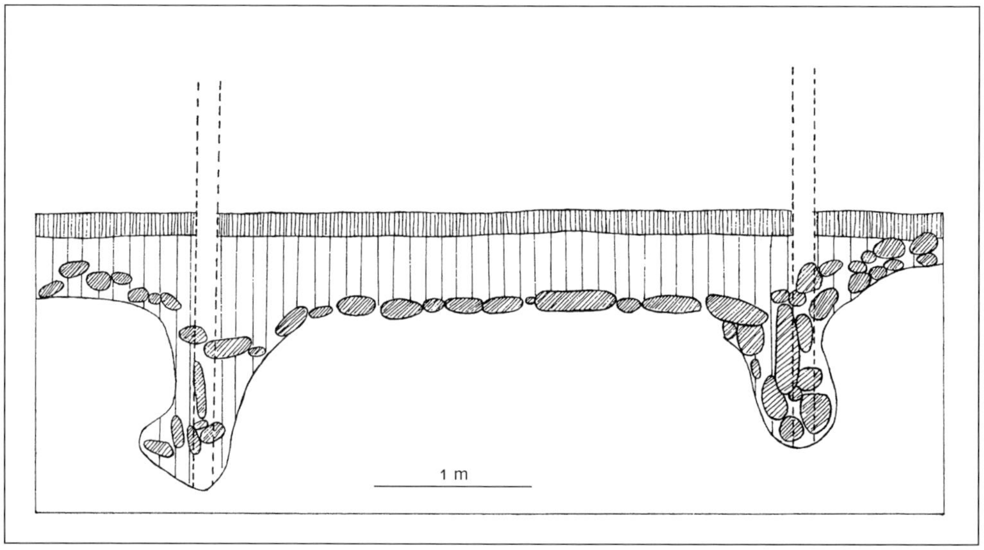

Fig. 9.1. *This longitudinal section through the Konens Høj grave shows the deep, stone-lined postholes beneath the stone pavement of the earth grave. In 1966, the excavator believed, erroneously, that the postholes formed part of the grave's construction.*

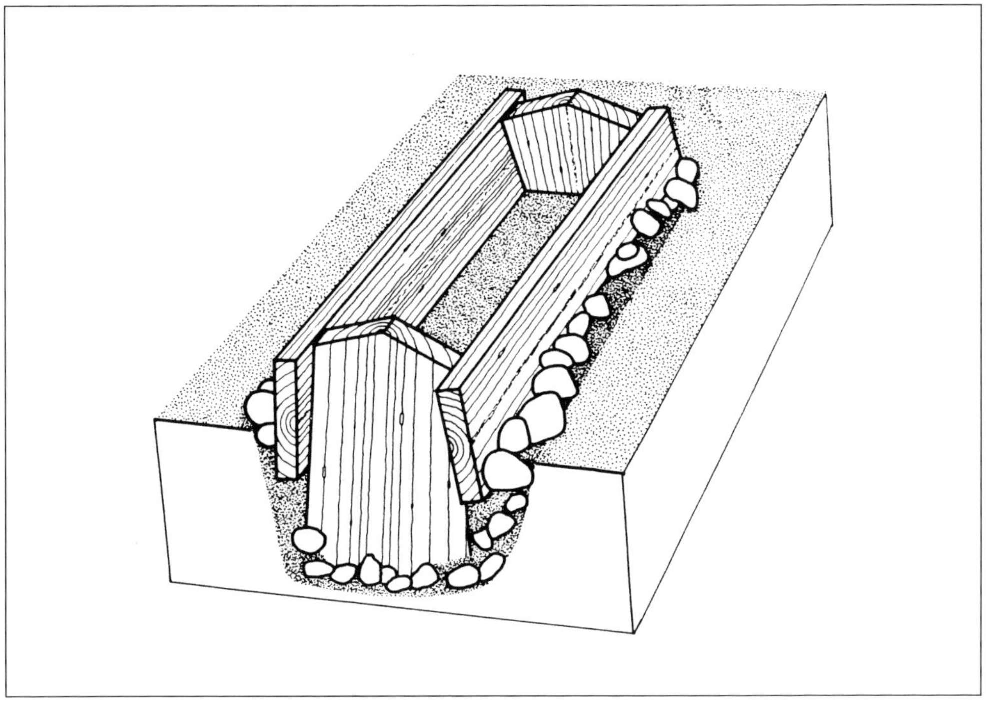

Fig. 9.2. *This is how David Liversage imagined the appearance of a grave of Konens Høj type in 1983. The sturdy plank cist has deeply-founded planks at the gables, because it was still thought at that time that the postholes formed part of the grave's construction.*

vertical wooden gables that, at each end of the grave, have terminated the inner grave space, and it seems reasonable to assume that between these gables there has been an horizontal ridgepole … the two parallel stone rows on each side of the cobbled area have functioned as a support for a roof, such that this has rested on the inner stone row and has been held in place by the outer."[6]

The excavation at Konens Høj revealed that the presumed simple earth graves could actually be quite complex constructions and perhaps had tent-like superstructures. However, the excavator's proposed reconstruction of the grave was found not to be tenable. David Liversage, of the Danish National Museum, came nearer the truth around 1970, when he was responsible for the investigation of a rather damaged mound containing a dolmen chamber and a long barrow with traces of plank-built cists at Lindebjerg, near Kalundborg.[7] The former – the mound with a dolmen chamber – had been surrounded not by kerbstones but, according to David Liversage, by thick planks set lengthwise. This interpretation is based on rows of stones, which to one side formed a straight line, as supports for the now decayed planks.[8] Similar indirect plank traces could also be observed alongside one of the two wooden cists in the long barrow.[9] Here there were parallel rows of stones, separated by stone-less strips, where the now vanished planks that formed the sides of the cist could once have stood. The cist, which had internal dimensions of 3.6 m in length and 80 cm in width, was of Troelstrup type, as it had been open at one end, i.e. not a structure like Konens Høj with a completely closed cist of the same dimensions. In his reconstruction, David Liversage suggests that the Lindebjerg cist was made of thick planks and was supported by stones.

The reconstruction of the Lindebjerg cist, and the considerations associated with this, led David Liversage in 1983 to propose a completely new theory about the possible appearance of cists of the closely-related Konens Høj type (fig. 9.2).[10] The stone rows at each side supported a thick plank that stood on edge. The gables also consisted of planks, which stood solidly in the deep pits and leaned slightly inwards – a detail based on the sloping cross-sections evident in these pits. The cist was closed by one or more heavy planks being laid on top.

David Liversage's proposed reconstruction met with general acceptance, but there were still some inherent problems. Important information in this respect was provided by the site of Bygholm Nørremark near Horsens. Here, in 1977-78, Preben Rønne of the Danish National Museum was responsible for the investigation of a ploughed-down long barrow that had originally been 75 m long, 13 m wide and up to 3 m high.[11] In its final phase in the Neolithic, the long barrow had covered a small passage grave, but before this there was here a more than 1 m high mound framed by a trapezoid arrangement of posts set in a foundation trench (fig. 9.3). At the eastern end of the framed area was a transverse ditch which had served as the foundation for some sturdy posts. In the middle part of the long barrow, in a large pit, were the remnants of a wooden chamber and four burnt skeletons. In the eastern part of the barrow was a further grave, a plank-built cist, holding the remains of an individual of 13-15 years of age and also containing a large amber bead and a transverse arrowhead. Around the grave were traces of a two-aisled house. Houses like this are typical of the Neolithic and are characterised by only having one row of roof-bearing posts running along the middle of the building, on its longitudinal axis. Together with load-bearing wall posts, these supported the roof of the house. A remarkable aspect of Bygholm Nørremark is that the grave was placed between the house's two central roof-bearing posts. It must therefore be later than the house, but not by much, as it was evident that the earthen fill of the postholes for these roof-bearing posts had

Fig. 9.3. *Plan of the initial phases at Bygholm Nørremark, where the structure was delimited by a post-built fence set in a ditch (light grey). The presumed transverse, north-south-oriented house at the eastern end (yellow) is more likely a façade ditch (dark yellow) with sturdy posts (yellow) belonging to the long Barkaer-structure. To the west of this is a decayed plank cist within the ground plan of a two-aisled house (green broken line). Further again to the west of this is a decayed wooden chamber containing four slightly burnt skeletons (black) and then a cluster of features (yellow), interpreted by the excavator as the traces of another house.*

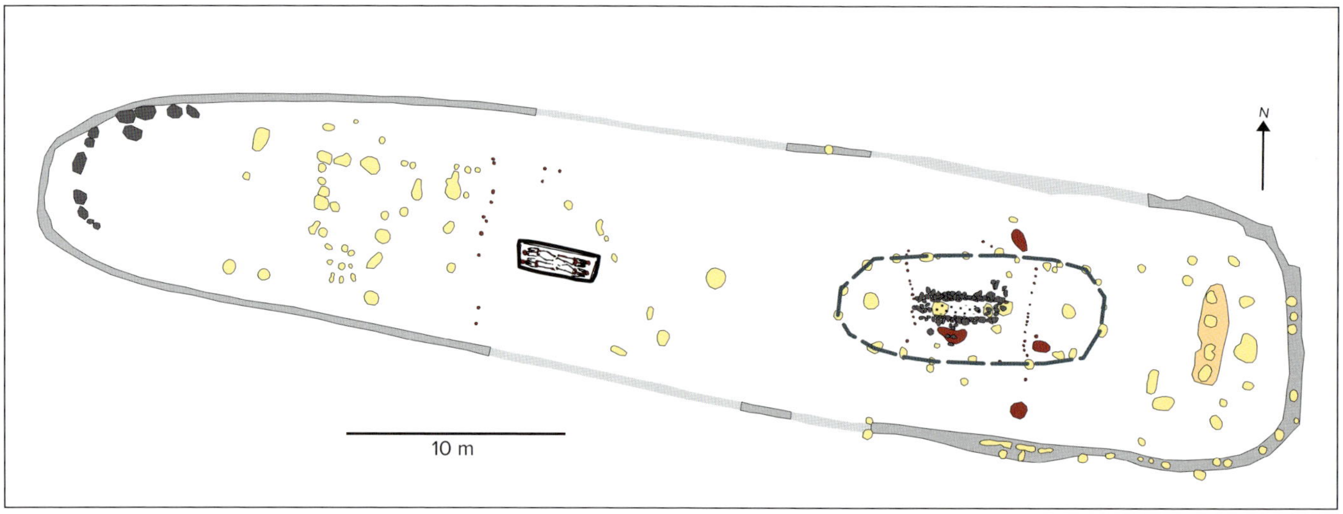

settled, drawing with it fill from the ends of the grave bed.[12] As no clear settlement traces were found around the building, the house site was interpreted by Preben Rønne as some kind of ceremonial building that had a function shortly before the burial and was subsequently demolished prior to construction of the grave.

In 1988, Flemming Kaul of the Danish National Museum published excavations of several Neolithic structures at Onsved in northern Zealand, including a presumed earth grave similar to those found at Konens Høj and Bygholm Nørremark. Here, it is clear that a post had stood at each end of where the grave came to lie, and that these posts were pulled up and the postholes back-filled before the grave was constructed.[13] Flemming Kaul makes comparisons with structures in England, where a similar sequence of events had taken place, and concludes that there need not have been a tent-like construction with central posts, but perhaps just a pair of free-standing posts, which were removed when the grave was established.

In the Konens Høj grave, a longitudinal section through the grave (see fig. 9.1) shows that the grave's cobbled base covered postholes at the gables, and that the cobbles had sunk down into these, corresponding to the situation observed by Preben Rønne at Bygholm Nørremark. The postholes are also seen to slope inwards towards the grave, a phenomenon that led David Liversage to suggest that the plank cist had sloping end walls which tilted slightly inwards (see fig. 9.2). However, it should be considered whether this simply shows that the posts were rocked forcibly back and forth in order to extract them from their postholes. The posthole on the left can, at least, be interpreted in this way.

In England during the Neolithic, coeval with the Danish plank cists described here, similar structures were built in long grave monuments, both with and without a mound, and these also had sturdy posts at the ends of the cists. The Scottish archaeologist Gordon Noble remarked in 2006 that the longitudinal axis of the cist is, in several cases, offset relative to a line running between the two postholes at the ends of the cist, for example at Fussell's Lodge, Wayland's Smithy and Haddenham.[14] Like Flemming Kaul, Gordon Noble believes these postholes contained posts that had a function and were involved in a context prior to construction of the grave.

Graves and houses

The most recent contribution to an understanding of these structures comes from an excavation undertaken in 2009-12 at the locality of Frydenlund, between Hårby and Strandby in southwest Funen. As part of the Sarup project (see chapter 20), an investigation was carried out by one of this book's authors, Niels Andersen, of two elongate structures of the same type as those found at Barkær and Bygholm Nørremark. The two Barkaer-structures at Frydenlund had, however, been very badly damaged by modern cultivation practices.[15]

One of the Barkaer-structures at Frydenlund – structure B – was 31 m long and 7.5 m wide (fig. 9.4). There were no traces of a covering mound, but the structure was framed by a foundation trench in which posts had stood. At its western end was a façade trench with traces of sturdy posts or, more correctly, cleaved, vertically-

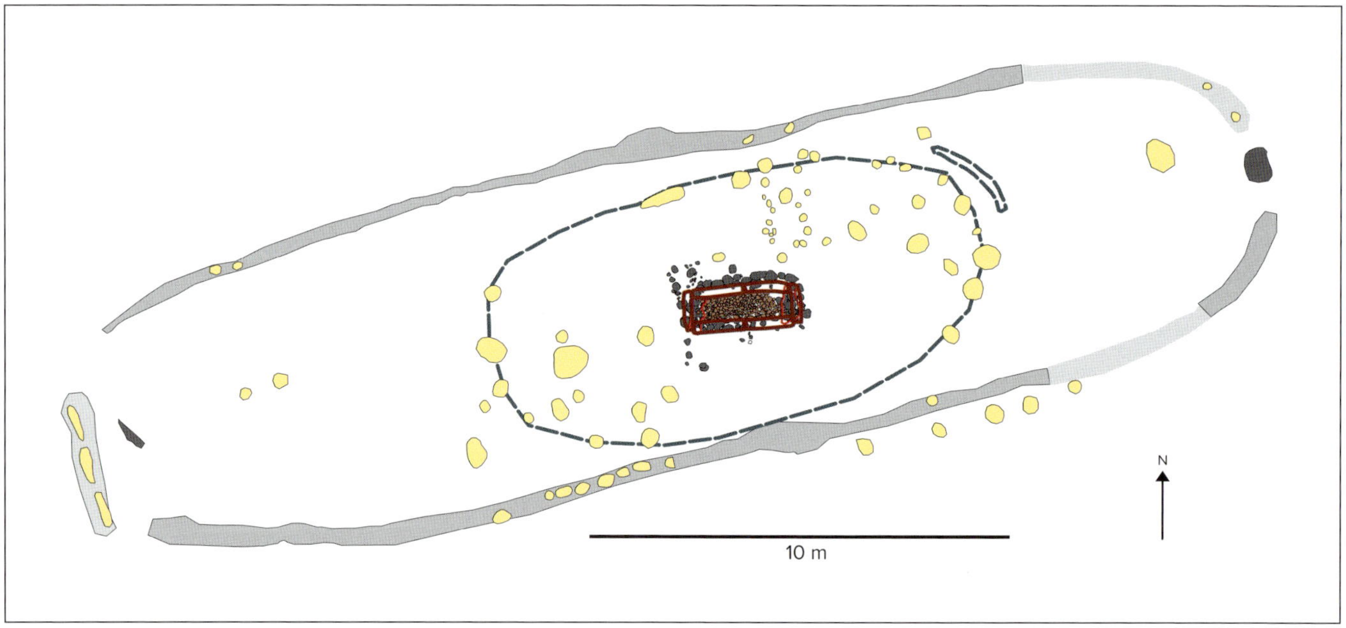

Fig. 9.4. *Ground plan of Frydenlund structure B, showing traces of a 31 m long post-enclosed Barkaer-structure (grey) with a façade ditch to the west containing three sturdy vertical planks (light yellow). In the middle of the structure is a decayed plank cist (red-brown). This is located where a two-aisled house (green dotted line) had previously stood. The house is the earliest structure on the site, and when it was demolished, the grave containing the plank coffin was built precisely over the former positions of the building's central posts.*

standing planks. Approximately in the middle of the monument lay a grave which, at the surface, was 2.9 m long and 1.7 m wide. The base of the grave, which measured 2 x 0.7 m, consisted of small stones on which, at the western end, lay two polished flint axes that presumably had been placed by the deceased's shoulders. In the presumed chest region were two transverse arrowheads, at the waist a large amber bead and by the right foot a further polished flint axe and a collared flask. No traces were, however, found of the individual interred here. Around the grave bed were decayed traces of planks that had been supported by head-sized stones (fig. 9.5). The elongate planks had been set about 10 cm into the subsoil and were probably not very high, no more than 50 cm.[16] All of this is consistent with a wooden cist measuring 2.5 x 0.7 m and made of horizontal planks. The lid could have been a single large plank.

At the ends of the grave bed, below the plank remnants, were a couple of elongate postholes that were offset relative to the longitudinal axis of the grave, as seen in the other grave structures described above. Some of the small stones of the grave bed had sunk slightly into the back-filled postholes, and the planks at the ends of the cist had extended partially over the latter. When the postholes were sectioned, no trace could be seen of the actual posts. The postholes were found to be almost hourglass-shaped in section, a form that arises when a post has been rocked back and forth in order to extract it from the ground.

At Frydenlund, we were again confronted with a wooden plank-built cist, partially constructed over two large, back-filled postholes. Inspired by Preben Rønne's excavation at Bygholm Nørremark, we began to look for possible traces of a house site, as this could explain the presence of the postholes. The subsoil around the grave was very gravelly, so observation conditions were not ideal. Postholes from Neolithic structures can often be extremely difficult to find, as topsoil has rarely become deposited in them. Had this occurred, it would of course have made them darker in colour and thereby easier to find, relative to the surrounding soil. By cleaning the surface carefully three to four times, photographing the cleaned surface on several occasions and then studying the resulting images under different conditions, where we altered the contrast, colour and many other factors, it became possible to detect the contours of a two-aisled house (see fig. 9.4).

We thereby obtained confirmation of the fact that a house had stood at Frydenlund, and that this was demolished, with the central roof-bearing posts being pulled up, before a grave was constructed in the middle of where the row of posts had stood. As mentioned above, Preben Rønne believed that the absence of settlement material associated with the house at Bygholm Nørremark meant that this should be interpreted as a ceremonial building. At Frydenlund, however, there were more than 14,000 settlement-related artefacts – predominantly potsherds and flint, but also abundant charred grain and fragments of quernstones. So this house very probably formed part of the habitation at the site. An excavation at Damsbo, just less than 2 km to the south of Frydenlund, also revealed house remains beneath grave structures (see chapter 20 and fig. 20.11). Two of these house sites lay under long dolmens, and in both cases a small dolmen chamber had been constructed between two postholes for roof-bearing posts in an earlier house. A third house site lay beneath the western half of a round barrow that had contained a small passage grave. Here too were houses prior to the megalithic structures being constructed. Only a few hundred artefacts were found around the Damsbo house sites. This shows that there could have been a settlement here which – considering the number of artefacts – was kept relatively clear of refuse.

It is worth considering whether a number of the peculiar, deep holes found next to plank cists in earlier excavations could possibly be postholes for the central roof-bearing posts of unrecognised longhouses. It takes great patience and good fortune

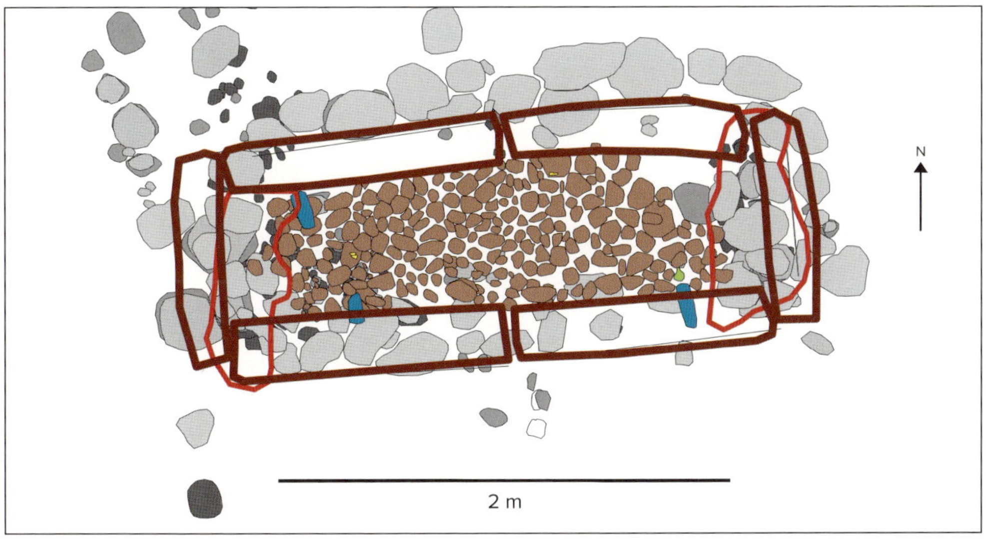

Fig. 9.5. *In Frydenlund structure B there was a fine, cobbled base for the plank cist, on which lay three flint axes, a collared flask, two transverse arrowheads and an amber bead; no traces were found of the deceased. The large grey stones supported the planks of the cist, the outline of which is shown in brown. The postholes at each end, marked in red, are earlier than the grave and belonged to a house.*

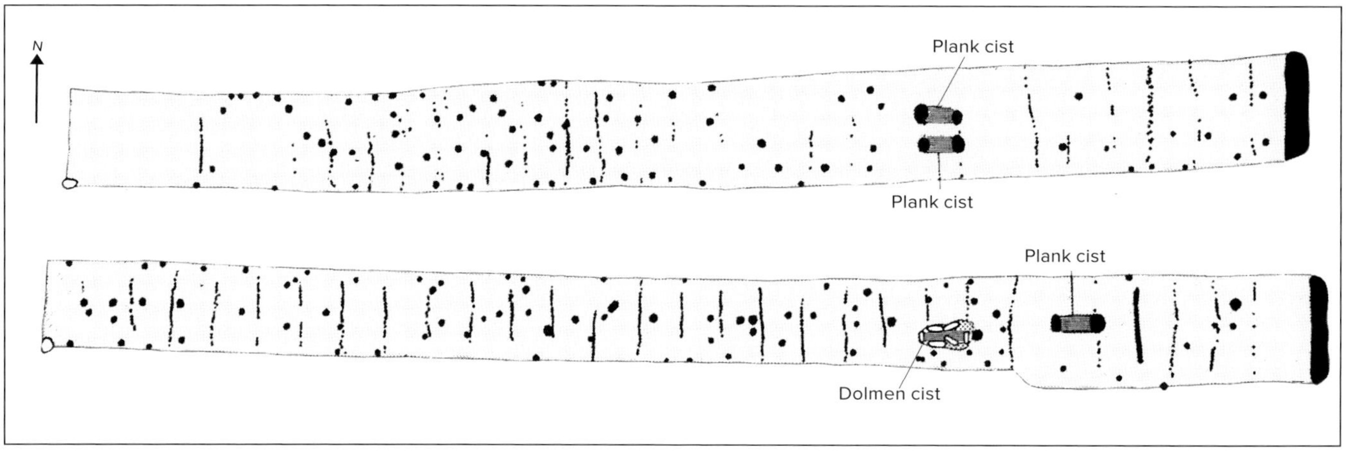

Fig. 9.6. *The two 90 m long structures at Barkær lay parallel, 10 m apart. In the eastern part of each structure were a couple of graves: In the northern structure these comprised two plank cists, in the southern there was a plank cist and a dolmen cist. Long grave structures of this kind are now termed Barkaer-structures. They can, as here at Barkær, have a robust façade ditch at one end, in which sturdy posts once stood.*

to detect Neolithic house sites, and only when excavations are undertaken under optimal conditions, can we hope to be able to identify the faint traces of them.

This account of research into the construction of Early Neolithic graves shows how work over a 50-year period, bracketed by investigations of the Konens Høj and Frydenlund structures, has reached its present state: Earth graves were most often plank cists, built on, and apparently associated with, the former sites of demolished houses, with the ends of the cists located on top of postholes for two of the roof-bearing posts. The previous interpretation – of graves with particularly deeply-founded gable planks and/or a tent-like superstructure – has now been replaced by the view that the graves took the form of simple plank cists covered with a flat, wooden lid.

Stone cists

Barkær is one of the best known Danish Neolithic localities thanks to P.V. Glob's investigations, which he completed in 1949. The site lies next to the now drained lake Korup Sø, a couple of kilometres north of Feldballe on Djursland. Here, P.V. Glob and his team found two almost 90 m long and 6.5-7.5 m wide east-west-oriented structures, separated by a c. 10 m wide stone pavement. Glob interpreted these as the remains of two longhouses built by the first farmers in the country, with a street or road running between them – Denmark's oldest village (fig. 9.6).[17] Later, in 1975, he completely revised his view and now saw the two structures as long barrows from the Early Neolithic,[18] an interpretation that has since become generally accepted.

However, it is not these two long structures, which have given their name in archaeological terminology to the so-called Barkaer-structures, that are of interest here, but the graves that lay within them: i.e. two earth graves in the northern structure and an earth grave and a stone cist in the southern one. P.V. Glob saw the stone cist as being much later than the long barrows and their earth graves.[19] This relative dating was disputed by David Liversage in 1992 when, after Glob's death, he published the Barkær investigations. According to David Liversage, the stone cist is coeval with the three earth graves, which had all contained plank-built cists.[20]

The stone cist was found in 1925 by a labourer who split the capstone with a large hammer. One, perhaps two pots lay in the cist, the interior of which is said to have been completely free of earth. Unfortunately, the pottery vessels had disappeared by the time 17-year-old P.V. Glob turned up three years later, accompanied by his father, to take a closer look at the stone cist. They investigated what remained of the cist and found half an amber bead. On that occasion they were also told that there had been 50 cm of soil above the tops of the side stones.[21] In 1931, the stones of the cist were tipped slightly backwards, allegedly by P.V. Glob! The cist then remained in this rather ruined state until re-excavated and restored by David Liversage in 1988. The restoration was a very simple process, merely involving re-erection of the stones (fig. 9.7). The cist consists of six stones of granite and gneiss, two at each side and one at each end (fig. 9.8). It is oriented east-west and is long and narrow, with an internal length of 2 m and it is 60 cm in both width and height. The stones are interesting in

Fig. 9.7. *The Barkær dolmen cist after restoration in 1988. The stone at the far end lacks part of its top.*

that they can almost be described as heavy flagstones with a thickness of 20-30 cm. One of the stones on the southern side appears rather small, due to erosion. It must originally have been larger and closely abutted its two neighbours. The two stones at the ends are somewhat taller than the side stones. Consequently, in order to give a more or less uniform height for all the stones in the cist, the stones at the ends are set deeper in the earth than those at the sides. Even so – according to David Liversage's description and survey data – the end stones intentionally project about 15 cm above the tops of the other stones. Neither do they have flat tops: The eastern stone is rounded uppermost, while the top of that to the west, from which a large fragment has unfortunately been split in recent times, is roof-shaped like an upturned V.

David Liversage argues, convincingly, that the stone cist is actually a plank cist converted to stone. The stone slabs of the Barkær cist are reminiscent of heavy cloven wooden planks, and they are set close together. David Liversage rejects the idea that the Barkær cist had a capstone as a lid, despite the old accounts, because how could a man possibly smash a capstone with a hammer? And how could there possibly have been room for a capstone when there was only 50 cm of soil above the cist, measured from the top of the side stones? David Liversage proposes instead that the cist had been closed with two longitudinal planks, which were fitted to the rounded/pointed tops of the end stones and which met at an angle, like a pitched roof.[22]

Pointed or rounded end stones projecting above the side stones are not unique to the Barkær cist. They are also evident in some hybrid forms between earth graves and dolmen chambers, for example at Try Møllegård in Vendsyssel, investigated by H.C. Broholm of the Danish National Museum in 1929 (fig. 9.9).[23] The sides here are made of stacked slabs and stones, while each end consists of a single stone that projects upwards and even comes to a point.

Another illustrative example, this time a dolmen chamber proper, is the Skavange dolmen, located 20 km west of Sæby, also in Vendsyssel (fig. 9.10). The dolmen was

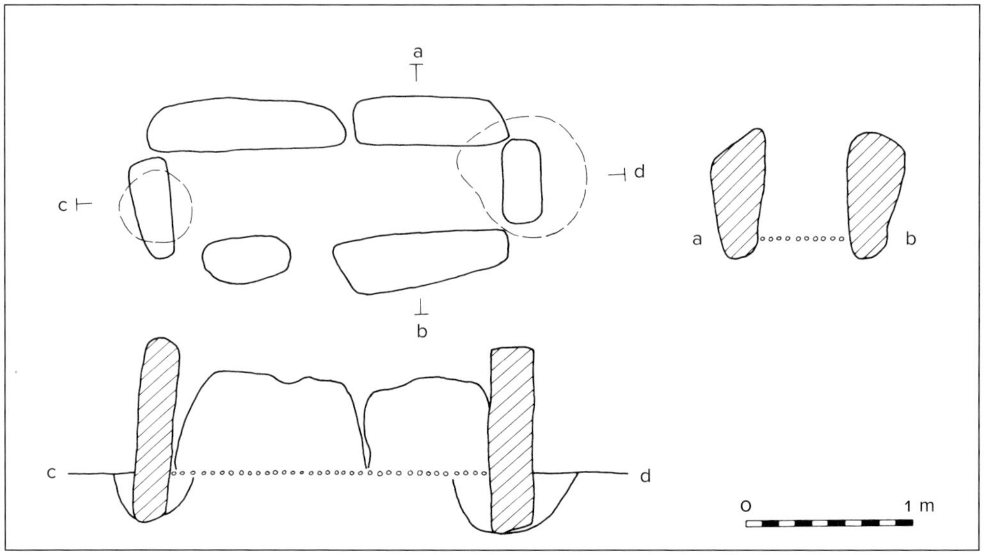

Fig. 9.8. *The Barkær dolmen cist in plan and section.*

Fig. 9.9. *The Try Møllegård grave, with its taller, pointed end stones, is reminiscent of the dolmen cist at Barkær, but the sides are of a completely different construction.*

discovered in 1953, when Holger Friis of Vendsyssel Historiske Museum investigated a ploughed-down barrow.[24] The chamber was of the broad, northern Jutish type, as much as 2.8 m in length and 1.8 m in width, and built of six orthostats: two at each side and one at each end. The entrance was marked by a couple of passage stones. The orthostats at the sides and the end stone by the passage were of equal height, c. 50 cm, while the opposing end stone was 80 cm higher, i.e. 1.3 m. With their height of 90 cm, the passage stones were 40 cm taller than the stones of the chamber, apart from the high end stone at the opposite end to the entrance. There was no capstone, and according to Poul Kjærum, who published the investigation, there appears never to have been one before the protective mound was built around the dolmen in the Late Bronze Age. If a capstone had been present and had been removed in recent times, Poul Kjærum believed that the chamber would have been disturbed at the same time, in search of artefacts, but this proved not to be the case. On the contrary, the investigation yielded several finds from beneath a quantity of stones: a collared

Fig. 9.10. *In the dolmen chamber at Skavange, the two passage stones and the end stone furthest from the entrance stand much higher than the five other stones that make up the chamber. The three higher stones are marked in grey. The capstone or capstones – there could well have been two over the 2.8 x 1.8 m chamber – are missing. But when they were in place, they must have rested on the five stones mentioned above.*

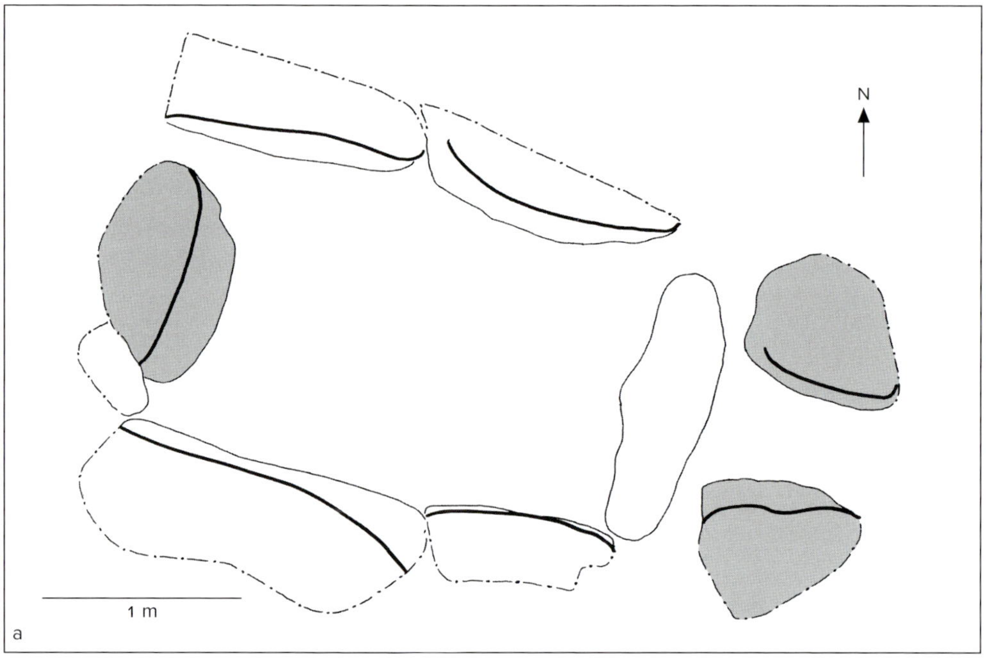

flask, a thin-butted flint axe and a number of amber beads dating from the first use of the chamber. There were no indications whatsoever of later activities. In his reconstruction in 1971, Poul Kjærum follows excavator Holger Friis' proposal, namely that the dolmen chamber was covered with a pitched-roof-like structure of sticks and branches, which accommodated the tall gable and passage stones so it was actually possible to enter. The many stones found within the chamber could originally have lain on top of this roof.

Barkær and Skavange therefore provide us with examples showing that stone cists and early dolmen chambers, as well as closely related stone-built graves such as that at Try Møllegård, apparently could have been covered with a pitched roof made of wooden planks or a higher construction of branches and sticks. However, these pitched-roof interpretations emerged at a time when archaeologists still believed in a close association between earth graves and tent-like superstructures, a perception that since has proved to be erroneous.

In the case of the Barkær cist it is not reasonable, as David Liversage does, to dismiss information that there was a capstone over the cist and that this was smashed with a sledgehammer. As seen in the chambers of the two long dolmens at Kellerød and Grøfte (see chapter 6), the capstones could very well have been slab-like and not particularly thick. Furthermore, the capstone of the Barkær cist may have suffered erosion and consequently been easy to smash by a man with a large hammer.

With regard to the Skavange dolmen, Poul Kjærum himself raises the possibility that the chamber may have been covered by one or two capstones, so that the stone closest to the tall end stone lay up against this, and he refers to a nearby dolmen chamber at Dronninglund. This is built of six stones, two at each side and one at each end, and has internal dimensions of 1.4 m in length, 0.8 m both in width and height (fig. 9.11).[25] A stone has, however, been removed from one of the sides. The capstone, which has been pushed to one side, measures about 2 x 2 m, and is therefore large enough to cover the entire chamber. The special feature of the chamber is that one end stone, marked in black on figure 9.11, projects 20-30 cm above the rest. As a consequence, when the capstone was in place, it did not necessarily rest on all the stones of the chamber. It probably did not lie on top of the taller end stone, but was pushed tightly up against it.

It therefore seems likely that the Barkær cist had a capstone that rested on the orthostats at the sides and abutted the two end stones. But just how old is the Barkær cist? It is very reminiscent of a plank cist – simply a version made in stone. There is therefore nothing, either technically or typologically, to hinder it being coeval with the three plank cists in the two long Barkaer-structures at Barkær. The contemporaneity of the four graves is underlined by their relative positions within the two Barkaer-structures (see fig. 9.6). In the northern structure were two plank cists located side by side, and their uniformity and symmetry about the long axis suggests they could be coeval. There were also two graves in the southern structure, but these lay in continuation of one another, 5 m apart. The grave to the east was also a plank-built cist, while that to the west was a cist of stone. The latter was slightly displaced relative to the long axis of the structure, but lay directly opposite the two graves in the northern structure, indicating that all four graves must, by and large, be coeval.[26] This means, accordingly, that plank cists and stone cists were built at the same time, and evidence of this is provided by other structures of Barkaer-structures, for example that at Troelstrup near Fjelsø in Himmerland, mentioned below.

The plank-like stone cist at the Barkær site has several parallels in Denmark. Similar Early Neolithic cists, built either of stone slabs and/or double-sided flat stones of

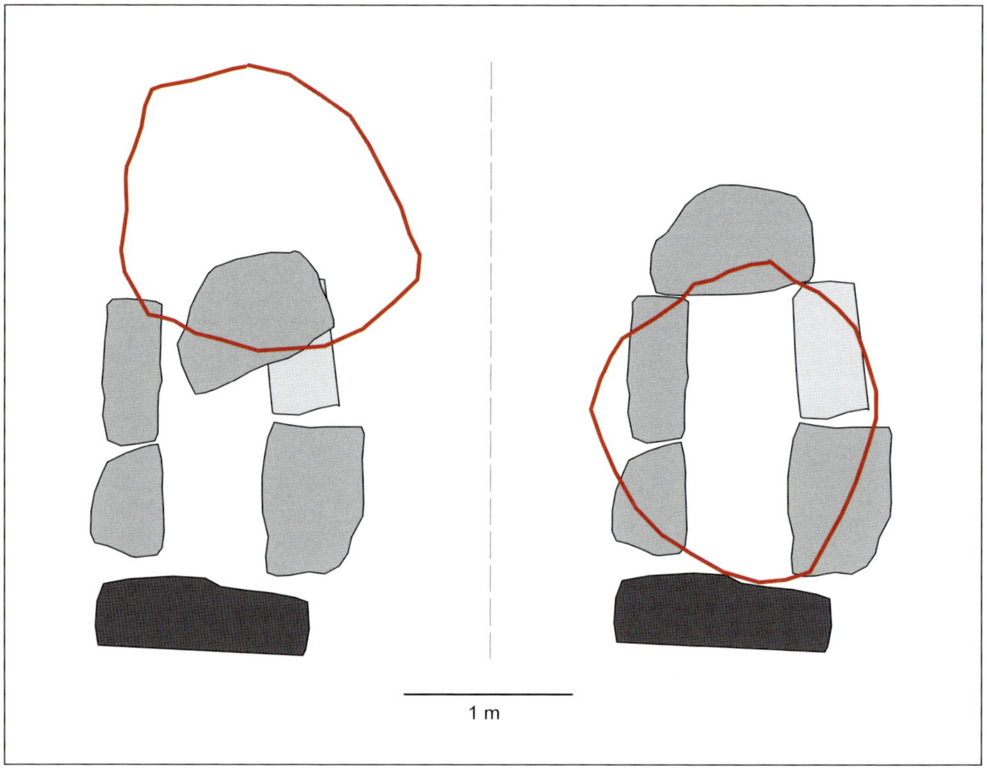

Fig. 9.11. *The capstone of the Dronninglund chamber is preserved but has been pushed to one side. One of the chamber's six side stones is missing, shown in light grey on the plan. Its neighbour, the end stone, has slipped somewhat into the chamber. The large dark-grey end stone at the opposite end is 20-30 cm higher than the side stones, so when the capstone was in place – see drawing on the right – it simply abutted the higher end stone rather than resting upon it.*

modest thickness, no more than 50 cm, are known from Kellerød in western Zealand, Rude near Odder in eastern Jutland, Havnbjerg Skov on Als and Skelde on Broagerland, both southeast Jutland (fig. 9.12).[27] In all of these instances, the cists are narrow and rectangular with a stone at each end and two or three orthostats of equal height at each side, so the cists were closed when the capstone was laid in place.

Dolmen cists and dolmen chambers

Dolmen chambers proper, and thereby dolmens as a whole, were built of large stones, each with at least one flat side facing in towards the chamber. Stone flags and slabs were mostly only used at the ends, and always at an opening or entrance, if there is one. Otherwise the orthostats usually have a domed "reverse", like the commonly thick and substantial capstone. Conversely, stone cists like those at Barkær, Kellerød etc. were built of large slab-like stones, often 20-30 cm thick, and have been covered by a large, slab-like stone or stones of roughly similar thickness. As mentioned elsewhere, these stone cists are referred to as dolmen cists (see chapter 5).

Dolmen cists, which are related to the plank-built cists and could be coeval with these, thereby dating from the time of the Barkaer-structures, are generally earlier than the dolmen chambers. As yet, however, a grey zone remains between dolmen cists and the earliest dolmen chambers. Some dolmen chambers can actually be built of slightly thicker, rather more than 50 cm, slab-like stones so they resemble a "more robust version" of the dolmen cists. It has already been shown, in the account of the

Grøfte long dolmen, that a dolmen cist and a dolmen chamber can lie side by side in the same long barrow and be coeval (see chapter 6).

The narrow, rectangular dolmen chambers of types I and II, constructed of four to eight orthostats and covered by a capstone, are considered to be the earliest dolmens in Denmark. These "primeval dolmens" occur in large numbers in eastern Denmark, especially on Zealand, but are also known from the rest of the country (fig. 9.13). The concentration of these dolmens, of which the smallest is less than 1.5 m in length, has prompted some researchers to maintain that the earliest dolmens are to be found on Zealand, from where they spread to the rest of Denmark.[28] Today, however, the view is that new site visits to re-examine these chambers, combined with precise, modern analyses of the finds and finds circumstances, are required before such a far-reaching interpretation can possibly be confirmed. Moreover, this view represents a very questionable interpretation of the distribution map. There are actually dolmens of types I and II across the entire country, and Jutland has more of their earlier predecessors – the dolmen cists!

In Denmark, a typological development can therefore be observed from wooden plank-built cists to dolmen cists made of stone slabs, and then on to dolmen chambers built of thicker moraine boulders with a single flat side facing in towards the chamber. It seems probable that dolmen chambers were developed locally within Scandinavia.

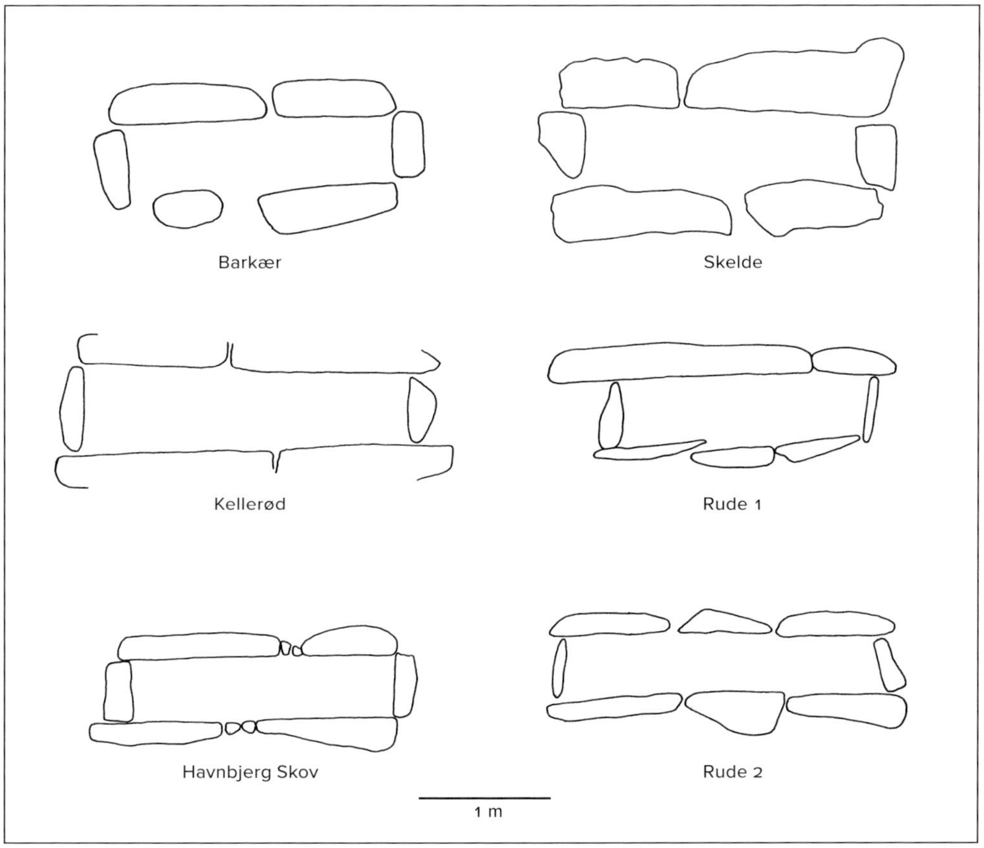

Fig. 9.12. *Plans of the six dolmen cists that, with their thin slab-like stones, all resemble plank cists and thereby differ from dolmen chambers proper, with thicker stones that bulge outwards.*

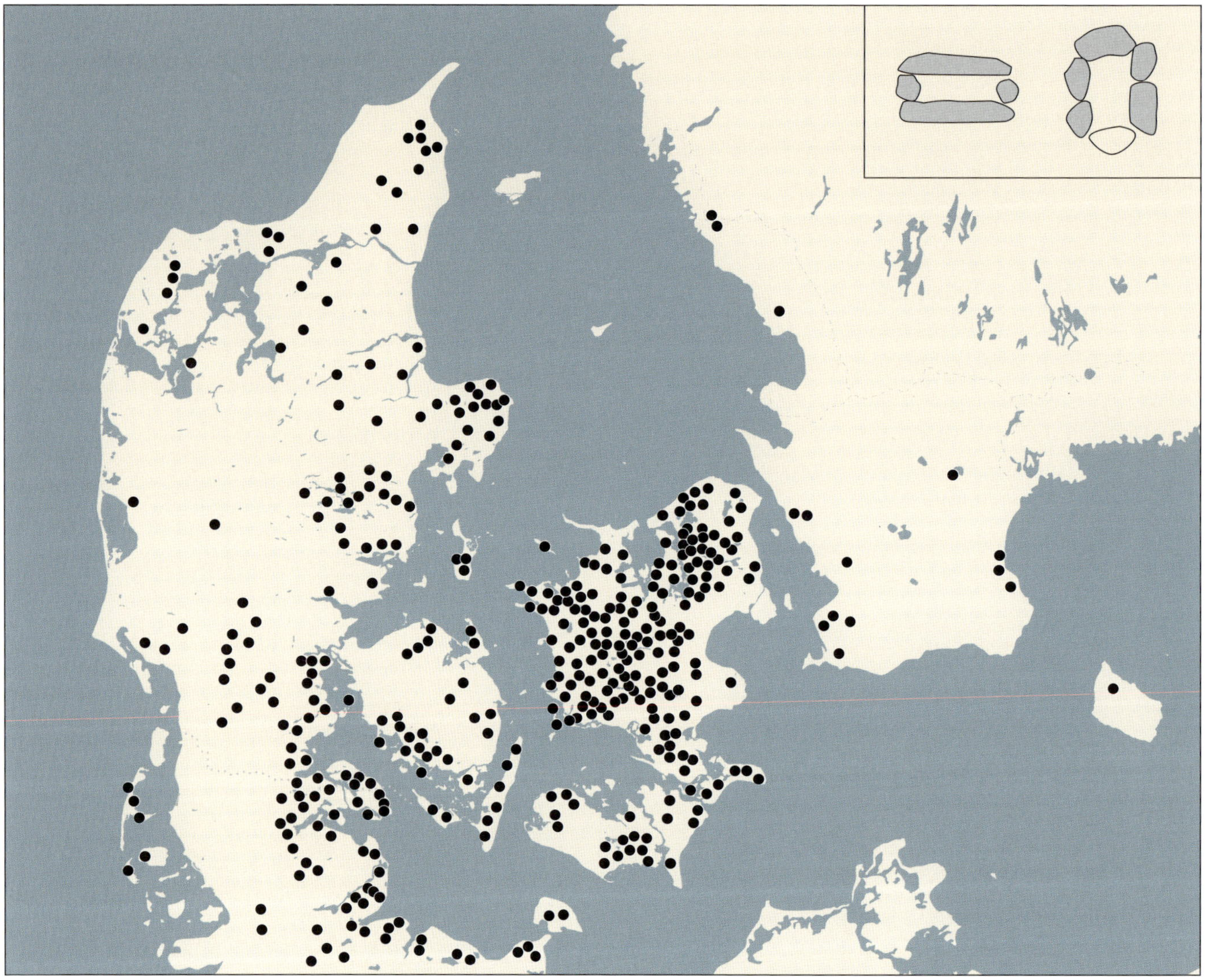

Fig. 9.13. *Distribution map for the earliest dolmens, types I and II. Each dot marks a parish with one or more dolmens of these types.*

From Barkaer-structures to long barrows and long dolmens

In early excavations of Early Neolithic earth graves, only the graves themselves were investigated. Excavators were not aware that these formed part of a larger structure: a Barkaer-structure, i.e. an elongate, rectangular or trapezoid area, the perimeter of which was marked with wooden fences or cut ditches. The interior of this fenced or ditched area could be covered with earth, forming a low mound, or could also be completely free of earthen material, i.e. no mound.

Today, we know of 84 Barkaer-structures, i.e. long barrows and long fence- or ditch-framed areas.[29] They are often oriented east-west and can vary from 14-89 m in length and 2-16 m in width.[30] In these structures there are frequently, and almost always at the eastern end, traces of a sturdy, wooden façade which has burnt down.

By this façade are often potsherds, from a number of vessels deposited here. Other common features include segmented division of the internal surface into a longitudinal series of smaller spaces, observed for the first time at Barkær, and the fact that the structures have frequently been extended in length. Furthermore, the earth graves which, as outlined previously, are "super-terrestrial" plank cists, mostly lie oriented along the length of structures. These Early Neolithic framed spaces and long barrows are complicated structures, where excavations often reveal a dynamic development involving two or more phases that may culminate with the raising of a long dolmen containing one or more dolmen chambers or passage graves.

A good example of this is the already frequently mentioned and well-investigated long barrow at Bygholm Nørremark near Horsens. It was possible here to distinguish four main phases, extending over more than half a millennium.[31] Bygholm Nørremark has, since its excavation, been mentioned time and again in reviews and articles. Its construction history has been examined from all angles, and alternative proposals have been made relating to its structures and the sequence of events that unfolded there, as done earlier in this chapter. To cut a long story short, the major developments from fence to barrow are as follows: A wooden plank cist was constructed between two postholes that had held the central roof-bearing posts of a recently demolished house. This was then enclosed within a post-built fence, after which part of the enclosed area was covered by a low earthen mound. Later, the entire monument was covered by a further mound, delimited by a chain of kerbstones. A passage grave was constructed in this mound and finally a row of large standing stones was erected along each long side.

Another interesting locality is the Troelstrup long barrow at Møldrup, 20 km north of Viborg, which was investigated in 1970-73 by Erik Johansen and Poul Kjærum of Moesgaard Museum. Here it was possible to follow the interaction between the five graves – two plank cists and three dolmen chambers – arranged in a line, and the development of the monument from a small, ditch-enclosed, slightly trapezoid 28 m long and 10-12 m wide Barkaer-structure with a post-built façade, to a fully complete 59 m long and 12 m wide long dolmen. In step with construction of the graves, the east-west-oriented structure was extended to the east in two operations (fig. 9.14).[32]

A third and very different long barrow is Mosegården, located 10 km east of Horsens, which was investigated by Torsten Madsen of Aarhus University in 1978-79.[33] The excavation revealed two polygonal dolmen chambers (type IV) within a 16 m wide and at least 102 m long Barkaer-structure, along the sides of which had stood a sturdy fence. Impressions of wooden posts, varying in width between 0.5-1.2 m and in thickness between 15-50 cm, revealed that the posts had been cloven.

Several further examples could be given of excavations of demolished long barrows and long dolmens that have yielded surprising findings showing extensive variation and dynamic in the development of these monuments, albeit within certain fixed limits and frameworks. In chapter 20, an account is given of some of the Barkaer-structures and long barrows that were investigated in southwest Funen in connection with the Sarup project.

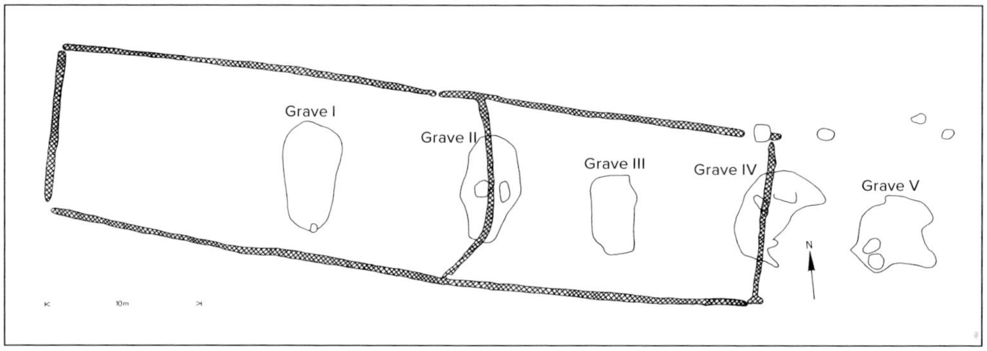

Fig. 9.14. *Plan of the Troelstrup barrow and its extension phases. The long dolmen with kerbstones is not included. The latter encompassed the entire monument, including the two eastern dolmen chambers IV and V.*

From wood to stone – from fence to mound

The development from plank-built cists within fenced enclosures or low earthen mounds surrounded by wood, i.e. Barkaer-structures, to long dolmens proper with dolmen chambers is by no means a purely Danish phenomenon. Structures resembling Danish Barkaer-structures are found across central Europe, from the Paris area in the west to the southern part of Poland in the east. These structures are often a couple of centuries earlier than the Danish examples, and we presume that the inspiration for the Danish monuments came from here.[34]

In these more southerly areas, the structures often lie in large groups or clusters, corresponding to a kind of burial ground or cemetery. The monuments, almost exclusively enclosures with a little earth or a mound raised over the graves, can be up to a couple of hundred metres in length and are either roughly keyhole-shaped or rectangular. It has commonly been assumed previously that they imitate the form of the houses in the settlements. This is an intriguing idea, and possibly also correct. In Denmark, we see a clear link between demolished houses, graves and Barkaer-structures, with the grave being built soon after the house has been removed, and the entire complex then being framed by a Barkaer-structure.

When we look at scheduled dolmens in Denmark today, for example the impressive 158 m long dolmen at Lindeskov near Ørbæk, southwest of Nyborg (see photo on page 96), we know that this monument, with only a single visible dolmen chamber close to one end, like many other long dolmens probably contains several concealed graves and remains of other structures. This impressive dolmen is likely the end result of repeated extensions, undertaken in several operations. Initially, it would have been much smaller, with one or more plank cists surrounded by posts, and completely without a mound.

Danish dolmens are the result of an extended developmental process, which probably took place, or was initiated, under the influence of similar structures further south in western Europe. In the Mesolithic, the dead were buried in pit graves in the earth, but only a couple of centuries into the Neolithic the deceased were now interred in plank cists, built on the ground surface. Interestingly, these cists appear to have been placed on the site of a house that had been demolished only a short time before. These plank-built wooden cists are often found in the more or less monumental Barkaer-structures, and they are very different from the earlier pit graves. Plank cists were subsequently replaced by similar structures that were now built of flat stone slabs. i.e. perishable wood was replaced by indestructible stone, resulting in what we here refer to as dolmen cists. Dolmen cists then developed into dolmen chambers proper, in which, at least at the sides, use was made of thick moraine boulders with only one flat side facing in towards the chamber itself. The occurrence of both wooden plank-built cists and stone dolmen cists at Barkær shows that these two early types could have been built at the same time. In the Grøfte long barrow we also see that dolmen cists and dolmen chambers can be coeval. The long, and in some cases post-fenced, Barkaer-structures with their plank-built and/or dolmen cists may be covered by an earthen mound or a stone pavement, at which point they are referred to as long barrows. If, in turn, these long barrows become framed with large kerbstones, they are known as long dolmens.[35]

10. Long dolmens with abundant mound fill

Many long dolmens containing dolmen cists or dolmen chambers of the possibly earliest type, type I, have exceptionally large amounts of mound fill, such that the surface slopes up from the tops of the kerbstones and conceals both cists and chambers. In cross-section, this is apparent as a strongly domed mound. As these long dolmens and their cists and chambers correspond closely in date to the Barkaer-structures, it seems natural and appropriate to take a closer look at them before moving on to the dolmens, which were constructed slightly later.

No archaeological investigations involving excavated sections have so far been undertaken of these long dolmens with abundant mound fill. But some of these monuments will, nevertheless, be presented in the following in order to give an idea of how much fill they actually contain. In 2010, we surveyed the surface profiles of three of them: Valbygård Skov, Langben Rises Høj and Kellerød, all located on Zealand.

In all three cases, two profiles were surveyed: one running over the chamber (red) and one over the intact mound surface close by (green) (fig. 10.1). The mounds could originally have been higher than the dimensions given below, as material may have slipped downwards and outwards from the top of the mound.

Valbygård Skov

In Valbygård Skov, east of Slagelse, two long dolmens stand side by side (see box 3 on page 125). One of these monuments is a completely open dolmen with two chambers of type II, but it is the other, rather longer structure that is interesting in the present context, because it contains an exceptionally large amount of mound material.

The latter long dolmen, which is oriented SSW-NNE, is 46 m in length and almost 11 m in width (fig. 10.2). It has apparently not been restored, so several of the kerbstones still lie fallen or covered by soil creep. The mound within the kerbstones is an impressive structure that, from the profile, can be seen to have a height of 2.5 m, which is 1.2 m higher than the tops of the kerbstones (see fig. 10.1a). There are now several overgrown holes in the surface of the mound resulting from previous digging activities. In one of these, in the middle of the long dolmen, lies the only known chamber.

The chamber, which lies along the longitudinal axis of the mound, has internal dimensions of 1.4 x 0.7 m. It is built of four stones of equal height. The thickness of the stones at the sides cannot be measured as these are concealed within the enclosing mound, but they are at least 40-50 cm thick, and probably more. The chamber is

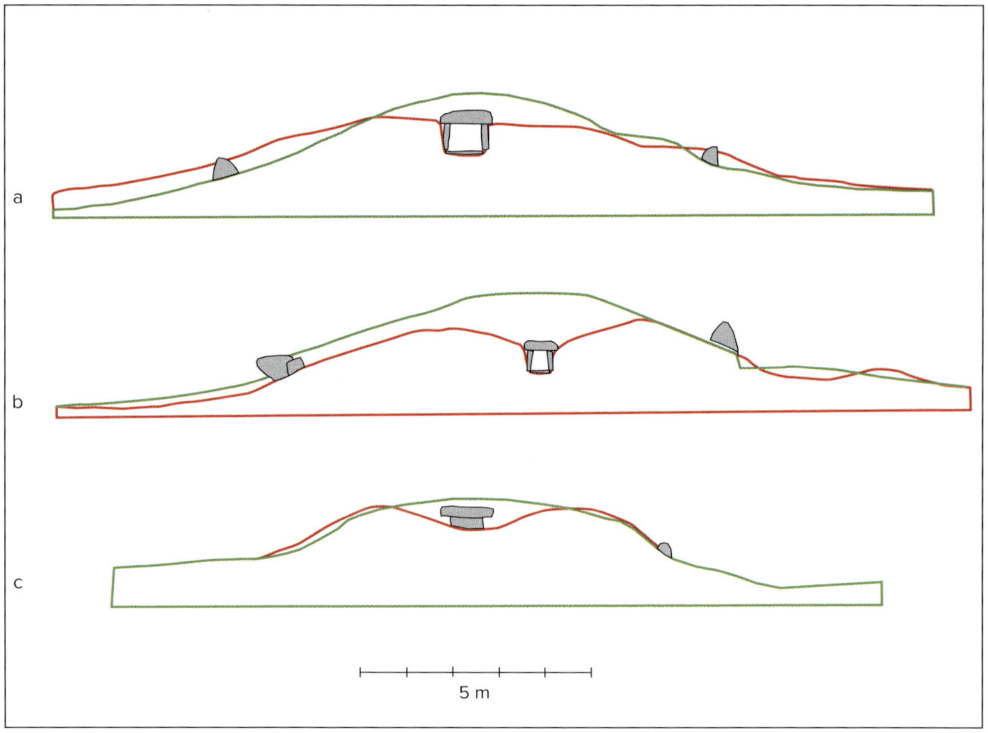

Fig. 10.1. *Cross-section showing the surface profiles of the long dolmens Valbygård Skov (a), Langben Rises Høj (b) and Kellerød (c). Shown in red are the profiles that cross the actual chamber. The areas around the chambers are all disturbed by earlier digging activities and, concomitant with that, the removal of mound material. In order to illustrate the course of the mound surface prior to these interventions, the nearby undisturbed surface of the mound is shown with a green line. The flat capstones, which were not demonstrated at Langben Rises Høj, have been added for effect.*

presumably a dolmen chamber of the earliest type, type I. It has no capstone, but just beside it is a 1.5 m high stone, 30-45 cm in thickness, which stands erect on the surface of the mound. This is very probably the capstone, in which case it is of modest thickness. The tops of the chamber's orthostats lie 70 cm below the surface of the mound. So if the presumed capstone is put back in place, it would be covered and concealed by the mound.

The chamber's present measurable height is 60 cm, but its true height is clearly greater. If the orthostats stand on the Neolithic soil surface, the chamber would originally have had a height of 1.7 m, which is considerable, but there are other examples of chambers of this type having a similar height.[1] The chamber could, however, have been built on a natural hillock or elevation, which would reduce its ceiling height somewhat.

Langben Rises Høj

The long dolmen Langben Rises Høj stands in the forest Klosterskov at Birkede, west of Køge, directly by the very busy railway line that links the capital, Copenhagen, with Funen and Jutland. A number of toppled kerbstones and three old holes dug in its surface suggest that this dolmen has not been restored either. One of these holes could well have been dug rather more than 350 years ago, as *Den Danske Atlas* reports that "On Daastrup Mark the renowned giant Lange Beenriser is thought to be buried. The burial place is 60 alen [37 m] long and 12 alen [7.5 m] wide and surrounded by 56 great stones. In 1658, M. Erasm. Enew. Brochmand, Rector Universit., had the ground opened and found under a vault of great stones an urn holding ash and some bones."[2]

This impressive long dolmen, which is oriented approximately north-south, is just less than 52 m in length and 10 m in width and has a height of 2.5 m (fig. 10.3 and photo on page 116). About 13 m from the northern end, in a hollow, lies the only identified chamber in the monument. But there was probably also a further chamber, now destroyed, in the large hole located roughly in the middle of the mound, and possibly another in the third plundering pit.

Fig. 10.2. *In Valbygård Skov, two long dolmens stand side by side: one with two chambers and no mound material and the other with abundant mound material and a single chamber, located in a hollow in the top of the mound. Beside this chamber, a stone is stood on end, which is very probably the capstone.*

Fig. 10.3. *At Christmas, a garden gnome is placed on Langben Rises Høj. The dolmen chamber can be seen at the base of a large hollow in the mound; its capstone was removed long ago.*

The small, narrow chamber, which is 1.3 m long and 0.4 m wide uppermost, lies along the longitudinal axis of the long dolmen. It consists of three orthostats of equal height, i.e. one at each side and an end stone to the south. As the chamber appears today, it is of type II, but the end stone to the north could very well have been removed later, so the chamber was originally of type I. No capstone is preserved. On the profile surveyed across the mound and chamber, it can be seen that there has been almost 1.25 m of mound fill above the tops of the chamber's orthostats, i.e. sufficient to cover a capstone of moderate thickness (see fig. 10.1b). Relative to the tops of the kerbstones, the top of the mound, measured on the profile, is 60 cm higher.

It cannot be determined for certain whether the long dolmen contains a dolmen cist or a dolmen chamber, because the stones extend into the mound. But it probably has a dolmen chamber, standing on what was the original soil surface in the Neolithic, in which case the chamber is rather more than 1 m in height.

Kellerød

The Kellerød long dolmen offers a broad view out across the lake Tystrup Sø, southeast of Slagelse, and with its length of 120 m, it is one of Zealand's longest dolmens (fig. 10.4). Unlike the two other long dolmens described above, it stands in an open field. The monument is oriented north-south.

It is framed by a chain of relatively small kerbstones, though there are some larger stones at each gable. With its height of 1.5 m, the mound exceeds the tops of the kerbstones by about 1 m. The monument is 7.5 m wide.

The otherwise neatly-trimmed and tidy long dolmen – it was restored by the National Museum in 1934 – has only one hollow in its surface, 25 m from its northern end. Here lies a dolmen cist that was found in 1933, i.e. prior to the general scheduling of barrows in 1937, when it was excavated by the farm's archaeologically-interested sons, one of whom was Harald Andersen, who later became a professional archaeologist. The only visible trace of this dolmen cist today is a single large stone. However, we have a good description of its appearance in 1933, and that of the long dolmen, because the discovery was reported to the Danish National Museum and the site was visited by Knud Thorvildsen, who also wrote a report.[3]

The chamber, which was covered by and packed within a heap of stones, was sealed by a capstone, the top of which lay 50 cm below the surface of the long dolmen. The 3 m long and up to 1.6 m wide capstone was very special in that it was of limestone and only 35-50 cm in thickness, which is very thin for a capstone. It covered a dolmen cist that lay in the middle of the mound, aligned along its longitudinal axis. The cist consisted of six stones of equal height, two at each side and one at each end (see fig. 9.12). Internally, it measured 2.5 m in length and was slightly trapezoid in shape, with a width of 60 cm to the south and 75 cm to the north. The height of the cist from its base to the lower surface of the capstone was only 60 cm.

Knud Thorvildsen does not mention the thickness of the side stones, but it is evident from a sketch in his report that these were not particularly thick, being almost slab-like (see fig. 21.1). On this sketch, the end stones are shown as being around 20 cm thick and the stones at the sides 25-30 cm.

The relationship between mound, kerbstones and cist is clearly evident on the profile surveyed across the mound in 2010 (fig. 10.1c). The only visible larger stone in the hollow is also included. This could be an end stone, but we do not know for certain. Knud Thorvildsen considered that the base of the chamber rested on the subsoil. On the profile, the present – estimated – height of the long dolmen is 1.6 m, which is consistent with the finds circumstances in the cist: 50 cm mound fill over the capstone plus a 35-50 cm thick capstone and a 60 cm high cist, giving a total of 1.45-1.6 m.

Fig. 10.4. *The Kellerød long dolmen with its crest of trees occupies an impressive and spectacular position in the terrain. The trees stand in two rows, one on each side of the monument. Early 20th century maps show a road running across the top of the 1.5 m high long dolmen at that time.*

Directly on the floor of the cist, which was paved with flat stone slabs, lay the skeleton of a 30-40-year-old man. This is described in more detail in chapter 21. There was also a pottery vessel, a flint blade and a small collection of snail shells.

In conjunction with the Danish National Museum's restoration of the monument in 1934, the top of the mound was excavated along its length in search of further stone chambers. None were, however, found, but there was a stone heap that may well have covered a plank cist.

Relationship to the Barkaer-structures

Common to all three of these long dolmens with abundant mound material – Valbygård Skov, Langben Rises Høj and Kellerød – is that they contain a dolmen cist or a dolmen chamber of early type and their chambers, with capstones, were completely concealed by mound material. At two of these, Valbygård Skov and Kellerød, the capstones are slab-like and 35-50 cm thick. The same is, incidentally, true of the monument at Grøfte (see chapter 6) which, with its earth-covered dolmen chamber and dolmen cist closed by a thin capstone, its location in a long barrow and its modest height, shows clear associations with the Barkaer-structures and their cists of wood and stone.

As pointed out in chapter 9, the dolmen builders' conscious selection of flat capstones for these dolmen chambers and dolmen cists must be due to their relationship to similar, coeval cists of wood, and to the clear intention that the cists, both those of wood and those of stone, should ultimately be covered with earth so they were no longer visible. The total concealment of these dolmen cists and early dolmen chambers suggests a conscious desire in the Neolithic to shut these structures off and conceal them completely. In Brittany's thousand year older long barrows, which also contain stone cists, a similar sequence of events can be seen to have taken place (see chapter 18).

It is possible that some of the Danish long dolmens that have a remarkable abundance of mound material, covering dolmen cists or early dolmen chambers, were given the extra mound material during the Passage-grave epoch. This is certainly true of Bygholm Nørremark, though not of the relatively low-profiled Kellerød long dolmen, where a longitudinal trial trench along the entire length of the mound revealed no trace of a passage grave. It would be obvious to investigate some of these mound-rich long dolmens with the aim of dating the mound material they contain.

If we are to attempt to outline the general course of developments, we must begin in the time of the Barkaer-structures, when elongate structures were established, framed by a fence or ditch and containing one or more plank coffins. Gradually, and at a varying pace, these structures were transformed into long barrows, at which point they also contained dolmen cists. In some instances, the Barkaer-structures ended up with very large amounts of mound material that concealed the cists. With their modest height and flat capstones, the latter did not project very far up in the mound and the tops of the kerbstones also stood significantly lower than the mound's apex. If a large, more or less flat stone is observed today in the top of a long dolmen, as for example in Niels Halses Høj on the island of Samsø, this could very well be the capstone of a dolmen cist.[4]

This tradition of transforming open, elongate structures into closed long barrows continued in the Dolmen epoch, when the first and earliest proper dolmen chambers appeared, built of large boulders and fitted with massive capstones. The mound fill, potentially comprising material from two or more phases, shows that this was still more than a one-off event, but the mound did not extend higher than to the upper edge of the orthostats on which the large, but now no longer slab-like, capstone rested.

If the developmental stages through which such a dolmen could progress were, for some reason, interrupted at some point, the chamber or chambers in it would stand partially exposed and the kerbstones would also project far above the inner surface. A long dolmen of this kind is presented in the next chapter.

Valbygård Skov

In Valbygård Skov, east of Slagelse, a pair of long dolmens stands deep in the forest, directly beside Rosted Skovvej and a couple of hundred metres east of the forest cottage Enebo. These long dolmens are very interesting and relevant to the theme of this book – dolmens with and without mounds. The longest of the long dolmens contains an extremely large amount of mound material and it is described in more detail in this chapter. The other, shorter long dolmen has no mound material whatsoever. The difference between the two long dolmens is very striking, as they stand side by side only 10 m apart.

The longer long dolmen is 46 m in length, just less than 11 m in width and 2.5 m in height. There are several holes in its surface as a result of earlier digging activities. In one of these holes, in the middle of the monument, stands a narrow, elongate dolmen chamber of the earlier type, type I. The erect stone beside the chamber is possibly its toppled capstone. When the capstone was in place, and the mound was undisturbed, nothing would have revealed the presence of the chamber beneath the mound surface. The long dolmen has clearly, and fortunately, avoided restoration, as several of the kerbstones have toppled outwards to some extent and the holes in its surface remain unfilled – it is a magnificent ancient monument.

The shorter long dolmen is 21 m long and 6 m wide and is, as already mentioned, completely without mound material. On the other hand, it has two handsome, totally exposed and visible chambers of type II, with intact capstones. The chambers, which are 1.7-2 m long and 1.2 m wide internally, are each built of 3-4 orthostats and are fitted with a threshold stone at the open end. The two chambers, which are aligned side by side transversely across the monument, resemble each other so closely that they must have been constructed at the same time.

The kerbstones, several of which have toppled over, are remarkably small relative to those of the longer dolmen. This could perhaps be due to a shortage of suitable large stones in the area following construction of the latter.

It is tempting to imagine that the shorter long dolmen was just as open in appearance in the Neolithic as it is today. And we tend towards this theory, though it cannot be tested without undertaking an archaeological excavation. But common sense speaks in its favour, because any mound that potentially extended up to the lower surface of the capstones has not left the slightest trace. With its two intact chambers and numerous kerbstones, the monument appears relatively undisturbed and remains in a state that can be traced back to 1820, when it was sketched for the first time.

In the time that elapsed between construction of the longer and the shorter long dolmen, a mental shift took place in the minds of the dolmen builders, which saw physical expression in the appearance of the two monuments. The oldest of the two monuments is the long dolmen with abundant mound material and a chamber that was intentionally concealed in the Neolithic, while the later, shorter dolmen has not the least amount of mound material and a pair of totally exposed chambers.

Around 1820, J. Thiele sketched the central part of the shorter long dolmen with the two chambers seen from the rear accompanied by a picturesque old oak tree. In 1857, he drew the dolmen again, this time from the other side. The oak tree had been felled in the intervening period. The fact that this monument is totally devoid of mound material is clearly evident from both drawings, in which the rather naïve sketching style means that onlya few of the kerbstones are depicted. In the background of the most recent sketch, the other, longer long dolmen can be seen, and digging activity in a hollow here has revealed a couple of stones that protrude above the surface – this is probably where the exposed chamber stands today.

11. The Gunderslevholm dolmen

In one of the forests belonging to the manor of Gunderslevholm, Borup Ris, at the southern end of the lake Tystrup Sø, southeast of Slagelse, stands the long dolmen that inspired N.F.S. Grundtvig's deeply romantic poem *Gunderslev Wood* (see page 143).[1] Accompanied by his friend Christian Molbech – both were 25 years of age at the time – Grundtvig was rowed across the lake Sorø Sø on the morning of 26th August 1808. The two young men then walked 16 km south for the sole purpose of visiting this dolmen, so it must already have enjoyed a certain degree of fame in the early 19th century. Just less than a month later, Grundtvig's poem was published in the weekly paper *Nyeste Skilderie af Kjøbenhavn*, in which Christian Molbech had, in the previous issue, already given a lively account of their antiquarian walking trip, together with a detailed description of the Gunderslevholm monument.

For the last couple of centuries, the long dolmen has stood in a clearing in the deciduous woodland. Previously, a few large trees grew on the dolmen itself, but now it is almost completely free of plant growth, both woody and otherwise. The 55 m long and around 8 m wide monument stands oriented east-west on the edge of a plateau which, to the east, grades down towards a stream, so that one end of the dolmen lies directly by the slope, where old hollow ways cut into the hillside.

The Gunderslevholm dolmen has often been highlighted as being largely undamaged, and as it has successfully avoided the excavation and restoration activities of both enthusiastic archaeologists and noble landowners, it apparently appears today – with the exception of some fallen and leaning kerbstones – as it did in the Neolithic (fig. 11.1 and photo on opposing page). As the dolmen has very little mound material – mostly stones of various sizes – it is a typical example of an open dolmen and consequently of great relevance to the question of dolmens without mounds. Many other long dolmens also have very little mound fill, but this particular monument is of special interest due to the many exposed stones in its interior. This is a very special feature of the Gunderslevholm dolmen and the reason that we, and others, have been so interested in it. But the degree to which it is a *genuine* open dolmen – i.e. a dolmen that also had very little mound material in the Neolithic – is the subject of differing opinions.

In the following, we will first take a look at early descriptions and drawings and then present our survey and description from 1999. This is followed by an account of an archaeological excavation undertaken in 2008, and we conclude with a discussion of whether this monument actually is a genuine open dolmen.

Fig. 11.1. *The internal surface of the Gunderslevholm dolmen is unique, being covered by 40-90 cm diameter stones with no earth between them. The fact that the monument has completely avoided restoration is apparent from the numerous toppled kerbstones.*

Early descriptions

The aforementioned article by Christian Molbech, published in *Nyeste Skilderie af Kjøbenhavn* in 1808, provided the first written description of the dolmen: "It consists of an elongate stone frame, which is 70 paces in length and 10 to 12 paces in width. The kerbstones, of which most have a height over the ground of a couple of alen [1.3 m] and more, are 89 in number. About 20 paces from the western [must be eastern] end, a gigantic stone heap [the chamber] rises up, consisting of a capstone, the uppermost point of which is around 3½ alen [2.2 m] above the ground; so that if one stands in front or behind it, one cannot see those who are on the other side. It is about 13 alen [8.2 m] in circumference, and rests on four partially buried stones; its form approaches that of a triangle." (fig. 11.2).

And further with respect to the chamber: "Between that [the capstone] and two of the orthostats there is at the front … an opening, so large that one can without much difficulty crawl down into the cavity beneath the stone, where two to three seated people could be accommodated."

Of the area to the east of the chamber, Christian Molbech writes: "The rearmost part of the stone frame is, a short distance from the offering altar [the chamber], separated from the remainder by a gap, marked by four large stones that on both sides stand further apart than the rest … Through these openings runs a footpath." There then follows a description of the two narrow ends of the long dolmen and its internal surface:

"At both ends of the stone frame is a recognisable opening or entrance, formed between two cornerstones of impressive size, but as if this entrance should be closed, a stone of pointed form and of greater height than the others has been erected in the middle [of each of them]. Of these [stones], one slopes somewhat inwards; the other at the western [must be eastern] end lies flat on the ground, presumably having toppled over. All the internal space the stone circle encloses is as if cobbled with large closely-spaced stones; such that it is only possible with great difficulty to walk from one end to the other.

According to this description the experts must judge how reasonable the view is of which I am to this moment completely convinced: that here in this dolmen, which stands so completely untouched that perhaps not a single stone from it has been removed, we have one of heathen times' handsomest and best preserved offering places. The monument's unsullied state through so many years is testified to by the thick encrusting of the common green moss, with which almost every stone is covered and which makes not a modest contribution to giving the whole a venerable appearance."[2]

As mentioned in chapter 5, in 1808 the Danish Royal Commission for the Collection and Preservation of Antiquities had asked Denmark's local clergy to report on the ancient monuments that occurred within their parishes. In March 1809, the Reverend Niels Hee submitted a very comprehensive report for Skelby and Gunderslev parishes. He reported 86 barrows and megalithic graves, and he asked for the

Fig. 11.2. *The earliest known drawing of the Gunderslevholm dolmen was probably made in 1808 by Christian Molbech, following his visit to the monument together with N.F.S. Grundtvig. Note the footpath running across the long dolmen just to the right of the chamber. Stones have been removed from the course of this path at both long sides of the monument. The path is mentioned by Molbech in his contemporaneous description, as are the large gable stones, one of which has toppled over.*

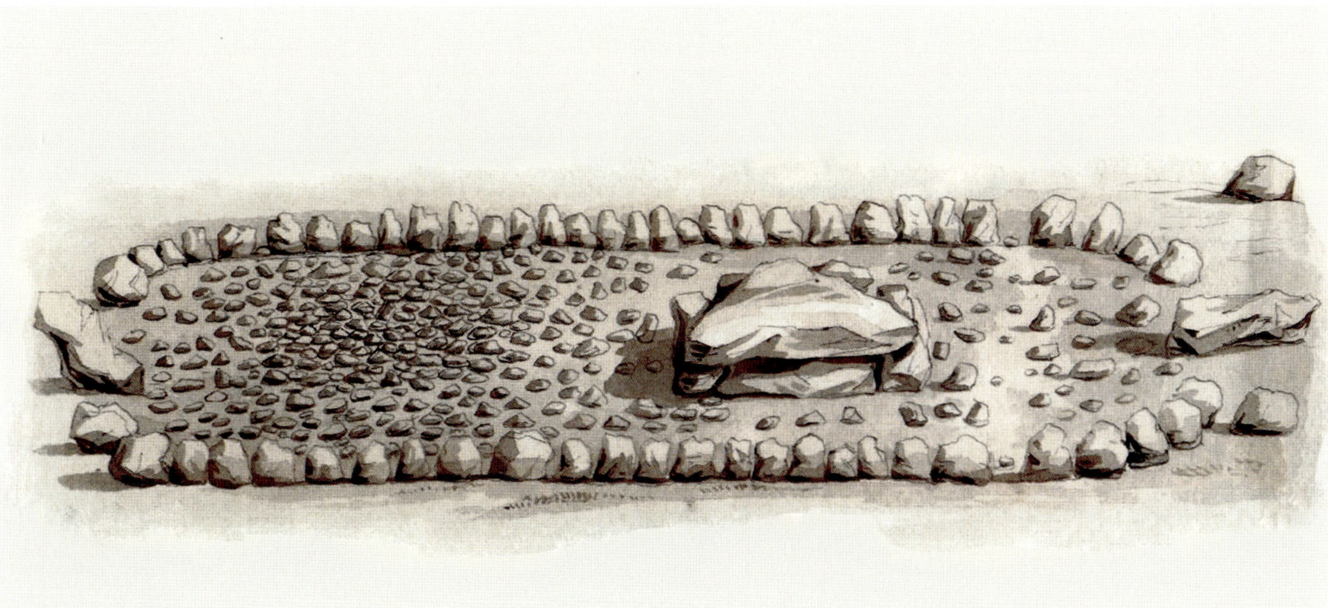

Fig. 11.3. *In 1857, Jacob Kornerup drew the Gunderslevholm dolmen when he visited the monument together with archaeologist J.J.A. Worsaae, who is seen posing by the mighty capstone over the chamber.*

commission's assistance in "the protection of" ten of these, including the Gunderslevholm dolmen: "in plane surface 108 alen [67.8 m] long and 15 alen [9.4 m] wide – surrounded by very flat stones, has to the southwest a very large upright stone. Everywhere densely covered with common stones which one man can hardly lift. Here and there some hollows and a large capstone supported by four stones – the only one of its kind here in the realm."[3] With the strange expression "in plane surface" that Reverend Hee uses in reference to this and other long dolmens, he probably means that they have a flat interior rather than a domed mound.[4]

Between 1809 and 1811, on the basis of the clerical reports, the commission identified 135 ancient monuments considered worthy of protection across the length and breadth of Denmark. The actual scheduling took place through the Danish Chancery, which administered Denmark's internal affairs. The Gunderslevholm dolmen was one of the monuments scheduled. In this regard, it was described as: "In Gundersløv forest a very magnificent, exceptionally and totally well-preserved offering place. About which there is a published description in Kjøbenhavns Skilderie."[5] These schedulings, referred to as "chancellery schedulings", were not legally binding on the landowners and a large number of the 135 ancient monuments were subsequently demolished.[6] Fortunately, this was not the case for the Gunderslevholm dolmen, the owner of which, Counsellor Peter Johansen de Neergaard, fully accepted and supported the scheduling in 1809.[7]

In 1857, archaeologist J.J.A. Worsaae and artist Jacob Kornerup visited "the renowned great long dolmen". While the archaeologist looked on and posed by the chamber, the artist produced a wonderful picture showing the interior of the long dolmen with virtually no fill or mound and the chamber standing tall, together with the kerbstones, several of which lean heavily inwards (fig. 11.3). On the accompanying ground plan, the kerbstones at the sides have been straightened out to form two parallel and completely straight rows, and the following text has been added in handwriting at the bottom of the drawing: "92 alen [57.8 m] long, 12½ alen [7.8 m] wide, frame consists of 88 large stones". This is true – there are also 88 kerbstones on the ground plan.

Less than five years later, the monument was again visited by an archaeologist and an artist, this time embodied in one and the same person, Captain A.P. Madsen. He drew a picture of the dolmen, epigonically viewed from the same angle as his predecessor Kornerup (fig. 11.4). A.P. Madsen also described the long dolmen: "This exceptionally fine and well-preserved long dolmen … The dolmen's length from east to west is 92 alen [57.8 m], and its width, north to south, 14 alen [8.8 m]. The kerbstone frame, which is virtually undamaged, consists of 88 large stones. The dolmen has only one burial chamber, which lies c. 30 alen [18.7 m] from its eastern end. The chamber has four wall stones [orthostats], of which three bear a mighty ceiling- or capstone. The entrance to the chamber is from the west. There is almost no earthen

Fig. 11.4. *Five years after Kornerup sketched the Gunderslevholm long dolmen, it was drawn again, from the same angle, by A.P. Madsen. Note the low internal surface between the chamber and the kerbstones.*

fill in this dolmen, conversely the space within the kerbstones is covered with many large and small stones."[8]

Titular Councillor of State J.V. Neergaard had the long dolmen scheduled by registration in the land register in 1886. The declaration contains a description, as usual written by one of the Danish National Museum's archaeologists, which – fortunately – is in places rather long-winded and elaborate. We are given an excellent impression of the appearance of the long dolmen in 1886. It was 175' long and 24' wide, corresponding to 55 x 7.5 m. There then follows a description of the chamber, before moving on to the kerbstones and the internal surface: "The kerbstones comprise: To the east 2, both fallen, one is 8'3" [2.6 m] long, to the west 4 (3 fallen), the height of the standing stone is 5' [1.6 m]. Along the north side 44 (20 fallen, the remainder leaning heavily inwards), along the south side 33 (7 fallen, most of the others leaning inwards), along the south side 33 (7 fallen, most of the others leaning inwards), all impressive c. 4' [1.3 m] high stones. In the second kerbstone from the east on the north side, a long, ground, deepened furrow can be seen; a fragment has been split off. There is no earthen mound within the kerbstones, but notably in the western part there is a large quantity of loose stones, of a size to be borne by two men, of a kind that usually forms the basal layer in the mounds of long dolmens. The dolmen is overgrown with large trees, several of the kerbstones are almost completely enclosed within their roots."[9]

This is then followed and concluded by the scheduling declaration: "The thus described long dolmen is hereby scheduled with respect to both the current and future owners such that it must never – under a penalty of 5 barrels of barley – be damaged by digging, cleavage of stones or in any other way." In conjunction with the scheduling of 1886, the scheduled ancient monuments marker stone was erected that still stands today by the northern side of the monument, opposite the chamber.

In 1904, A.P. Madsen revisited the long dolmen, this time in the course of a district survey. His description reads as follows: "Long dolmen 55 m long from east to west, 7½ m wide. The dolmen is without mound fill within the kerbstones. It has a free-standing burial chamber of elongate, rectangular form, 1.82 m east to west and 0.9 m wide with 2 side stones and 2 end stones, with a large capstone over these. As for the kerbstones, there are 2 fallen to the east, 1 standing and 3 fallen to the west, along the north side are 22 standing and 20 fallen."[10]

The captain, who by this time was 82 years of age, forgot to mention the kerbstones on the south side, but otherwise it is clear that the metric system of measurement had now been introduced to Danish archaeology.

In 1940, the dolmen was again visited by a professional archaeologist in the line of duty, this time P.V. Glob, on a scheduling survey trip. His description is, as is the norm for scheduling texts, very brief and relies heavily on the text from the parish record: "Long dolmen, 55 x 7.5 m. No mound; but the space within the kerbstones is filled up with boulders. Kerbstones: E. 2 (fallen) W. 4 (3 fallen) N. 44 (20 fallen) S. 2. Free-standing chamber of 4 orthostats and 1 capstone. (Should be restored. Absolutely worth visiting)."[11] Apart from the error with regard to only two kerbstones being present to the south, the big surprise is the recommendation that the long dolmen be restored. This opinion should be viewed in the context of the great surge in popular dolmen restorations that were undertaken across the country by the Danish National Museum in the 1930s and 40s, with conservator Julius Raklev at the helm (see chapter 7). Today, we should be grateful that P.V. Glob's recommendation to restore the Gunderslevholm dolmen was not acted upon.

In the above, seven descriptions of the Gunderslevholm dolmen have been reproduced, dating from 1808 to 1940, from Christian Molbech to P.V. Glob. In these, the monument's length and width vary from 54.8 to 57.8 m and from 7.5 to 8.8 m. When Reverend Hee reported the much greater length of 67.8 m and width of 9.4 m in 1809, this must have been because he measured to the outer edge of the fallen kerbstones. In 1808, Christian Molbech gave the number of kerbstones as being 89, in 1857 and around 1862 a total of 88 were recorded and in 1886 mention is made of 83 kerbstones. One could therefore be led to believe that there actually was a decrease in the number of kerbstones and that stones had been removed subsequent to the first description of 1808. This is, however, not the case. The six stones that were "lost" between 1808 and 1886 were simply not visible at the time of counting, year for year, probably because they had fallen and become covered and hidden by earth. The number of kerbstones today is 87, with a further couple of examples just outside the frame of kerbstones, see below for more details.

In 1808, Christian Molbech believed that the long dolmen was undamaged, while A.P. Madsen, half a century later, refers to the kerbstones as virtually undamaged, and in the scheduling declaration of 1886 reference is made to a few damaged kerbstones. With regard to the internal surface, this is said to be without, or with only very little, earthen fill, such that the kerbstones and the chamber stand free and exposed. In none of the descriptions is it mentioned that the mound-free interior could be due to the removal of earth and stones.

Survey and description 1999

In October 1999, we undertook a survey of the long dolmen. It is a large structure with numerous stones and there was dense bramble scrub over the easternmost third that had to be cleared, so the survey took three days. It was undertaken using a pantograph and a theodolite. We were then able, for the first time, to look at a precise and exact plan of this monument (fig. 11.5). Described first below are the kerbstones, then the dolmen chamber, followed by the surface between the chamber and the kerbstones. Finally, an evaluation is given as to whether the Gunderslevholm dolmen is one of the "tricky" open dolmens.

The number of kerbstones which stand in situ, or approximately in situ, is 87 (nos. 1-87). Further to these are a couple of cloven kerbstones (nos. 88-89), which lie outside the row of kerbstones, giving a total of 89 kerbstones. Judging from the large gaps in the kerbstone frame, between 13 and 15 stones are missing, so the monument originally had 102-104 kerbstones (fig. 11.6).[12] An average standing kerbstone has a height

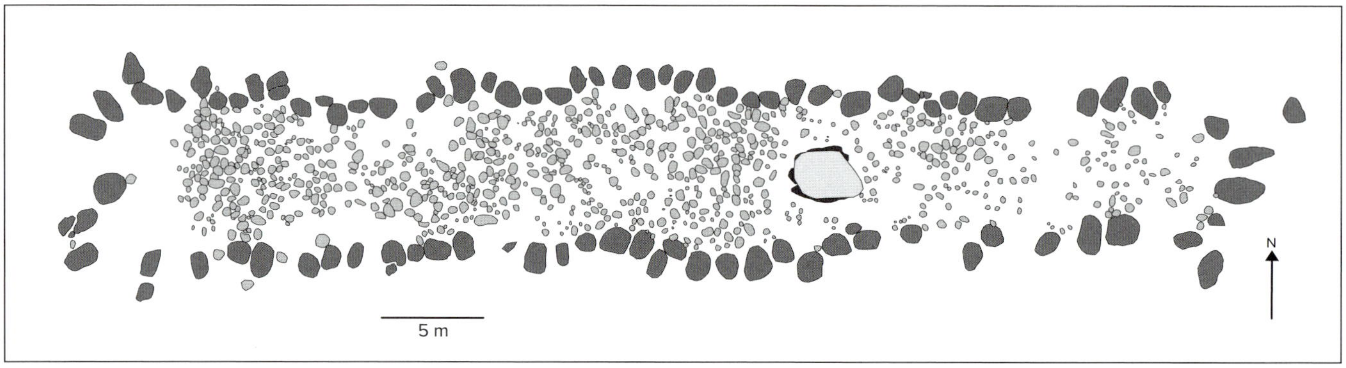

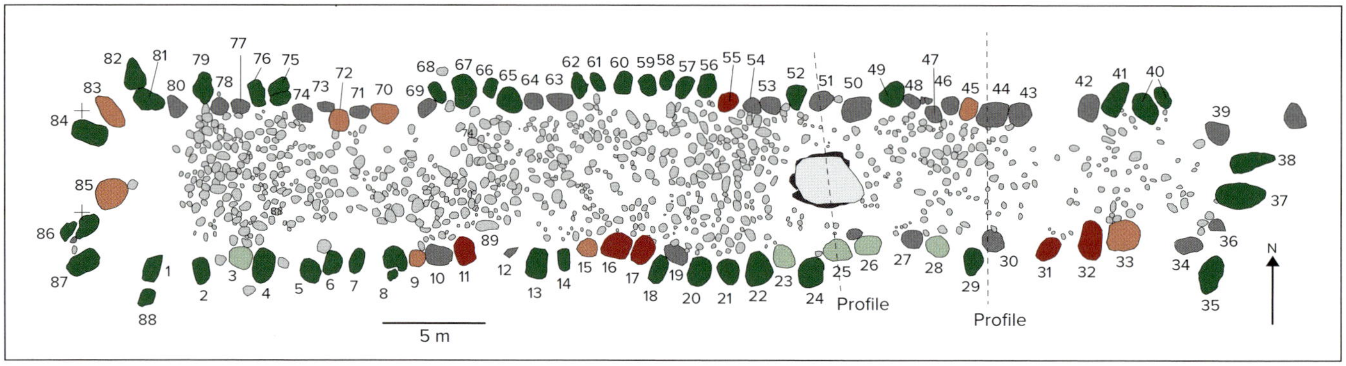

Fig. 11.5. *The first precise survey of the Gunderslevholm dolmen was undertaken in 1999, as part of the project "Dolmens without mounds".*

Fig. 11.6. *Plan of the long dolmen showing the inwardly and outwardly fallen stones marked, together with the positions of the two profiles, surveyed in 1999. Dark green: leaning strongly outwards. Light green: leaning slightly outwards. Dark red: leaning strongly inwards. Pink: leaning slightly inwards. Grey: in situ. The 89 kerbstones are described in note 12.*

of 1.5-1.8 m, and the largest stones, up to 2.6 m in height, have stood at the gables of the monument. Of the 87 kerbstones, 16 have been damaged by cleavage, though only three to any major extent. A couple of kerbstones (nos. 39-40) have 60-65 cm long cleavage furrows carved in them for the purpose of splitting the stones, which has not, however, been carried through. One of these cleavage furrows is mentioned in the scheduling declaration of 1886 as "a long, deep, ground furrow". The technique, involving long, carved cleavage furrows, is known from the 16th and 17th centuries and was in use on Zealand as late as the 1970s.[13] Apart from a further cloven kerbstone (no. 75) showing traces of a couple of 10 cm long cleavage holes, no cleavage marks are evident on the other split kerbstones.

The removed or damaged kerbstones stood primarily near the gables of the long dolmen, such that a longer section on both sides of the chamber remains largely untouched. In the south, these are kerbstones nos. 13-30 and in the north nos. 43-68. Within this entire zone, there is only one missing and one cloven kerbstone to the south and only one cloven kerbstone to the north.

As is the norm with dolmens that have not been restored, many kerbstones can be seen to have toppled outwards completely, or have a slope in that direction. This is also true of the Gunderslevholm dolmen, where there are 40 outwardly fallen or partly outwardly fallen kerbstones and five which slope outwards. Unlike the usual situation, however, the Gunderslevholm dolmen also has seven kerbstones that slope *inwards* and, in some cases, the lower part of these stone has, consequently, slipped outwards. Further to these are eight kerbstones that lean *inwards* to an exceptional degree. Thanks to the many kerbstones which, nevertheless, remain standing in situ, it is possible to draw the approximate original outline of the long dolmen and determine its form and dimensions. Its external length was 54.5 m and its form was slightly trapezoid with a width in the west of 8.6 m and 7.4 m in the east.

The dolmen chamber lies on the long axis of the long dolmen and its centre is displaced 9 m towards the east, relative to the centre of the monument. There are no visible traces of other stone-built chambers within it. The chamber is of the early type with a narrow, rectangular interior (figs. 11.7 and 11.8). It is built of four orthostats, but although these are of equal height, only three support the capstone today, while the fourth – the end stone to the west – has a gap above it. This is due to the capstone having weathered to the west, and an attempt has possibly been made to split it, leading to the disappearance of a large fragment. The capstone must originally have closed the chamber completely, and it is therefore of type I. The interior of the chamber is free of earth down to a level of 1 m below the capstone, and here it is 2.1 m long and 80 cm wide. The stones of which the chamber is built are of considerable size. The two that constitute the sides are at least 2.3-2.9 m in length and around 1.7 m high, corresponding to the chamber's internal height, as measured during the excavation in 2008. The up to 90 cm thick capstone measures 3.6 x 2.7 m and probably weighs around 15 tonnes.[14]

The internal surface of the long dolmen is scattered with large and small stones, most around 40 cm in diameter, with the largest being 90 cm. The upper layer of stones lies freely exposed without earth or smaller stones between them. The tops

Fig. 11.7. *The chamber of the Gunderslevholm dolmen is built of four stones of equal height, covered by a mighty 3.6 m long capstone. The photo is taken from the northwest.*

Fig. 11.8. *Plan of and profile across the chamber of the Gunderslevholm dolmen, surveyed in 1999. Both kerbstones in the section stand in situ, the one to the east has been pushed a little outwards. It appears as if the capstone does not rest on one of the orthostats, but it does in reality, just not at the point shown in the cross-section. The relatively large amount of mound material around the chamber is due to packing and stabilisation of its large stones so they do not slip or topple.*

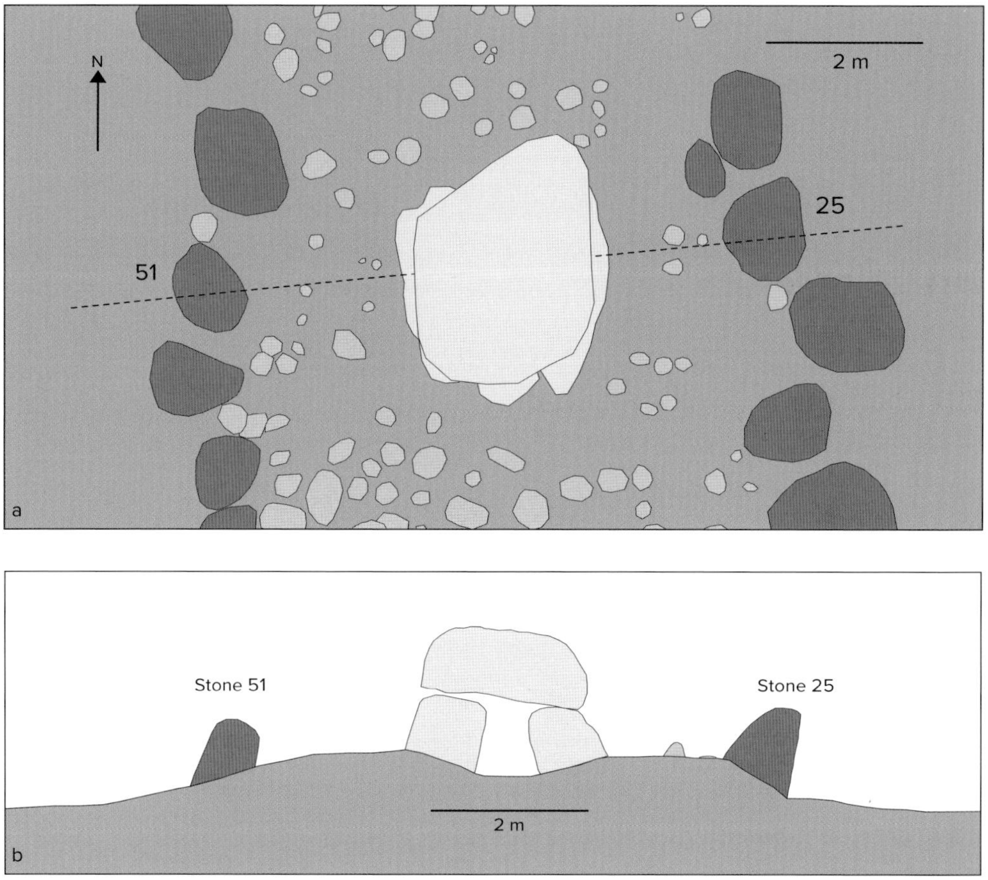

of deeper-lying stones are visible below the stone-free areas on our plan of the long dolmen, giving the impression of further stones below. In 1808, Christian Molbech mentioned a footpath running across the dolmen. Its course is clearly evident from the missing kerbstones between kerbstones nos. 30 and 31 in the south and nos. 42 and 43 in the north (see fig. 11.2). The concentration of stones on the surface is not uniform, as there are virtually none in the westernmost 4 m of the monument. Similarly, there are fewer stones in the eastern part, from and including the old footpath. The few stones at both gables should presumably be seen in the context of the abovementioned destruction in and removal of kerbstones from these same areas. Some of the monument's inner stone fill could also have been removed here.

A profile across the eastern part of the long dolmen, including two kerbstones that stand in situ, gives a good impression of the relationship between the internal space and the kerbstones, which here project 65-100 cm above the surface (fig. 11.9). In general, the internal surface appears uniform in height along the entire length of the monument, though with a slightly higher area evident around the chamber (see fig. 11.8b), with a slope up towards this, beginning 9 m to the west and 5 m to the east of the chamber. It should also be noted that there are no traces of split or fragmented stones among the stones occupying the interior of the monument.

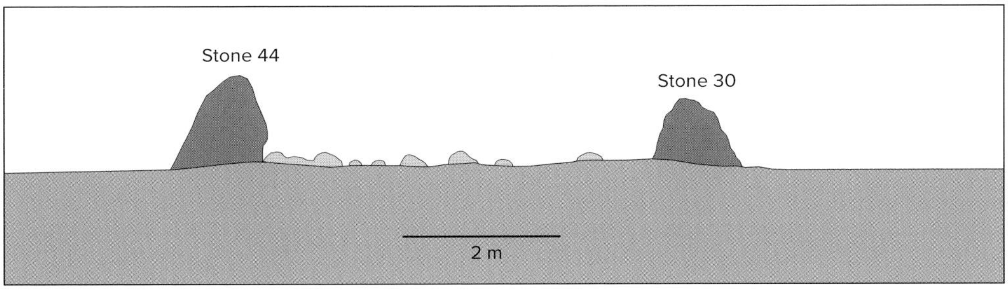

Fig. 11.9. *The profile across the Gunderslevholm dolmen just 6 m east of the chamber gives a good impression of the low, stone-scattered surface between the large kerbstones.*

What was the appearance of the monument in the Neolithic? The kerbstones stood erect and close together, and the gaps between them were closed with dry-walling, but we don't know how far up this extended. The inner surface of the dolmen was much like today, i.e. scattered with large and small stones. The fact that the dolmen lacked a mound at that time is evident not only from its inner surface but also from the many kerbstones that have toppled inwards. This would not have been possible had there been mound material present. The dolmen chamber was just as free-standing and exposed then as it is today, but the gaps between the stones may have been closed with stones or other material, so the chamber was sealed and dark. It is difficult to determine whether the dolmen was built in one single operation. Like many other dolmens, it probably comprises two or more phases. For example, we can imagine that the many stones on the inner surface are the result of one or more events or actions subsequent to the dolmen's actual construction. Ultimately, these stones could very well have formed the actual fill and surface in the mound. We should not let ourselves be distracted by our modern sense of order, the dolmen users had other aims and objectives and did not intend to produce a flat, cobbled surface comprised of closely-spaced stones. A long dolmen such as Capeshøj also has abundant stones in its fill. If we look at the exposed surface of this latter monument, which has been sealed ever since a mound was raised over the long dolmen in the Early Bronze Age, the stone scatter is also seen to be extremely uneven (see fig. 6.6).

In the Middle Ages, the Gunderslevholm dolmen did not stand in a forest, but was surrounded by cultivated fields.[15] It is tempting to believe that the many stones in the dolmen's interior originated from these fields, gathered up and placed out of the way by being discarded within the dolmen's kerbstones. This explanation does, however, appear unlikely because many of the stones are very large and lie far from the edge of the monument. On the other hand, if they were placed here in the Middle Ages, or for that matter later, the dolmen's interior would, prior to this, have been even lower than today.

The excavation in 2008

During the survey work in 1999, and again in 2006, the part of the dolmen east of the chamber was found to be very overgrown with brambles and other vegetation. But in 2008, the bicentenary of Christian Molbech and N.F.S. Grundtvig's visit to the site, the monument was cleared of trees and scrub by the local branch of the Danish Society for Nature Conservation after permission for public access to the dolmen was granted by the owner, Claus de Neergaard, Gunderslevholm. The agreement with the owner also included permission to undertake an archaeological excavation. This investigation took place in 2008, under the auspices of the Danish National Museum, which at that time was responsible for the maintenance and restoration of scheduled ancient monuments. The aim of the investigation was to discover whether this apparently very open dolmen had originally been earth-covered.[16] The investigation was directed by Svend Hansen who has, since 1986, been responsible for the maintenance and restoration of scheduled dolmens and passage graves.

After the necessary scheduled monument consent had been granted by the Danish Agency for Culture, the excavation was able to commence on 25th March 2008, when a thin covering of newly-fallen snow lay over the area. Due to our declared interest in open dolmens, we were invited to participate in the investigation, which concluded on 17th April. The two excavation trenches were then back-filled, covering any trace of the interventions, and later in the summer, on the 26th August, the 200th anniversary of N.F.S. Grundtvig and Christian Molbech's visit, the dolmen was opened for public access in a well-attended ceremony.

In the investigation, two 1 m wide trenches, trenches 1 and 2, were cut. Trench 1 extended from the north side of the long dolmen, between the kerbstones nos. 51 and 52, and up to the exterior of the chamber. Trench 2 passed transversely through the monument at the kerbstones nos. 16 and 17 in the south and nos. 58 and 59 in the north and extended beyond the kerbstones at each side (see fig. 11.6).

In trench 2, in addition to the large conspicuous stones on the surface, a quantity of small stones and crushed flint was observed uppermost in the fill. This stone layer (layer 3) had a thickness of 60 cm and rested on a 10 cm thick stone-less layer (layer 2), which lay on top of an equally thick buried soil horizon (layer 1). The buried soil represented the topsoil on which the dolmen was constructed in the Neolithic. The mound fill in the dolmen therefore consists – at least in this particular area – of two clearly distinct layers, with a combined thickness of 70 cm. Outside the kerbstones in trench 2, this topsoil layer was absent; it could have been removed in conjunction with construction of the dolmen, perhaps to render the latter more monumental in appearance. There were, however, indications that there had been a c. 2 m wide stone "pavement running externally alongside the kerbstones", which subsequently became overlain by collapsed dry-walling slabs and stones. The dry-walling between the kerbstones was beautifully preserved in its lowermost parts, which in 2008 lay below ground level. The quantity of collapsed slabs appears to be so great that the kerbstones may well have had dry-walling extending all the way up to their tops.

Trench 1, running at right angles to the dolmen chamber, also revealed several interesting phenomena. Around the dolmen chamber there was, in the 1 m wide excavation trench, an arc of stones that lay just under or at the present ground surface. These stones presumably form part of a circle of stones around the chamber. The 1 m thick layer of mound fill running up to the dolmen chamber was, as

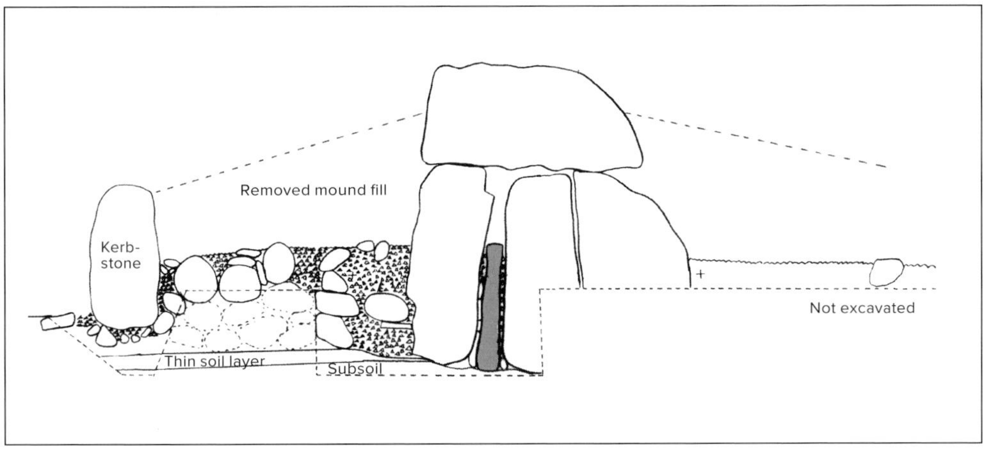

Fig.11.10. *Simplified drawing of the section through the Gunderslevholm dolmen from the excavation in 2008. The section, which is seen from the west, includes three of the chamber's orthostats. The gap between two of these is closed with a long stone slab, marked in grey, set on end. The broken line, showing the presumed height of the mound, reflects Svend Hansen's interpretation.*

expected, slightly – i.e. 30 cm – thicker than that in trench 2. This difference can, as already mentioned, be readily observed. Trench 1 also included the corner formed between the chamber's gable stone to the west and the orthostat to the north. These two stones, which are slightly sunk into the old ground surface, do not quite meet and the gap between them is, from the level of the Neolithic topsoil, closed with a flat stone slab standing on edge and extending 10 cm above the present ground surface (fig. 11.10). The chamber could then be measured from the outside, revealing an internal height of 1.7 m. The 80 cm of fill material in the chamber was not investigated.

Svend Hansen's interpretation of the findings from the excavation is that the dolmen has been severely altered in modern times by the removal of large quantities of stones. As Svend Hansen writes, his "own conclusion … is completely clear. The dolmen chamber had been constructed and encased in a completely sealed mound fill, at least up to the capstone – perhaps even higher! So the chamber was completely covered by a house-shaped long barrow with tall gable stones. The row of vertically standing kerbstones with walling between them have had the appearance of a house wall." (fig. 11.11).[17] He has three main arguments in support of this interpretation:

Firstly, he maintains that the tall wedge-shaped stone between the chamber's western end stone and northern side stone, i.e. orthostat, shows that the dolmen builders aimed to seal and encapsulate the chamber totally, and he therefore assumes that the chamber was covered by a mound. Secondly, the many collapsed, loose stone slabs found externally along the sides of the monument are interpreted as showing that the dry-walling between the kerbstones had extended high up, far above the level of the present inner surface. The wall of kerbstones and dry-walling is presumed to have held the inner mound material in place. However, by erosion, in combination with stone robbing, most of the mound material has disappeared and the dry-walling slabs and stones have therefore collapsed outwards. This is then linked with a third argument: That quantities of stones constituting the upper part of the mound material were removed for use in building a stone dyke that forms the boundary of the forest to the east and which can be seen on the cadastral map of 1791.

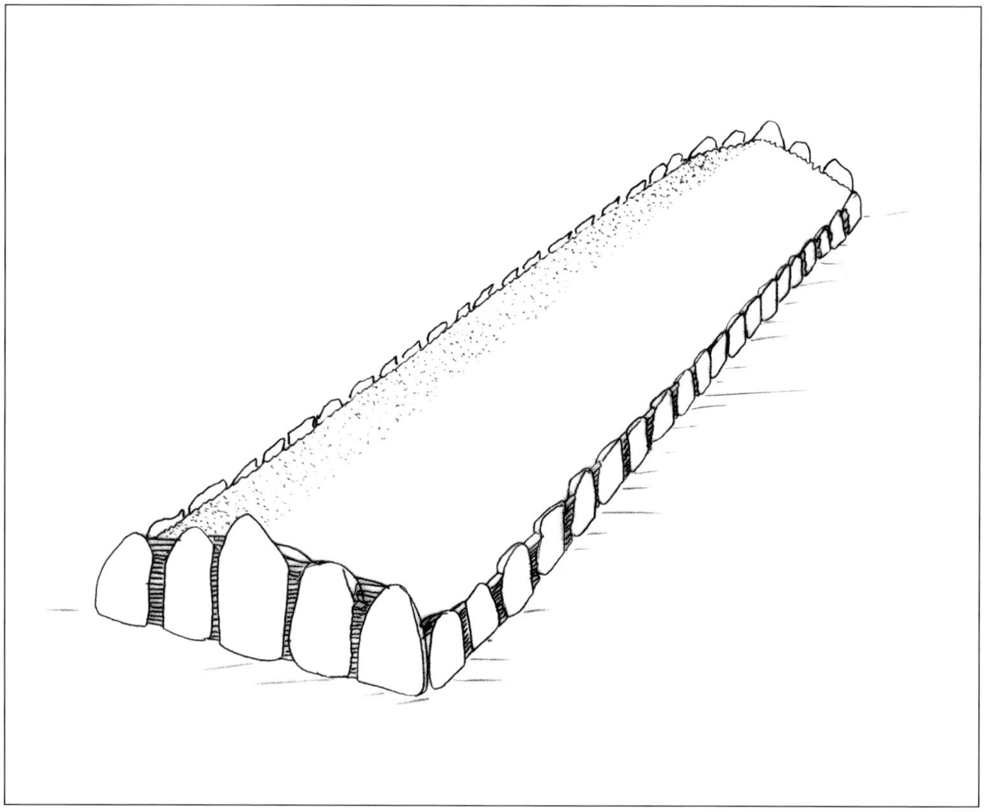

Fig. 11.11. *This is how the director of the 2008 excavation, Svend Hansen, imagines the appearance of the Gunderslevholm dolmen in the Neolithic.*

Svend Hansen's colleague of many years' standing, Torben Dehn, also arrives at very much the same conclusion: "These constructional elements are basic and quite normal in megalith construction and show that the Gunderslevholm dolmen was fundamentally constructed in the same way as all other megalithic tombs: with a sealed dry chamber, solid packing around the chamber and apparently also dry walling between the kerbstones to hold a mound structure in place. The reason that it has had its present appearance for the last 200 years is down to factors to which all building works can be exposed: alteration, wear, destruction and decay."[18]

An open dolmen after all

On the basis of our own observations during the 2008 excavation, we are unable to accept these conclusions. Let us first examine Svend Hansen's three main arguments in favour of the Gunderslevholm dolmen not being an open dolmen:

The present closure of the chamber, with stone slabs inserted between its orthostats, only extends up to the present mound surface (see fig. 11.10). This in no way demonstrates that the dry-walling originally continued up to the lower surface of capstone. But it is possible, probable even, that the chamber was completely sealed in the Neolithic, without it necessarily being surrounded by more fill material than it is the case at present.

There could well have been dry-walling extending up to the tops of the kerbstones, without the mound itself necessarily extending this far up. In this case there would be more of a free-standing kerbstone frame with the mound fill only extending about halfway up the inner surface of the kerbstones (fig. 11.12). A frame of this kind was, in part, documented at the round dolmen Poskær Stenhus in 1770 (see chapter 12). It is clear that frames of this nature are extremely susceptible to decay and, therefore, do not survive to the present day. The discovery of collapsed dry-walling slabs *behind* more or less toppled kerbstones could be an indication of a free-standing dry-stone wall. This situation was observed in trench 2 at the Gunderslevholm dolmen, where several dry-walling slabs were found behind kerbstone no. 59.[19]

That the stones were removed in order to build a stone dyke is an assertion – a hypothesis. The nearest "modern" stone wall is a forest dyke bordering the field just less than 100 m to the east of the monument. Between the dyke and the dolmen is a steep valley in which a stream flows, a difficult feature to cross when transporting stones. It would appear much more logical, practical and useful to have built this stone wall using stones gathered from the fields. Moreover, there are exceptional numbers of surface stones in the area, so why cross the stream to obtain them?

If we attempt to quantify a hypothetical situation where mound material has extended up to the underside of the capstone – and perhaps even higher up – it would mean that the mound layers had a total thickness 75-100 cm greater than at present. If we replace the fill that has slipped out over time, we still lack a 65-90 cm thick layer of stones, corresponding to the removal of 250-350 m^3 – a very considerable amount.

Fig. 11.12. *The Gunderslevholm dolmen as the authors believe it could have appeared in the Neolithic.*

Removal of stones from the dolmen of this magnitude would unavoidably have left its mark, but any indications of human intervention are only evident in the two areas at the ends of the long dolmen. The present surface of the monument – apart from the irregular stones and a couple of stone-free areas – follows an even course. If the fill in the hypothetical upper part was of the same character as the present material, a quantity of small stones, shattered flint and earth would have been deposited over and between the stones presently on the surface, but these are exposed and free-standing, with no earth etc. between them. This feature is quite remarkable, because a surface of this kind is not evident at any other Danish dolmen. What is the reason behind it? One possibility could be that the stones were intentionally placed on the monument in connection with cult activities performed during the Neolithic. This would also explain why the greatest number of stones lies close to the chamber – "the inner sanctum".

A further three arguments can be presented in favour of the Gunderslevholm dolmen being an open dolmen – a dolmen without a mound. The first is that when Christian Molbech and N.F.S. Grundtvig visited the monument in 1808, the stones on the internal surface were covered with a thick layer of moss, and this can be taken as showing that they had lain untouched for a very long time. Secondly, the 15 more or less inwardly toppled kerbstones would not have been able to lean inwards if there had been more mound material inside the dolmen than is the case now. Thirdly, there is the matter of the stratigraphy of the layers and deposits in dolmen. At the base of trench 2 in the 2008 excavation, over the old ground surface/topsoil, lies a 10 cm thick stone-free layer, which in turn is overlain by a 60 cm thick layer of earth and stones. This clear bipartite division could very well be due to the fact that the mound material was added during at least two phases.[20]

We therefore do not believe that the 2008 excavation provided any evidence in favour of there once being a now vanished mound over the Gunderslevholm dolmen, but that it, instead, offers support for our theory that the dolmen, at the end of its period of use in the Neolithic, had largely the same appearance as it does today.

Gunderslev Wood

Tell me, O wood, what so closely you clasp,
to your breast what so firmly embrace!
Tell me, O wind, as you glide through this place,
as you drift with light grace
over yonder great oaks,
as you look here below
through the branches and leaves!
O, but doubtless you know
what receives its embrace!

The tops of the oak trees
are shaking and vying,
with wind in the tree-tops
all soughing and sighing,
like tongues from the North;
and I am deciph'ring
the whisp'ring and crying
that stream from the North!

So then it is you, you gnarled oak-trees,
that fence in the circle where fire-flames leap
and the victim lay bleeding on those holy stones!

O sun! You that blaze so high up in the air!
You have seen and you know
even perfumes so rare
of sweet flow'rs could not slow
my quick steps on the earth;
nor the soft, gentle lake
my ardour could slake
for the long-vanished North;
I strode with a view
over the hillside and dale,
and my burning gaze flew
over fields like a gale
to discover the place
where the oak-trees' embrace
had gathered around
the holy ring-mound.

Gentle my friend,
move to the woodland!
Lightly now touching
sanctified earth!
Here mid the oak-trees reside
gods of the North, long departed;
slumbering sweet they abide,
will not be disturbed by your footsteps!
See how the water-drops trickle
so little
there in the dale!

When the Aesir of old in their power
ruled where the high mountains tower,
within their pale,
waters flowed there with thundering voice,
the Aesir to praise, in the groves to rejoice.
Nor through the dale they but trickle
so little,
ancient stone kissing,
silence here wishing,
whisper their blessing,
lulling those gods into far deeper sleep.

See the hill rise higher thither,
broader there the oak-trees' fissures,
gloomier the wood is here,
with the gods' own altar near!

Time to leave this beaten path!
It leads not to th' altar garth;
where the herd rush forth pell-mell,
gods do not choose homes to dwell.
Here I see a path lie hidden –
under grass the faintest track
trodden here by foot so rare;
gallant friend, we go as bidden.
If to th' altar in the North
only lead faint tracks of earth,
we must with a keen gaze testing
what our sight may find perplexing
trace a path to our old North!
Follow, friend, and do not turn!
Still the tracks I can discern.
Strangely have they left their imprint
on the stems of grass so light.
Here an ancient giant-shadow
surely passes by at night.

See, the track so faint has vanished,
as it were by my word banished,
by my breathing blown away.
O sorry day!

Stop, my foot,
here upon this oak-tree root!
Cast, my eye, your glance high curving!
If you find yourself observing,
boldly see
through the grove, and past each tree!

My teardrops are flowing!
What rises there showing
itself to my gaze?
O, is it not stones of the moss-covered altar,
vaulted by oaks which enclose where they quiver?
It is! – O, I shiver,
I tremble with joy;
a holy devotion wells up in my breast.
I hurry, I hurry on light-wingéd feet,
and kneel at the Aesirs' great altar to greet
and honour the gods long departed!

N.F.S. Grundtvig

The poem *Gunderslev Skov* – "Gunderslev Wood" in English – was first published in the weekly paper *Nyeste Skilderie af Kjøbenhavn*, 5th vol., no. 101, Tuesday 27th September, 1808.

Edward Broadbridge (translator and editor): *Living Wellsprings* – The Hymns, Songs and Poems of N.F.S. Grundtvig, Aarhus University Press 2015, pp. 225-228.

BOX 4

12. Kjallesten and other dolmens with internal stone circles

The area between the dolmen's kerbstones and the chamber has had its own special significance and symbolism. In rare instances, this is seen reflected in intentionally laid out and carefully formed circles of stones around the chambers or transverse rows of stones running across long dolmens. Finds such as pottery, resulting from activities in front of the dolmen chambers, also point in the same direction. These internal structures and artefacts are important with regard to the question of open or closed dolmens, because they constitute evidence of activities that took place here during the Neolithic, when the dolmens were in active use.

The construction of a dolmen is conventionally perceived as consisting of three mutually linked elements: chamber, kerbstones and an intervening layer of packing and/or mound fill (see page 46). The packing layer is seen as something that stabilises the chamber and the kerbstones, and the kerbstone circle or frame, sealed with dry-walling, as something that holds the packing layer and mound fill in place. This focus on practical function overshadows the fact that these were structures with a deeper significance, the nature of which we are unable to decipher today. The circular or rectangular frame formed by the kerbstones around the chamber presumably encloses a "sacred" area, a view that the author Martin A. Hansen has so clearly expressed in prose (see chapter 3). In the following, we will examine a couple of Danish examples in this respect.

In 1879-80, archaeologist Conrad Engelhardt and artist Magnus Petersen were engaged on a district survey on the island of Lolland (see chapter 3).[1] Here, where there are numerous megalithic tombs, there was plenty to see to and the artist was kept busy. Among Magnus Petersen's many drawings from Lolland are four of megalithic tombs that are particularly relevant here, i.e. Kjallesten, Hydeskov Fredskov, Frejlev and Lille Guldhøj.

Kjallesten

Magnus Petersen drew a plan of the round dolmen Kjallesten, which stands in Toreby Skov, east of Sakskøbing (fig. 12.1 and photo on opposing page). At the bottom of the drawing he has added a note in brackets: "Only very slightly elevated over the surrounding ground surface". Conrad Engelhardt briefly described Kjallesten: "Stone dolmen with one capstone encircled by stones in two concentric circles – in an earthen mound".[2] Eleven years later, in 1890, Kjallesten was scheduled and in the accompanying text it was described in a little more detail: "Round dolmen surrounded by a double stone circle, the outermost 33 feet [10.4 m] wide, the inner-

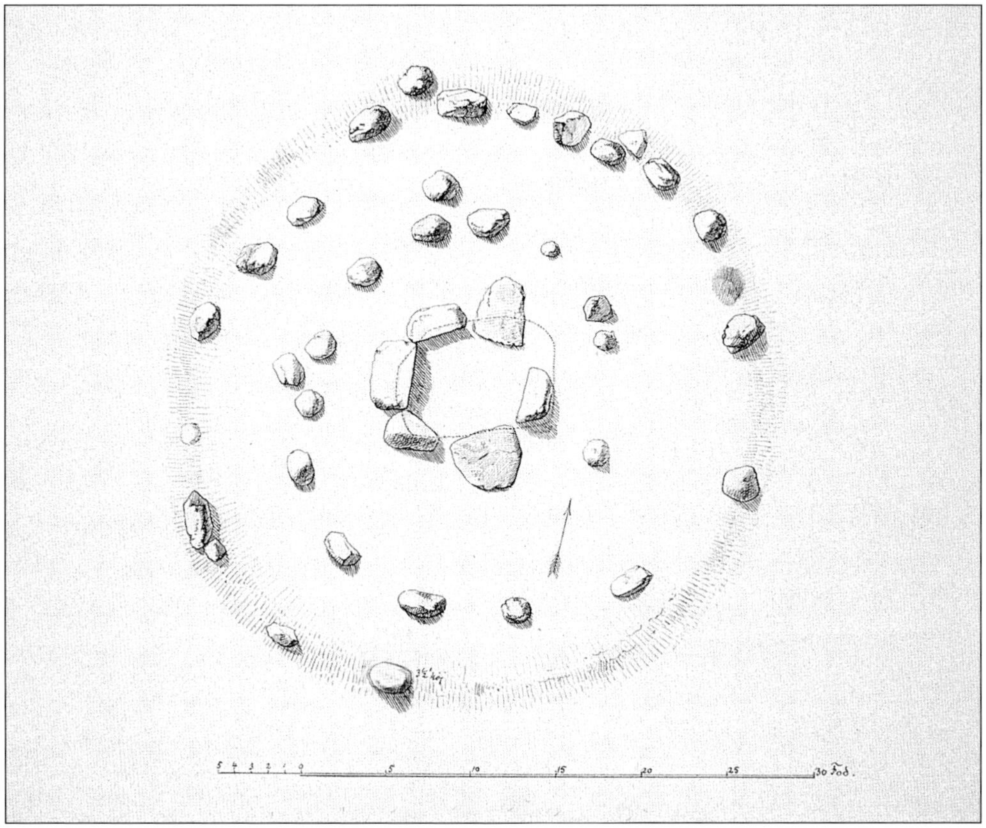

Fig. 12.1. *The inner ring of stones in the Kjallesten round dolmen was reasonably well-preserved when Magnus Petersen drew a plan of the monument in 1879. He noted on the drawing of the dolmen that it was "only very slightly elevated above the surrounding ground surface."*

most 19 feet [6 m] wide. The chamber is built of 6 side stones in polygonal form 5 feet 8″ [1.8 m] and 5 feet [1.6 m] wide. Two of the side stones lie fallen – a piece has been split off one of these. The capstone lies inclined."[3]

From these two descriptions and Magnus Petersen's drawing we can see that Kjallesten is a polygonal chamber consisting of six orthostats and a capstone, with a small opening but no passage stones. The dolmen chamber stands in the middle of a round dolmen with a low, shield-shaped mound, surrounded by about 20 kerbstones. Between the kerbstones and the chamber is an inner, slightly irregular circle of 15-16 stones. On the whole, it can be said that the inner stone circle, by way of the descriptions and the drawings, is well-documented, even though one should be aware that Magnus Petersen's drawings are not always completely correct.[4]

At the time of the scheduling survey in 1954, the inner stone circle was no longer so conspicuous that it was included in the scheduling text. Therkel Mathiassen noted that there were 18 very small kerbstones and that the chamber, in addition to a large capstone, consisted of four orthostats. In his haste, he must have forgotten the two fallen examples. The mound is stated to have a diameter of 10 m and a height of 1 m.[5]

In 1999, we visited Kjallesten and surveyed its profile. In the chamber were large holes dug by foxes or badgers, who had pushed up a large heap of earth in the process.[6] Scattered over the internal surface between the chamber and the kerbstones lay a number of stones that must belong to the inner stone circle. To the right on our

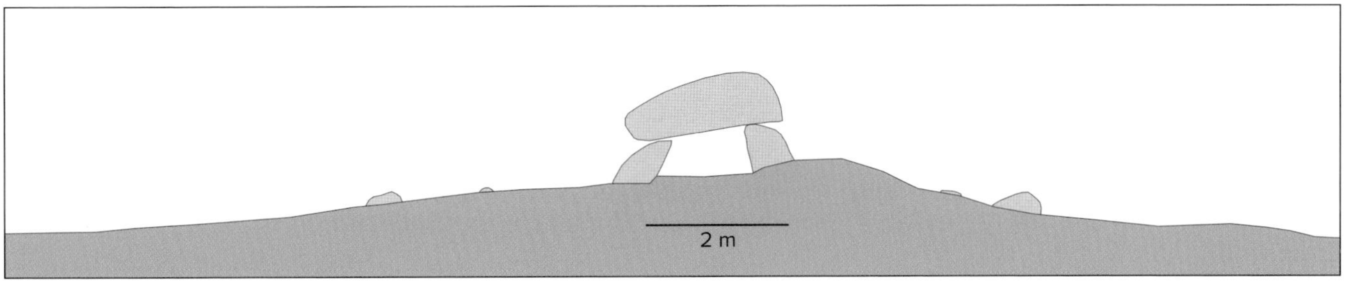

Fig. 12.2. *Profile, surveyed in 1999, of the Kjallesten dolmen shows that there is only about 50 cm of mound fill. The heap of soil to the right of the chamber has been dug out by a fox making its den.*

profile drawing (fig. 12.2), a higher area is evident beside one orthostat, as a result from the earth dug out from the animal burrows. The left side of the drawing gives a good impression of the low mound surface in relation to the capstone, the lower face of which lies 75 cm above the surface of the mound. A couple of smaller stones – one on each side of the chamber – could belong to the inner stone circle. Measured between the outer surfaces of the two outermost kerbstones, the mound has a diameter of 11.5 m.

Kjallesten is to date the only known scheduled round dolmen in Denmark with a polygonal chamber surrounded by an inner, preserved stone circle. Poskær Stenhus has also had an inner stone circle, as we shall see later in this chapter.

Hydeskov Fredskov

Another example of an inner stone circle is seen in a small, almost quadratic long dolmen that stands in Hydeskov Fredskov, southeast of Sakskøbing (fig. 12.3). Magnus Petersen's drawing from 1880 shows the monument both in plan and in profile and gives several measurements for stones, distances and dimensions. In the middle of the monument stands the disturbed chamber, of which only a 1.6 m long orthostat and the displaced capstone, which measures 2.1 x 1.5 m, seen from above, are visible. Around the chamber is a circle of stones, which number eight on the drawing. This circle has a diameter of only 4.5-5 m. It is, in turn, framed by a square of stones, which we perceive as the actual kerbstones. This long dolmen, with internal dimensions of 7.8 x 5.6 m, has 18 kerbstones: Almost all its kerbstones are therefore present and in situ, though two have toppled. In the middle of one of the two gables stands a kerbstone that is slightly taller – 1.2 m; for comparison see figure 5.12. Two other kerbstones are of the same height, but otherwise, with heights of 30-90 cm, the kerbstones are on the small size. The stones of both the circle and the square are free-standing, each situated at a distance from its neighbours. From the longitudinal profile it can be seen that the monument has no packing or mound whatsoever, so the chamber is probably set into the natural soil surface.[7]

Conrad Engelhardt's contemporary description is somewhat laconic: "Dolmen with quadratic enclosure of erect stones. The burial place partly disturbed."[8] The inner stones, which form a circle on the drawing, are not mentioned at all. In general, Engelhardt's accompanying descriptions to his colleague's drawings were often very brief.[9]

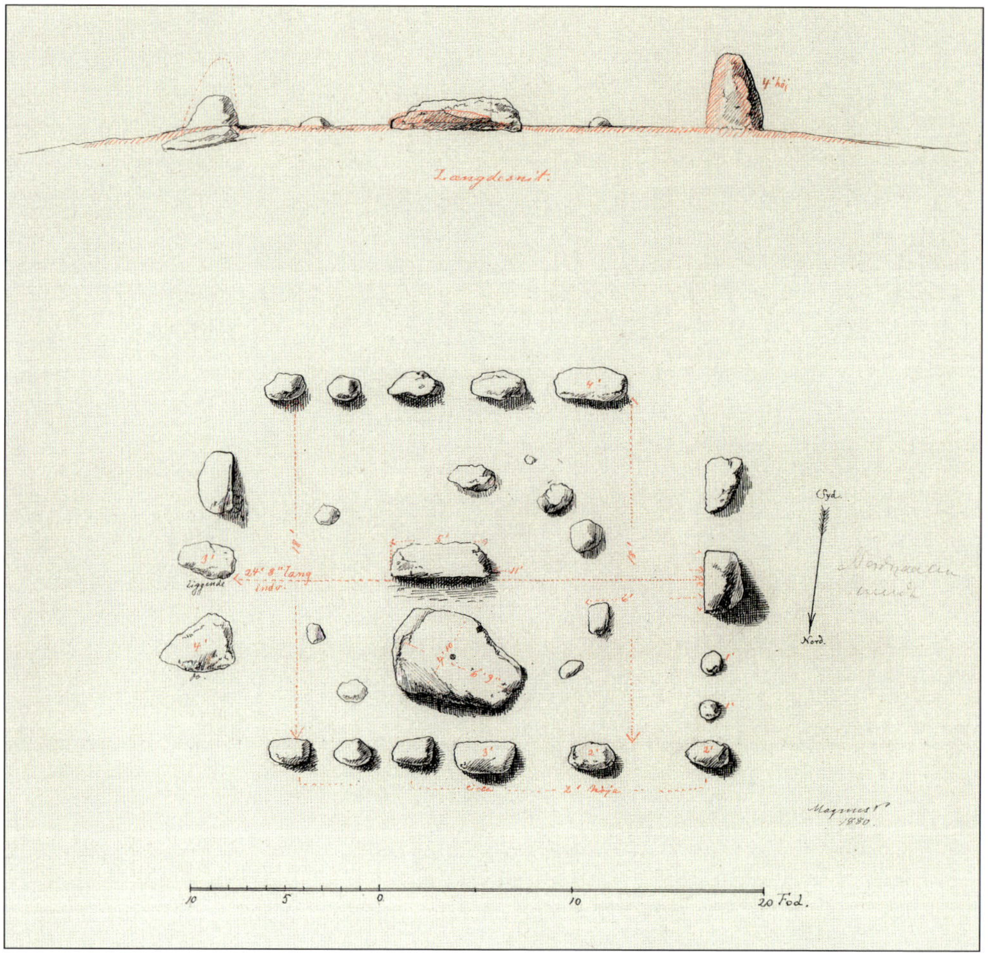

Fig. 12.3. *In Hydeskov Fredskov stands this small long dolmen, the surface of which is only slightly raised above its surroundings. Around the chamber, of which only one orthostat and the displaced capstone can now be seen, is a small circle of stones. When Magnus Petersen drew the monument in 1880, he mistakenly drew the north arrow in the opposite direction.*

In 1926, Hans Kjær visited Hydeskov Fredskov and described the dolmen: "Small dolmen. See plan. Most of the stones appear still to be present, but in less and less regular order than on the plan. Heavily disturbed. Not suitable for scheduling."[10] The plan referred to is Magnus Petersen's drawing. It was possibly Hans Kjær who noted on the drawing that the north arrow is pointing in the wrong direction.

In connection with the scheduling surveys in 1954, Therkel Mathiassen stated that the monument must have been demolished. So it was the usual sad old story – one would think! But in 1986, the dolmen was rediscovered and it was described in the following year by Karen Løkkegaard Poulsen, Lolland-Falsters Stiftsmuseum, now Museum Lolland-Falster, who had found an unrecorded dolmen in Hydeskov Fredskov which corresponded to the 1879 description of Therkel Mathiassen's "vanished" monument. The fact that the monument was recorded as probably demolished by Mathiassen on the scheduling survey was actually due to it, at some time, having been marked incorrectly on the map. The correct location was 400 m further to the east. The "newly found" dolmen fits with the earlier description and drawing, and it must be the same monument as that which Magnus Petersen drew. Because "the dolmen stands close to a large forest road and is visible from this. It is unlikely that it has not been recorded previously."[11]

In the rediscovered dolmen, according to Karen Løkkegaard Poulsen's account, the 17 kerbstones form a rectangular stone frame, measuring 6 x 11 m, with six stones to the south, five to the north and three to both the west and the east. The middle stone on the eastern side is somewhat taller than the other kerbstones. Otherwise the kerbstones have a height of 60-75 cm. An earthen mound within the stones can only just be made out. Around 1 m inside the kerbstones to the east is a row of five stones, and at a similar distance inside the kerbstones to the west are two stones, of the size of kerbstones, standing parallel to the latter. Some of the stones in the monument appear to occupy their original positions, others have toppled outwards or inwards, relative to the course of the stone frame. In the interior, near the south side, there is a 1.5 x 1 m stone, which must be interpreted as the toppled capstone of the chamber. Opposite the capstone, but further to the north, the very narrow edge of a large stone protrudes from the ground. This appears to be one of the chamber's orthostats. Karen Løkkegaard Poulsen also draws attention to the fact that it is not known whether an earthfast stone located 2 m outside the kerbstones has anything to do with the monument.

The inner stone circle, which Conrad Engelhardt described and Magnus Petersen drew in 1880, was therefore not visible in 1987, but the five stones in a row to the east and the two stones to the west must be remnants of this. The owner of the forest would unfortunately not give his permission for us to undertake a survey and description of the monument in 2011.

Frejlev and Lille Guldhøj

The third megalithic tomb with an inner stone circle drawn by Magnus Petersen on Lolland is a trapezoid long dolmen at Frejlev. The capstone is in place and conceals the chamber, which is surrounded by a small circle of stones (fig. 12.4). The monument measures 16 x 8 m and one end of it is damaged. Only a few stones appear to be missing from the stone circle, which has a diameter of 5-6 m. From the longitudinal profile it can be seen that this long dolmen has had a fair quantity of mound material and that the stones of the circle are placed on the surface of the mound. Conrad Engelhardt wrote the following about this dolmen: "Longish, four-sided enclosure of large stones; orientation WNW-ESE. Inside a large capstone, surrounded by a circle of small stones."[12] The dolmen was recorded in connection with scheduling in 1954, when it was described by Therkel Mathiassen as "Long dolmen? Elongate stone setting, 16 x 8 m. Within this a circle of smaller stones, in which there is a large stone (capstone?)."[13]

The fourth megalithic tomb with stone circles drawn by Magnus Petersen on the Lolland trip is Lille Guldhøj, which stands a little to the east of the Frejlev dolmen. Lille Guldhøj has no less than three stone circles, of which the outermost, with the largest stones, must be seen as being the kerbstones. The innermost circle, which like

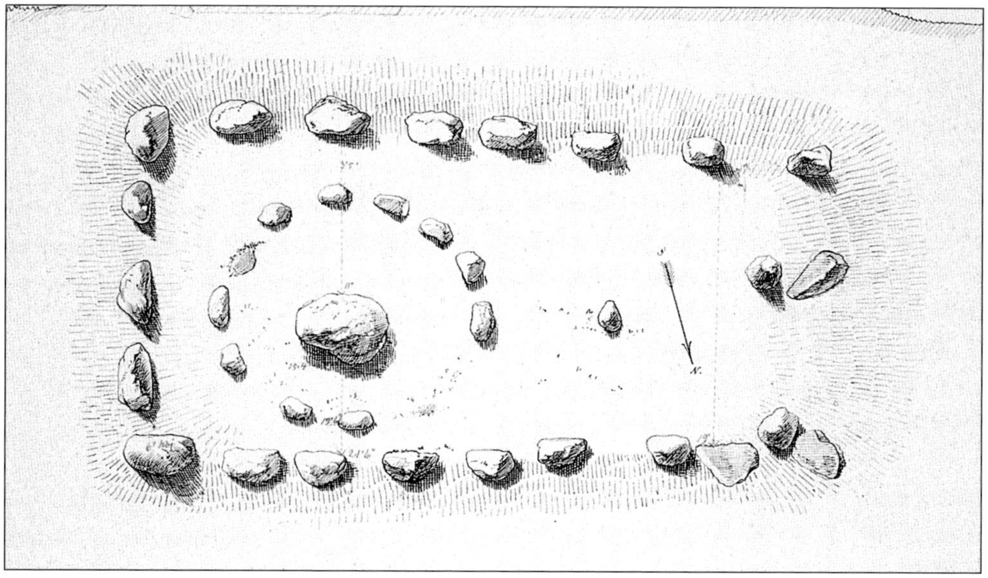

Fig. 12.4. *The Frejlev long dolmen has an inner stone circle around its chamber. Unlike Kjallesten and Hydeskov Fredskov, there is a good amount of mound material in this monument, drawn by Magnus Petersen in 1879.*

the other two circles is only partially preserved, encircles very close to the chamber. Conrad Engelhardt described it as: "Lille Guldhøj; a small earthen mound with numerous stones in concentric circles – and a collapsed stone chamber."[14]

The monument was scheduled in 1888. In 1923, the chamber was investigated by G.A. Rosenberg of the Danish National Museum. It proved to be a small passage grave – 3.5 x 2.4 m, with a 4.5 m long passage in a round barrow with a diameter of 22 m. The excavation resulted in finds of skeletal parts belonging to at least 30 individuals, in addition to various grave furnishings, including four flint daggers. So the stone circles at Lille Guldhøj actually stand on a mound containing a passage grave. This does not render them any less interesting, as stone circles have not otherwise been observed in association with Danish passage graves.

Syllinge Skov

Syllinge Skov, which is part of the forest Fyrendal Skov, lies to the north of the highway between Skælskør and Næstved. Here, in level terrain, stands a small and rather unusual long dolmen (fig. 12.5). It was recorded very late, not until 1937, and was scheduled that same year. Therkel Mathiassen described it as a "Long dolmen with a double row of kerbstones. The monument is oriented east-west. The outer row of kerbstones forms a rectangle, 9.5 x 6 m; to the west 5, to the north 6, to the east 4 and to the south 6 kerbstones, generally quite large, upright stones. Within this an oval of smaller stones, 8 x 5 m. In the middle is a narrow, elongate chamber in E-W, built of two stones at each long side and one at each end; its internal dimensions are 1.4 x 0.65 m. No capstone. No trace of mound."[15]

The artist Klaus Bo Poulsen was very familiar with Syllinge Skov and its ancient monuments. In 1968, he went to the Danish National Museum to deliver survey sketches and photographs of the dolmen and some other stone monuments in the forest.[16] His sketch of the dolmen gives a good impression of the monument and, astonishingly, adds a totally new dimension that had previously been overlooked (fig. 12.6): The dolmen actually has "horns", because the kerbstones at both long sides continue, with a further one or two stones, past the narrow western end. This phenomenon is known from a few other Danish megaliths, of which the most renowned is the passage grave mound Kong Svends Høj on Lolland.[17] The 21 kerbstones present in the dolmen in Syllinge Skov in 1937 are still there today. The inner stone circle comprises 18 stones, and as one stone is missing, there were originally 19 in total.

When we surveyed the dolmen in 1999, one of the "horn stones" on Klaus Bo Poulsen's drawing had disappeared (fig. 12.7). The form of the inner stone circle is – as shown on the drawing – not a circle and not a square, rather something in between. The surveyed profile, which includes the stone circle, kerbstones and the chamber, shows that the internal ground surface is slightly raised above that of the surrounding terrain, probably due to internal packing fill.

Fig. 12.5. *In Syllinge Skov there is a small, well-preserved dolmen, consisting of a chamber, though with no capstone, surrounded by a circle of smaller stones which, in turn, are enclosed within a rectangular frame of larger stones.*

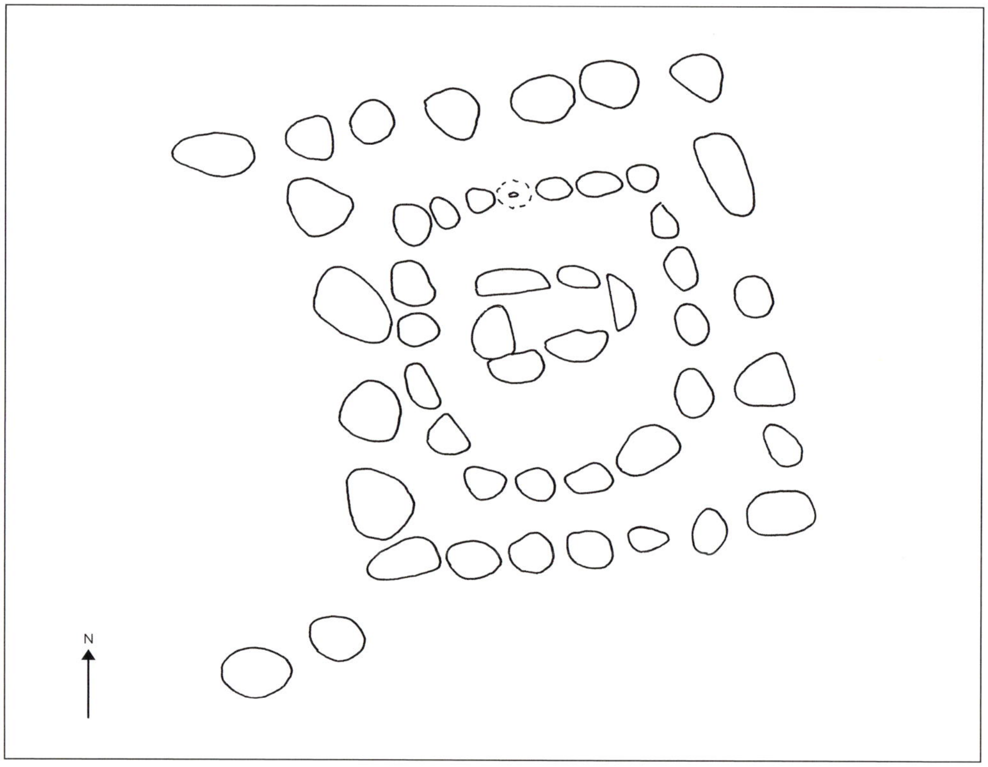

Fig. 12.6. *From the plan of the dolmen in Syllinge Skov, surveyed by Klaus Bo Poulsen in 1968, it is evident that the dolmen has "horns", as one or two stones continue at each side.*

Poskær Stenhus

The round dolmen Poskær Stenhus has already been referred to and presented several times, for example in chapter 2, and with good reason. Poskær Stenhus is not only Denmark's most famous dolmen, it is also the prototype for the open dolmen (fig. 12.8). However, it does not appear quite so monumental today as it did on the drawing from 1878. During restoration work undertaken in 1943, earth was laid up against the outer surface of the kerbstones in order to stabilise them and prevent them from slipping outwards, because at that time the surrounding field was ploughed very close to the monument. This means that the kerbstones do not appear as large and impressive as they did previously.

In 1995, we undertook a survey and description of Poskær Stenhus (fig. 12.9). The circular kerbstone frame consists of 23 – originally 24 – kerbstones and has a diameter of 15.5 m. The dolmen chamber, which stands in the eastern part of the monument, consists of five orthostats that carry the mighty capstone, which weighs 16.3 tonnes. The polygonal chamber has a floor area of 5 m^2 and, towards the east, there is an opening flanked by a couple of passage stones. The profile through the round dolmen shows that the kerbstones and the orthostats are free-standing, and that there is very little mound material. The lower surface of the capstone is more than 1 m above the inner surface of the dolmen.

The earliest description of Poskær Stenhus was published in *Den Danske Atlas* in 1768: "Among the many pagan burials found in this parish, there is one known as

Posekier Steenhuus, where on top of five large [stones] lies a much larger stone, some way away from here are set about 20 more ordinary stones, and some paces from there a further 24 boulders in a circle."[18]

Already in 1770, we have the first plan and detailed description of Poskær Stenhus. This is thanks to master draughtsman Søren Abilgaard who, for a royal commission, travelled around "our kingdoms and lands" between 1756 and 1776 in order to draw and describe *monumenta patriate* – the monuments of the fatherland, and he too visited this later so renowned dolmen (fig. 12.10). Søren Abildgaard's description reads as follows: "Immediately outside a farm in Knebel east-northeast of the town is an impressive dolmen known as Posekiær Steenhuus, this is a round enclosure of encircling large erect stones that are 24 in number, though here and there are a few smaller stones placed between the large ones, enclosing a round space, the diameter

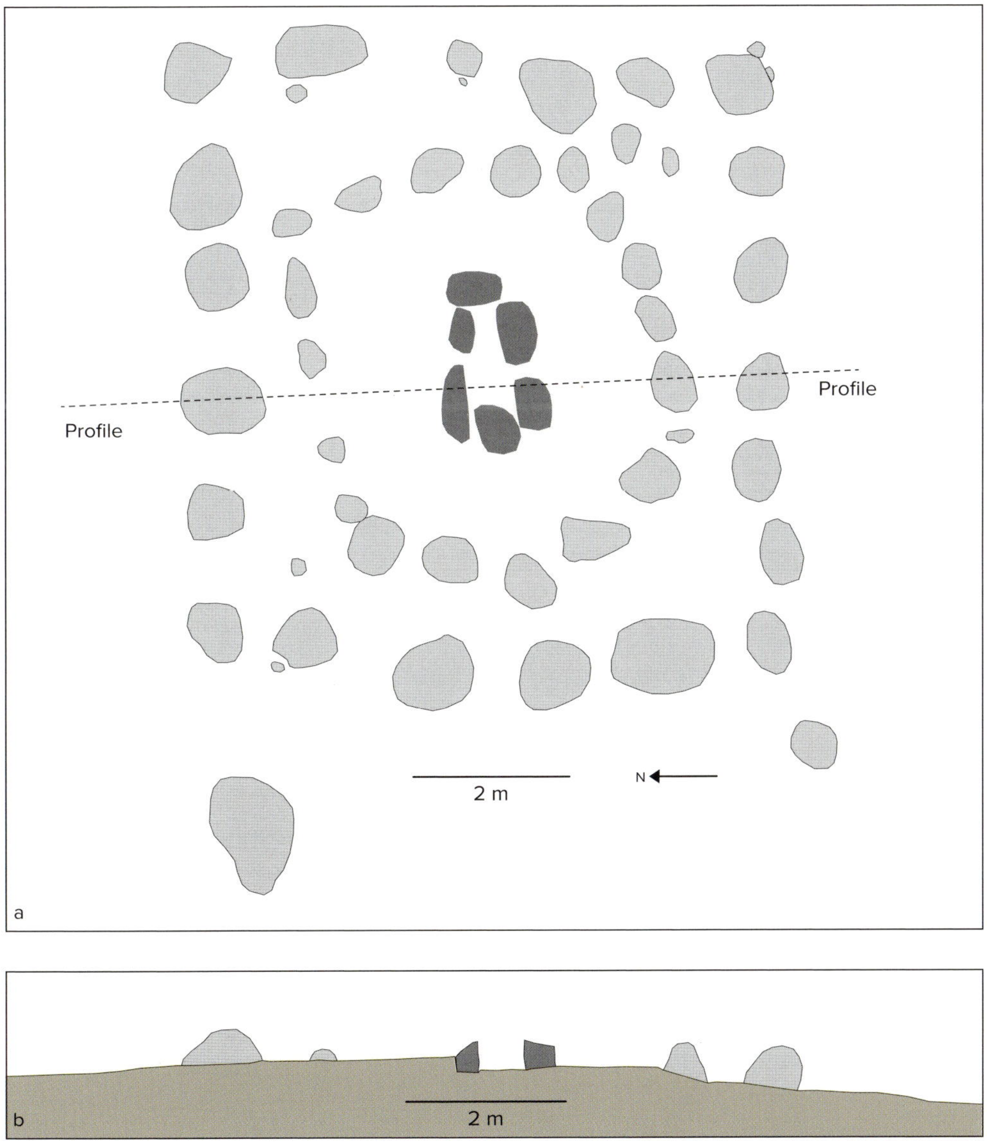

Fig. 12.7. *Plan and profile of the Syllinge Skov dolmen, surveyed in 1999. It is clear from the profile that the monument has no mound material.*

Fig. 12.8. *The round dolmen Poskær Stenhus is built of stones of impressive size, taller than a man. This drawing from 1878 is by Erik Schiødte.*

Fig. 12.9. *Plan and profile of Poskær Stenhus. Note the very low internal surface.*

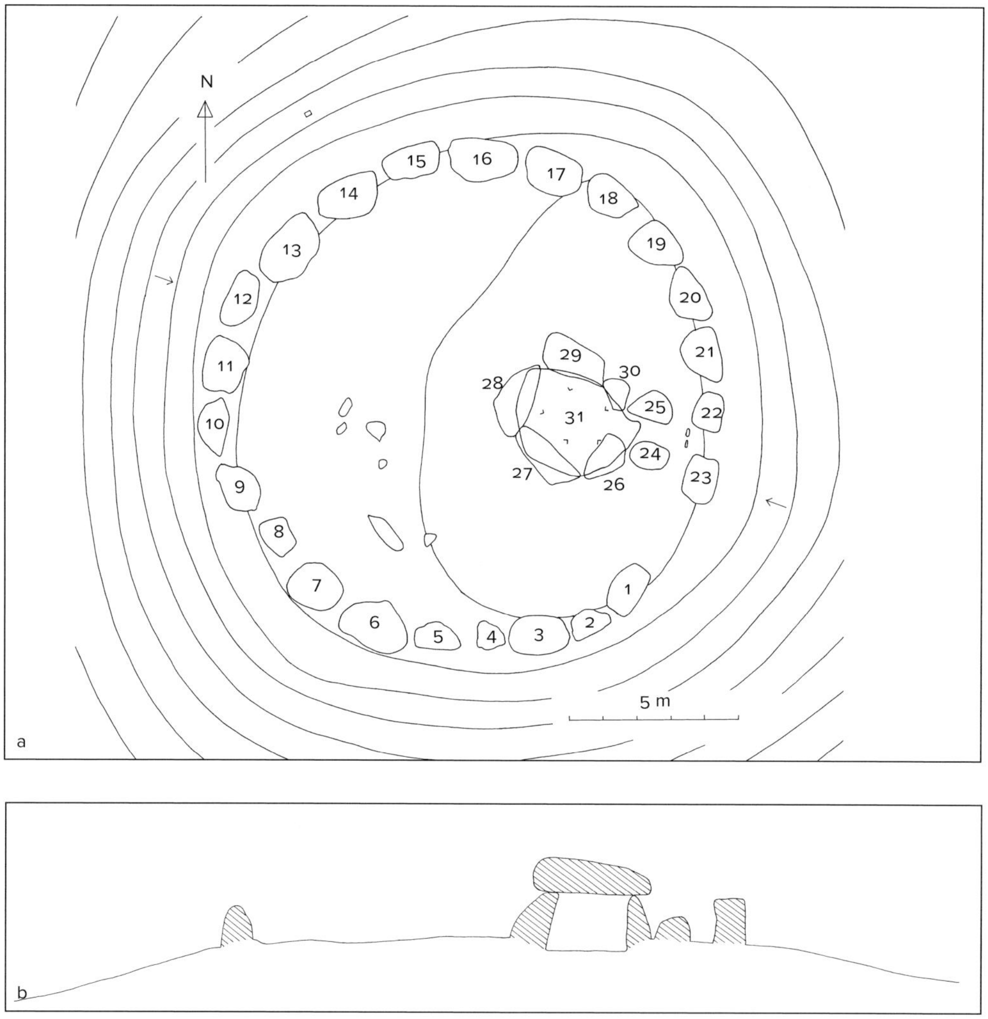

of which within the stone enclosure is 22 alen, at the northeastern edge, within the stone enclosure, a stone altar has been built of 5 large upright stones 2½ alen high and below ½ to 3 alen wide, but narrower above, on these rests a very large flattish stone 16 alen long and 4½ alen wide 1½ alen thick."[19] One alen corresponds to 0.63 m.

These early descriptions and the sketch of Poskær Stenhus from 1768-70 contain several constructional elements that have since disappeared, probably in connection with a change of ownership in 1859.[20] Firstly, the circle of kerbstones is complete, as there are 24 stones, compared with 23 today. Secondly, there is an inner circle of 20 smaller stones. Thirdly, the comment "though here and there are a few smaller stones placed between the large ones" is interpreted to mean that in the gaps between the kerbstones were remnants of dry-walling that protruded from the inner surface of the monument. In general, one gains the impression from the terms "enclose" and "stone fencing" that the kerbstone circle forms a fence or wall around the chamber. So Poskær Stenhus was still unspoiled almost 250 years ago, and its surface was sealed by the inner stone circle (fig. 12.11).

Dolmens with inner stone circles

This account of five scheduled dolmens and a passage grave with inner stone circles shows that these circles consisted of stones that are 40-50 cm in diameter and which are, consequently, rather smaller than the kerbstones in the monuments within which they lie. There is therefore no suggestion that these inner stone circles represent earlier kerbstone circles that have remained standing on expansion of the monument. Neither do they have any functional significance, as they are exposed and free-standing and do not have to retain any fill material. These inner stone circles must therefore have had a symbolic significance that we are unable to decipher today.

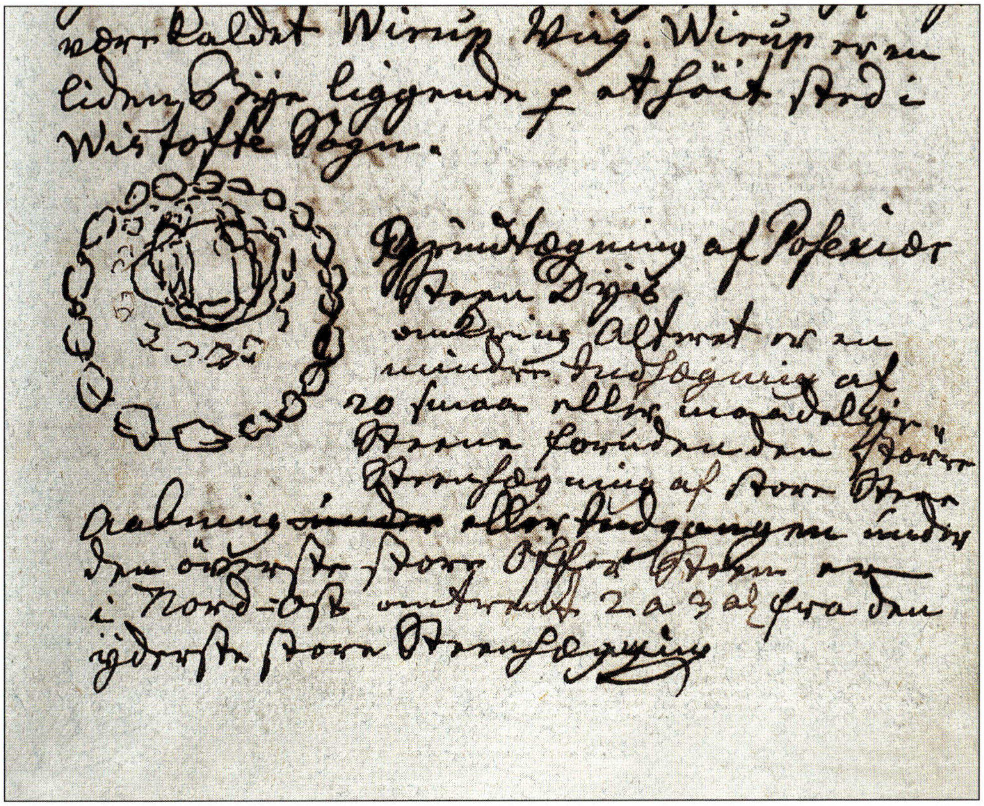

Fig. 12.10. *In 1770, Søren Abildgaard visited Poskær Stenhus and made this small sketch of the monument's plan, accompanied by the following description: "Ground plan of Posekiaer Steen Dys. Around the altar is a small enclosure of 20 small or ordinary stones, in addition to the larger stone fencing of large stones. The opening or entrance under the upper large offer stone is to the northeast about 2 to 3 alen from the outer large stone fencing." This is the only known drawing of the inner stone circle before it was removed, probably just prior to the monument being scheduled in 1860.*

Fig. 12.11. *Poskær Stenhus as it may have appeared in the Neolithic.*

The six megalithic tombs with inner stone circles are far from unique. The early archaeological literature contains numerous drawings of now vanished dolmens with inner stone circles (fig. 12.12). Similarly, the phenomenon of inner stone circles around dolmen and passage grave chambers is exceedingly common in megalithic monuments across Europe, including Ireland, where at Carrowmore in Sligo there are several round dolmens that closely resemble the Danish examples. The Irish round dolmens have inner stone circles and no mound material (see chapter 18).

The inner stone circles in the Danish megalithic monuments must be seen as an integrated part of the monuments in which they are found. Or, to put it in another way: They are coeval with them. But one should, of course, be critical of this interpretation. It was common practice for megalithic monuments also to be used later in the Neolithic, for example in the Late Neolithic. Could it be that the stone circles date from this time and that they are, consequently, later than the actual construction of the monuments? Only more detailed archaeological investigations will be able to resolve this question, and it has only been sparsely illuminated by recent excavations. One of the latter was undertaken at the Gunderslevholm dolmen (see previous chapter). The stone circle here was clearly established in the Early or Middle Neolithic, as is evident for example from the crushed flint embedded between the stones; a constructional feature that is characteristic of dolmens and passage graves and not known later in prehistory.

Even though some stone circles associated with Danish dolmens should date from a later period of prehistory – we do not believe this to be the case, but let us follow this line of argument – the point is actually the same relative to our main argument

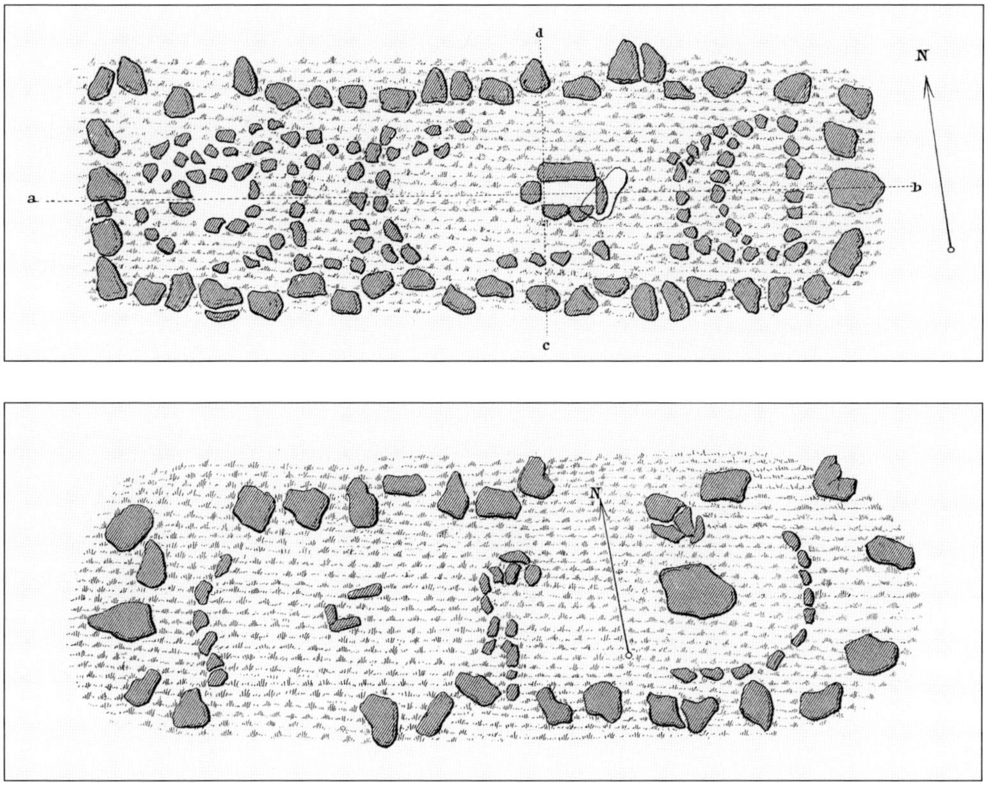

Fig. 12.12. *A couple of examples of long dolmens – Bøsøre and Voermark in southeast Funen – with inner stone circles. These monuments are just less than 30 m in length. They were drawn for F. Sehested's impressive book from 1878* Fortidsminder og Oldsager fra egnen om Broholm.

here: A stone circle constitutes a temporal seal on the surface on which it lies. If we assume for example that the stone circle at Poskær Stenhus was established in Late Neolithic times, this simply means that the dolmen had, at that time, a low, level internal surface – and therefore no mound.

In the next chapter, we will take a look at a very special dolmen with inner stone circles.

13. Videdysse – a long dolmen with stone circles and two mounds

Between Roskilde and Ringsted lies the village of Birkede. On the western edge of the village, in the garden of a small property – a former smallholding – stands the long dolmen Videdysse (fig. 13.1). According to tradition, its name derives from that of the killer of Langben Rise, Videric Verlandsen, who is reputed to be buried here. And the unfortunate Langben Rise is said to have been laid to rest just less than 1 km to the south, in another scheduled long dolmen that bears his name (see chapter 10). Perhaps this legend is the reason attention became focussed on Videdysse at such an early stage, because it is depicted in the earliest known illustration of a Danish dolmen, in Ole Worm's great work *Danicorum Monumentorum Libri Sex*, from 1643 (fig. 13.2).[1]

Ole Worm's book does not contain a more detailed text or accompanying description for the picture of Videdysse, so we do not know whether he saw the monument for himself. He probably did not, because many of the ancient monuments – primarily rune stones – that appear in his work were presumably only known to him from reports submitted by clergymen around the realm. The image of Videdysse, a woodcut, shows a rectangular frame of stones, which are the kerbstones for the long dolmen. Inside the long dolmen, three mounds stand in a row, thereby occupying the entire length of the monument. The central mound is the largest, and on top of this stands a dolmen chamber, surrounded by a small stone circle. Along the edges of the mounds, in the foreground of the picture, a row of stones runs parallel with the sides of the monument.

This stone row is though very puzzling, because even though there are examples of transverse rows of stones in long dolmens, as yet there are no records of a longitudinal stone row in this type of monument.[2] If one takes a closer look – as Torben Dehn has done – at this row of stones on Ole Worm's picture of Videdysse, one discovers that it does not follow a straight line.[3] The stones form three arcs, corresponding to the three mounds, and it is evident that the "stone row" continues in between the mounds. So they do not represent one straight row of stones, but three stone circles that, like kerbstones, each encircle one of the three mounds.

In 1763 – 120 years later – Videdysse was again depicted, this time in *Den Danske Atlas* by Erik Pontoppidan (fig. 13.3). The illustration is based on the earlier drawing in Ole Worm's book, being merely a new version modernised in the fashion of the time and in copper print. Similarly, there is no detailed text in *Den Danske Atlas*.

The first actual description came in 1808, when Professor Børge Thorlacius went to Dåstrup parish in the company of two local clergymen to visit Langben Rise's

Fig. 13.1. *Videdysse as it appears today. In the foreground is the small mound at the north end of the long dolmen.*

grave, Videdysse and other of the "place's curiosities". In his report to the Danish Royal Commission for the Collection and Preservation of Antiquities, Børge Thorlacius writes the following: "… a majestic dolmen called *Videdyss*. On a mound of great extent, much elongated and now overgrown with bushes, there is in the middle a large capstone more than 3 alen [1.9 m] in length, almost 2 alen [1.3 m] in width and 1½ alen [0.9 m] high, of this form [sketch of the capstone seen from the side], resting on 4 large pyramidal stones; the mound is, presumably due to their weight, sunken at this place, and the altar surrounded by stones of the same size as the altar orthostats. On both sides of the altar are elevations with stone settings; and the mound's entire length is similarly oval, surrounded by pyramidal stones … From this place, almost nothing appears to have been taken away."[4]

Here we are provided with some useful information on a number of aspects: The dolmen chamber (the altar) consists of four orthostats, on which the great capstone rests, i.e. it is a chamber of type I. The chamber stands on level ground. Strangely enough, Børge Thorlacius does not doubt his predecessors – in his report, just prior to the above quotation, he mentions Erik Pontoppidan's illustration – but explains the missing mound beneath the dolmen chamber as being due to the stones of the chamber presumably being so heavy that they pressed down through the mound and flattened it out! The fact that the dolmen chamber is shown, first by Ole Worm and later by Erik Pontoppidan, standing on a mound, is due to this being how a "pagan altar" was depicted at the time. That is, as a structure which, both in a spiritual and a literal sense, was elevated to some degree. Børge Thorlacius also mentions the two mounds, one on each side of the chamber, as shown in the early illustrations, and he confirms that they are encircled by stones. The chamber is also said to be surrounded by stones of the same size as the orthostats. The latter could, on the face of it, be perceived as one of the stone circles shown around the dolmen chamber on the early illustrations.

Børge Thorlacius had a great interest in dolmens and was an excellent observer. His book, *Bemærkninger over de i Danmark endnu tilværende Hedenolds-Høie og Steensætninger*, provides the first overview of Denmark's barrows and megalithic tombs. It was published in 1809 and was based on clerical reports to the Royal Commission for the Collection and Preservation of Antiquities. Of Videdysse it states: "This wonderful monument between Roskilde and Birke, close to the latter, has, further to the entire mound's encircling, also a circle around each of its triplet mounds and also a stone circle on top of the middle one, the tallest, around the altar; that is 3 stone circles."[5] Videdysse was one of the ancient monuments selected for scheduling by the Danish Chancery in 1810, in connection with which it is described as "as yet untouched".[6]

In 1887, A.P. Madsen drew a plan and a longitudinal profile of Videdysse (fig. 13.4). Fourteen years later, in 1901, he again visited the dolmen in Birkede during a district survey. His drawings and description are highly informative with respect to the appearance of the monument at this time: "The long dolmen "Videdysse", 33 m long (NW to SE) 8.4 m wide. In the middle a stone-set grave, 1.8 m long, 1.21 m wide, with 3 side stones, open towards SE. Over the grave a large capstone. Around the

Fig. 13.2. *This woodcut of Videdysse from Ole Worm's great work on Danish monuments, published in 1643, is the earliest known depiction of a Danish dolmen.*

Fig. 13.3. *The first topographic description of Denmark* – Den Danske Atlas *of 1763 – also contains a depiction of Videdysse, as the only dolmen in this major work, which otherwise contains a wealth of information on dolmens.*

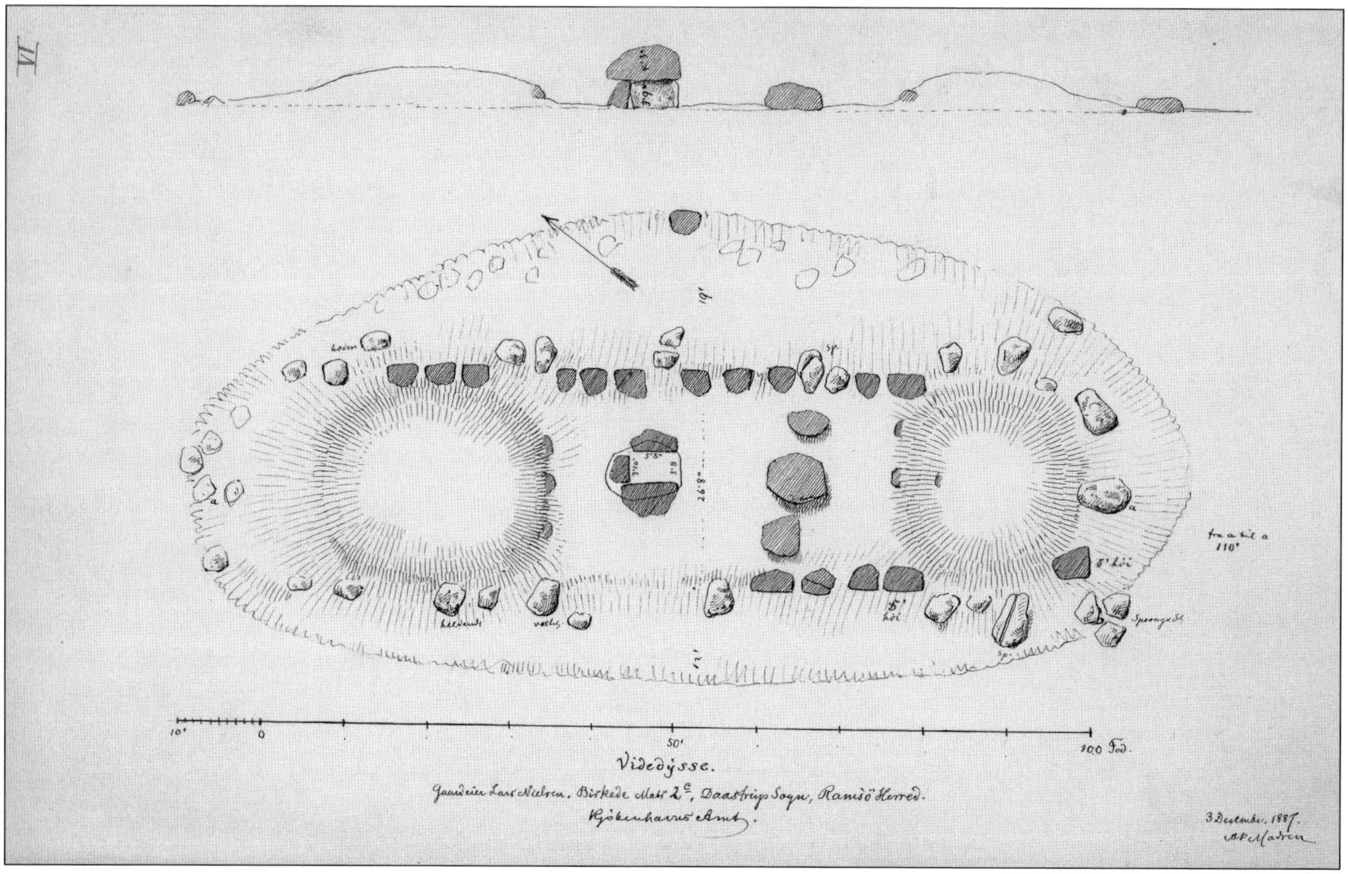

Fig. 13.4. *Videdysse, drawn by A.P. Madsen in 1887. Unlike the earlier drawings, the dolmen chamber is now shown down at ground level. The two small mounds, one at each end of the long dolmen, are very conspicuous. Stones can be perceived on the margins of both of them.*

dolmen are 16 standing kerbstones, several fallen and some split. A little southeast of the grave lie 3 large stones in a row across the dolmen. The mound fill is insignificant in the middle section of the dolmen, higher at both ends."[7]

A.P. Madsen's drawing clearly shows the 16 standing kerbstones, the chamber and the row of three stones across the long dolmen. He does not mention that there is a small mound at each end of the monument, simply that the mound fill in the long dolmen is higher towards the ends. On the drawing this is shown as two small mounds, both furnished with two to three visible kerbstones. But otherwise it seems that the 19th century had not been kind to Videdysse. At the beginning of the century, it had been described as more or less intact, but now several of the kerbstones were missing and many others had been split by stone masons (fig. 13.5). Near one of the corners of the long dolmen, the drawing shows a toppled-out kerbstone in which a stone mason has carved a long furrow, but for some reason it has not been split. Just beside it lies a broken kerbstone in three pieces. And there are only three orthostats in the chamber; one is missing – taken by the stone masons. Perhaps the missing orthostat is the middle stone in the row that runs across the monument, because this row is a 19th century architectural invention, as it does not feature in the earlier descriptions.

Videdysse was not scheduled until 1937, and in the scheduling declaration the Danish National Museum reserved the right to "undertake a possible minor improvement of the dolmen".[8] At this point, its appearance was more or less the same as in 1884. The number of preserved kerbstones is given as 17 at the northeast side, two at the southeast end, seven at the southwest side and none at the northwest end. The false row of three stones is also included in the description as follows: "at a similar distance from the NW end there is a corresponding row of 3 somewhat smaller stones across the dolmen". Again, no mention is made of the two mounds at the ends of the long dolmen, it merely being stated that: "The mounding of the earth is insignificant in the middle of the dolmen, such that the chamber is completely free of earth, but somewhat higher, up to ¾ m at the ends." In the same year that Videdysse was scheduled, it was restored by Julius Raklev of the National Museum, who re-erected the fallen kerbstones.

"Time erases all traces", goes the old saying, and this is also partly true of the memory of the appearance of Videdysse. The two mounds, surrounded by stone circles, at each end of the long dolmen, lost their identity after A.P. Madsen's visit in 1884 and became reduced to something resembling mound fill following an unsubstantiated assumption that the mound material had been removed from around the chamber in the middle part of the monument.[9]

Before we reach a conclusion about the appearance of Videdysse in prehistory, mention will be made of a couple of other long dolmens which have a round mound at each end.

Fig. 13.5. *Despite its early renown, Videdysse was not scheduled until 1937. At that point, many stones had already been removed or split. This remnant of a kerbstone with wedge holes – the upper hole still contains a piece of an iron wedge – can be seen on the west side of the long dolmen.*

One of these is Tingstedet, by the village of Store Rise on Ærø. This long dolmen was described by Henry Petersen in the district survey of 1884 and was also drawn by A.P. Madsen (fig. 13.6).[10] Today, the monument, which is 54 m long and 8.5 m wide, has two preserved dolmen chambers of early type. Between these two chambers there has probably been a third chamber, which was demolished before A.P. Madsen drew the monument. It is relevant in this respect that one end of the long dolmen was covered by a round barrow, which measured 15-20 m in diameter and was 1.5 m high. According to a description of Ærø from 1834, the round barrow was encircled by kerbstones. It presumably contained a burial from the Bronze Age.[11] This quite unique structure was ruined in 1945, when the round barrow was removed in the course of restoration work undertaken by Julius Raklev of the National Museum.

The other long dolmen is Harald Hildetands Grav, at Gammel Lejre. A drawing from 1758 shows a round barrow at one end of the monument (fig. 13.7). The monument is now scheduled, but this happened so late that both the dolmen chamber and the small barrow had been demolished and removed, and, similarly, most of the kerbstones were gone or had been split. Compared to the barrow on Tingstedet, the little mound on Harald Hildetands Grav was smaller and was confined within the kerbstones of the long dolmen.

The two small mounds at each end of Videdysse may, like the round barrows at Tingstedet and Harald Hildetands Grav, very well have been added at a later point in prehistory. At Videdysse, this could possibly be confirmed by an archaeological excavation of just one of the mounds, and at the same time it would be possible to check whether there were still traces of the small kerbstones around the mound. There is a

Fig. 13.6. *The long dolmen Tingstedet on the island of Ærø was drawn by A.P. Madsen in 1884. A round barrow had been built over one end of the long dolmen; this barrow was removed in 1945.*

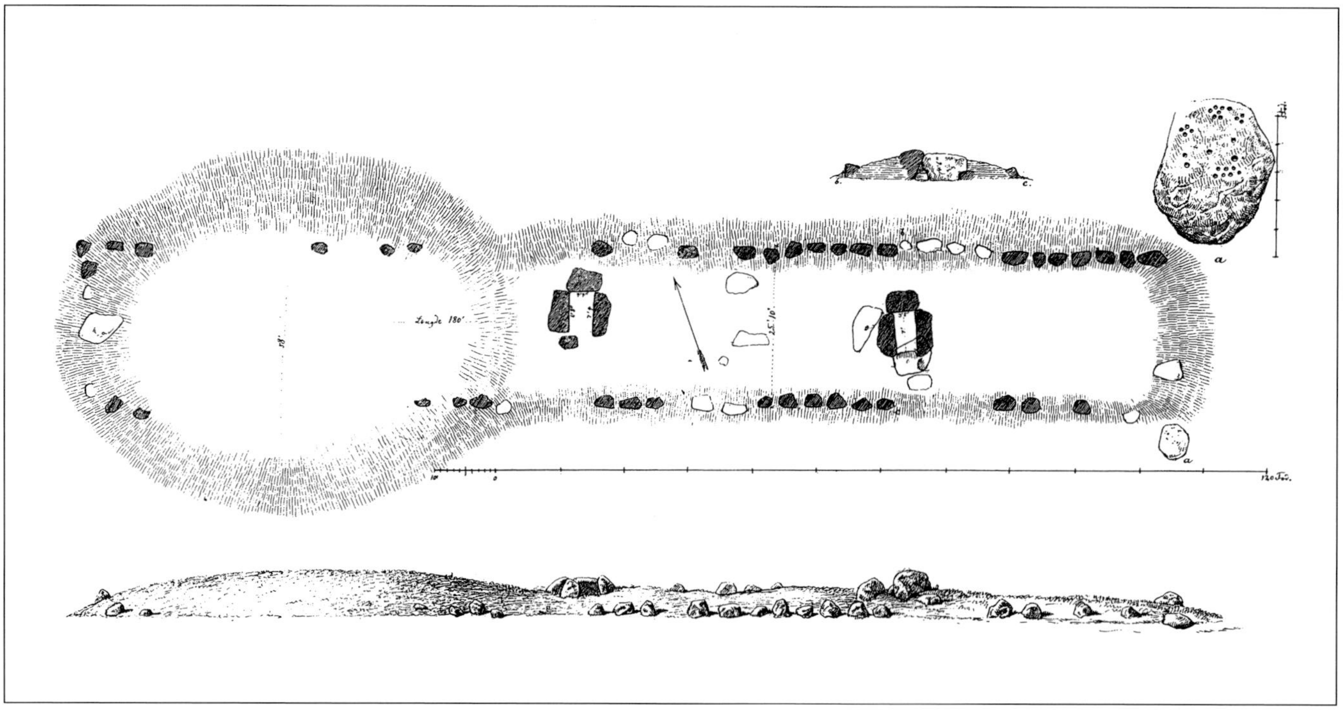

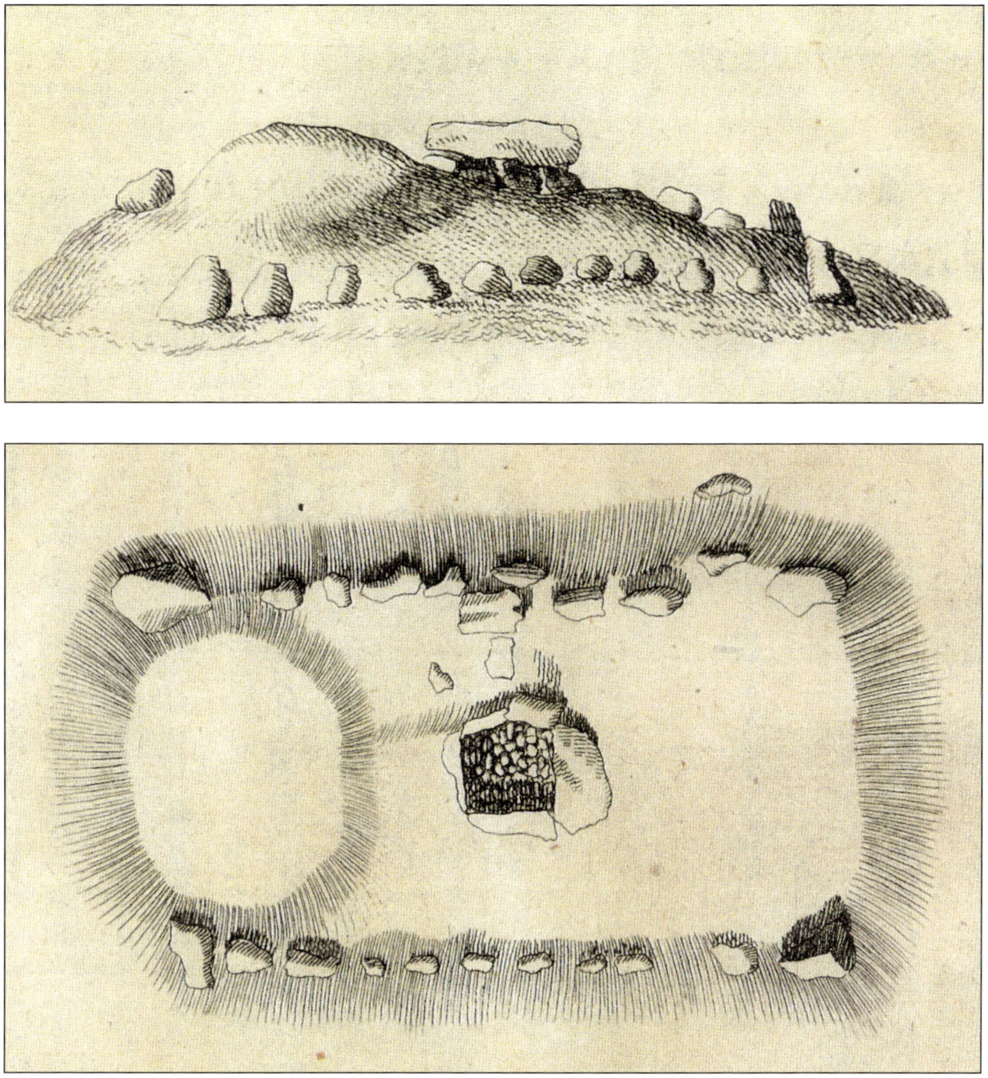

Fig. 13.7. *The long dolmen Harald Hildetands Grav also had a barrow at one end, though here, as at Videdysse, it was located within the kerbstones. The drawing was made in 1758 by L.A. Gebhardi. The long dolmen is now scheduled, but the barrow, dolmen chamber and many of the kerbstones are long gone.*

good deal to suggest that Videdysse was an open dolmen in the Neolithic and, much later in prehistory, the long dolmen was also used in the grave cult by the building of a small mound at each end of the monument. These two mounds were then encircled by small kerbstones and in the middle, on the original Neolithic surface, stood the dolmen chamber, which was surrounded by a stone circle, too.

14. Stenhus – a dolmen on a mound

In Denmark, a dolmen chamber that stands elevated, almost like a crown on top of a small hill or barrow, is almost only found in the form of modern memorial and ornamental dolmens, or depicted in cartoons, adverts and the like. Modern builders and drawers of dolmens have clearly been inspired by the scholars of the 17th and 18th centuries (see previous chapter). In the real world, you have to look very hard and long to find a Neolithic dolmen that corresponds to this modern concept. Nevertheless, it does exist.

On Mols, rather more than 6 km south as the crow flies from Poskær Stenhus, stands another scheduled dolmen, known simply as Stenhus. Like its famous namesake, there is no mound of any consequence here. The monument does though have some properties that are significant relative to an understanding of the original appearance of this and similar dolmens.

Stenhus stands a little way out into the field, directly east of the road linking the two villages of Torup and Strands. The terrain is evenly undulating and much less strikingly steep and hilly than at Poskær Stenhus. But Stenhus at Strands is just as conspicuous, as it stands elevated, high up on top of a small hillock (fig. 14.1 and photo on opposing page). This topographic situation is not typical for Danish dolmens, which normally stand neither high or low, but on a suitable surface somewhere in between, as in the case of Poskær Stenhus.[1]

Its remarkable situation on the top of a steep-sided, rounded hillock, which measures 20 x 22 m and is 3 m high, is the reason Stenhus is so well preserved. Here, it was out of reach of the plough and fortunately no spruce trees have been planted either, so the dolmen on the hill has stood undamaged as far back as we can trace in archives and on maps.[2] As part of the National Museum's district surveys, archaeologist Sophus Müller and architect Erik Schiødte visited Mols in 1877-78 to map, describe and draw the district's ancient monuments and selected historic monuments. Both men were exceptionally competent in their field. Sophus Müller was an excellent observer and produced careful, sometimes almost punctilious, descriptions, while Erik Schiødte's drawn documentation and sketches of dolmens are some of the best in the genre. One day, in August 1878, they visited Stenhus at Strands:

"Handsome and well-preserved round dolmen standing on a low elevation on an even surface. The round mound which surrounds the chamber is 35-40 feet [11-12.6 m] in diameter and about 3 feet [94 cm] high; mainly built of stone; no actual kerbstones. The mound covers the side stones of the chamber up to 2-3 feet [63-94 cm] from their upper edge. The small angled chamber is formed of 5 stones and has a 2 feet wide

Fig. 14.1. *Stenhus stands tall and handsome atop a small, round hillock, exactly like the dolmens drawn by children and cartoonists.*

entrance to the east, outside which are 4 passage stones, which are about 2 feet lower than the side stones of the chamber. The chamber is dug out; its internal height is now 4½ feet [1.4 m], but originally was somewhat lower, as the cobbled floor is now broken up. There does not appear to have been an actual door stone. The passage is probably not fully dug out. Handsome capstone about 4 feet [1.3 m] thick."[3] (fig. 14.2).

Like the other archaeologists who embarked on the district surveys, Sophus Müller had instructions to attempt to persuade landowners to have the most exceptional ancient monuments scheduled. We do not know how much effort he invested in this aspect of the matter on Mols, but the results were far from impressive with respect to megalithic tombs. Sophus Müller employed a local middleman, the parish executive officer in Agri, Niels Thuesen, whose task it was to negotiate with the farmers with regard to scheduling of their barrows and dolmens. As it was common knowledge in the area that smallholder Ole Hansen had received 200 kroner in 1860 to allow Poskær Stenhus to be scheduled, apparently no one was willing to allow their ancient monuments to be scheduled without payment. Only one dolmen was scheduled in 1878, the Grovlegård dolmen, against a payment of 200 kroner, in addition to the two Stabelhøje barrows, which went for 90 kroner. It was not until 1895 that ancient monuments were again scheduled on Mols. On this occasion it was the unusually fine barrow group of Trehøje, which the state bought for scheduling.[4]

The person we have to thank for the fact that many dolmens at Mols have, nevertheless, survived to the present day is local archaeological enthusiast Frederik Just, who was a grocer in Knebel. His interest in prehistory came from his father who, sometime in the 1890s, took his son out to see a large round dolmen, which stone masons were in the process of breaking up into rubble. This made such a deep impression on the boy that he promised himself, when he grew up, he would work to prevent similar vandalism. He kept his promise. Of the 31 scheduled dolmens on Mols in 1963, grocer Just was involved in the scheduling of 14 of them, prior to the passing of the Ancient Monuments Act of 1937.[5] One of these was Stenhus, which was scheduled voluntarily in 1925 by farmer S. Sørensen of Solhøjgård. In apprecia-

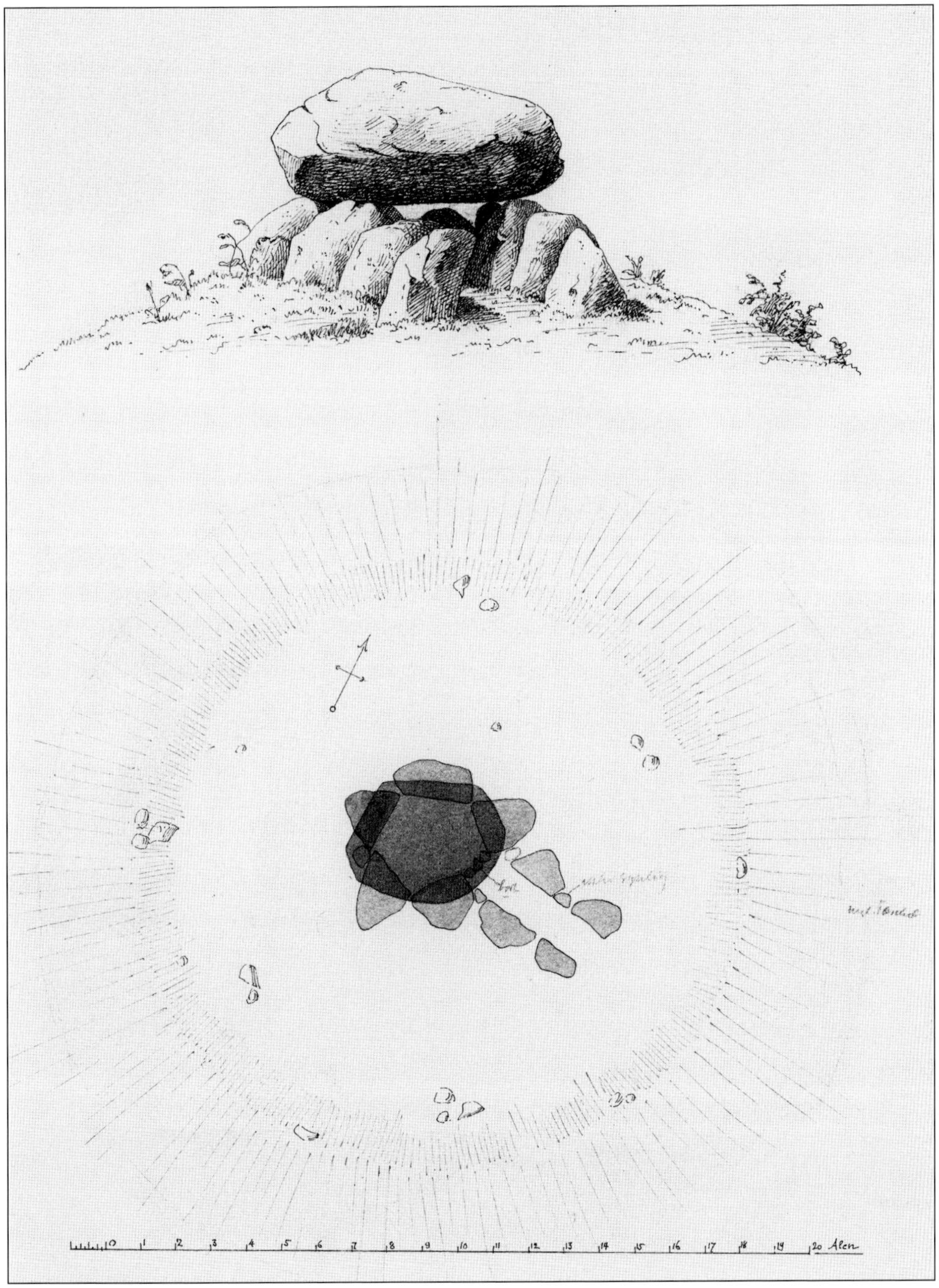

Fig. 14.2. *During the district survey of Mols in 1878, Stenhus was drawn by Erik Schiødte. Quite exceptionally, the polygonal chamber has two sets of passage stones.*

Fig. 14.3. *On the plan of Stenhus, surveyed in 1996, the outermost stones can, with a little imagination, be seen as the kerbstones of a round dolmen. The contour interval is 0.5 m.*

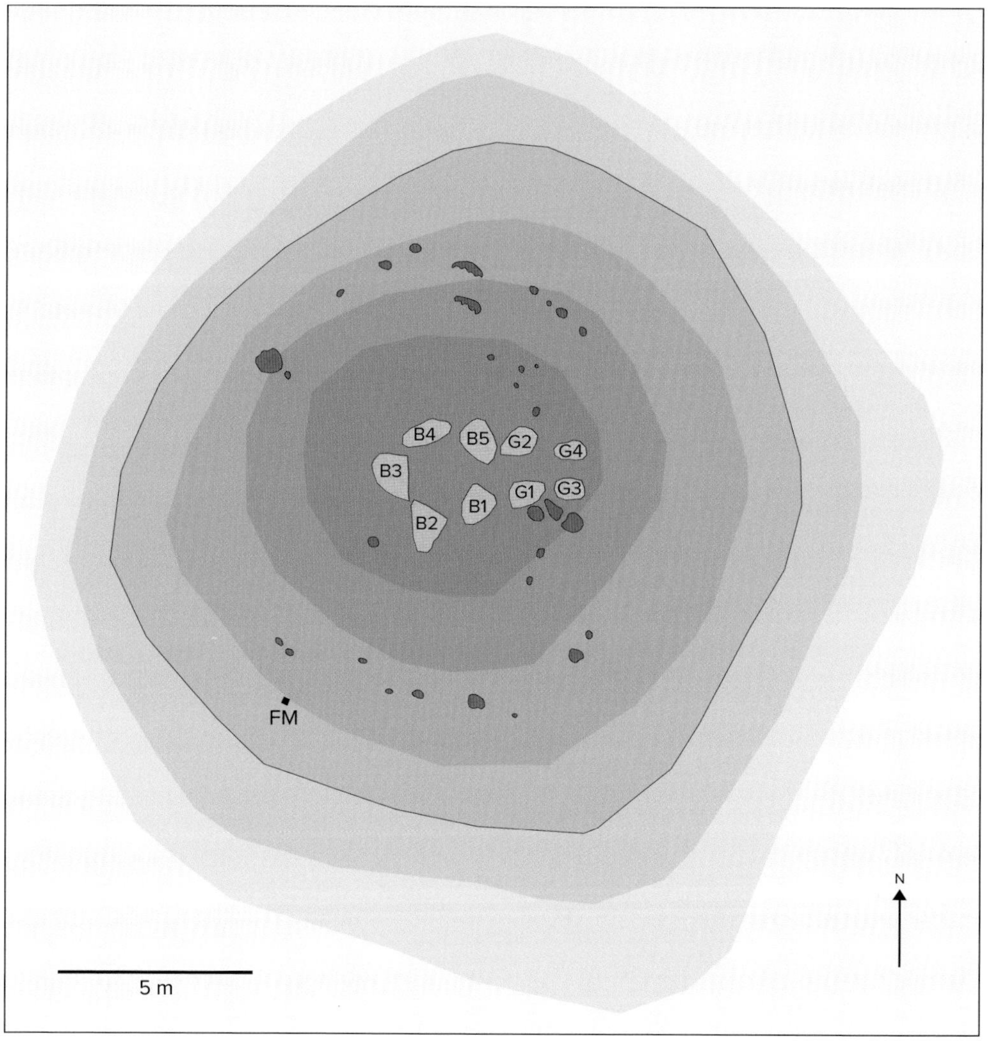

tion of the scheduling, the National Museum gave farmer Sørensen a silver beaker bearing an inscription commemorating the event.[6] Prior to the scheduling of Stenhus, Solhøjgård's owners had fortunately taken good care of their handsome dolmen.

The scheduling declaration of 1925 brings us to the next description of Stenhus, written this time by Hans Kjær of the National Museum: "'Stenhus' is a rounded hillock, 20-22 m in diameter, on top of which stands a dolmen chamber with passage. The hillock rises c. 3 m above the surrounding surface. The foot stands, in part, rather steeply and there are some stones here and there. In the northern side is a minor depression. In the middle stands a fine and impressive dolmen chamber with capstone and passage, surrounded by an 11 m wide stone circle, of which about 14 stones, c. 2/3 m in size, are visible on the surface. Only the upper part of these stones is visible; they are almost completely covered by earth. The polygonal chamber, in contrast, is clearly visible, hexagonal, formed of 5 large, up to 1.3 m wide, orthostats, sloping slightly inwards, while the passage opening, 0.65 m wide, makes up the sixth side, approximately to the east. No threshold is evident; 1.5 m below the capstone, the chamber is 2 m wide externally, the upper 0.7 m of the stones is visible. The capstone is flat on its lower surface, upper surface ridged; it is 2.55 x 2.45 m wide, 1.3 m thick. The passage is formed of 2 pairs of stones, the innermost 0.25 m lower than the orthostats, the outermost a further 0.25 m lower. The passage is 2.7 m long, partially earth-filled, especially externally, 0.5-0.75 m wide. Of the outer stone pair c. 0.65 m is visible, of the inner c. 0.75 m. The outermost is c. 0.65 m, the innermost c. 0.9 m wide, insofar as they are visible, at the base broader. Up to the SE outer surface lie 3 large stones."[7]

This distinctive and well-preserved dolmen subsequently enjoyed a relatively anonymous existence, until we became aware of its potential significance in relation to the project on dolmens without mounds, and in 1996 it was surveyed and described (fig. 14.3).

Stenhus, the hillock with the dolmen on top, just stood there, unchallenged, as when Sophus Müller and Erik Schiødte had visited it 118 years earlier. Only the grass seemed more luxuriant than back then, when the hillock was probably grazed by cattle.

The chamber

The chamber is of the polygonal type, constructed of five orthostats that, together with the entrance, form a hexagonal chamber, covered by a large capstone. The entrance, marked by two pairs of passage stones, faces east.

The interior of the chamber is free of earth and the floor has possibly, as Sophus Müller believed, been broken up, but this is not certain because he does not mention the extent to which he investigated this by excavation. Today, the gravelly base of the chamber lies 1.5 m below the uneven but nevertheless level lower surface of the capstone. In 1878, the height of the dolmen chamber was measured as 4½ feet, corresponding to 1.41 m – i.e. more or less the same as today.[8] The orthostats, which are probably about 2 m high, stand solidly anchored and packed in mound fill, so the stones of the chamber have probably not moved at all since 1878. One can just compare Erik Schiødte's drawing of the dolmen, seen from the southeast, with a photograph taken today from the same angle (see figs. 14.2 and 14.4). The approximately circular floor surface of the chamber has a diameter of c. 1.8 m, giving it an area of rather more than 2.5 m^2, which corresponds to half the size of the chamber in Poskær Stenhus. All the orthostats have flat internal surfaces which slope slightly inwards to accommodate the weight of the capstone (see fig. 14.3). Only one of the orthostats (B1) has a flat surface that could result from the stone being split.[9] The orthostats, which are 1.1-1,5 m wide, stand close together and are locked together by the construction, with exception of two of the orthostats (B2, B3), between which there is an 8 cm gap. The vertical distance from the floor to the surface of the surrounding fill around the chamber is 60-80 cm, seen from inside. The gaps between the orthostats are packed with stacked field stones, in up to four courses, to keep out the mound material. So

Fig. 14.4. *Stenhus today, seen from the same angle as Erik Schiødte's drawing made 135 years ago.*

there is no actual dry-walling built of stacked stone slabs, though the gap between two orthostats (B1, B2) is closed with a large, slightly sloping flagstone.[10]

The well-proportioned capstone rests horizontally on four of the five orthostats, as the top of one of the orthostats (B3) is 10 cm short of the capstone. This was also the case in 1878, when Erik Schiødte drew the chamber. The capstone, which is 3 m long and up to 2.4 m wide, has an estimated volume of 4 m^3 and weighs therefore just less than 11 tonnes.[11]

The passage

A 60 cm wide opening between a pair of orthostats leads out to an equally broad passage of around 2.5 m in length, marked by two pairs of passage stones. These have a flat, vertical or slightly sloping side facing in towards the passage. One of the stones (G2) has a surface that could have arisen from the stone being split. The largest and tallest passage stones are the innermost pair, with a width of up to 70 cm and a height 12-22 cm below the top of orthostat B5 at the entrance to the chamber. The outer pair are not quite as tall, as they are 31-40 cm short of the top of the aforementioned orthostat.[12] The very large gaps at both sides, between the passage stones themselves and between passage stones and orthostats, could originally have been closed with stacked stones, as shown in three places on Erik Schiødte's ground plan (see fig. 14.2). On later visits, these had possibly become overgrown so they were no longer visible, something which is also noted in a later handwritten note on the actual drawing.

Sophus Müller and Hans Kjær both noticed that there does not appear to have been a door stone. The three smaller stones that lie in a row on Erik Schiødte's drawing, in the place where there could have been a door stone, have nothing to do with this. Whether Sophus Müller was right can only be determined by an archaeological excavation, as his comment that "the passage is probably not fully dug out" is still true. At least there is a large amount of now grass-covered earthen fill in the passage.

Has the passage been covered by capstones? The passage stones are tall enough in this case for it to be possible to crawl or walk bent over into the chamber. At the innermost set of passage stones, the height – if it is presumed that the floor of the passage was on a level with the present floor in the chamber – has been around 1.3 m. The three stones that lie to the south of the passage, and which Hans Kjær also noticed, are not split, and are not large enough to be capstones.

Another, similar dolmen with a polygonal chamber and a passage covered by capstones has also existed on Mols. The monument, known as Sognefogedens Dysse,

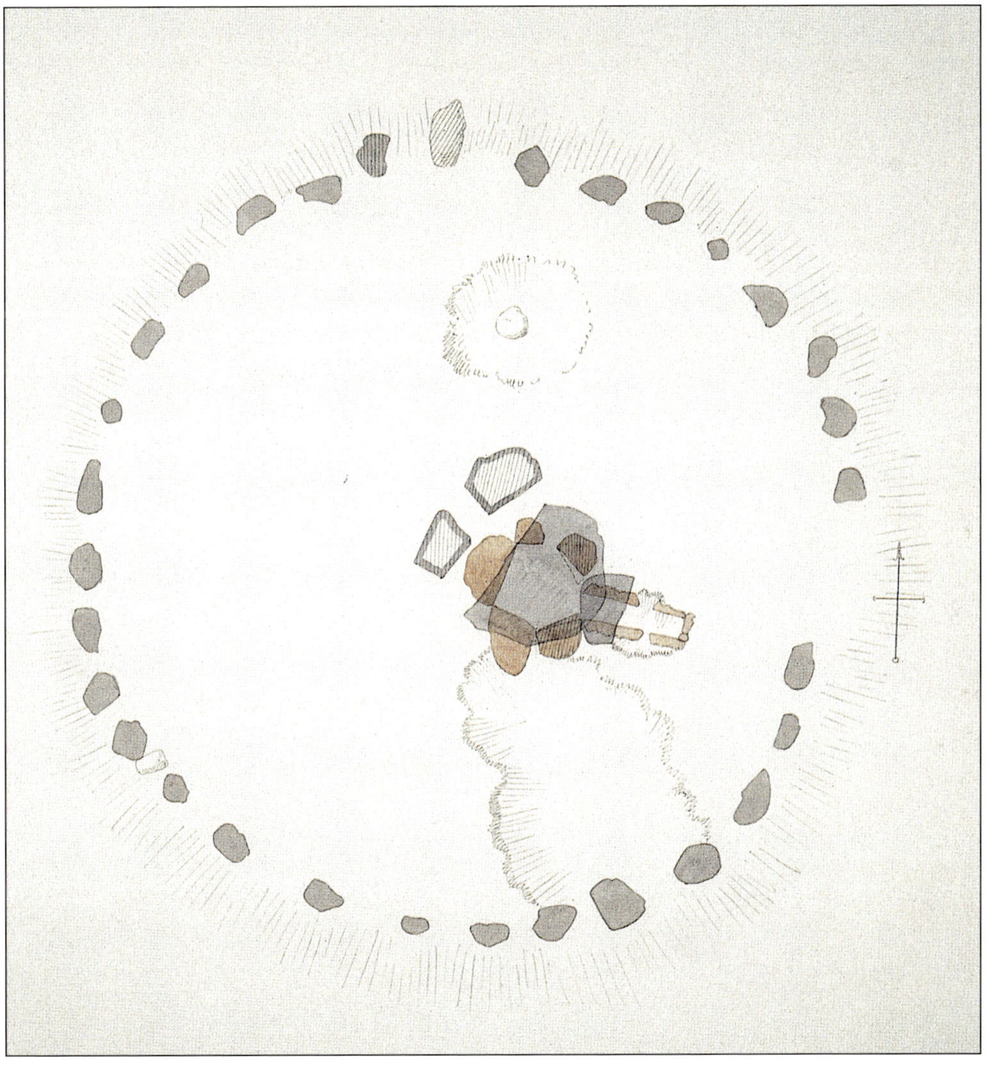

Fig. 14.5. *Sognefogedens Dysse was also drawn by Erik Schiødte in 1878. The passage made of stone flags was probably added in Late Neolithic times as a burial cist.*

was located 400 m west of Poskær Stenhus. It, too, was recorded by Sophus Müller and drawn by Erik Schiødte in 1878 (fig. 14.5). At that time, a large capstone lay over the chamber and a smaller capstone covered the innermost part of the passage. A piece had been split off the large capstone, and this lay beside it. Strangely, Sophus Müller did not comment on the capstone over the passage.

Unfortunately, the chamber was later destroyed and a more detailed study must be based exclusively on the record from 1878. Measured from the drawing, the passage was 2 m long, with an internal width of 45 cm. It was set of two stones at each side. Outwards, to the east, it appears that the passage was terminated by one, perhaps two, transverse stones. The side stones in the passage appear to have been very thin, almost like broad flagstones set on edge. The passage had been dug out in a recent, non-archaeological intervention. The capstone over the passage measured – based on the drawing – just less than 1.3 x 0.7 m, but the stone had probably been a good deal larger as the edge facing away from the chamber had a broken surface resulting from a piece being split off.

With respect to the capstone over the passage, there are two possibilities: The passage and the capstone could have been original, constructed at the same time as the chamber, or – more likely – the passage could have been added on or altered in the Late Neolithic, to form an actual stone cist. The latter explanation is favoured by the flagstone-like passage stones, the termination across the passage to the east and the fact that in the Danish Late Neolithic it was very common practice to use the passages in passage graves for burials in this way.

Finally, it should be noted that the entrance to the chamber and the passage in Stenhus faces directly east, towards sunrise at the equinoxes, the only two days of the year when day and night are of equal length. Stenhus has also been known as Solhøj (Sun barrow), but this name for the monument cannot be traced further back than the 20th century.[13]

The mound

When Sophus Müller visited Stenhus in 1878, he could see that the chamber was surrounded by a round manmade mound with a diameter of 11-13 m and a height of just less than 1 m. He also noted that the mound was, to a significant extent, built of stones and that there were no actual kerbstones. Back then the conditions for observation of the mound's surface and height were better, because the vegetation on the mound was sparser and more open than today. Erik Schiødte's plan supports his colleague's description, but only a few of the smaller stones are included, and he has drawn the round mound with a diameter of just less than 17 alen, corresponding to 10.7 m. In concurrence with Müller's description, no kerbstones are shown on the drawing. It is important, however, that neither the description nor the drawing shows or makes the least reference either to split or missing stones, or holes or irregularities in the mound surface, resulting from destructive digging activities or similar. Mound, chamber and passage all appear intact.

In the scheduling declaration of 1925, Hans Kjær remarks expressly that there were around 14 almost completely earth-covered stones, each of which was around 75 cm "in size", which formed a circle with a diameter of 11 m. Probably due to their modest size, Hans Kjær does not refer to them as kerbstones, even though such small kerbstones are not unknown on Mols. Sognefogedens Dysse also had very small kerbstones, perhaps because all the large stones in the neighbourhood were used to build Poskær Stenhus.

In the plan from the modern survey, a number of stones are drawn in on the mound, especially at its periphery (see fig. 14.3). With a little imagination, the stones to the south and north can be presumed to be located at the edge of the mound, as they all lie at a distance of 5.6 m from the mound's centre, in the middle of the chamber. These must correspond to the stones that Hans Kjær took to be kerbstones. The mound has thereby a diameter of around 11 m, which corresponds to the observations made in 1878 and 1925.

Based on the modern survey, we can draw a profile of the mound (fig. 14.6). We have manipulated the profile a little, without altering the main impression, and marked the lower boundary of the mound with a broken line, as we presume that the kerbstones to the south and north rest on the old Neolithic land surface. The mound fill slopes evenly up towards the chamber, where, with a thickness of 85-90 cm, it reaches its maximum, corresponding very well to Sophus Müller's 3 feet (94 cm). But the mound could well be 1 foot higher, because we presume that the kerbstones stand on the old Neolithic surface and that these stones are 50 cm tall, meaning that the mound fill is around 1.2 m thick at the chamber.

The general term "mound fill", used in the context of dolmens, can encompass several layers that may have been formed in various ways. As described in chapter 5, at least four categories can be identified, i.e. packing layers, cult layers, fill layers and natural deposits. Often two or more of these categories interact with each other, but this situation can only be detected by an archaeological excavation. At Stenhus, it seems likely that some of the mound fill, if not all of it, can be attributed to packing layers that were intended to support and stabilise the large stones of the chamber and passage, possibly combined with a thinner cult layer that was formed as a consequence of one-off events or successive cult activities at the dolmen.

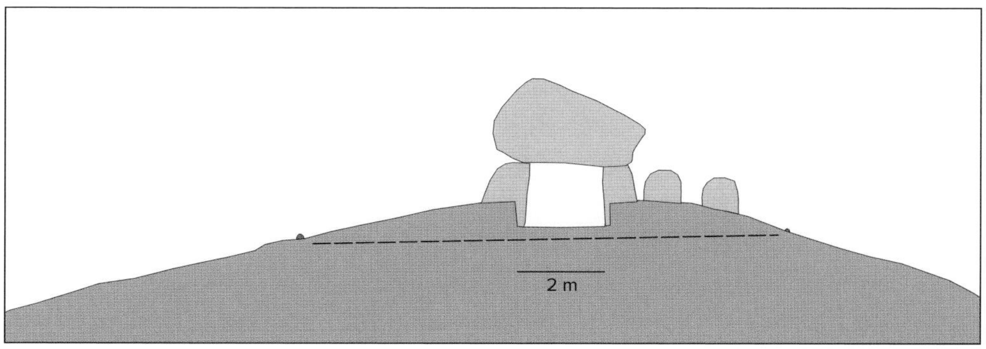

Fig. 14.6. *The profile through Stenhus shows the difference in height between the chamber, passage stones and the possible kerbstones. The kerbstones are joined with a horizontal broken line. The profile has been adapted by projecting on the passage stones.*

Fig. 14.7. *Stenhus as it may have appeared in the Neolithic.*

A dolmen without a mound standing on a mound

Under this rather cryptic heading, the results of the presentation and analysis of Stenhus at Strands will be summarised.

On the top of a hillock with relatively steep sides, a polygonal dolmen chamber with two pairs of passage stones was built on the level surface. The chamber stands in the middle of a shield-shaped mound that is 11 m in diameter and 90 cm in height. The mound, which was probably built of small stones used as packing, has been surrounded by small kerbstones. As there are no traces of destruction or removal of stones, or the removal of mound fill, it must be assumed that the dolmen and its mound have stood undamaged since prehistory. Towards the north, however, there is today a depression that could be the result of earlier digging activities or settlement of the earth. Since the dolmen ceased to function as a cult place, a layer of turf has formed over the surface of the mound which, during the time it was in active use, could have appeared as a stone-covered surface. The mound fill has extended up to the middle of the orthostats, so their upper halves stood exposed, when seen from outside the chamber.

Had the mound fill extended up to the lower surface of the capstone, it would have resulted in a rather steep mound that subsequently must have been removed or eroded away. There are no traces of either of these processes. Similarly, a mound of this kind would have demanded very special measures to keep the passage free of soil, measures of which there is not the least indication at this or similar dolmens with polygonal chambers (fig. 14.7).

Stenhus is referred to here as a round dolmen, but it should be noted that the kerbstones are very modest and insignificant. Sophus Müller even wrote that actual kerbstones are not present. As such, Stenhus, with its free-standing chamber, located in the middle of an 11 m diameter circular stone setting, is related to the completely free-standing dolmen chambers that we will examine more closely in the next chapter.

15. Trollasten and other free-standing dolmen chambers

In many places across Denmark, it is possible to see dolmen chambers that stand completely solitary, exposed and isolated, without either a mound or kerbstones (fig. 15.1). In some cases, they are almost the only visible ancient monuments, standing one after the other, as on the Refsnæs peninsula, near Kalundborg, or on Helnæs, south of Assens. These dolmen chambers are impressive in appearance and they have, as we saw in chapter 1, become part of the Danish national consciousness as the mental image and symbol of a dolmen.

Of the 1061 scheduled dolmens included in *Vore Fortidsminder*, 255 are free-standing dolmen chambers without a mound and kerbstones. This corresponds to 24%, or a quarter of all scheduled dolmens. In comparison, long dolmens comprise 55% and round dolmens 15%, while the remaining 6% monuments are so damaged they cannot be identified to type.[1] The total number of scheduled dolmens is, however, around 1800, so this means there are even more free-standing dolmen chambers, and remnants of these, than the aforementioned 255.

Some people perhaps think that these isolated dolmen chambers originally stood in a mound surrounded by kerbstones, and that the kerbstones and mounds have been removed in order to exploit the area for agricultural cultivation and use the great stones for other purposes. Subsequently, the chambers have been allowed to stand untouched, probably in veneration, but also because they look so imposing and they don't, after all, take up so much space in their amputated state (fig. 15.2). Numerous early descriptions and drawings bear witness to the fact that this may well have been the course of events in many cases. There are plenty of examples, of which only one will be mentioned here, Hylledysse, which stands near Gadstrup, 6 km south of Roskilde.

Hylledysse is an impressively large dolmen chamber with a mighty capstone (figs. 15.3 and 5.5). Its round chamber has an internal diameter of 3 m and is constructed of seven orthostats. Today, the chamber stands surrounded by a slight elevation on an otherwise level field. But this is far from how it appeared previously. It is apparent from a description written by Børge Thorlacius in 1821 that Hylledysse was once one of three dolmen chambers, which stood in a 21 m long and up to 9 m wide long dolmen that was surrounded by a double row of kerbstones. The long dolmen was scheduled as early as 1808, and in 1823 it was scheduled for a second time. But these early protective measures were not particularly effective and on the watercolour

Fig. 15.1. *The free-standing dolmen chamber Knøsen, depicted here by Jacob Kornerup in 1893, stands on the east coast of the island of Samsø, out towards Samsø Belt.*

Fig. 15.2. *On the right of this aerial photo is the scheduled dolmen chamber Grydeshøj, located south of Dreslette in southwestern Funen. The chamber stands in a demolished and ploughed-out long barrow containing traces of two further, now removed, chambers. The elongate, rectangular, light-coloured dolmen footprint is clearly evident in the cornfield. To left of the long dolmen, possible traces of four demolished megalithic tombs can just be perceived.*

from 1877 reproduced here, only one of the original three dolmen chambers remains (fig. 15.3). The third and final scheduling took place by voluntary declaration in 1889 and related to the remains of the monument that still stand there today.[2]

There are, however, many isolated dolmen chambers for which there are no early descriptions or drawings to reveal their original appearance and whether or not they stood in mounds with surrounding kerbstones. It is remarkable that many of these dolmens only have a little mound material associated with them. The stones therefore stand very exposed and the dolmens have, as such, no visible signs of destruction in the form of surface holes left by dug-up stones or the remains of stones that have been split. In some cases, the traces from destruction could be hidden or have

Fig. 15.3. *The impressive dolmen chamber Hylledysse now stands exposed, but previously it stood in a long dolmen together with two other dolmen chambers. This watercolour, from 1877, is by Jacob Kornerup, who painted and drew many dolmens in the vicinity of Roskilde, where he lived.*

been erased, but it is also possible that these are actually undamaged monuments which have survived from the Neolithic until the present day in more or less the form that they now have. This possibility can only be confirmed by careful archaeological excavation, ideally of reasonably well-preserved dolmens.

Only a very few investigations of this type have been undertaken in Denmark. This is partly due, as previously mentioned, to the fact that new excavations are only exceptionally undertaken in scheduled dolmens, and partly because for them to provide a satisfactory answer, the investigations must include the surrounding mound or the area extending up to the dolmen chamber. Finally, there must be no evidence of kerbstones, as the dolmen chamber must have stood freely exposed. Only a couple of scheduled Danish dolmens, Lunden on the island of Langeland and Ormslev near Aarhus, satisfy these conditions, while the now free-standing Tustrup passage dolmen is a round dolmen, where the kerbstones are no longer preserved (see chapter 16). These investigations of demolished dolmens do, however, show that the otherwise severely ploughed-down monuments nevertheless often contain clear and very informative evidence of free-standing dolmen chambers (see chapter 20).

Trollasten

Even though it is nearly 50 years ago, in 1968, that Märta Strömberg of the University of Lund published her investigation of the Scanian dolmen Trollasten in her book *Der Dolmen Trollasten*, this work, with its thoroughness and richness of perspective, remains unsurpassed in the literature on Scandinavian megaliths. Mention will be

Fig. 15.4. *The Scanian dolmen chamber Trollasten under excavation in 1965.*

made here of only a few of the aspects of Trollasten that are of greatest relevance for the question of dolmens with or without mounds.

Trollasten, which would be called The Troll Stone in English, is a free-standing dolmen chamber standing on a level field near Ystad in Scania, southern Sweden (fig. 15.4). In the years prior to the excavation, which took place primarily in 1965 with a couple of follow-up investigations in the subsequent two years, the field was cultivated right up to the chamber, resulting in stones being ploughed up from the soil. This prompted Märta Strömberg to carry out an archaeological investigation of the surroundings of the dolmen chamber that were most at risk. Even though the investigation, as a consequence, had the character of a rescue excavation, it was in fact a piece of research which formed part of Märta Strömberg's Hagestad project; a project that, to a major extent, focused on the megalithic tombs in the study area.[3]

The dolmen chamber is of polygonal type, where the capstone rests on six orthostats (fig. 15.5). Its internal dimensions are 2.4 x 2 m. One of the orthostats is, moreover, a passage stone in the short passage. Only one side of the passage, comprised of two stones, is preserved. The passage is so low that there has not, in a traditional sense, been a covered passage as evident in passage graves. According to Märta Strömberg, it was more probably an uncovered path or passageway.[4] The dolmen has no fewer than three threshold stones: one opposite the gap between the two stones in the passage, one at the passage/chamber transition and one a little further inside the chamber itself. The orthostats, as is usual for the later dolmens, stand on their narrow ends, and are fairly tall, with a height of 2 m. As the surrounding ground surface only reaches up to the middle of the orthostats, the chamber appears strikingly free-standing and monumental with its massive capstone, and with its orthostats set a good way down into the ground, it is solidly anchored. This also means that the floor of the chamber lies 60 cm below the old Neolithic surface (fig. 15.5 section). Special note should be taken of this, because no mound was evident around the chamber, and neither was a mound necessary to support and stabilise the chamber.

An area of just less than 200 m² was investigated. The chamber construction, which without the south-facing passage covers an area of 12 m², stands in the middle of a rectangular stone pavement. In the publication, written in German, Märta Strömberg refers to this as a *Tablett* – a word that in the Danish and English versions *tablet* can also mean a platform (fig. 15.5).[5] Only the easternmost part of the platform was exposed, while the western part, on the opposite side of the chamber, was merely localised and delimited with a stone probe. Together, the chamber and platform have an extent of about 4.7 x 10.7 m. The platform consists of one layer of stones, with carefully laid sides and right-angled corners. It does not extend all the way into the cham-

Fig. 15.5. *Excavation plan of Trollasten and a cross-section through its chamber. The square stone pavement – the platform – seen east of the chamber probably has a matching partner on the opposite, uninvestigated side. On and outside the semicircular stone pavement in front of the chamber were potsherds (black dots), as well as burnt bone, flint axes and other artefacts (circles with black triangles) or just flint axes (black triangles).*

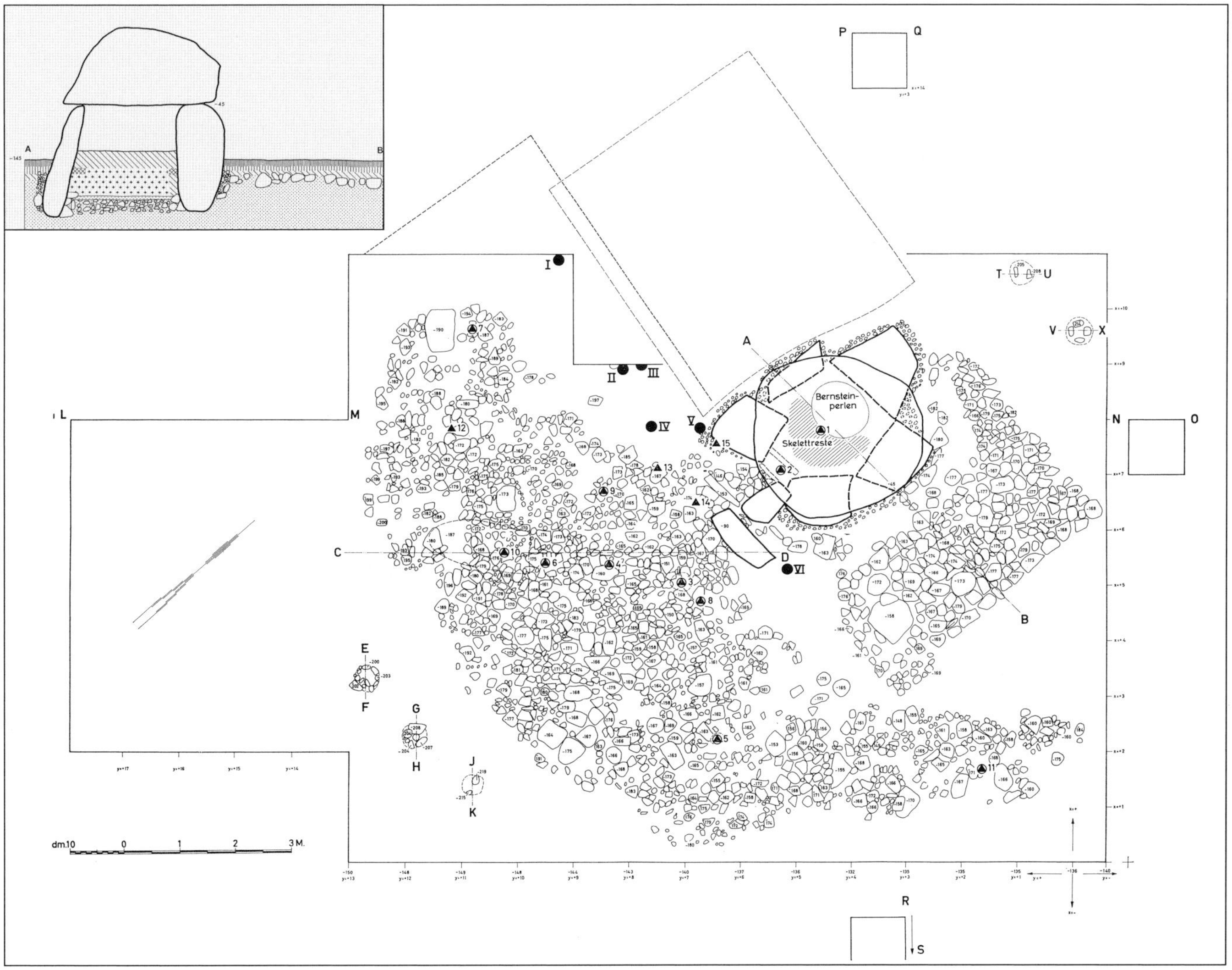

Fig. 15.6. *The stones in the crescent-shaped stone pavement in front of Trollasten could have been placed there in multiple operations. In the background to the right, a more regular stone pavement, the platform, is evident. These stone pavements constituted the surface around the dolmen, when it was in active use during the Neolithic.*

ber, around which is consequently a stone-free zone. The stones of the platform lie directly on yellow sand and only a few artefacts were found on it – just 30 potsherds, of which 14 were ornamented. The chamber and the tablet/platform are considered by Märta Strömberg to have been built at the same time in one single operation. The chamber itself was investigated and emptied of finds in the 19th century.[6]

In front of the chamber, a crescent-shaped stone pavement was uncovered that abutted the mouth of the passage but otherwise was separated from the platform and chamber by a stone-free zone (figs. 15.5 and 15.6). This stone pavement, which was 15 m in length and had a maximum width of 5 m, consisted mainly of one to two layers of stones, but in several places there were though more than two layers. It was much less clearly delimited than the platform, but its external edge does, nevertheless, describe an evenly rounded curve. The stone pavement lay on a 10 cm thick cultural layer, which consisted of dark, soot-mixed sand containing a few burnt stones and artefacts. Beyond the stone pavement, and further away from the dolmen chamber, the cultural layer reached a thickness of as much as 40 cm, but otherwise it was limited in extent to the area by the dolmen.

There were no traces of kerbstones. On the other hand, five stone-lined postholes were found: three in front of the stone pavement, but separated from this by a stone-free zone, and two behind the dolmen, beyond the platform. According to Märta Strömberg, it is possible that posts stood here which had a function corresponding to kerbstones or monoliths. However, the fact that no further postholes were encountered argues against this interpretation. But this could be due to the other postholes not being stone-lined and therefore not as easy to identify, so they may very well have been there.[7]

In and on the stone pavement were 5797 potsherds and 821 flint and stone artefacts, clearly a substantial finds assemblage. Rather more than half of the potsherds came from ornamented vessels. The cultural layer yielded 2890 potsherds, of which a third were ornamented, and 723 flint and stone artefacts. In several cases, sherds from the same vessel occurred both in the stone pavement and in the cultural layer. There were sherds from more than 200 vessels, none of which was found intact, and many were just represented by smaller or larger fragments. A distribution plan of sherds from six different vessels shows that they were smashed and spread out across the area in the Neolithic.[8] The pots can be dated to late EN and MN I-IV/V, with a predominance of vessels from MN II.

The fact that the stone pavement in front of the dolmen remained fairly intact, despite modern ploughing, is demonstrated in particular by the discovery of 11 small portions of burnt human bone, together with burnt artefacts, including fragments of flint axes that typologically belong to MN II-IV/V.

In the stone-free area between the dolmen chamber/platform and the stone pavement, remains were found of six different vessels (I-VI), in different locations. They all date from late EN-MN I and are considered to be a kind of votive vessel coeval with the construction of the dolmen.

Inside the actual chamber and passage which, as already mentioned, was emptied in the 19th century, the finds included pottery from the Battle Axe culture, corresponding to the Danish Single Grave culture, and the Viking Age.

Märta Strömberg has, on the basis of her excavation findings, attempted to describe the course of events in the Neolithic: "In the beginning, people undertook burials and offerings on a number of occasions, resulting in the formation of the cultural layer. At that time, the dolmen stood within the quadrangular stone pavement [the platform] and had perhaps some kind of function in relation to the undertaking of the offerings in front of the entrance, though there was at this time still no large stone cairn. There was, therefore, a structure that could be referred to as a "cult settlement" [*Kult-Siedlung*]. Probably associated with this were the postholes … Some degree of destruction of the previously offered objects likely took place during the extended period when offerings were made. If this had not been the case, they would not have been so widely scattered. At the end of the period of active use, the earlier structures were in disrepair and the large stone pavement was then laid. Subsequently, the burnt bones, axes etc. were placed on the stone pavement and in the chamber and passage ... A pottery vessel of the Battle Axe culture was placed in the chamber ... After the final use, the entire terrain around the dolmen was covered ... most likely by shifting sand ... The dolmen still protruded, however, and people visited it sporadically during the Late Neolithic ... If the cup marks [on the capstone] were not already made, they could perhaps have been produced at this time."[9]

The excavation of Trollasten clearly demonstrates an isolated dolmen chamber which is free-standing today and which stood just as free in the Neolithic. The many special finds of burnt bones, together with the burnt flint axes lying in small "caches" within the stone pavement, show that there was no mound during the dolmen's period of active use, which, with respect to artefacts and offerings, stretched over a period of 400-500 years, up until the end of the Middle Neolithic Funnel Beaker culture.

Ormslev

"The Ormslev dolmen – a free-standing dolmen?" is the English title of Nina Nielsen's article published in *Kuml* 2003. The article is based on an investigation of the Ormslev dolmen in 1975, directed by Torsten Madsen of the University of Aarhus. This was a research undertaking, forming part of his project on the Funnel Beaker culture in eastern Jutland.[10]

Fig. 15.7. *The Ormslev dolmen, seen from the south.*

Fig. 15.8. *Excavation plan of the Ormslev dolmen. The chamber is of type III, an extended dolmen, and despite not being very large, it has two capstones.*

The dolmen, which was scheduled in 1894, stands near Ormslev, on the southern side of the river valley Aarhus Ådal (fig. 15.7). The chamber is formed of six orthostats and covered by two capstones. The passage consists of a couple of passage stones that are of the same height as the chamber orthostats. According to Torsten Madsen, there are strong indications of a further two passage stones in continuation of those now present. In the outer part of the passage is a threshold stone, and in the inner part a "door stone". The ground plan of the dolmen chamber is almost trapezoid with a maximum internal width of 1.5 m and a length of 2.4 m; it therefore belongs to type III, an extended dolmen. To the east is a 50 cm wide opening into the passage (fig. 15.8). The dolmen stands with very freely-exposed, prominent stones on a small mound that at the time of the investigation was heavily affected by ploughing.

The excavation, which covered 66 m^2, was concentrated on the area around and in front of the passage, as shown on the excavation plan. Directly around the chamber and passage was a chamber packing layer. In front of the passage was a predominantly stone-free zone that extended to both sides. Unfortunately, there was a major modern disturbance in this area. The stone-free zone was succeeded outwards by a 2 m wide stone pavement, the sides of which were curved about a central point in the chamber area. It is possible that this stone pavement, which consisted of one to two layers of hand- to head-sized stones, had continued all the way around the chamber (fig. 15.9). There was not the least trace of kerbstones so it is very unlikely that the chamber was encircled by a kerbstone chain. Beneath the 9 m long, preserved stone pavement were five pits, two of which contained pottery from the Funnel Beaker culture. At the edge of the stone pavement were three cooking pits that could well date from the Neolithic.

In the area in front of the dolmen, beneath the grass turf, the original old land surface, on which the dolmen was built, was discovered. In this layer was a large concentration of potsherds. Further away from the dolmen, directly beneath the plough soil, was a layer of dark, humus-rich sand that overlay the original land

Fig. 15.9. *Part of the stone pavement in front of the Ormslev dolmen chamber, which can be seen in the background.*

surface. The stone pavement lay in this sand layer, and within it was a considerable quantity of pottery from the Funnel Beaker culture – primarily in the lower part. The actual chamber and passage were disturbed down to the level of the subsoil. This disturbance could possibly result from an excavation undertaken in 1870, the finds from which included several flat-flaked flint daggers and some pottery vessels; two surviving daggers and a vessel can be dated to the Early Bronze Age.

The finds from the 1975 excavation were heavily dominated by potsherds. Further to these were two flint arrowheads and sickle blades from the Late Neolithic/Early Bronze Age. From the area outside the chamber, 950 heavily fragmented potsherds were recovered, of which 450 sherds were included in the further analysis. The pottery could be assigned either to an early group (MN I-II/III) or a late group (MN IV-IV) in the Funnel Beaker culture. Further to these were a few sherds from a later period of the Neolithic. There were rim sherds from 30 vessels, of which 14 belonged to the early group and seven to the late group. The remaining nine vessels also belong to the Funnel Beaker culture, but cannot be dated more closely within this period.

The majority of the early pottery was found on the original surface in the area immediately south of the entrance to the dolmen, concentrated rather more than 1 m south of the place where the presumed outer passage stones would have stood. Conversely, the late pottery from the end of the Funnel Beaker culture was associated with the curved stone pavement located further away from the dolmen entrance. Finally, there are potsherds from three later vessels, from the Single Grave culture and the Late Neolithic, which lay in the same area and at the same level as the early pottery from the Funnel Beaker culture.

The finds and their circumstances will not be dealt with in detail here, and reference is made to the publication. It will, however, be highlighted that the pottery is interpreted as arising from a mixture of vessels placed in front of and by the entrance, on the old surface, as well as the clearing-out of vessels from the chamber, after which these were then covered by the stone pavement. Clearance probably took place during the Single Grave culture or the Late Neolithic.

The investigation of the Ormslev dolmen shows that the monument was involved in cult activities from period MN Ib to MN V of the Funnel Beaker culture. In the Late Neolithic and Early Bronze Age, the dolmen was also used for burials. The location of the pottery, and the finds circumstances in general, suggests that the surrounding terrain during the monument's period of use had more or less the same form as when it was excavated in 1975, i.e. "that the dolmen has never been covered by a mound!".[11]

Lunden

Following his appointment at Langeland Museum in 1971, Jørgen Skaarup began an ambitious project on the Neolithic period on the islands south of Funen. There was already a strong tradition of research into the settlements and megalithic tombs of the Funnel Beaker culture at the museum, undertaken first by Jens Winther and later by Hakon Berg. Jørgen Skaarup collated all this material, supplemented it with infor-

Fig. 15.10. *The Lunden dolmen chamber under excavation in 1974, seen from the east. The capstone had been pushed to one side sometime in the 19th century. Following the investigation, the capstone was replaced over the chamber.*

mation from the archives and undertook a large number of research investigations of, in particular, dolmens and passage graves, both demolished and scheduled. In 1985, he concluded his large-scale and far-reaching project with the publication *Yngre stenalder på øerne syd for Fyn*, most of which is taken up with information on and analyses of 579 megalithic tombs.

One of these 579 monuments, Lunden, which was investigated as part of the project, is of particular interest with respect to the question of dolmens with or without a mound. We can let Jørgen Skaarup himself describe:

"In the small coastal woodland of Lunden, near the southern tip of Langeland, a newly-found dolmen chamber was investigated in 1974 (fig. 15.10). The chamber stands in the middle of a low, shield-formed *elevation* with a diameter of about 9 m. This elevation is built of 0.1-0.8 m diameter field stones, which do not form a particular compact layer, and which, next to the chamber in a 50 cm wide zone, are accompanied by large quantities of flint rubble – possibly a technical feature intended to stabilise the packing immediately up against the orthostats (fig. 15.11). Apart from this function, the elevation appears only to have been built to level the terrain, which slopes W, in advance of construction of the chamber and thereby give the latter a more monumental setting. With the aid of several trial trenches around the elevation, and a section through it, it was securely established that there had never been kerbstones around the elevation.

The chamber is small and intact, apart from the capstone which, sometime in the 19th century, was toppled towards N. This has now been put back in place. The rectan-

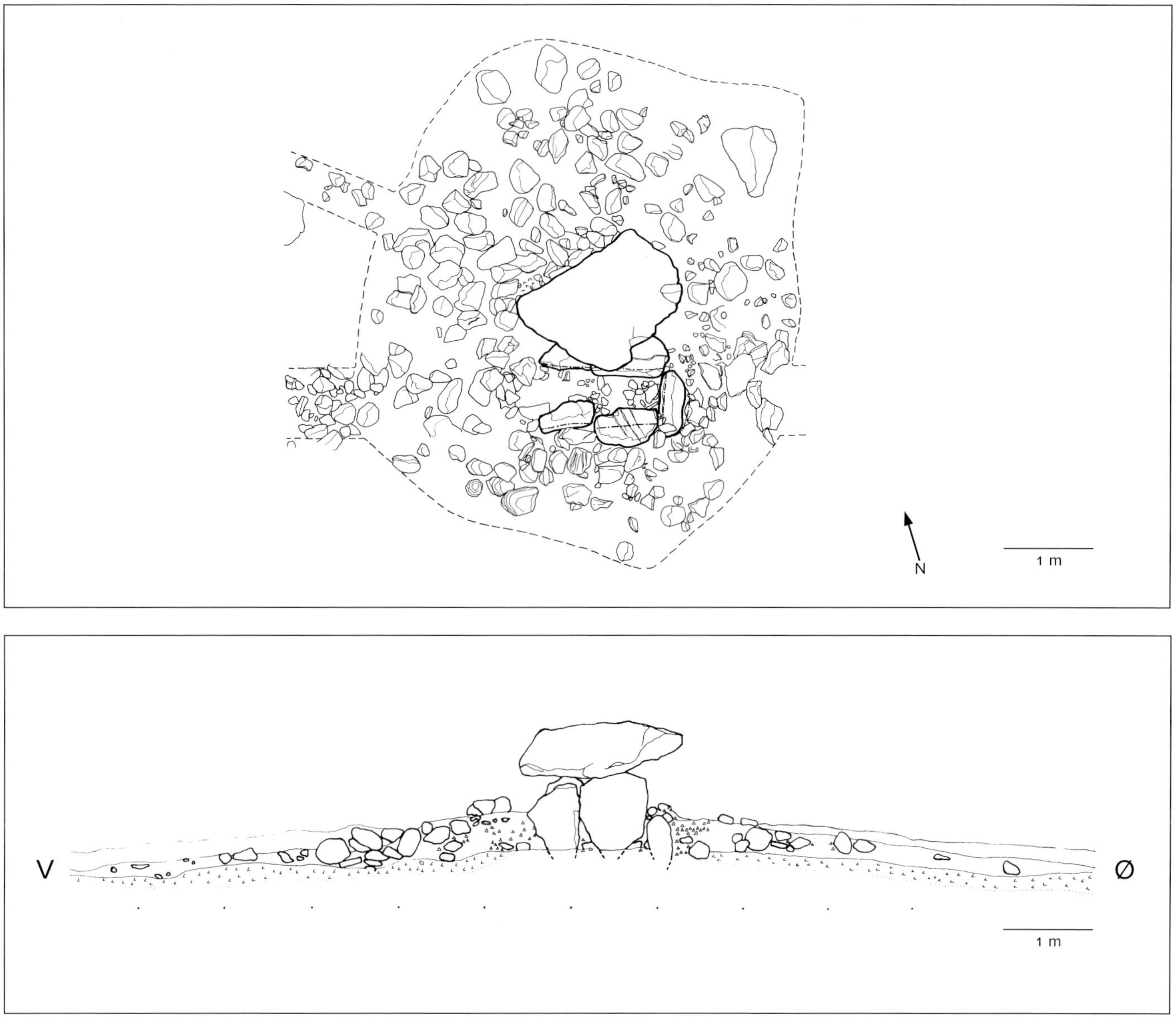

Fig. 15.11. *Plan and section of the Lunden dolmen after the capstone had been put back in position.*

gular, c. E-W-oriented chamber is comprised of 4 orthostats, 2 at each long side, and a low gable stone to the E. The tops of the orthostats lean distinctly inwards. The base of the grave, which lies 0.85 m below the tops of the orthostats, measures 1.4 x 0.7 m.

The chamber's entrance to the W was closed by a substantial flint and stone packing, which extended up to 1 m from the west end of the chamber and was c. 1 m wide and 0.6 m high."[12]

So much for Jørgen Skaarup's description, which concludes with an account of the extremely sparse finds from the lowermost layer – the burial layer – in the dolmen chamber, where there lay only a few rim and side sherds from vessels of the early Middle Neolithic Funnel Beaker culture. Outside the chamber, the only find was a flint blade discovered between the stones in the packing slightly south of the chamber.

Free-standing dolmen chambers

The above account of three investigations of randomly selected dolmen chambers – the two later dolmen chambers Trollasten of type IV and Ormslev of type III, and the typologically earlier dolmen chamber Lunden of type II – shows that some dolmens, both in the Neolithic and later, had stood as free-standing chambers without a mound and without kerbstones. At the same time, it is apparent from the investigations that these monuments are not restricted to the actual chambers, but that stone pavements were laid out and depositions were made outside the chambers. The previously mentioned dolmens of Stenhus (see chapter 14) and Tårup in its first phase (see chapter 6) have many features in common with these completely free-standing dolmen chambers.

Fig. 15.12. *Many scheduled dolmen chambers – like this example at Kongstrup on Røsnæs, northwest of Kalundborg – stand in cultivated fields. Ploughing close to these monuments destroys stone pavements and other structures next to the chambers.*

It is very worrying to think of how many scheduled, solitary dolmen chambers there are in Denmark. Around these chambers, only a 2 m wide zone is protected and must be kept free of cultivation. But this narrow zone is far from adequate, because the structures and activity areas clearly extend much further out than this. If scheduled dolmen chambers are not given a special, larger protected zone, they will become, as many already have, mere torsos, amputated and trimmed by modern, deep-draught ploughs (figs. 15.12 and 22.1).

16. The passage dolmen at Tustrup

Just less than half a kilometre west of the village of Tustrup in northern Djursland, on a plateau out towards the Hevring Å river valley, stands a cluster of megaliths: a passage grave, two dolmens and a cult house. While the three megalithic tombs were scheduled as early as 1887, and have therefore long been visible and known, the overgrown ruin of the collapsed and burnt-down cult house was first discovered in 1953.

It was investigated in the following year by Poul Kjærum of the Prehistoric Museum, now Moesgaard Museum, in Aarhus. It was found to be a completely new and, at that time, unique and sensational type of structure, which was coeval with, and had functioned in conjunction with, the dolmens and the passage grave. In order to clarify this remarkable relationship, investigations of the passage grave and the dolmens were undertaken in 1954-57 and in 1961. On conclusion of these excavations, all the structures, including the site of the cult house, were restored. Since then, this scenic area with its fascinating group of monuments has been an attractive destination, helped along by scheduling of the area in 1956 (fig. 16.1).

Since the investigations in the 1950s, Tustrup has enjoyed great renown in the archaeological world, and it is difficult to imagine a book or a TV programme on European megaliths or the Funnel Beaker culture without some mention of the site. This is due, first and foremost, to the cult house, whereas the passage grave, actually one of the largest in Jutland and with a subsidiary chamber, and the two dolmens, which – as we will see later – are also remarkable, have not received anywhere near the same degree of attention.

Immediately following the investigations, Poul Kjærum published a couple of articles on the preliminary results of the Tustrup project.[1] These contain only scant reference to the two dolmens. In subsequent years, when time permitted between expeditions to the Arabian Peninsula, lecturing at the university, relocation of the museum from Aarhus to Moesgaard, duties at the museum etc., he worked on various analyses and the production of a manuscript for the academic publication of the investigations at Tustrup.

In 2008, in connection with our project on dolmens with or without a mound, Poul Kjærum gave permission for us to have access to and write about the results of his investigations of the two dolmens at Tustrup. These monuments, referred to as the *passage dolmen* and the *round dolmen*, are actually crucial to the question of dolmens with and without mounds. Already during the investigations in the 1950s, they were recognised by Poul Kjærum as originally being quite free-standing and mound-less

Fig. 16.1. *The Tustrup site, seen from the air on 13th July 2011. The four megalithic monuments stand close together. Lowermost to the right stands the round dolmen, followed clockwise by the passage grave, the passage dolmen and the cult house.*

at the time of their construction and use in the Neolithic; a realisation he develops and clearly expresses in his reports and analyses of the excavation findings relating to the two dolmens. The following brief account of the investigation of the two dolmens and the interpretation of the excavation findings is based primarily on Poul Kjærum's preliminary manuscript on Tustrup.[2] It is limited to circumstances that are significant to an understanding of the original appearance of these monuments.

The passage dolmen

Passage dolmen is a term used time and again by Poul Kjærum in reference to the northernmost of the two Tustrup dolmens (fig. 16.2). As the name suggests, this monument has a passage leading to its chamber, but it could not be seen before the excavation began that the chamber had also stood within a round dolmen. The other dolmen, located further south, is also a round dolmen, but its chamber has no passage.

Chamber and passage

The free-standing, solitary chamber is hexagonal in shape, when the entrance to the chamber is included, and was originally constructed of six orthostats of which one is now missing (fig. 16.3). The length and width of the chamber at the original floor level is, respectively, 2.9 and 2.6 m. The missing capstone must therefore have been extremely large as it very probably covered the entire chamber. In early descriptions prior to 1900, a solitary stone of the correct dimensions is mentioned in the vicinity.[3] The orthostats, which lean slightly inwards towards the chamber, are impressive, as the distance from floor level to the top of the tallest orthostat is 1.9 m. The stones are though actually taller than this, up to 2.5 m, as they are set in a 40-50 cm excavated ditch, solidly packed with stones and burnt, crushed flint. In order for the tops of the orthostats to be on the same level, they stand at varying depths in the ditch: The largest stone is set at a depth of 70 cm, while the shortest, a 1.7 m long stone, is not sunk into the ground at all. This "short" orthostat (B6) had also become dislodged and slipped slightly into the chamber. The gaps between the orthostats have been sealed with dry-walling. The floor, which was greatly disrupted, consisted of flat stones laid directly on the sandy subsoil, so the topsoil must have been removed in advance of construction by the dolmen builders.

The 1 m wide passage was constructed with one stone at each side, and the floor was cobbled with ordinary field stones and delimited by two threshold stones; one at the outer limit of the passage and the other at the transition to the chamber. In rela-

Fig. 16.2. *The Tustrup passage dolmen as it appears today, seen from the south-west. The missing orthostat is marked by a piece of timber.*

Fig. 16.3. *Plan of the excavated area around the Tustrup passage dolmen. In the eastern quadrant, the small kerbstones that encircled the inner stone pavement are marked in red. Outside these, the large, exposed standing stones are marked in blue. The excavator believed that both the circles of kerbstones and of standing stones continued all the way round the chamber. Orthostat B1 had been removed at some time prior to the excavation. Directly outside the stone pavement were a couple of stone-filled pits, shown here in brown. The stone pavement is shown in grey.*

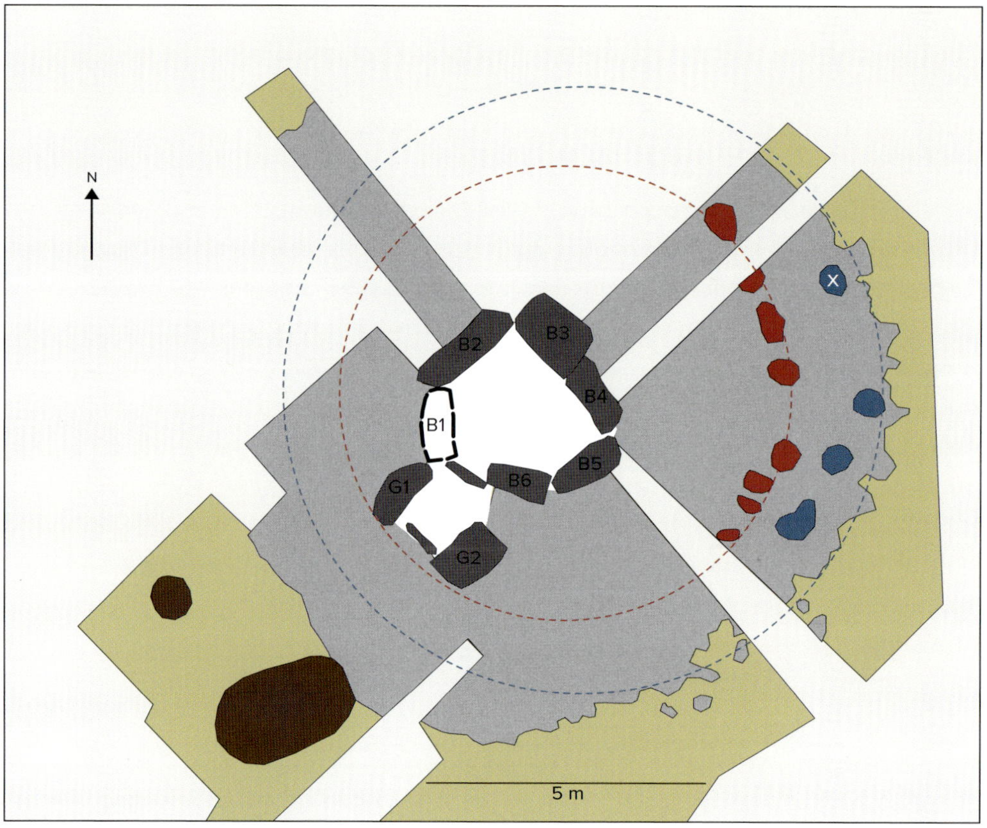

tion to the tops of the passage stones, the height of the passage was 1.17 m outermost, decreasing evenly inwards to 1.24 m at the inner threshold stone, so the floor was then on level with that in the chamber.

Unlike other dolmens with significantly lower passage stones, it would have been possible to enter the chamber in the passage dolmen, given the passage was fitted with a capstone. But as there was no mound over the chamber and passage – see below – this capstone would have had no function. Just as with the other free-stranding polygonal dolmen chambers, such as Trollasten, Poskær Stenhus and Stenhus at Strands, the passage stones constituted more of a marker for the opening and an entrance to the chamber.

The capstone and the missing orthostat must have been removed from the chamber a long time ago, because the two stones were already absent when the earliest description of the passage dolmen was recorded in 1887. Otherwise, the chamber is undamaged, with the exception of the orthostat directly opposite the entrance; this has been split transversely by a carved, horizontal furrow. The split-off top is wedged fast between the lower part of the stone and the two neighbouring orthostats, and for some reason the stonemason did not continue his work. The actual technique employed – cleavage with the aid of a long, carved furrow – suggests that this operation was undertaken in the 16th or 17th century.[4]

Appearance prior to excavation

At the beginning of the investigation in 1955, the dolmen chamber stood freely exposed, only surrounded by a low elevation, overgrown with grass and heather. The orthostats protruded 1.1-1.3 m above the immediately adjacent surface outside the stones. The elevation – or mound, you could say – had a diameter of c. 14 m and a maximum height of only 20-30 cm above the surrounding, level terrain. The surface of the elevation bore no traces of secondary digging in recent times. The inside of the chamber was free of soil, apart from a 20 cm layer of fill over the damaged floor.

The investigation

About three-quarters of the area directly around the chamber and extending 6-8 m out from it was investigated, corresponding to a substantial area in front of and on each side of the passage as well as the eastern quadrant behind the chamber (see fig. 16.3). The northern quadrant was not investigated. Three sections secured a record of the composition of the elevation. These were laid out in an approximate T-shape.

Directly beneath the upper turf layer was a 10 cm thick layer of shifting sand, followed by a layer of crushed stones within an earlier vegetation horizon, and then again shifting sand covering a stone pavement. The latter, which had a circular outline, was about 12 m across and consisted of stones up to 35 cm in diameter (fig. 16.4). This stone layer, which constitutes the "mound fill" in the dolmen, had generally a thickness of only 30-40 cm, so the largest stones effectively constitute a single course. The stones were placed on the surface of the subsoil or on dug-up fill from

Fig. 16.4. *The stone pavement in front of the passage dolmen at Tustrup.*

Fig. 16.5. *In the eastern quadrant at the Tustrup passage dolmen, the largest stone in the foreground is the lower part of a broken standing stone, marked with an X on the plan shown in figure 16.3. Behind this is the stone-free zone before the stone pavement; the three large stones at the edge of the latter are kerbstones.*

the sockets for the orthostats. The Neolithic topsoil had been removed by the dolmen builders, both in and around the chamber, but was partially preserved beneath the fill thrown up from the sockets.

Two important elements were discovered in the eastern quadrant: the boundary of the outer stone pavement and, 1-1.15 m outside this, a circle of standing stones (fig. 16.5). Poul Kjærum interpreted this situation in terms of the inner stone pavement's outer, rounded edge being surrounded by "mini-kerbstones", most of which were larger (or taller) than the stones of the stone pavement. Seven of these "kerbstones" were preserved in the eastern quadrant, and there was a further example in the 1 m wide excavation trench to the northwest of it.

The standing stones had, on the other hand, been less fortunate. In the eastern quadrant there were traces of three stones that had been removed, as well as a stone – marked with an X on figure 16.3 – which had been broken into pieces but of which the lowermost part was preserved (see also fig. 16.5). Sections through the stone sockets and by the broken stone showed that the stones had stood in 60-70 cm diameter pits, with a depth of 25-40 cm. On the basis of this, Poul Kjærum believed that the stones had been of considerable size, up to 2 m high, corresponding to the kerbstones of the round dolmen located just less than 100 m away.

The stone-encircled stone pavement and the circle of standing stones could, according to Poul Kjærum, have continued all the way around the chamber, but due to the poor conditions for preservation, later structures added in front of the passage and – again according to Poul Kjærum – the excavators' lack of attention during an early stage of the investigation, these were not recorded. The row of large edging stones – "the mini-kerbstones" – around the inner stone pavement was, however, probably turned inwards toward the entrance, as opposite each passage stone there were larger stones that could have been associated with these.

The 1-1.15 m wide zone between the standing stones and the inner stone pavement was, according to Poul Kjærum, originally free of stones. The fact that, on excavation, it was found to be covered with stones was attributed to erosion and slippage from the stone pavement described above.

Between the two layers of shifting sand, the lowermost of which covered the stone pavement, there was a vegetation horizon containing granite debris and rubble (fig. 16.6). This layer was seen by Poul Kjærum as being connected with the destruction and breaking up of the standing stones; an activity that may well have taken place in the Middle Ages, when there was a huge demand for stone for the construction of churches.

Apart from a piece of a polished stone axe, the finds comprised exclusively potsherds and fragments of pottery ladles. Poul Kjærum has identified almost 30 individual vessels as well as two ceramic ladles. There were no intact vessels or ladles, and on the whole the material was greatly fragmented, with very few sherds

Fig. 16.6. *In the section running up to orthostat B5 of the Tustrup passage dolmen – which can just be seen to the left – two very different stone layers are evident. Lowermost, and directly over the surface of the subsoil, lies an up to 30 cm thick layer of ordinary stones, while uppermost is a thin layer of granite debris and rubble.*

from each pottery vessel. Sherds from the same vessel were sometimes widely scattered. The vessels comprise footed bowls, funnel beakers, shouldered bowls and coarse storage jars.

Only very few sherds were found in the chamber and passage, both of which must have been dug through long before the investigation. The majority of the sherds were found up against the east side – the rear side – of the eastern passage stone and extending outwards from here, in the southern quadrant, to the edge of the stone pavement. There were also concentrations of pottery in a smaller area in front of the passage and to the rear of the second passage stone. The pottery is dated by Poul Kjærum to the Klintebakken phase, MN Ib, which he believed also gave the construction date for the dolmen.

The appearance of the passage dolmen through time

Poul Kjærum concluded that: "The hexagonal dolmen chamber has therefore, according to the available observations, been surrounded by a low, apparently almost level heap of stones [the inner stone pavement], delimited by an 8-9 m diameter stone circle that can almost be considered as a supporting wall. As a further enclosure, a free-standing stone circle [the circle of standing stones] with a diameter of c. 11 m surrounded the overall monument. The stones in this latter circle were of unknown dimensions, but the size of their sockets permits the conclusion that they are unlikely to have been shorter than the c. 2 m high kerbstones in the round dolmen at the same locality. The chamber cannot have been mound covered, as the area between the inner and outer circle of stones was free of soil at the time the structure began to degrade and the stones of the outer circle slipped outwards. This conclusion is further supported by the finds circumstances for the pottery, as the sherds within the inner stone circle were found on top of the stone heap, whereas outside this, they lay directly on the subsoil, covered by stones."[5]

To a very great extent, we agree with Poul Kjærum's conclusions, but in the following we will comment upon and supplement these with some interpretations and observations of our own, relative to a few specific aspects.

It is possible that the area between the two stone circles was originally free of stones. However, due to the almost level surface on which the dolmen was built, it is unlikely that this subsequently became covered with stones that had slipped outwards from the very low stone pavement. The stones in the area between the two stone circles were more probably placed there by the dolmen builders in connection with various rituals.

The outer circle of standing stones has several parallels in stone rows evident at and around long dolmens.[6] Conversely, there is apparently only one other example in Denmark of a round dolmen containing a dolmen chamber or a passage grave, where there is a circle of standing stones outside the kerbstones.[7] If we look abroad, the best known example is the mighty Irish passage grave mound of Newgrange. This is surrounded by a circle of standing stones that were erected during the Beaker period, corresponding to the Late Neolithic in Denmark.[8] We tend most towards the view that the circle of standing stones around the Tustrup passage dolmen was erected long after the construction of the dolmen, possibly in the Late Neolithic.[9]

It is therefore possible that the passage dolmen has several construction phases: chamber – stone pavement – standing stones. But could there be further phases? This seems possible. The stone pavement around the chamber had lain exposed, but gradually became overgrown and covered by shifting sand. The mound – and the monument – changed appearance due to natural forces, and following a sandstorm it could have appeared as a whitish-grey elevation around the mighty dolmen chamber. This fascinating, almost virginal, sight attracted the descendants of the dolmen builders and, perhaps several centuries later, they carefully covered this new surface with a layer of granite rubble. This activity corresponds fully to the stone layer found in the shifting sand at the nearby round dolmen, which is presented in the next chapter.

17. The round dolmen at Tustrup

As part of Poul Kjærum's investigations at Tustrup in the 1950s – see chapter 16 – the round dolmen was excavated in 1956. In 1957, the investigation was described in brief in a presentation of the preliminary results,[1] though not in sufficient detail to have a major influence on the restoration work carried out in 1994, which is discussed at the end of this chapter. A more comprehensive publication, based on new analyses of Poul Kjærum's investigations, is in preparation. Only some of the most important excavation results, as interpreted and described by Poul Kjærum in his report, will be presented here.[2]

Appearance before excavation

Prior to the excavation in 1956, the surface of the round dolmen was covered with grass (see photo on opposing page). At some stage, though long before the dolmen was scheduled in 1887, a couple of kerbstones were removed and the capstone was split. A large piece of the capstone lay on the ground beside the chamber and a small piece actually inside it. Further to this were a couple of other relatively minor incidences of damage. There must originally have been 15 kerbstones but, as stated above, two had been removed, eight had more or less toppled over and only the remaining five stood as they had been placed in the Neolithic. It is remarkable that these stand side by side in the northern part, with a single toppled kerbstone between them. The question is whether the toppled stones in the southern part, where there are also two missing stones, are a consequence of human activities?

Both the chamber's orthostats and the kerbstones protruded prominently, i.e. about 1 m, above the inner surface of the round dolmen, between the chamber and the kerbstones. In the untouched northern part, the surface was level, but in the disturbed southern part it sloped slightly downwards, and beyond the kerbstones there was also an even downward slope.

The investigation

The round dolmen was built on almost level ground. The Neolithic topsoil was preserved below the monument, having been only dug away in the area of the chamber and the kerbstones. The large stones were primarily placed on the surface of the subsoil, directly beneath the stripped topsoil.

The chamber stands in the middle of the monument, which has a diameter of 8.5 m and is relatively small for a round dolmen. Stones of impressive size, around 2 m in

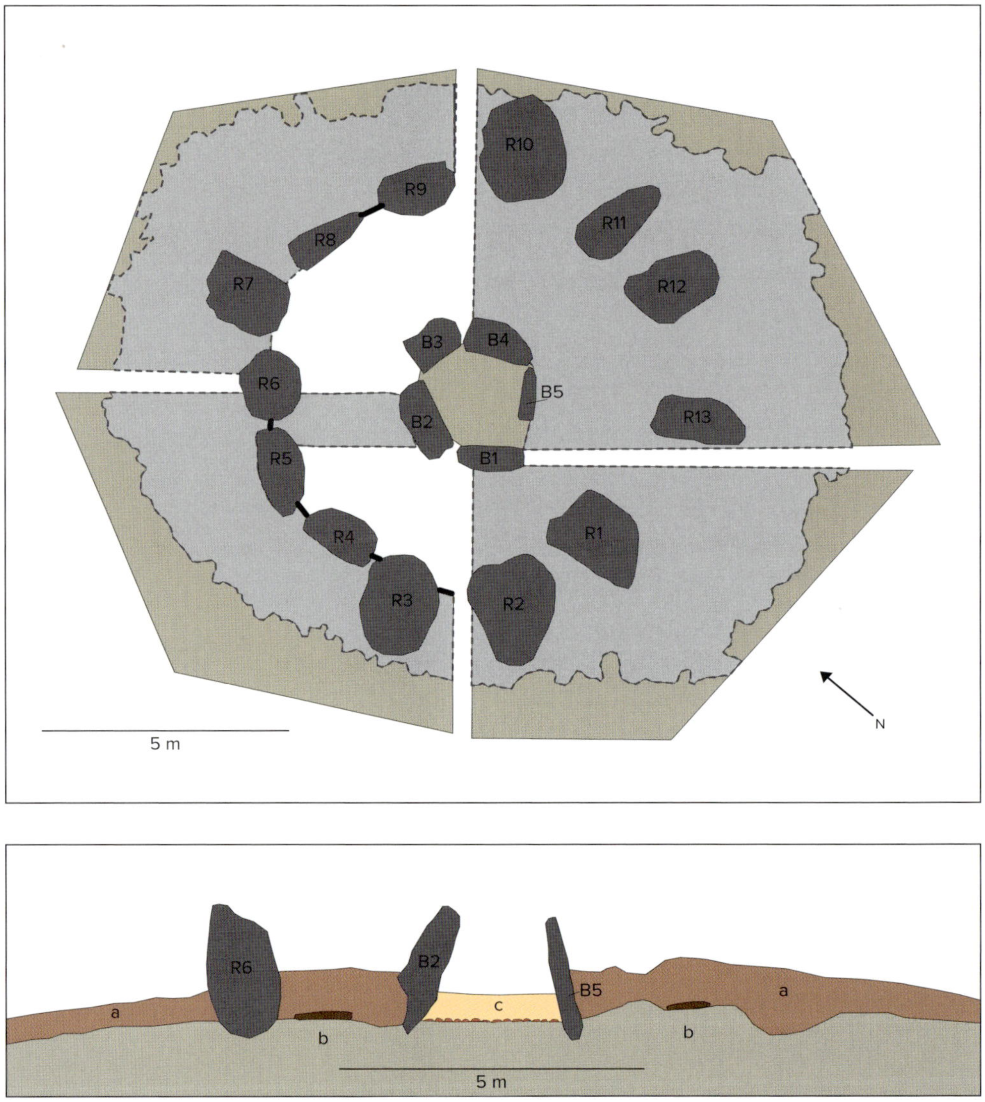

Fig. 17.1. *Simplified plan and section from the investigation of the round dolmen at Tustrup. All the kerbstones with the exception of five – R 4-6 and R 8-9 – have fallen over. Beneath the grass turf, the surface of the dolmen was covered with stones. The extent of this stone pavement is shown in grey. On the section below, the fill, including the modern topsoil, is labelled a, while b denotes the topsoil on which the dolmen was built.*

height, have though been used for both the chamber's orthostats and its kerbstones. The pentagonal chamber is built of five orthostats and has an opening towards the south. There are no passage stones or indications of entrance markers. The floor of the chamber consisted of flat stones placed directly on the surface of the subsoil. The floor surface measures 2.2 x 2.2 m and the chamber has a height of 1.8 m, so both are of a good size.

The round dolmen, and the stone covering around it, which extends 3.5 m beyond the kerbstones, was investigated by laying out four quadrants with intervening baulk sections (fig. 17.1). In the interests of further investigations in the future, most of the western quadrant and all of the northern quadrant were not investigated in the area between the chamber and the kerbstones.

A stone pavement turned up directly beneath the surface turf. This consisted of fist-sized stones, mostly in a single layer extending from the chamber and out beyond the kerbstones (fig. 17.2). The stones in this *upper* stone pavement lay on or in fine sand, interpreted as shifting sand, which in the form of a more or less thin layer overlay a second stone pavement (fig. 17.3). The *lower* stone pavement consisted of stones that were larger and coarser than the stones of the upper layer, and in the area between the kerbstones and the chamber there was also crushed, burnt flint and gravel between the stones. The lower stone pavement apparently extends out beyond the kerbstones. Poul Kjærum believed, however, that it had originally been limited to the area within the kerbstones and that the stones outside had in some way slipped or rolled out from the inner area.

This very simple stratigraphy, with a total maximum thickness of 75 cm, was demonstrated and recorded in all the sections. Only two of these sections will be shown here; one from the inner area, the other from the area outside the kerbstones (figs. 17.4 and 17.5). In both sections, the upper stone pavement of smaller stones can be seen directly beneath the grass-clad surface. This layer is just visible in the outer section, and other sections and observations confirm that it also extends over fallen kerbstones.

The shifting sand layer, in and on which the stones of the upper pavement lie, is very thin in the inner area but has a very considerable thickness in some places outside the kerbstones (see fig. 17.5).

The lower stone pavement consists, as already mentioned, of larger stones mixed with flint and forms a more compact layer than the upper stone pavement. Outside the kerbstones it is different, less dense, and the excavator was of the opinion that it was of a completely dissimilar character.

Fig. 17.2. *The exposed upper stone pavement in the Tustrup round dolmen.*

Fig. 17.3. *The lower stone pavement in the Tustrup round dolmen consisted of slightly larger stones than those evident in the upper stone pavement.*

In the 15-40 cm gaps between the kerbstones, the lowermost part of the dry-walling was preserved in situ, and outside the gaps were quantities of collapsed dry-walling slabs. The number of slabs by each gap was so great that the excavator concluded that the dry-walling, when intact, had almost reached the tops of the kerbstones.

The chamber had been dug through long before the investigation, so no finds of pottery or other artefacts were encountered. Potsherds were, however, discovered by and outside the kerbstones to the south. Poul Kjærum has identified sherds from 26 different pottery vessels and three pottery ladles. With the exception of one vessel and one ladle, all of these were ornamented, and where the ornamentation can be identified, according to Poul Kjærum it is executed in Klintebakke style, corresponding to period MN Ib. Two flint blades and the butt of a battle axe of Fredsgård type were also recovered.

The numerous sherds of Neolithic pottery lay in the sand directly beneath the lower stone layer, and were also found deeper in the sand. The pottery finds on and in the sand outside the kerbstones show that this surface represents the ground surface directly following completion of the dolmen. This is further confirmed by the fact that the lowermost of the collapsed dry-walling slabs also ended up here.

Fig. 17.4. *The different character of the two stone layers is clearly evident from the section running up to orthostat B 1 in the Tustrup round dolmen. Uppermost is the upper layer of smaller stones, which is separated from the lower stone layer by a layer of shifting sand. The lower layer increases in thickness in towards the orthostats in order to provide support.*

Fig. 17.5. *The layer of shifting sand between the two stone layers was thicker outside the kerbstones of the Tustrup round dolmen. The stone layers each represent a period in the dolmen's history and appearance. To the right is kerbstone R 13.*

The appearance of the round dolmen through time

Based on the excavation findings, Poul Kjærum wrote about the original height and appearance of the mound surface: "From this stratigraphic sequence it is apparent that only the large field stones at the base can belong to the original dolmen structure, while the upper layer of small stones must have been added later, after the dolmen had begun to degrade and seemingly after the kerbstones had fallen over, as these small stones were not found beneath the kerbstones that were found lying on the surface. A calculation of the volume of the original materials, i.e. the stones in the lower stone layer outside the kerbstones, leads to the conclusion that the degree of cover of the chamber was more or less the same as at the beginning of the excavation, because the layer of small stones and the overlying sand layer must be excluded. As shown by the sections, there was no significant secondary sand layer outside the kerbstones, therefore the situation clearly appears to be that the chamber was not covered by a mound of earth or stones, but simply surrounded by a flat stone pavement, just like the passage dolmen."[3]

After first outlining the construction of the chamber and then the raising of the kerbstones, Poul Kjærum describes the original appearance of the kerbstones and the dry-walling as follows: "Finally, the gaps between the stones were closed with shaped stone slabs, so that the kerbstone circle around the chamber became a compact wall of the same height as the chamber. The tallest kerbstone, R 6, is 11 cm higher than the tallest orthostat, B3. It has not proved possible to establish whether this wall was also completely closed in front of the entrance to the chamber as two or more kerbstones had been removed from this particular area in recent times. It is possible that there has been access between stone R 13 and the missing stone R 14 or R 15, corresponding to the situation at passage dolmens and passage graves with large kerbstones or façade stones."[4]

These observations were published by Poul Kjærum in 1986, not – unfortunately – in an archaeological periodical, but in *Turistmagasinet*, where, in reference to the two dolmens at Tustrup, he writes "... the easternmost of them is still surrounded by its stone circle, consisting of boulders with a height close to 2 metres. This has originally stood as a solid wall, with all the gaps closed with shaped flat stone slabs, as a monumental enclosure of the tomb."[5]

So we now have a good idea of the original appearance of the dolmen, according to the excavator: The polygonal chamber with its capstone towered a good way above the inner, stone-clad surface. The kerbstones, together with the dry-walling, formed a round, walled enclosure, which encircled the round dolmen and also towered above its interior (fig. 17.6). Outside the kerbstones, the soil surface was bare sand and the stones found here had slipped or rolled out from the inner part of the dolmen. On the latter point, however, we disagree with the excavator. These stones, or at least a large number of them, could have been brought here as part of the cult activities. Deliberately placed stone pavements and "collars" are very common features of dolmens and passage graves.[6]

In prehistory, the dolmen decayed, stones fell over – or were toppled, dry-walling collapsed outwards, and a whitish-grey covering of shifting sand spread over the

Fig. 17.6. *Poul Kjærum's article in* Kuml *1957 contains a drawing of the possible appearance of the Tustrup round dolmen in the Neolithic. The kerbstones have been erected, the gaps between them filled out with dry-walling and a capstone has been placed over the chamber.*

monument. Later, activity resumed at the site, and the sandy surface became covered with a carefully laid carpet of smaller stones. In more recent times, the capstone was split and a couple of kerbstones were removed and a further two stones bear marks left by the stone masons, who fortunately abandoned their efforts. Grass and heather then spread over the round dolmen, which finally was scheduled.

Then came the archaeological excavations of the 1950s and "following the conclusion of the investigation, the excavated parts of the monument were again covered over. Within the kerbstones, the excavated area was back-filled with stones and sand up to the level evident in the northern part of the mound … which was not affected by the excavation. The leaning or completely toppled kerbstones were all – apart from [the split] kerbstone R 13 – righted." Finally, the missing kerbstones were "built up with a low wall of grass turves to achieve a natural, not too rigid appearance of the monument, following collapse of the turf and vegetation growth" (fig. 17.7.).[7]

An open dolmen

The Tustrup round dolmen is the only scheduled Danish round dolmen where the mound has been investigated in recent times.[8] This thoroughly documented excavation is extremely valuable relative to an understanding of the possible original appearance of a well-preserved dolmen, and how this developed over time.

Particularly significant in this respect is the upper stone pavement, which was laid out like a carpet over the surface of the dolmen and out past its kerbstones. This stone layer, which is very well preserved and uninterrupted, lies like a chronological lid over the dolmen. The fact that its outer limits are beyond the kerbstones and that, in some instances, it partly covers fallen kerbstones, shows that it was not part of the original mound construction, but was added on top of a layer of shifting sand, some time after construction of the original monument.

The chamber belongs to the group of polygonal dolmens, type IV, which together with the extended dolmens, type III, constitute the latest dolmen forms. Polygonal dolmens actually have their main distribution on Djursland and the adjacent part of northwestern Zealand, but are otherwise found all across Denmark.

Fig. 17.7. *After the excavation, the round dolmen at Tustrup was carefully restored by Poul Kjærum. A kerbstone was left lying as it had been split in two, and its two absent neighbours were not replaced with new stones.*

Only six of the 254 megalithic tombs with polygonal dolmen chambers have been dated – to the end of the early Neolithic – but it "is likely that [their] construction continues up into MN Ia".[9] To these six we can now add the Tustrup round dolmen, which has been dated by Poul Kjærum to MN Ib.

An apparently surprising feature of the Tustrup round dolmen is that it lacks a passage. The best known of the polygonal dolmens, Poskær Stenhus, which lies 30 km directly south of its smaller relative in Tustrup, does have a passage, but nationally just less than half – 122 out of 254 – of the polygonal dolmens lack this feature. This is a surprisingly large number, given the immediate conclusion that the absence of a passage is due to its later removal. At present there is no reliable information on this situation: "The existence of a type of polygonal dolmen without a passage cannot be demonstrated."[10] However, there were apparently no passage stones at the Tustrup dolmen and not the least indication was found during the excavation of any special marking of a passage.

Poul Kjærum's commendably meticulous restoration of the Tustrup round dolmen was, in an exemplary fashion, based on the facts uncovered during the excavation. This restoration is, however, no longer visible.

Chaos – seen from a modern perspective

In summer 1994, the round dolmen at Tustrup was again restored as part of a national campaign aimed at maintaining, restoring and communicating Denmark's megalithic tombs. The task at that time lay under the auspices of the Ministry for the Environment and was undertaken by two experienced megalith restorers, Torben Dehn and Svend Hansen.[11]

It was decided to reconstruct the round dolmen a second time in order to show the possible appearance of a dolmen in the Neolithic before decay and dilapidation had set in. In advance of the reconstruction of the round dolmen, Poul Kjærum was consulted and the plans and drawings from his excavation were studied.

The dry-walling was built up all the way to the tops of the kerbstones, using slabs of Nexø sandstone. Earth was then added to the newly-created space between the kerbstones and chamber so the interior of the monument was completely filled up, forming a level surface that extended from the tops of the kerbstones to the tops of the chamber's orthostats. Finally, a large stone was brought from a nearby field boundary and placed as a capstone over the chamber (see fig. 3.4). From a dolmen without a mound, the dolmen had become a dolmen with a mound.

This restoration has subsequently been criticised,[12] also by the present authors.[13] Our disagreement with the restoration team with regard to the original appearance of dolmens did, however, have a positive outcome, in the form of our joint involvement in the investigation of the Gunderslevholm dolmen (see chapter 11).

In a popular article, Svend Hansen explains the construction of the dry-walling as follows: "... this reconstruction has been carefully undertaken according to the excavation plans from the 1950s and consistent with the numerous remains of original dry-walling that are still preserved in the dolmen and which are present at the base of the reconstruction."[14] We cannot disagree with Svend Hansen on this point.

The disagreement relates to the mound fill. Judging from the excavation plans there was actually not much collapsed mound fill to be taken up and replaced on the surface of the mound. Figure 17.8 shows a section through the dolmen to the northwest. The section goes through the best-preserved – and very probably undisturbed – part of the round dolmen, from the chamber's orthostat B 2 out to kerbstone R 6, which stood there since the Neolithic, and then further out through the stone pavement outside the kerbstones. The inner surface between the chamber and the kerbstones lies 1.2 m below the tops of the orthostats and kerbstones. But the layer of "slippage" outside the kerbstones is only 50 cm thick, so when this is replaced on the inner surface – level 3 on figure 17.8 – there is still 90 cm of free space. Included in this is the fact that the modern turf/vegetation layer on both the inner and outer surfaces, 20 cm in total, must be subtracted. Consequently, prior to the "slippage", the inner surface was only 30 cm higher than level 2, the modern inner surface prior to reconstruction.

Furthermore, the way we and Poul Kjærum interpret this section, there is virtually no slippage. The fill in the space between the chamber and the kerbstones consists of two completely different kinds of material – deposits A and B shown on figure 17.8. The surface of both of these could potentially also have constituted a surface in prehistory, such that the inner surface of the dolmen, in its final appearance, was covered by a layer of smaller stones, as when the investigation began in the 1950s (fig. 17.8 level 2). The upper stone layer here probably corresponds to the upper stone layer evident in the other sections through the round dolmen (see figs. 17.4 and 17.5).

The fill constituting the "slippage" is of the same character as the upper fill layer A in the interior of the dolmen and the two layers were described as one by Poul

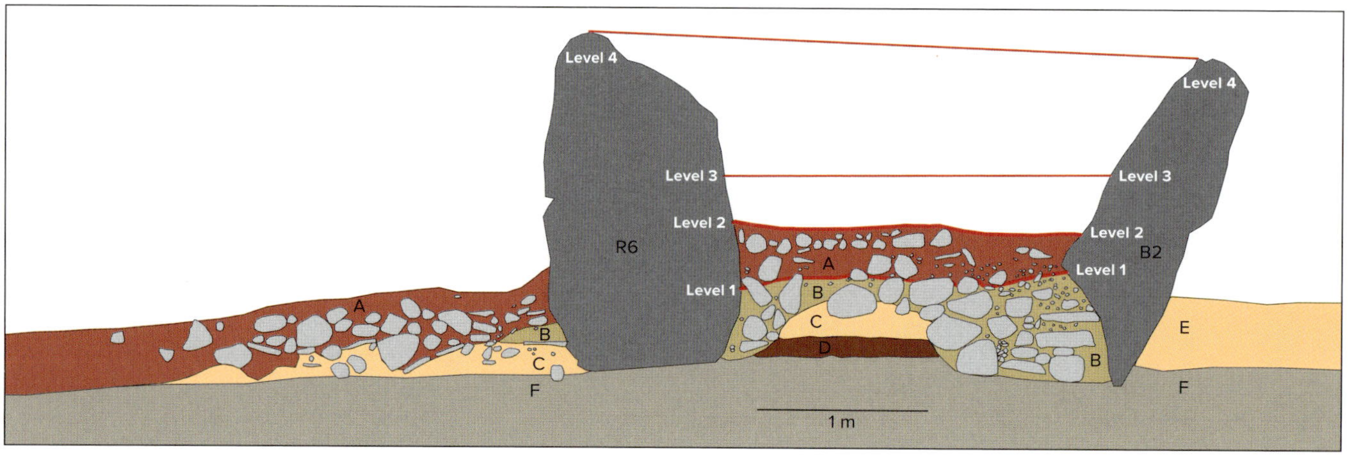

Fig. 17.8. *Section through the Tustrup round dolmen showing various possibilities with regard to the original height of the inner surface between kerbstone R 6 and orthostat B 2 in the chamber. – Levels: Level 1: Primary surface. Level 2: Secondary surface, stone pavement directly below the modern turf layer. Level 3: The surface when the "slippage", i.e. eroded fill from the inner surface (A), is added on, minus the thickness of the modern turf layer. Level 4: The surface when the space between the chamber and the kerbstones is completely filled up to the tops of the stones. – Stratigraphy: A: Between the stones grey sand, uppermost elevated humus/organic content. Almost black when wet, lighter grey when dry (shifting sand?). B: Between the stones brownish-yellow sand mixed with a good deal of gravel and large quantities of crushed flint. C: Yellow sand, thrown up from digging the sockets for the large stones. D: The Neolithic topsoil, i.e. old land surface. E: Fill outside the chamber. F: Sand, subsoil.*

Kjærum. Parts of this layer outside the kerbstones could have been added much later than the construction of the dolmen.

Furthermore, as mentioned previously, caution should be exercised in interpreting the quantities of stones in front of the kerbstones as slippage. These could have been intentionally placed here as part of cultic activities. Moreover, it is a myth that closely-packed stones, which lock into each other, can roll and move around on their own.[15]

In his article "Open dolmens – a matter of decay?", Torben Dehn has argued that the collapsed mound fill would, if put back in place, reach up to the tops of the kerbstones and orthostats.[16] We believe we have disproved this possibility above.

The dry-walling also constitutes an important aspect of the reconstruction of the Tustrup round dolmen as a mound-covered dolmen, from the point of view that it was built as robustly as possible because it was intended to stand for a long time. The latter is best achieved – as seen in the case of the kerbstone circles around the mounds of passage graves – by stabilising the dry-walling and its associated kerbstones with a rear packing of stones, clay, crushed flint and so on. In support of this argument, also with respect to the Tustrup round dolmen, reference can be made to a reconstruction drawing in an article written by Poul Kjærum in 1958 (see fig. 17.6).[17] This drawing was transformed into the present reconstruction, being used almost as a working plan. But if the artist had, instead, viewed the dolmen slightly from above, he would, according to Poul Kjærum's specifications, have drawn the upper part of the kerbstone circle as a free-standing *wall* or *enclosure*, rising above the internal surface (fig. 17.9).

As mentioned above, Poul Kjærum was aware that the dry-walling between the kerbstones could be free-standing without the support of fill behind it, but he did not publish this otherwise innovative observation. Things decay, and things disappear. The Neolithic people apparently did not attempt to either prevent decay or repair it. In some ways, they promoted these, in our view, chaotic circumstances. Today, we are very aware of intentional and frequent depositions of fragments of vessels, of

Fig. 17.9. *This is how the Tustrup round dolmen may have appeared in the Neolithic.*

deliberate destruction and burning down of cult houses, of pottery vessels smashed with stones in front of megalithic tombs, of the rapid decay and swift back-filling of the large system-ditches at causewayed enclosures, of ritual treatment of skulls and human bones at both megalithic tombs and causewayed enclosures. From this, a picture emerges of intentional fragmentation of bones and pottery vessels and a "laissez-faire" attitude to these monuments.

So why should the dry-walling not collapse quickly outwards? Two years after the restoration of the Tustrup round dolmen in 1994, one of the participants, Lars Holten, received a gold medal at the University of Copenhagen for his prize-winning paper with the thought-provoking title: "Religiøs praksis: kaos eller organiseret uorden? Dødekult i tragtbægerkultur belyst ud fra megalitgrave" (Religious practice: chaos or organised disarray? The death cult in the Funnel Beaker culture as illuminated by megalithic tombs). Decay, destruction and chaos are, to modern eyes, negative actions and events, but we have a very poor understanding of the original intentions of the dolmen builders.

18. Dolmens without mounds in Britain, France and Ireland

Chris Scarre

In 1865 a dramatic engraving of the megalithic monument of Pentre Ifan in south-west Wales appeared in the periodical *Archaeologia Cambrensis* (fig. 18.1).[1] It showed a couple on horseback resting under the massive capstone, profiled against the distant backdrop of hazy mountains. The artist had carefully emphasised the delicately propped nature of the stone, resting on the pointed tops of three tapering orthostats that barely seemed capable of supporting its weight.

Seven years later, a similar image was reproduced in *Rude Stone Monuments in All Countries*, written by the architect James Fergusson.[2] Fergusson's book provided one of the first general surveys of megalithic monuments, covering not only western and northern Europe, but also Asia and the Americas. One of his key objectives was to explain why early societies had chosen to build monuments of megalithic construction, using massive blocks of stone. In that context, his comments on Pentre Ifan were especially salient, and bear directly upon the question of chambers and mounds. For, he observed, "men do not raise such masses and poise them on their points for the sake of hiding them again ... The mode of architectural expression which these Stone men best understood was the power of mass. At Stonehenge, at Avebury, and everywhere, as here, they sought to give dignity and expression by using the largest blocks they could transport or raise – and they were right; for in spite of their rudeness, they impress us now; but had they buried them in mounds, they neither would have impressed us nor their contemporaries."[3]

These engravings of Pentre Ifan are typical of the large numbers of paintings and drawings of the late 18th and 19th centuries that portrayed Neolithic chambered tombs as megalithic skeletons, devoid of any covering of earth or stones. They include paintings by Romantic artists such as Johan Christian Dahl (*Hünengrab nahe Vordingborg im Winter* 1825) and the famous Caspar David Friedrich (for example *Hünengrab im Schnee* 1807 (see figs. 1.2-1.3) or *Spaziergang in der Abenddämmerung* c. 1835). The same Romantic tradition is represented in Britain by paintings of Stonehenge by William Turner (1825) and John Constable (1835). In all cases it is the power of the stones that takes centre-stage, set against a dramatic natural background of stormy sky or brooding twilight. This focus on the stones, however, masks an important issue. How many of these structures were ever intended to be visible in that

Fig. 18.1. *The portal dolmen of Pentre Ifan in southwest Wales. Engraving from 1865. The photo on page 216 is of the same dolmen.*

way? Stone circles such as Stonehenge were free-standing monuments, but were not the many chambered tombs – including Dahl and Friedrich's *hünegräber* – originally covered by mounds or cairns?

In Britain, it was the publication of the first English edition of Worsaae's *Primeval Antiquities of Denmark* in 1849 that appears to have sparked the debate. William Collings Lukis questioned Worsaae's contention that the Danish tombs consist of a "stone chamber ... perched upon the top of the mound", with the stones exposed. He noted by contrast that the British "cromlech" is "enclosed in a mound, and is either planted upon the level of the surrounding earth, or raised a little above it."[4] Lukis attributed the absence of a surviving mound (where that is the case) to processes of natural erosion: "the superincumbent earth will be carried by rain through the interstices of the cap stones and their supports, and in process of time fill up the chamber of the tumulus. The action of the elements will also tend, in course of ages, to carry the earth down the sides of the mound. This will account partly for two facts which are apparent to us now, viz. – the denudation and exposure of many cromlechs, and their being, in some cases, more or less filled with earth or silt."[5] Lukis concludes "that all cromlechs, of whatever form, were originally enclosed in mounds of earth or stone."[6]

The debate took a similar course in France. In one of the earliest descriptions of the prehistoric monuments of the Morbihan department of southern Brittany, the Abbé Mahé drew a distinction between "dolmens" (megalithic chambers) on the one hand, and "barrows" and "galgals" (earthen mounds and stone cairns) on the other.[7] That distinction was followed by subsequent writers, such as the Chevalier de Fréminville who distinguished the cairn-covered 'tombelle' of Mont Héleu (Er Grah) at Locmariaquer from the exposed "dolmen" of La Table de César (Table des Marchand).[8] It lived on in the Baron de Bonstetten's *Essai sur les dolmens* of 1865, one of the first general surveys of monuments of this kind. He divided "dolmens" into two principal categories: "dolmens apparents" (visible dolmens) and "dolmens couverts d'un tumulus en terre ou en cailloux' (dolmens covered by a mound of earth or stones). Bonstetten was at pains to defend his conclusion that "dolmens apparents" are not megalithic structures that have lost their mounds, and that no process can reasonably be envisaged that would have led to the removal of those mounds if originally they had existed.[9]

Yet not all French or francophone writers saw matters in these terms. In the 1850s Alfred Fouquet had argued that the exposed or free-standing "dolmens" of the Morbihan were in fact merely the denuded remnants of formerly covered monuments. Take the Gavrinis passage tomb and remove its covering cairn, he suggested, and one would be left with a "dolmen" like the Table des Marchands: "more complete and more decorated; but, within several centuries, the weather and human action will assuredly turn it into a simple dolmen."[10] By the 1870s, this had become the prevailing view. In *La France préhistorique d'après les sépultures et les monuments* (1889) Émile Cartailhac affirmed at the very outset that these monuments were originally "furnished with a covering of pebbles, stones or earth and buried beneath a mound of greater or lesser height." He contrasted this original design with the condition to which many megalithic chambered tombs had ultimately been reduced: "Over time the monument has become degraded and the covering has disappeared. The blocks have been exposed and the chamber, which has been emptied, is itself often ruinous."[11] He repeated this view a few years later in *Les* âges *préhistoriques de l'Espagne et du Portugal.* The Romantic image of the free-standing monument was deceptive: the megalithic structure deprived of its covering was a monument in ruins.[12]

Scandinavian prehistorians were unconvinced. Cartailhac drew criticism from no less an authority than Oscar Montelius, who like Bonstetten preferred to distinguish a category of free-standing dolmens (*freistehende Dolmen*) from buried or below-ground chambers with entrance passage or entered via a vertical shaft.[13] In Britain, by contrast, the arguments advanced by Lukis and others had, by the early years of the 20th century, won general acceptance. Thus in the last (seventh) edition of *Prehistoric Times* (1913), John Lubbock observed: "We may regard a perfect megalithic interment as having consisted of a stone chamber, communicating with the outside by a passage, covered with a mound of earth, surrounded and supported at the circumference by a circle of stones, and in some cases surmounted by a stone pillar or 'menhir'."[14] Allowance was made for occasional exceptions,[15] but the concept of the "normal" megalithic tomb encased within its mound was firmly established. It remained so through the middle decades of the century. Gordon Childe, in the last edition of the *Dawn of European Civilization*, puts the matter straightforwardly: "Built chamber tombs, when not erected in an artificial excavation, were probably always put underground artificially by burial in a mound or cairn."[16]

Within recent decades, however, such a standardised view of the "classic" chambered tomb has come increasingly to be questioned. The basis for this re-evaluation is twofold: first, a growing wariness of "normative" concepts within archaeology, accompanied by a new and greater emphasis on the uniqueness and diversity of individual monuments; and secondly, new excavations leading to a heightened awareness that Neolithic monuments are often multi-phase structures that reached their final form only through successive stages of addition and modification. Thus it is a combination of theory and field observation that has reopened the question of chambered tombs and their mounds.

Megaliths without mounds in western Britain

Let us begin by returning to Pentre Ifan, the megalithic chamber at the heart of the 19th century debates (see photo on page 216). Its visual impressiveness, with massive but delicately poised capstone, has been taken up again by recent writers seeking to connect the monument with its landscape.[17] In particular, the orientation and inclination of the capstone has been compared to the profile of Carn Ingli, a rocky mountain outlined on the skyline 3.5 km to the west. The argument is that the builders of megalithic monuments intentionally referenced natural landforms in their layout and design, creating conscious links between chambered tombs and important and powerful places in the landscapes. Thus the capstone of Pentre Ifan, like the summit of Carn Ingli, is oriented north-south and dips downwards towards the north. This resemblance leads to the conclusion that "important architectural features of the monument appear to duplicate the incline of the mountain outcrop."[18]

The visual link proposed between Pentre Ifan and Carn Ingli is largely dependent on the visibility of the capstone, and the absence of a covering mound. James Fergusson had remarked the complete absence of side-walls, and the remoteness of the location that made it unlikely that local farmers had removed the cairn to take material for buildings or field walls.[19] This was dismissed by one contemporary as "unqualified nonsense"[20] but it was not until the 1930s that unequivocal evidence for an enclosing cairn or platform was discovered. Excavations in 1936-37 revealed the outline of an elongated structure extending back over 30 metres from the chamber (fig. 18.2). The edges of this cairn had been marked out by smaller upright stones, represented mainly by their empty sockets, though these extended for only 17 metres along the eastern and western sides of the cairn and did not appear to enclose the whole of the structure.[21]

These discoveries established the original presence of a structure surrounding the Pentre Ifan chamber but fell short of determining its height and profile. In the 1970s the idea was revived that portal dolmens (such as Pentre Ifan) had been essentially free-standing.[22] The multi-phase nature of Neolithic monuments was gaining wider recognition, and it was also suggested that Pentre Ifan had initially been set within a low cairn, and that the tall orthostatic façade was a later addition, along with the lengthening of the cairn.[23] An alternative view considers the megalithic chamber and façade to be the primary elements, with the whole of the cairn a later addition, and argues that the latter was of relatively low height.[24] The idea that the cairn may have been merely a platform around the base of the chamber is seductive but hard to substantiate. Other reconstructions adhere to the concept of a more substantial structure, enclosing the chamber although not necessarily concealing the capstone.[25]

Despite the continuing uncertainty, recent interpretations have largely accepted the proposal that Pentre Ifan and similar sites were not masked by mounds. The massive capstones raised on conspicuously slender pillars have conjured the evocative image of "stones that float to the sky" and have led to the suggestion that the purpose of these structures was not to create a closed funerary chamber but to venerate and display the capstones themselves.[26] These capstones, at Pentre Ifan and at the neighbouring site of Carreg Samson, may have been earth-fast boulders dug from the very spot on which the chambers were later constructed.[27] Hence the massive capstones that are typical of portal dolmens may have been symbolically powerful in themselves, and the surviving structures might be more than merely the megalithic skeletons exposed by the removal or erosion of cairns. In this class of tomb, such cairns may never have existed.

It must be emphasised, however, that in this respect portal dolmens may have been exceptional among the Neolithic chambered tombs of western Britain. Most megalithic burial chambers of this region were covered by mounds or cairns, and some remain so to this day. The Cotswold-Severn long mounds of southwestern England and south Wales, for example, enclosed megalithic chambers. Excavations at Belas Knap in 1929-30 revealed that the stone-built cairn had had a covering of overlapping slabs laid like roof tiles, and a ridged configuration can be envisaged.[28] A central ridge was also observed at West Tump, Cow Common Long and Lamborough Banks and most if not all may have been finished with a roof-like structure with central ridge and sloping sides.[29] What should be remarked in all these cases, however, is that construction of the chambers preceded the building of the cairn, and the chambers must therefore, for a short period at least, have been free-standing. This is confirmed by the sequence of constructional phases at Hazleton North and Ascott-under-Wychwood.[30] There is nothing to preclude the possibility that the chambers at these sites were used for burial from the very outset. Thus interment in a free-standing megalithic chamber could have been much more common than we now believe, even though in most cases those chambers were subsequently covered by a mound or cairn.

The well-known passage grave of Bryn Celli Ddu on Anglesey has a particular place in this debate by virtue of the diversity of interpretations that have been placed on its constructional sequence. Excavations in 1925-29 revealed that the passage and chamber, together with its oval mound and orthostatic kerb, concealed a series of earlier structures.[31] The most significant of these was an annular ditch with an arc or circle of stones on its inner edge. At its centre, immediately behind the chamber, was a pit and lying flat beside that (though originally upright) a single decorated block known as the "pattern stone". The multi-phase character of the sequence at this site was demonstrated not only by the fact that the pattern stone and stone circle had been entirely hidden by the mound. It was also clear that the orthostatic kerb had

Fig. 18.2. *Pentre Ifan: Plan of the monument showing the cairn footings revealed in 1936-37.*

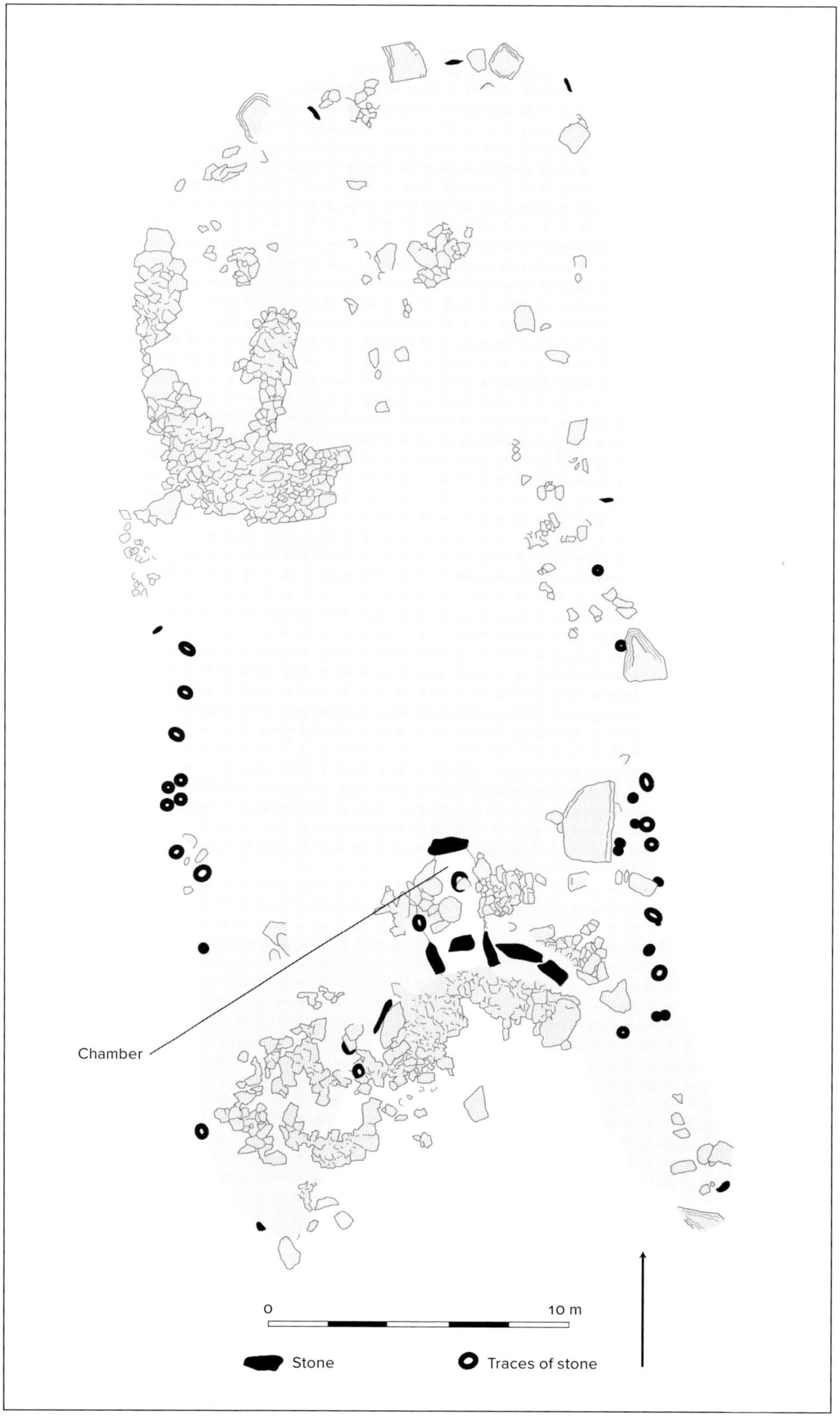

been built directly on the infill of the annular ditch. O'Kelly argued that a henge represented by the ditch and stone circle preceded the passage tomb.[32] Against this is the absence of a bank outside the ditch, and the likelihood that the digging of the ditch had furnished the material for the mound. Hence various alternative reconstructions propose a small initial mound enclosing the burial chamber, followed by enlargement to give an oval mound with orthostatic kerb overlapping the top of the earlier ditch.[33]

Documentary evidence confirms that the cairn, at least in its final form, enclosed the passage and chamber. This is shown by a schematic 1723 engraving that appears to show the mound intact, although from a later illustration it can be seen that by 1847 the mound was already badly degraded (fig. 18.3).[34] Some of the original mound material still survived on top of the capstone when excavations began in 1925,[35] though it was removed and later replaced by the modern replica mound that covers the chamber today. Recent proposals for a two-phase mound leave open the possibility, however, that the original smaller mound may only have lapped around the base of passage and chamber. Even the initial mound probably buried the "pattern stone", however, suggesting an initial mound-free stage. That may have been only of short duration. Cremated human remains were found in association with several of the stones in the stone circle and radiocarbon dates supported by Bayesian analysis indicate that these deposits predate by a short interval the deposits from the passage and chamber.[36] The overall impression is of a relatively rapid transformation from virgin site to stone structures (with human remains) and to mounded tomb. Passage and chamber may have appeared at a fairly early stage in this sequence. They may at first have remained visible, only partially enclosed by the small initial mound, even if some measure of support was essential from the outset to stabilise the shallowly bedded orthostats. Alternatively, the initial mound may from the outset have covered the chamber, with the expanded mound filling the remainder of the space within the orthostatic kerb later to form a lower platform.[37]

Bryn Celli Ddu provides an excellent example of the complexity underlying "finished" monuments. It also illustrates the difficulty of deciphering constructional sequences even where evidence from excavation is available. Above all, however, it draws attention to the changing appearance of the monument through time, and demonstrates that the addition or enlargement of the covering mound was often one of the final acts in a lengthy drama. In some cases, indeed, it may have been a mark of closure. We shall return to that concept below.

Free-standing megaliths in Ireland

Portal dolmens and passage graves are not restricted to western Britain but are also two of the principal types of megalithic tomb in Ireland (where they are known as "portal tombs" and "passage tombs" respectively). In Ireland, as in Britain, it has been argued that the builders of portal tombs intended the capstones to be visible. Of the 180 or so portal tombs in Ireland, 86 have traces of a cairn, and the greater scar-

Fig. 18.3. *The passage grave Bryn Celle Ddu stands on the island of Anglesey in North Wales. On this 19th century drawing, remains of the mound fill can be seen on top of the capstone.*

city of cairn remains in areas of fertile soil suggests that where they are missing their absence is due to human clearance.[38] In less intensively exploited regions such as the Burren, the outlines of kerbless cairns have been revealed by excavation and are visible today (fig. 18.4). In no case does the surviving remains of the cairn approach the height of the chamber, and they were most likely low bench-like structures, above which the capstone would always have been visible.[39] It is possible that the placing of the capstone required the construction of a full-height mound or ramp up which the massive slabs could be dragged; in which case the low bench-like cairn could be either the reduced remains of that structure, or an entirely separate construction.

Portal tombs seem generally to have been enclosed within a low cairn or platform. For wedge tombs, a late Neolithic monument type, the evidence suggests a less uniform arrangement. Wedge tombs consist of a slab-built chamber covered by one or more capstones, with an entrance at one end, and excavations at some sites have revealed the foundations of a substantial stone-built cairn edged by carefully laid blocks. At examples such as Baurnadomeeny in Co. Tipperary and Island in Co. Cork it is likely that an outer cairn covered and entirely enclosed the chamber save for the entrance.[40] At Island, however, it has been suggested that the outer cairn might be a Middle Bronze Age addition.[41] Furthermore, the majority of wedge tombs in south-west Ireland lack any trace of a covering mound, and while this absence is often explained in terms of natural erosion or deliberate "robbing", there is genuine doubt as to whether many of these sites were ever covered.[42] In some cases, the apparent cairns consist of modern field stones; in another case excavation showed the cairn to be unrelated to the chamber; while at Leenane the cairn may have been placed to provide structural support for the chamber orthostats.[43] Thus some wedge tombs may have been covered by cairns, but others – perhaps the majority – appear to have been free-standing with a low bench-like surround at most.

In contrast to portal tombs and wedge tombs, the two other principal types of Irish megalithic tomb – court tombs and passage tombs – are generally believed to have been originally covered by a mound or cairn. In some cases nothing survives. It has been observed, for example, that as many court tombs (some 50%) as portal tombs lack any trace of a cairn.[44] Excavated court tombs such as Ballyglass and Creevykeel make clear, however, that they had substantial kerb-defined cairns, and the relatively small chambers with their modestly proportioned capstones were probably originally covered. Thus while a denuded court tomb and a denuded portal tomb may bear some superficial resemblance to each other, they relate to structures that were initially very different in conception and design.

Irish passage tombs, too, appear generally to have been covered by a mound or cairn. This must be qualified, however, in two important respects.

First, there are exceptions, in particular the unusual passage tombs of the Carrowmore cemetery close to Sligo Bay in western Ireland. Most of this cluster of 25 surviving monuments (out of an original total of around 60) consist of a relatively simple megalithic chamber roofed by a single capstone, set within a boulder circle.[45] A

Fig. 18.4. *Irish portal tomb of Poulnabrone on the Burren, Ireland. Excavations in the 1980s revealed traces of a small oval kerb-less cairn, but it is unlikely that this would ever have covered the capstone.*

number of them are provided with a short entrance passage, but this does not reach as far as the encircling boulders and does not coincide with a break in the boulder circle (fig. 18.5). Excavations at several of the Carrowmore tombs in the 1970s revealed no traces of mounds or cairns within the boulder circles, and in the case of grave 27 the excavator concluded there can never have been a covering mound.[46] The chamber uprights had been supported by a packing of stones around their base but there was no evidence that this material had slipped or spread either within or beyond the limits of the boulder ring. The packing stones can have supported at most only a low platform. Earlier references to "cairns" at Carrowmore are either inaccurate, or relate to recent stone clearance from the fields surrounding the sites.[47]

Most Irish passage tombs do, however, appear to have had covering mounds or cairns, and the Carrowmore monuments are unusual in this respect. Yet as in western Britain, it is important to recall the chamber must inevitably have been constructed before the mound or cairn that covered it, and that for a period of time, all megalithic chambers must have been free-standing. In some cases, the mound or cairn may have been added immediately, without a break in the constructional sequence. In other instances, by contrast, the addition of the covering mound may have been an afterthought, and might have followed only after a period of several decades or centuries. This is the kind of sequence revealed at a number of Danish monuments. The evidence is not always easy to read. At Tårup in East Jutland, excavation was unable to provide definitive evidence that the megalithic chamber had initially been free-standing.[48] It can nonetheless be suggested that the original structure was only later covered by a turf mound before being enclosed in the Early Bronze Age in a much larger mound. A similar sequence may apply to Carrowmore tomb 51, which stands apart from the rest of the Carrowmore tombs, both in its position at the centre of the cemetery, and its morphology. It was the only Carrowmore tomb with remains of a cairn, but a significant interval may have elapsed between the completion of the tomb and the addition of the cairn.[49]

An even clearer demonstration of this phenomenon is provided by the tomb of Mound of the Hostages at Tara.[50] Here the passage grave is covered by a two-tier structure: an inner cairn of stones, and an outer mound of earth (fig. 18.6). The chamber remained accessible and continued to receive new inhumations into the Early Bronze Age, at which time individual burials were also inserted into the earthen mound. It is possible, indeed, that the earthen mound was added only at this period, which would provide direct analogy with the sequence documented at Danish sites such as Tårup (see p. 71). The "great mound" at Newgrange may have been added in the late 3rd or early 2nd millennium BC, enclosing and concealing the famous passage tomb and its decorated kerb.[51] It is the beginning of the sequence at Mound of the Hostages that is particularly interesting, however, since behind the orthostats, three small stone-slab cists were constructed. These contained cremated human remains that must have been deposited after the erection of the chamber but before the construction of the inner cairn. Radiocarbon dates and the presence of Carrowkeel bowls suggest that the deposits in the cists were contemporary with the initial burials within the chamber. This implies that the chamber at Mound of the Hostages was receiving human burials, as a free-standing structure, for an indeterminate but possibly extended period before the cairn was added. The potential parallels and contrasts with the sequence at Bryn Celli Ddu are particularly striking.

The decoupling of chamber and cairn suggested by the evidence of these British and Irish examples is more than a mere constructional detail: it goes to the very heart of what we consider a megalithic tomb to be. We shall return to that issue below, but first let us briefly review the evidence for cairns and mounds at Neolithic chambered tombs in northern France.

Cairns and mounds in northern France

Several of the early French antiquaries, as we saw above, drew a distinction between burial mounds on the one hand, and dolmens or megalithic chambers on the other, and considered the latter to have been free-standing structures. From the 1850s, however, it came generally to be recognised that the current condition of many mega-

Fig. 18.5. *Photo mosaic of excavations at Carrowmore tomb 27, Ireland.*

lithic tombs was the result of centuries of erosion and human interference. By the 20th century the concept of the free-standing megalithic chamber had been largely abandoned. Prehistorian Jean Arnal, for example, defined the "dolmen" as an "accessible burial chamber, generally megalithic, covered by a mound and intended to receive several inhumations."[52] He accepted that some may take issue with the presence of a mound in all cases, but he considered it impossible to envisage a weatherproof protective chamber for the dead without one.

In northwest France, many famous megalithic tombs have ample evidence for the existence or former existence of a covering mound. These are not mere dumps of earth and stone. It is now more than a century since Zacharie Le Rouzic noted the presence of concentric internal walls within the cairn covering the passage grave of Ile Longue,[53] and the internal structure of the Breton passage grave cairns achieved greater prominence following Pierre-Roland Giot's excavations at Barnenez in the 1950s. When Giot began work at Barnenez he was struck by the fact that the inner walls were visible high up the mound, standing to a greater height than the outer kerb of the monument. As he himself explains, "Such structural features had hitherto been considered part of the internal arrangements hidden within the cairns, evidence of phases and techniques of construction, and playing the role of retaining or supporting walls." It was this that led him to propose a stepped mound, and thus was the monument of Barnenez physically reconstructed at the end of his excavations. The published detail does not allow us to go further than this.[54] Reconstruction at several northern French passage graves has subsequently adopted the stepped concept to a greater or lesser degree, giving these monuments a very different appearance to that envisaged for most British and Irish sites.

Internally structured cairns are a recurrent feature of passage tombs in northern France but other types of monument tell a different or more ambiguous story. The Late Neolithic *allées couvertes* of the Seine-Somme region, for example, were megalithic chambers sunk into a trench, with little trace of a covering mound. At Méréaucourt, indeed, evidence indicates that the capstones were added only when the tomb was put out of use by being filled with sediment to the top of the orthostats. During the use-life of the tomb, the only covering may have been a lightweight structure of timber or thatch.[55] At the neighbouring site of La Chaussée-Tirancourt, the infilling of the chamber was followed not by the placement of capstones but (after an interval) by the systematic destruction by fire of the protruding upper parts of the orthostats. The orthostats fractured into thousands of fragments which were left littering the surface of the site.[56] The monument was essentially buried and forgotten.

The absence of mounds or cairns at Paris basin *allées couvertes* draws attention to the possibility that the *allées couvertes* of northwestern France may also have been free-standing. Excavations or other indications have however shown them to be systematically enclosed within the footings of a cairn.[57] In most cases, however, it remains difficult to determine whether this was a true covering cairn or merely a platform around the base of the structure. One exception to that uncertainty is provided by the *allée couverte* of Coat-Menez-Guen in southern Finistère, where the remains of the

Fig. 18.6. *The passage grave Mound of the Hostages at Tara, Ireland. Plan and section through the chamber.*

mound reach the level of the underside of the capstones,[58] but the curious morphology of this tomb raises other questions about its original appearance.

Recent investigations in the Channel Islands have shown that some of the megalithic tombs in the Guernsey archipelago lacked a covering mound. On the small island of Herm, the Robert's Cross tomb appears to be sunk within a mound, but excavation revealed this to be an accumulation of wind-blown sand of medieval origin. There was no trace of a mound or cairn, beyond a packing of granite blocks against the foot of the orthostats.

Probably the most impressive of all the megalithic tombs of northern France are the "dolmens angevins" of the Loire region. Here again, evidence for an enclosing structure has been found at some sites and conventional wisdom holds that these structures are the bases of cairns that originally covered the whole monument. At La Bajoulière near Saumur, a well-built kerb defined an oval inner cairn within a broader spread of material. The cairn material had been heavily robbed in Roman times, but in one place the pattern of the collapsed stones appeared to indicate that the kerb had stood to a height of at least 1.6 m.[59] It is hence not impossible that the cairn, despite the scanty surviving traces, did originally cover and enclose this large and impressive chamber, concealing it from view. That is somewhat surprising given the scale and appearance of the tomb, which one might assume was designed to impress the viewer (fig. 18.7). We must remember, however, that the chamber at La Bajoulière would have been built first, before the cairn was added. For a period of time it would have been exposed and visible, and there is nothing to preclude the possibility that (as at Mound of the Hostages) the chamber was receiving burials long before the cairn was built.

Cairns as closure

For most of the monuments discussed above, the presence of a cairn or mound did not in itself obstruct access to the funerary space. In other cases, however, the addition of the cairn was a definitive act of closure, preventing any further funerary deposition within the cist or chamber. The provision of a cairn or mound may not always have been part of the original design; and it may have marked the memorialisation of a previous burial space, not one that was still actively receiving new deposits.

A good, if spectacular, example is provided by the Tumulus de Saint-Michel at Carnac in southern Brittany. Its present form and dimensions are the product of successive actions or activities, the most obvious being the individual constructional phases: the cists and chambers on the original ground surface, the rubble core, the lake marl capping, the rubble outer layer and passage grave.[60] A gallery excavated between the centre of the mound and its eastern terminal at the beginning of the 20th century discovered four buried structures on the old ground surface: a circle of stone blocks and three cists. At the very centre, again resting on the original ground surface, were two megalithic chambers surrounded by a cluster of a further 21 small stone cists.[61] All of these structures were built and used before work on the cairn began. Once the cairn was in place, they were closed and inaccessible.

We find a similar sequence at the Tumulus du Moustoir, another of the massive "Carnac" mounds.[62] The earliest activity is represented by a stone-ringed hearth and a megalithic chamber. After a time, that chamber was sealed away within a conical mound, prohibiting access, and a second chamber was built alongside it in which funerary activity continued for a further period. That in turn was then sealed within the rubble core of a long mound, and another free-standing chamber (a large rectangular cist) was built just beyond its western end. Eventually, a capping of lake marl was laid over all of these structures, and an outer covering of rubble was added to enlarge the mound to its present height and length (fig. 18.8).

Thus the conventional image of the "chambered cairn" may be in many cases illusory. Chambers were not only built first, but may have functioned as free-standing structures, not waiting for the "completion" of a covering mound before burials were placed within them. In some instances, indeed, the mound or cairn may have marked the closure of the monument, and its transformation into a memorial. This was clearly the sequence at the non-chambered long mounds of southern and eastern Britain. These cover the remains of mortuary houses or other timber structures associated with burials. In most cases all that survives are post-holes, but waterlogging at Haddenham in the Cambridgeshire Fenland preserved a series of massive slabs of wood that invited comparison with the slabs of stone used in contemporary megalithic constructions.[63] At many of these long mound sites the timber structures had been intentionally destroyed by burning. The long mounds that mark their locations were hence not containers for the timber mortuary structures but memorials covering the places where they once stood. The long mounds themselves are not associated with new funerary deposition, but are essentially acts of closure.

Two key conclusions arise from this brief overview of megalithic sites in Britain, Ireland and northern France (fig. 18.9). The first is the importance of *sequence*: that in monuments where a chamber is covered by a mound, the chamber may have operated for a significant period before the mound or cairn was added. It is generally difficult to determine the length of that period, but free-standing chambers may have been much more common than conventional wisdom suggests. There will have been exceptions, notably in the case of corbel-vaulted burial chambers where paral-

Fig. 18.7. *La Bajoulière, a dolmen angevin at Saint-Rémy-la-Varenne, Maine-et-Loire, France.*

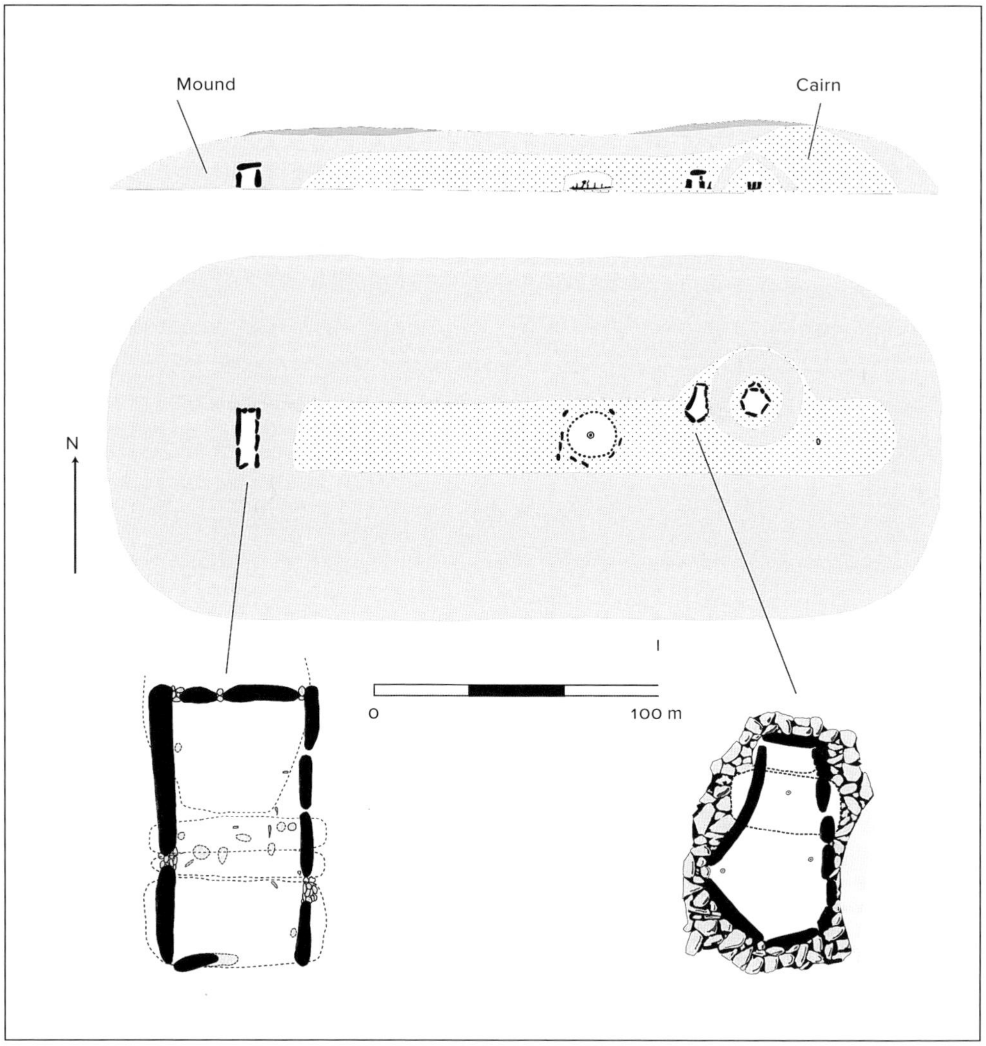

Fig. 18.8. *Constructional phases in the long mound of Le Moustoir, Carnac, Morbihan, France.*

lel construction of the chamber and cairn would have been essential to ensure the stability of the covering. In other cases, however, the building of a mound or cairn may have been the final stage in a multi-phase sequence of construction, use and abandonment.

In second place we have to recognise how difficult it is to reconstruct the original three-dimensionality of these monuments. Nineteenth century antiquarians were sometimes misled by the appearance of the surviving megalithic structures and overlooked issues of natural degradation and human interference. Absence of a visible mound does not necessarily indicate that one never existed. Furthermore, at many well-known sites the covering mound still survives, such as West Kennet in Wiltshire, Gavrinis in Brittany and Newgrange in Ireland. In the majority of cases, however, excavation may discover the base of a cairn-like structure but that discovery does not resolve the question of its original character. Was it merely a bench or platform, or did it rise above the capstones? Careful observation can sometimes

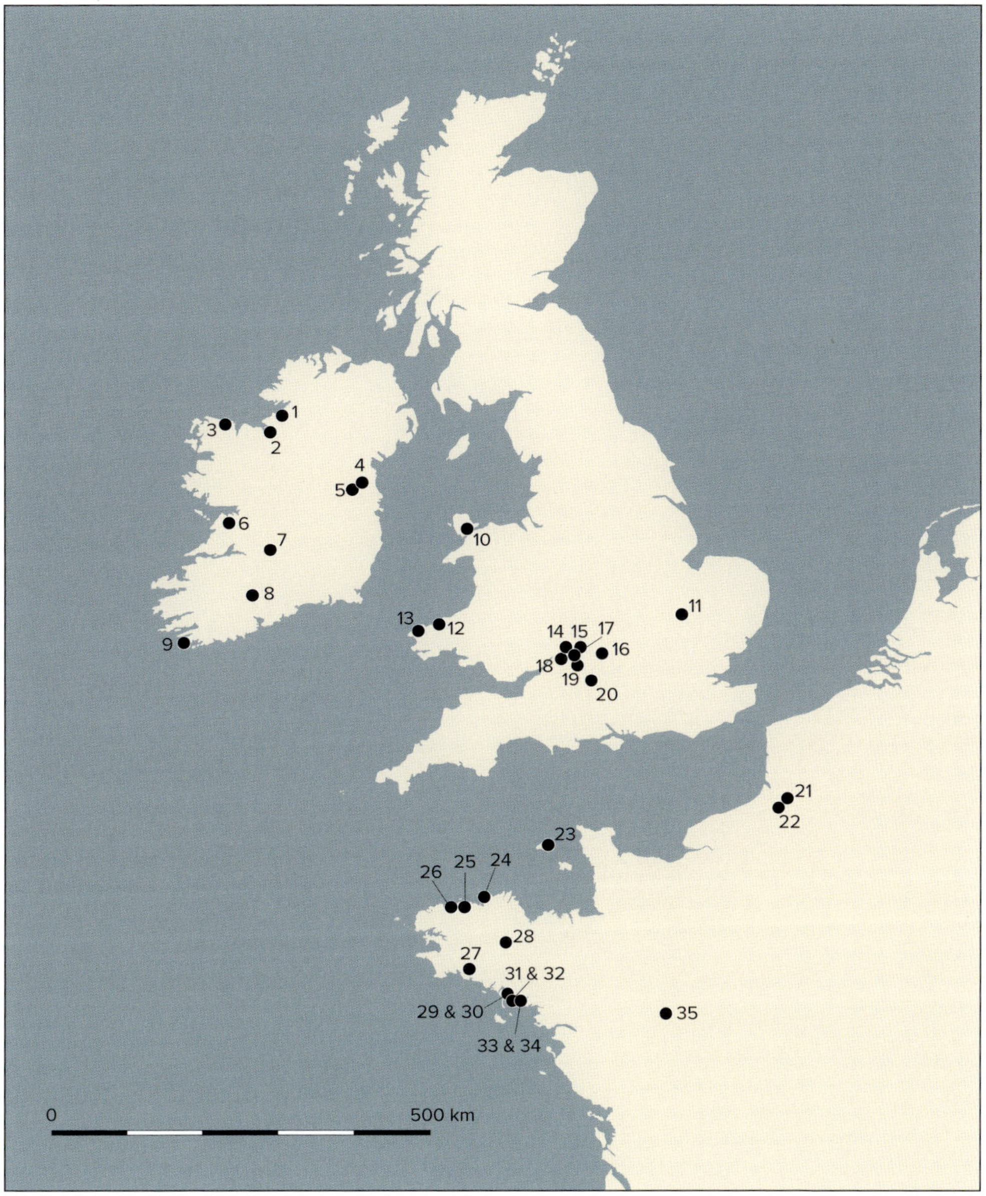

Fig. 18.9. *Map of the localities in France, England, Wales and Ireland mentioned in the text.*

1. *Creevykeel*
2. *Carrowmore*
3. *Ballyglass*
4. *Newgrange*
5. *Mound of Hostages, Tara*
6. *Poulnabrone*
7. *Baurnadomeeny*
8. *Island*
9. *Leenane*
10. *Bryn Celli Ddu*
11. *Haddenham*
12. *Pentre Ifan*
13. *Carreg Samson*
14. *Belas Knap*
16. *Cow Common Long*
15. *Hazleton North*
17. *Ascott-under-Wychwood*
18. *West Tump*
19. *Lamborough Banks*
20. *West Kennet*
21. *La Chaussée-Tirancourt*
22. *Méréaucourt*
23. *Robert's Cross*
24. *Prajou-Menhir*
25. *Barnenez*
26. *Kernic*
27. *Coat-Menez-Guen*
28. *Liscuis*
29. *Tumulus de Saint-Michel*
30. *Tumulus du Moustoir*
31. *Er Grah*
32. *Table des Marchands*
33. *Gavrinis*
34. *Ile Longue*
35. *La Bajoulière*

determine the issue, but not in all cases. What emerges is the diversity of forms that is encountered among the Neolithic monuments of northwest Europe, and the realisation that structures that look very similar in their current denuded state, or from the published plan, could have been strikingly different in concept and appearance.

19. Capstones

A visit to Troldkirken is an awe-inspiring experience. This long dolmen stands in the middle of arable land, undisturbed by settlement and visible from afar on a grass-clad hilltop that offers a broad view across Himmerland and the Limfjord to the north. As in the case of many other truly remarkable dolmens, Troldkirken has avoided restoration. It stands more or less as it has done for millennia, but the passage of time has nevertheless taken its toll. About half of its kerbstones are missing and there is a suspicion that the large stones in the monument's gables must have been re-erected at some point in time prior to its early scheduling in 1850. The latter is marked by a rather unusual scheduled monument marker stone, which was erected in the middle of the long dolmen in 1873.

But what makes Troldkirken very special is, first and foremost, its impressive capstone over a mighty dolmen chamber – one of the largest in Denmark – built of five orthostats and a shorter stone, over which there perhaps was access to the 8.5 m^2 interior (see fig. 5.5).[1]

The capstone's fascinating enormity and monumentality is underlined by the fact that it stands freely exposed and visible, silhouetted against the sky, high up on the chamber's orthostats (fig. 19.1). Despite its gigantic size – the capstone measures 4.3 x 3.5 m and has a circumference of 12.3 m – it does not appear heavy and static. It rises obliquely and elegantly up, like the bow of a ship meeting a wave. The resulting dynamism and movement were clearly not unintentional on the part of the dolmen builders. The stone, with its maximum thickness of 95 cm, is not particularly thick for a capstone, and its sloping appearance is due to a 50 cm difference in height between the orthostats at either end. There is a certain affinity between capstones of portal dolmens in Wales and Ireland (see chapter 18 and photo on opposing page) and that of Troldkirken: *Stones that float to the sky*. Moreover, markedly inclined capstones are an unusual sight among Danish dolmens (see fig. 15.1). Most capstones, in their elevated state, rest heavily and securely on the supporting orthostats, but make no mistake: Bumblebees *can* fly!

Around Denmark there is great variation in the form, composition and structure of dolmen capstones (fig. 19.2). Some are evenly rounded or rectangular in profile, others are comically humped, like the capstones on the Raklev dolmen near Kalundborg and the Skellerup dolmen north of Torup on Mols. Others, like the dolmen on Rungeløsebjerg – also near Kalundborg – display a dramatic series of folds, created in the formation of the stone. Most are natural grey or greyish-brown in colour, but grey and brown can be many things, a wealth of shades and tones, and these variations and nuances are best viewed when the sun's rays play across a rain-soaked surface. A few capstones stand out by virtue of their colour and the most remarkable example

Fig. 19.1. *The long dolmen Troldkirken's huge chamber is covered by a mighty capstone that has intentionally been mounted on a slope.*

of this is the white, almost 1.5 m thick and roughly pyramidal capstone on the long dolmen Grønsalen, located close to Fanefjord church on the island of Møn.[2]

No two capstones are quite alike – or are they? The capstones on Poskær Stenhus and the Grovlegård dolmen are originally from the same boulder even though these two dolmens stand 2 km apart.[3] Stones like these are known as twin stones and many instances are known from passage graves.[4] Twin dolmen capstones are on the other hand extremely rare, but the phenomenon is encountered at Kragedyssen near the village of Sørninge in western Zealand, where the two capstones covering the two chambers probably originate from the same boulder.

The size of the stone chosen as a capstone by the dolmen builders was determined by the shape of the dolmen chamber and the available stones left behind by the melting glacial ice (see box 2 "The great stones" on pages 54-55). Not only should the capstone have at least one large flat surface, it was not possible in Denmark, as in for example France and Spain, to quarry a stone of the desired dimensions. The largest known capstone lies over the Spanish passage grave Cueva de Menga. It weighs 180 tonnes, whereas the capstone of the Brownshill portal dolmen in Ireland "only" weighs 100 tonnes. Compared with these, even the largest Danish dolmen capstones, with a weight of around 20 tonnes, are rather on the small side. Troldkirken's capstone is of about this weight, as is the capstone for the Grovlegård dolmen, and the mighty stone over the Ristinge dolmen on the island of Langeland is also one of Denmark's heavyweights.[5] Poskær Stenhus belongs to this category too, with a capstone weighing rather more than 16 tonnes, but the majority of Danish dolmens have a smaller capstone weighing 6-10 tonnes.

As 1 m^3 of granite or gneiss, the rock types most commonly used to build dolmens, weighs 2.75 tonnes, it is "only" necessary to know the volume of a capstone for its weight to be calculated. As these stones are often very irregular in form, this calculation was previously associated with a fair degree of uncertainty. But nowadays the volume of freely exposed capstones can be determined very precisely by scanning (see box 6 on pages 246-247). Following a scan undertaken by architect Jens Vedel, the capstone of Poskær Stenhus was calculated to have a volume of 5.93 m^3, corresponding to a weight of 16.3 tonnes; it was previously estimated to have a weight of 11.5 tonnes.[6]

The more or less colossal and spectacular capstones over dolmen chambers fascinate, enchant and captivate us today, but has this always been the case? Were these capstones, in prehistory, partially or completely hidden and concealed by mounds that have subsequently disappeared?

It can be argued that dolmen capstones have always lain freely exposed and visible. The supporting evidence for this statement falls into two groups: An aesthetic-intuitive group, arising from the premise "to honour the dead", which appeals to one's feelings and perceptions but cannot be proved, and a rational, scientific group, which can be supported by hard facts.

Fig. 19.2. *Some dolmen capstones were selected due to their unusual form, characteristic folded structure or particular colour – circumstances that suggest they were intended to be seen. a) Raklev, b) Skellerup, c) Rungeløsebjerg, d) Grønsalen.*

"... a work in honour of the dead ..."

When one stands today in front of a dolmen with a mighty capstone, one senses the pride and satisfaction the dolmen builders must have felt when this chosen, named stone, perhaps enveloped in sorcery and taboos, was finally lifted and positioned in its intended resting place. "We did it – we did it!", the dolmen builders may have boasted, perhaps after having hauled and manhandled the enormous stone for several days in order to bring it to the construction site and then, by the chamber, finally to raise it up and slide it into place (see box 5 on pages 244-245). The event which marked that the dolmen had been completed and could now be taken into use may have been a great celebration, involving crowds of people, music, dancing and food, and lasting for several days. Hosting a celebration like this would have been bound up with enormous prestige and for the participants it would have been an unmissable event. Pure imagination? Not entirely! Because we know this is exactly what happened when dolmens were constructed no more than a century ago, in Indonesia for example.[7]

In chapter 18, about dolmens without mounds in Britain, France and Ireland, Chris Scarre outlines some of the many observations and considerations presented over time with respect to visible, i.e. freely exposed, capstones. Here, we will simply repeat a theory proposed by James Fergusson in 1872: "... men do not raise such masses and poise them on their points for the sake of hiding them again. ... The mode of architectural expression which these Stone men best understood was the power of mass. ... they sought to give dignity and expression by using the largest blocks they could transport or raise – and they were right, for, in spite of their rudeness, they impress us now; but had they buried them in mounds, they neither would have impressed us nor their contemporaries."[8]

Exactly the same point of view was expressed by Sophus Müller in 1897: "... that it was originally the intention that the capstone should lie exposed and visible is unequivocally demonstrated by its form. It is most often a very thick, high and domed stone, much more massive than necessary to cover the tomb – the placing of such a boulder high up on top of other stones must be perceived as a work in honour of the dead, and there would be no sense in immediately afterwards covering it all with earth."[9]

In 1942, P.V. Glob was of largely the same opinion and, as already quoted next to a photo of Poskær Stenhus, he writes: "These later and more complicated grave structures often lie exposed, merely concealed by an earthen mound around their foot. Together with the surrounding kerbstones, which can stand as high a man, the chamber forms an architectonic entity of great beauty when the monument has stood untouched since prehistory. This effect was to a great degree deliberate."[10]

Sophus Müller and P.V. Glob's views on freely exposed capstones are in no way to be seen as purely desktop archaeology. They both had enormous experience from innumerable site visits on behalf of the Danish National Museum, and they had both seen a great many dolmens. And their perception was shared and expressed by the author Martin A. Hansen in his book *Orm og Tyr* (see chapter 3).

In 1949, the renowned Danish furniture designer and architect Finn Juhl wrote engagingly and provocatively about the capstone on a megalithic tomb in Brittany, from a purely sculptural-aesthetic point of view: "We can only guess as to the original intentions behind the many stone structures from prehistoric times. The megalithic tomb in Brittany has, in my view, purely sculptural values on a par with Arp's torso. One is gripped by the powerful and daring effect achieved by allowing this enormous stone to rest on its fragile foundations at 3 points. Were this stone to lie on the ground, it would appear as heavy as a forgotten omelette. In this installation, it has become heavy in a threatening and resilient way, directly impinging on the imagination and senses. Barbara Hepworth's abstract sculpture works intensely with the relationship between 2 bodies, one resting, the other in unreleased movement. Like Arp's torso it contains, in contrast to the megalithic tomb, a depiction of a *movement*."[11]

Finn Juhl's text is accompanied by photos, including one of "Megalithic tomb in Brittany", which can easily be identified as the famous passage grave La Table des Marchands (fig. 19.3). The capstone here, which is a 5.7 m long, 4.2 m wide, 1.3 m thick and weighs around 50 tonnes, is a fragment of a menhir. Menhirs are long, slender, dressed, needle-like stones that have stood upright. Some of these stone phalluses date from the 5th millennium BC and are consequently the oldest megaliths in Europe. They can be very tall, i.e. long. The largest, Le Grand Menhir Brisé, was originally 20.3 m in length and weighed 300 tonnes. It now lies in four pieces next to La Table des Marchands, where the top of another large, impressive menhir bearing carved symbols forms the gable stone in the chamber. It is no longer possible to experience the fantastic sight of the huge capstone at La Table des Marchands, as its proud appearance had, in the 1990s, to yield to other ideas of how such a monument should look (fig. 19.4).

Fig. 19.3. *Finn Juel's photograph of "Megalithic tomb in Brittany" is a postcard which resembles the one shown here. Since the 18th century, the massive, raised, freely-exposed stone in La Table des Merchands – The Merchants' Table – has occupied and inspired many artists. Just think of Bjørn Nørgaard's model for a planned sepulchral monument for Queen Margrethe II and Prince Henrik in Roskilde Cathedral.*

Fig. 19.4. *The impressive and enthralling sight of the huge megalithic tomb La Table des Marchands depicted on the postcard shown in figure 19.3 can unfortunately no longer be experienced. Restorers and building contractors encapsulated the stones within a mound in the early 1990s. The fact that this intriguing and popular ancient monument had stood exposed for centuries and had its own very special value did not deter these meddlesome restorers.*

Facts

If we now take a look at the tangible arguments in support of the capstones having lain free and exposed, these include the many examples presented in previous chapters, where the focus was on demonstrating that dolmens were not necessarily covered by a mound from the outset. In particular, it should be emphasised *that* the numerous stones seen in the interior of the Gunderslevholm dolmen (chapter 11), and the inner stone circles evident in a large number of round and long dolmens (chapters 12-13), seal the underlying prehistoric surfaces, *that* the round dolmen Stenhus stands so high up on a small hill that it is difficult to see how its capstone could ever have been covered by a mound (chapter 14), *that* archaeological investigations of free-standing dolmen chambers show that some of them have always stood free and exposed (chapter 15) and *that* archaeological investigations of the two dolmens at Tustrup have confirmed that the chambers were not mound-covered (chapters 16-17).

Further to these lines of evidence are the numerous, well-preserved free-standing dolmen chambers and long and round dolmens with chambers, where the mound fill only covers the lowermost part of the orthostats and the capstones lie completely exposed, and do not show any traces of later interventions or of the occurrence of natural slippage of large quantities of mound material (fig. 19.5). There is not the least indication that these many monuments have suffered major disturbance, and the traditional perception of them as ruins lacks justification. Nevertheless, this is a myth that is difficult to dispel.[12]

It is obvious, furthermore, to compare the scheduled dolmens with the scheduled passage graves. Whereas the capstones of dolmens generally appear completely exposed, those of passage graves are usually more or less mound-covered and often completely concealed. Passage graves and dolmens have been exposed to the same degree of destruction and erosion over time. Nevertheless, unlike dolmens, many passage graves are still preserved within their mounds, which conceal both chambers and capstones. This can only be explained in terms of the many dolmens with visible chambers and capstones not originally having been covered by a mound.

Finally, it is worth drawing attention to the fact that the sides, and especially the tops, of capstones have been popular places for the carving of cup marks and other rock art, and must obviously have been exposed to some degree at the time for this to be possible (fig. 19.6). More than 200 Danish dolmens have capstones displaying cup marks. These phenomena are normally dated to the Bronze Age, but cup marks are also known from the Late Neolithic and some of them could perhaps be traced all the way back to the Dolmen epoch. The Landerslev dolmen chamber, a type II chamber that stands south of Jægerspris, has an orthostat completely covered in cup marks on the side facing in towards the chamber.[13] Cup marks and other carved symbols also occur frequently on the stones in the French, and especially Irish, passage graves, where these carvings are unequivocally coeval with the megalithic tombs.

Fig. 19.5. *The round dolmen at Tøstrup, north of Kolind, was drawn by Magnus Petersen in 1886. As in the case of many other dolmens, it has an even surface and there are no indications that the chamber has ever been mound-covered. In the Neolithic, the dolmen had the same appearance, apart from probably having had a covering of stones rather than the grass turf of the present day.*

Fig. 19.6. *The rock carvings of ships and wheel crosses on the capstone of the Dilhøj dolmen in Odsherred were discovered in 1830 and drawn shortly afterwards by Theofilus Hansen. The capstone, and probably the entire chamber, must have stood freely exposed in the Bronze Age, when the rock carvings were made.*

Visible – invisible

There is great variation in the thickness of capstones placed over Danish dolmens. Some are flat, slab-like and only 30-50 cm thick, while others are thicker, often more than 1 m, and domed in shape. These differences reflect, to some extent, the fact that flat capstones were covered by a mound already in the Neolithic, whereas it was intended that the more rounded capstones should be freely visible.

The flat capstones lie over dolmen cists and some of the related earliest dolmen chambers of type I. However, as many type I dolmen chambers, for example that in the Gunderslevholm dolmen, have massive orthostats and a thick capstone, the shift from thin and flat to thicker and more rounded capstones must have taken place during an early part of the Dolmen epoch.

In the case of the later, extended and polygonal dolmens – types III and IV – the capstones are intentionally and deliberately very exposed; a situation of which both Sophus Müller and P.V. Glob were aware. It was not until the Passage-grave epoch that stone chambers – passage graves – were built and then more or less immediately encapsulated and concealed within a mound. It is possible, however, that some of the passage graves previously referred to as large dolmens have always had a visible capstone (fig. 19.7). In conclusion, it should also be mentioned that several originally exposed capstones – and their associated dolmens – became concealed later, in the Early Bronze Age, in newly constructed mounds built over the earlier megalithic tombs.[14]

So the relationship between visible versus invisible, or concealed, capstones is not a matter of "either/or", but "as well as", and it can be arranged in a chronologi-

Fig. 19.7. *The capstone on the Bakkebølle dolmen, located southeast of Vordingborg, appears much larger in this watercolour by Ditlev Laub from 1876 than it is in reality; it is actually "only" 1.5 m high. In the 1820s, this megalithic tomb inspired J.C. Dahl to paint the picture shown in figure 1.3.*

cal sequence, where the exposure or non-exposure of the capstone was controlled by intentional aims inherent in the design of these monuments. This sequence begins with the concealed capstones on dolmen cists, followed by exposed and very conspicuous capstones on dolmen chambers and culminating with capstones hidden beneath the mounds of passage graves.

It was actually not Frederik VII who ...

There is a myth in Danish archaeology that it was the enthusiastic amateur archaeologist King Frederik VII who solved the puzzle of how capstones were raised up on to dolmens and passage graves in the Neolithic. It is true that the king was the author of an excellent little pamphlet On the Construction of "Giants' Houses" or "Cromlechs", which was published in Danish in 1857 and translated into quite a number of foreign languages, in addition to English. In this, Frederik VII suggested that an earthen ramp was built against the chamber, up which the capstone was hauled into place on rollers.

From ethnographic parallels, historical evidence and practical experiments, we know that it is possible to accomplish the task in this way. However, it is easier and more expedient to employ ramps made of posts and timber. And wooden ramps may well have been used when the dolmens were constructed, but no archaeological investigations have as yet located postholes that can definitely be linked to this practice. It is also difficult to imagine that earthen ramps were built up against free-standing dolmens, when the task can be accomplished in a much easier way.

The capstone could have been raised with the aid of levers, with timbers being pushed into the space beneath the raised part of the stone. By alternating from side to side, lifting the stone with the levers and inserting timbers, the stone was raised upwards on a gradually growing scaffold of crossed beams. When the stone, which was initially positioned directly beside the solidly timber-braced chamber, reached a height on a level with the tops of the orthostats, the lifting operation was halted. The stone could then be hauled or rolled over the chamber and into its final resting position. The latter operation could be easily accomplished with the aid of a so-called A-frame. Like the levers, this employs the principle of leverage, whereby a modest effort can be multiplied 10-20 times, according to the proportional relationship between the short and long arms of the lever or

A-frame. For example, a man or a woman who pulls down on a lever with a weight of 50 kg will affect the stone with 10-20 times this weight, corresponding to 0.5-1 tonne!

Experiments undertaken in 1994, which involved lifting stones weighing 10 tonnes up to a height of 7 m in order to show how the lintels at Stonehenge could have been put into position, demonstrated that a scaffold is much quicker and more efficient than a ramp. Included in this appraisal is the fact that the scaffold requires no preparation and is easy to dismantle. However, it has the disadvantage – seen from an archaeologist's point of view – that it does not leave behind the least trace.

In the early and mid-19th century there were clearly formulated theories circulating in the Netherlands about the use of earthen ramps, and in 1822, the Dutch clergyman and historian Westendorp mentions that Nordic scholars are also of the opinion that this method was employed in megalith construction.

It is true that the ramp theory belongs to Frederik VII, but the Danish king was not the originator. Neither did he claim this to be so. The origin of the theory has been attributed to him by posterity. The king himself ended his text magnanimously as follows: "I will not, however, deny that other methods may be conceived. If these are more reasonable, or more conformable to the degree of skilled knowledge which existed in ancient times, I shall go over to the side of their authors, and adopt them as the most probable. Whoever comes nearest the truth will be the man to whom I shall be the most willing to give my support."

References: Adams 2007, 2010. Eriksen 2002. Frederik VII 1857, 1862.

Dolmens are still built on Sumba. Here, the capstone has been raised on a scaffold and the men are in the process of rolling it over the chamber.

Volume and weight of a capstone

It was previously difficult to measure the volume and weight of a dolmen capstone, because it is not easy to place the stone in a large container and see how much water it displaces. However, the stone's volume can now be measured by scanning, and when the density of the particular rock type is known, its weight can then be calculated.

Surveying of the stone and calculation of its volume can be undertaken by using a laser scanner to measure the surface of the stone, leading to the generation of a "cloud" of closely-spaced points. As the laser cannot measure "around corners", it must be repositioned several times in order to obtain a comprehensive and representative point cloud.

A much easier, quicker and cheaper method is to undertake a photogrammetric scan. In this method, use is made of a digital camera and specially-developed software, e.g. PhotoModeler Scanner. The essence of this method is that an extensive series of photos is taken with a digital camera, such that all its surfaces are covered, ensuring an overlap of at least 60% between each individual image. When the images have been transferred to a computer, the programme calculates the changing positions of the camera, after which it can scan the entire surface of the stone. Where there is a match in the image structure between two photos, a point is fixed and in this way a point cloud is progressively formed. The point density can be specified by the operator. The point cloud can then be triangulated, so the surface consists of tiny triangles. If "texture" is selected, the model will appear "photo-realistic", because the programme automatically covers the small triangles with photo texture from the image that is closest and most perpendicular to each individual triangle. The inherent metric error for an object of 1 m is 0.3 mm and for an object of 10 m it is 3 mm.

The photogrammetric method is easy to apply because the only equipment required for the scan is a digital camera. It can be applied to everything from very small objects, less than a finger nail in size, to very large ones. For example, a video is available on YouTube showing how, over the course of several days, volcanologists are able to photograph an erupting volcano from the air and, from the resulting images, calculate the mass of the material ejected by the volcano per day. Furthermore,

unlike a laser scanner, the equipment does not require regular maintenance and calibration, and it is of course much easier and quicker to transport a camera. The 3D survey data can easily be exported to other CAD systems for further processing. If, during the photography of the object, images of three or more coordinating points are also included, the object can be exported to a national mapping facility such as GoogleEarth.

For our surveys, we used the programme PhotoModeler Scanner from Eos Systems Inc. This programme, which can be learned fairly quickly, is inexpensive and it has many useful features that are applicable in an archaeological context. In addition to dolmen capstones, artefacts can also be surveyed in 3D. Excavations can be photographed in plan, too, and the images combined to give large horizontal surfaces, and sections can be swiftly recorded to scale with attached photos.

Shown here are some of the pictures from the survey of the capstone on the Årslev dolmen, which stands near Brabrand in eastern Jutland. The survey and calculation of the capstone's volume and weight were undertaken by architect Jens Vedel of the company 3D Photo – http://www.3dphoto.dk.

Mosaic of photos showing the position of the camera for each of the 54 images.

This image of the 2.4 m long capstone on the Årslev dolmen is a combination of the 54 survey images. The granite capstone's volume has been calculated as 2.12 m³ and, as granite has a density of 2.75 t/m³, this means the stone weighs 5.83 tonnes.

Jens Vedel in the process of photographing the capstone of the Årslev dolmen at Brabrand near Aarhus. A total of 54 photos were taken over the course of half an hour.

20. Dolmens without mounds in the Sarup area

The many scheduled dolmens presented in this book have demonstrated that these are most often complex structures, whose history is best understood when it has been possible to undertake an archaeological excavation, as in the case of Trollasten and the two dolmens at Tustrup. Excavations in scheduled dolmens are though not normally permitted, and dispensation can only be given under very exceptional circumstances. Furthermore, it is clear that archaeology is constantly developing new and improved methods and analytical techniques, which can provide information that was not available previously.

However, this is not the only way of obtaining information on the history of the construction and use of dolmens. Investigating some of the many thousands of sites of demolished dolmens that are permanently under the plough can also prove to be informative. Denmark is a country where large stones constitute a scarce resource. When stone churches were built almost a millennium ago, and later in the construction of manor houses, bridges, roads and railways, it was therefore obvious to obtain the stones required from dolmens and passage graves. The road regulation of 1793 even includes a direct recommendation to do just this.

The site of a demolished and dismantled dolmen or passage grave can be evident today as a slight elevation on the surface of the field, with a dense concentration of fire-shattered granite stones, numerous sandstone slabs from the dry-walling, large quantities of burnt, crushed flint and possibly also lumps of clay that was used in the monument's construction (fig. 20.1). When a site of this type is investigated, and the plough soil is removed, the lower 20-30 cm of the megalithic monument is usually found to be preserved. This gives the opportunity to gather information on the form and layout of the structure, from for example impressions left by the large stones, and on the activities that took place there in the Neolithic. In fortunate cases there will be undisturbed activity layers and deposits, often because only the large stones have been removed. The chambers in the majority of extant dolmens and passage graves were emptied during the 19th century, when there was great interest in excavating these monuments. These "plunderings" have, unfortunately, almost always resulted in it now being impossible to know what originally lay in a particular megalithic chamber and certainly not how the artefacts lay in relation to one another – circumstances that are frequently more important than the artefacts themselves.

Only too rarely have excavations been undertaken in Denmark's many ploughed-down megalithic monuments. This is even more regrettable at the present time, when efficient agricultural practices employ machines that, with each sowing, remove about a centimetre of the overlying soil. Continued ploughing will therefore, year after year, cut deeper and deeper into the remains of the megalithic monuments

Fig. 20.1. *Traces of a ploughed-down megalithic tomb at Sarup. On a sandy field, a patch of clay can be seen, surrounded by burnt flint. The demolished monument – Sarup Gamle Skole I – was later excavated (see photo on page 248).*

that lie hidden beneath the topsoil. It is distressing to see just how much is being destroyed by the plough.[1]

A couple of research projects have, however, been undertaken in Denmark, where the aim was to investigate cultivation-threatened, ploughed-down dolmens and passage graves. One of these was carried out in the 1970s on the island of Langeland, where Jørgen Skaarup of Langelands Museum, with support from the Danish Research Council for the Humanities, investigated a large number of dolmens and passage graves over a number of years (see chapter 15). This research was published in exemplary fashion in 1985.[2]

The second project took place around Sarup in southwestern Funen, where one of this book's authors has, since 1971, undertaken investigations especially focussed on the Sarup site and its relationship to coeval settlement in the area.

The Sarup project – the Sarup site

At Sarup, there is a sandy promontory with an area of 9 ha, bordered by watercourses on two sides (fig. 20.2), which was well-suited to habitation. At least ten times during prehistory, between the Mesolithic and the Late Iron Age, people have occupied this site. Two of these events, dated to the Neolithic and more precisely to the period 3400-3200 BC, are however of particular interest. Through enormous communal efforts at that time, the promontory became framed by a palisade and complicated systems of ditches. All of this took place at the same time as people were also building dolmens and passage graves.[3]

Through excavations undertaken between 1971 and 1984 – primarily financed by the Danish Research Council for the Humanities – an area of 6 ha of this sandy promontory was uncovered and partially investigated. This resulted in an excellent understanding of a previously unknown monument type in Nordic archaeology. This is termed a *Sarupanlæg* in Danish, named after the locality, but referred to in international archaeology as a *causewayed enclosure* (fig. 20.3). A causewayed enclosure is an area of up to several hectares framed by one or more rows of so-called *system-ditches*, on the inner side of which there may be a post- or stake-built fence – a palisade. The

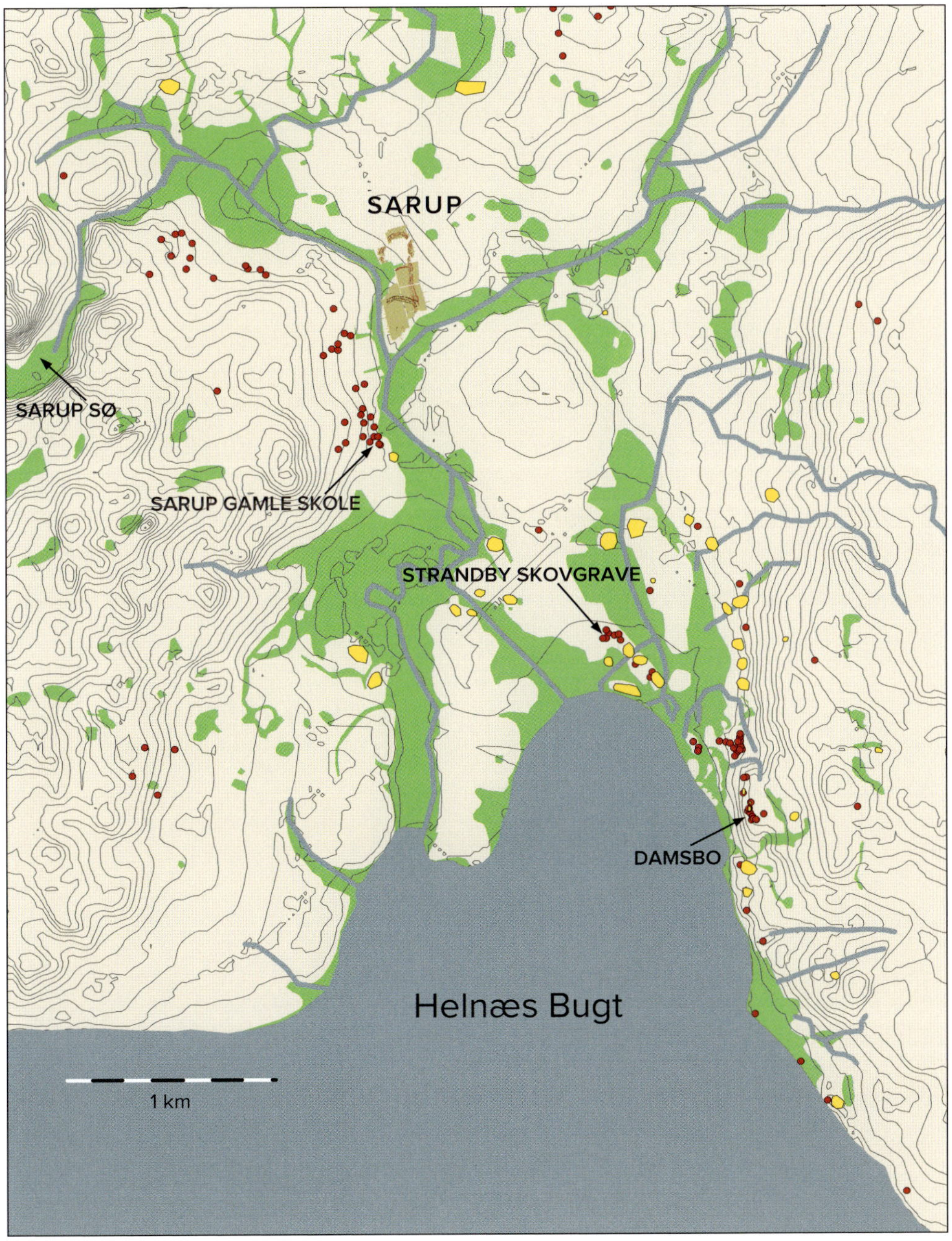

Fig. 20.2. *The Sarup area is in southwestern Funen, between Assens and Faaborg, only a couple of kilometres from Helnæs Bugt. The Sarup site is located on a sandy promontory, bordered by two watercourses. The locations of the area's known dolmens and passage graves are shown with red dots. Recorded settlements, which may be coeval with the megalithic monuments, are marked in yellow.*

Fig. 20.3. *Plan of the Sarup I and Sarup II causewayed enclosures. The Sarup I monument, from c. 3400 BC, consisted of a palisade (a), an entrance area with a 1.6 m opening and an access corridor (b) and two rows of system-ditches (c). The Sarup II monument, from c. 3200 BC, was much smaller and consisted of a kind of palisade formed of a wide belt of stakes (d) and two rows of system-ditches (e). Contour interval 0.5 m.*

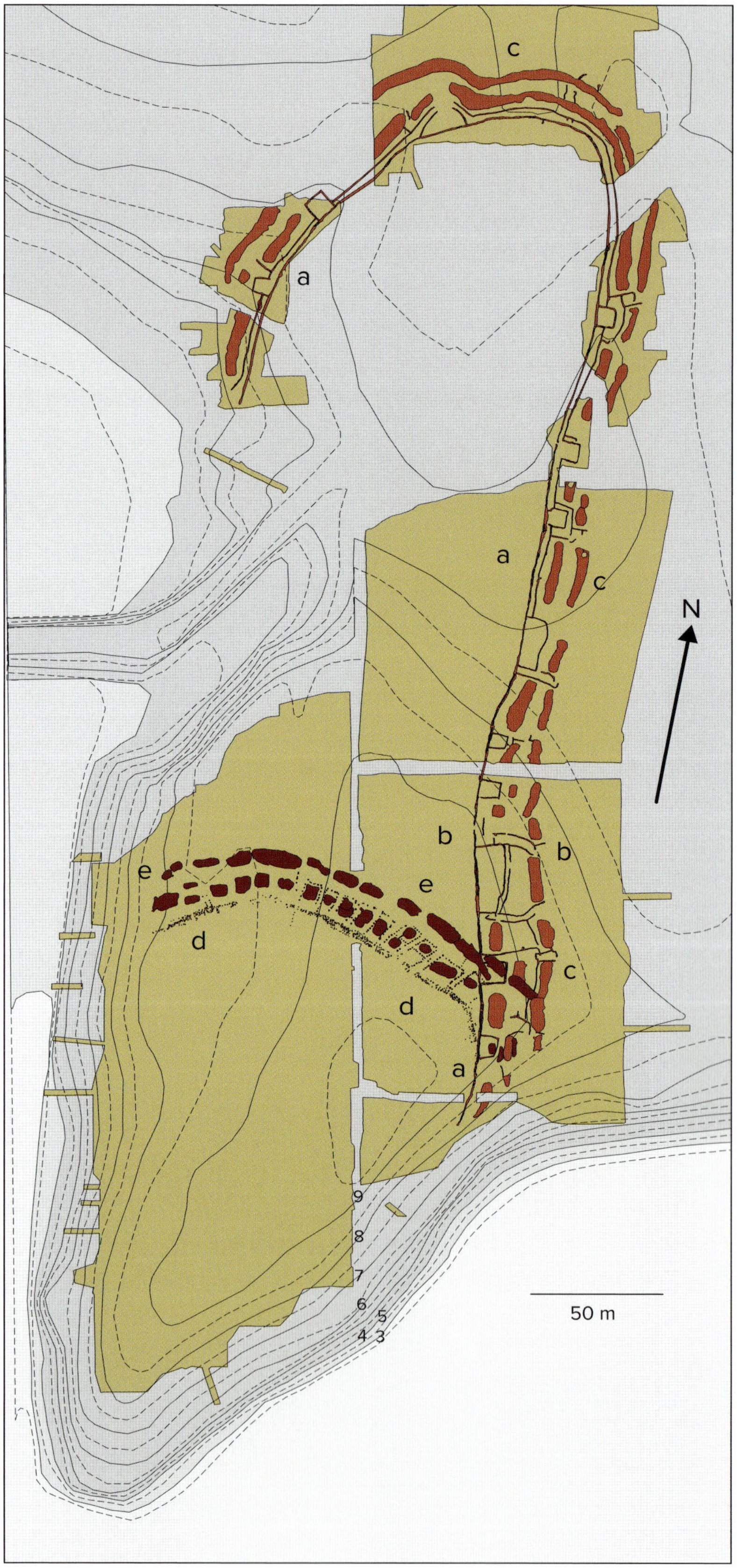

term system-ditch refers to rectangular pits that are usually 5 m wide, 5-20 m long and with an average depth of 1 m. It proved possible to uncover two causewayed enclosures on the Sarup promontory – Sarup I and Sarup II, constructed a couple of centuries apart. Sarup I dates from the Fuchsberg phase, i.e. around 3400 BC, coeval with the construction of dolmens, while Sarup II belongs to the Klintebakke phase, c. 3200 BC, the time when passage graves were built.

The establishment of these causewayed enclosures would have required the coordinated efforts of many hundreds of people. At Sarup I alone, almost 1500 m^3 of earth had to be dug out to create the system-ditches, and it was necessary to obtain and shape almost 3400 wooden posts for the 1430 m of palisade (fig. 20.4).

The finds, which mostly comprise the bones of humans and animals, pottery vessels, axes, charred grain, quernstones and grinding stones, are characterised by having been specially selected and by often only being represented by fragments. It is clear that these items have been subjected to special treatment, which involved intentional destruction. Furthermore, they must have been moved around several times prior to their final deposition in the system-ditches, by the palisade or in the few pits that lay on the otherwise almost finds-free inner surface.

As already mentioned, the Danish causewayed enclosures date from the time when dolmens and passage graves were also constructed. This means that, over the course of a few centuries, and in parallel with the construction of numerous megalithic tombs, other very major construction works took place that involved many hundreds of people. It is not known how many causewayed enclosures were built

Fig. 20.4. *This is how part of the Sarup I causewayed enclosure may have looked when in use.*

in Denmark. At present, we know of about 40 examples, but the original total could have been many hundreds. Detailed studies around Horsens Fjord and on Djursland have shown that these monuments usually lie about 5 km apart, a figure that corresponds with situations evident in other areas of Europe.[4]

The Sarup area

Following conclusion of the excavations at Sarup in 1984, it was decided to try to find evidence of coeval Neolithic habitation in order to understand how the causewayed settlements had functioned relative to the settlements, Barkaer-structures, megalithic monuments and possible votive sites in the area. The archives of Fyns Stiftsmuseum, now Odense City Museums, and the parish records at the Danish National Museum contained data on four megalithic tombs that all lay a couple of kilometres to the southeast of Sarup. Two of these had been demolished, while the two others – a dolmen and a stone cist – were scheduled. The stone cist is of a type that is more than a millennium later than the dolmens and is therefore of no interest here. There was also a record of a Neolithic settlement, but this referred to the actual Sarup site.

The plan was for investigation of the Sarup area to be undertaken in exactly the same way as that which Fyns Stiftsmuseum carried out at the same time in the Dreslette area, about 5 km to the west of Sarup.[5] The study area comprised a 4 x 5 km area centred on the Sarup site, and the central parts included a number of wetlands associated with the watercourse Hårby Å. At each side are high hills, which promote a slightly milder climate in the river valley. The area was – and continues to be – subjected to survey by systematic field-walking across all accessible places at 5 m intervals in order to record cultural remains that lie exposed in the newly-ploughed fields. In addition, all the farms were visited to record whatever they had in the way of collected artefacts; antiquarian collectors in the area were also contacted. Use was also made of aerial photos, though to a lesser degree. Through these combined and concerted efforts, several thousand artefacts were found and recorded, and several hundred features were documented. Of particular interest here is the fact that it proved possible to locate around 125 ploughed-down megalithic tombs and about 40 settlements dating from the same time as the Sarup I and II causewayed enclosures (fig. 20.2).

Through 16 excavation campaigns – some extending over several years – it has proved possible to uncover and investigate the remains of 29 megalithic tombs, four Barkaer-structures, parts of several settlements and a votive site. This large body of evidence is presently undergoing analysis. Rather than simply investigating many scattered single monuments, a high priority was given to examining entire clusters of monuments in order to discover how these possibly related to each other. In the following, three of the excavations will be presented as the evidence contributes to the picture of the emergence of dolmens in the Neolithic.

Sarup Gamle Skole

Just less than 0.5 km south of the Sarup site lies a field where, to date, a number of monuments coeval with the Sarup enclosures have been located and excavated (fig. 20.2). The field slopes east, down towards the wetlands around the watercourse Hårby Å. Remarkably, a row of system-ditches was found here too, belonging to a monument of the same type and of the same period as Sarup I (fig. 20.5 A33).[6]

Just 20 m to the north of these ditches lay a trapezoid enclosure that proved to be a foundation ditch with traces of posts (fig. 20.5 A4). The structure was 58 m long, 7.2 m wide to the west and 11.2 m wide to the east. Parts of the enclosure had been destroyed by cultivation and soil erosion. From the north side of the enclosure, a 23 m long foundation ditch ran eastwards, down to the bank of Hårby Å (fig. 20.5 A30).

One of the ditch's postholes contained a piece of oak charcoal, with a "wood age" of 40-80 years, which has been radiocarbon dated to 3650-3380 BC.[7] Another similar piece of charcoal gave a date of 3940-3650 BC, but this date is thought to be too old, relative to the finds located by the palisade.[8] These two very different dates show how cautious one must be with respect to radiocarbon dates. Optimally, a number of dates should be obtained from the same structure or layer so it is possible to identify inconsistencies or detect possible mixing of material.

The posts in the foundation ditch were round in cross section, about 20 cm in diameter, and on average set 20 cm down into the ditch, measured from the excavated surface. In most places, the ditch was c. 10 cm deeper than the postholes. This must be because it was necessary to be able to vary the depth of the posts so they were all of the same height. The posts were spaced at intervals of 15-40 cm, and these very wide gaps mean that the fence did not constitute a closed barrier. It can be presumed that the fence did not exceed 1 m in height.

In the middle of the enclosed area were the remains of a small dolmen chamber (fig. 20.5 A3). This was evident as an east-west-oriented, 1.8 x 0.6 m patch of soil that differed from the sandy subsoil. On this lay a number of stone slabs, measuring c. 20 x 20 cm, that had constituted the floor of the dolmen chamber; they were surrounded by the traces, i.e. sockets, of four large stones. At each side of the chamber there had been a very broad, flat stone, and at the eastern end there had sat a large, round stone, while to the west was a smaller, flat stone. The dolmen chamber was of an early type and it had been built parallel to the longitudinal axis of the post-built enclosure. There were no traces around it of an earthen mound or bank to support the orthostats. All of this could of course have been ploughed away, but the discovery of several potsherds on the excavated surface and stone base of the chamber shows that some material remained. All the evidence suggests that the dolmen chamber in the middle of the enclosure had stood on the soil surface as an exposed stone cist, i.e. a dolmen cist like the one at Barkær.[9]

Opposite the north side of the dolmen chamber, in the middle of the post-built fence, lay an earthfast stone, just less than 1 m in length and with a flat face upwards. On excavation, it appeared that this had functioned as a kind of threshold stone into the enclosed area.

Fig. 20.5. *At Sarup Gamle Skole, on a field sloping eastwards, down towards the watercourse Hårby Å, a number of Neolithic structures were discovered and excavated. The former positions of large stones are marked in green. – Structures: A1: Non-megalithic grave. A2: Site of a rectangular dolmen chamber. A3: Site of a small, rectangular dolmen, possibly a dolmen cist, in the middle of fenced enclosure A4. A4: Fenced enclosure, 58 m long. A30: Additional fence running from the fenced enclosure A4 and down to Hårby Å. A33: Row of system-ditches belonging to a causewayed enclosure. A34: Site of a polygonal dolmen chamber. B: Two sites of passage-grave chambers in a long barrow framed by kerbstones.*

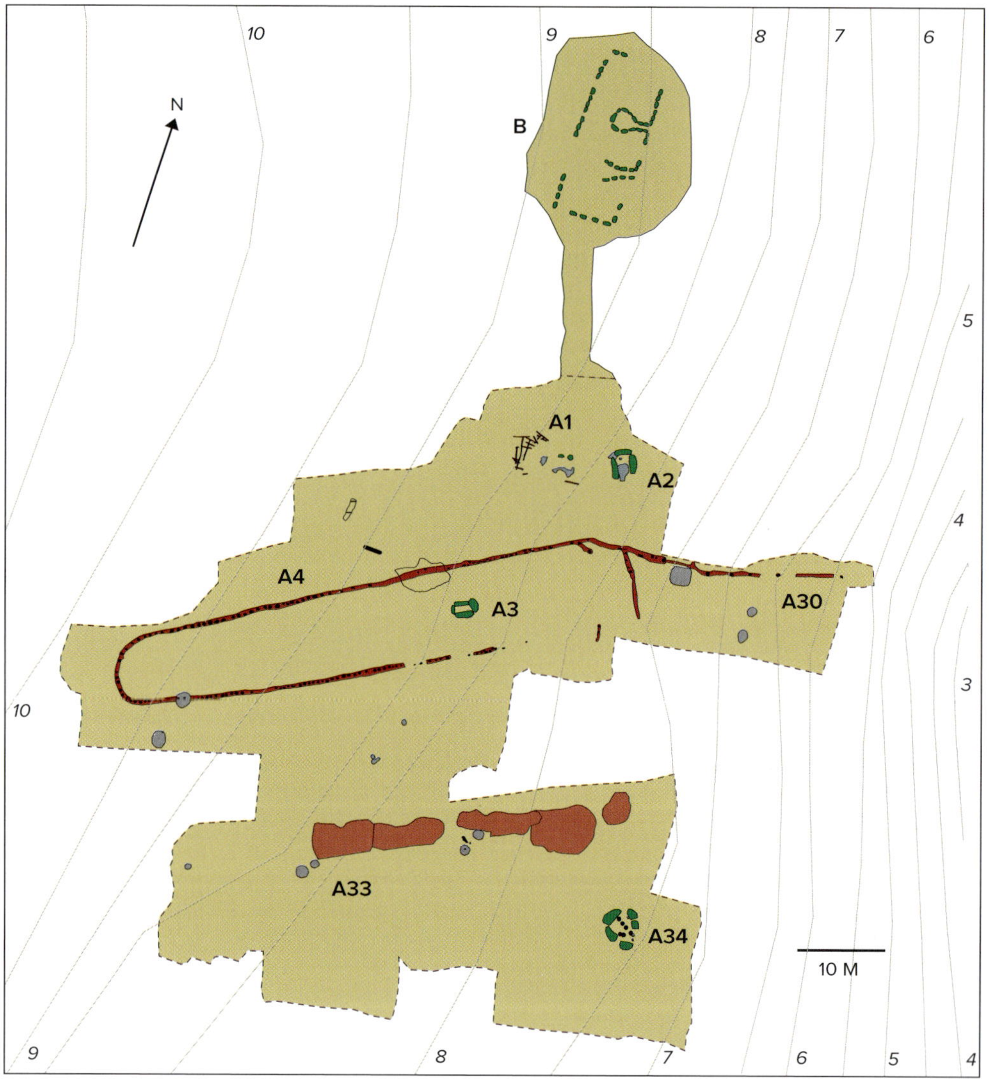

Up against the fence, especially to the northeast, there was a great deal of pottery – though only fragments of vessels – ornamented in Fuchsberg style.[10]

A large pit had been dug overlapping with the north side of the foundation ditch, causing its partial removal, though not the lowermost part with post traces, which lay below the base of the pit. The pit contained a quantity of flint debitage and a great deal of pottery, also datable to the Fuchsberg phase, i.e. coeval with the pottery found in front of the foundation ditch.

It seems that the fenced enclosure quickly lost its significance and a pit was dug overlapping it, though this probably did not happen before the posts had rotted away. This also shows there could not have been any overburden here at the time.

There is therefore nothing to indicate that the trapezoid enclosure had, at any point in time, earthen fill within it (fig. 20.6). The dolmen chamber does not appear to have been supported with stones and soil, and opposite the chamber there was an entrance in the fence that allowed access to the enclosed area. Moreover, the fence was set of small posts which stood so far apart that they could not possibly have retained soil within the area. As already mentioned, a large pit was also dug overlapping the foundation trench, which extended into the enclosed area.

The enclosure corresponds to those found at Barkær and also to the type that is evident at a number of sites in northern and western Europe, for example that recently published from Łódź in Poland by Seweryn Rzepecki. He calls this kind of monument a long barrow of *Niedźwiedź* type. These monuments are characterised by only being enclosed within ditches, possibly foundation ditches, with posts constituting the frame, not large stones as in long dolmens.[11]

Remains of a dolmen chamber were found on each side of the trapezoid enclosure at Sarup Gamle Skole. One of these (A2) lay 6 m to the north (fig. 20.5). The chamber was badly damaged and it only proved possible to find impressions of the three orthostats that had stood to the west, north and east, as well as parts of the chamber floor. The elongate chamber, with a preserved floor measuring 3.2 x 1.2 m, was oriented north-south. Some flint blades were found here, as well as some brick rubble! The chamber lay 4 m to the east of a possible inhumation grave (A1) (fig. 20.5).

The other solitary chamber (A34) lay in the southern part of the excavated area (fig. 20.5). Here, remains were found of a polygonal dolmen with traces of five orthostats and an opening towards the southeast. The chamber floor was slightly basin-like and had been covered with flagstones, interspersed with fine flint. There were no indications that the dolmen chamber had been surrounded by an earthen mound or a stone circle. A few potsherds were found in the area immediately around it.

On the basis of what has been excavated and analysed to date from Sarup Gamle Skole, a picture emerges – see figure 20.5 – suggesting that around 3500 BC a possible

Fig. 20.6. *Reconstruction of the Barkaer-structure A4 with dolmen cist A3 at Sarup Gamle Skole, seen from the northeast.*

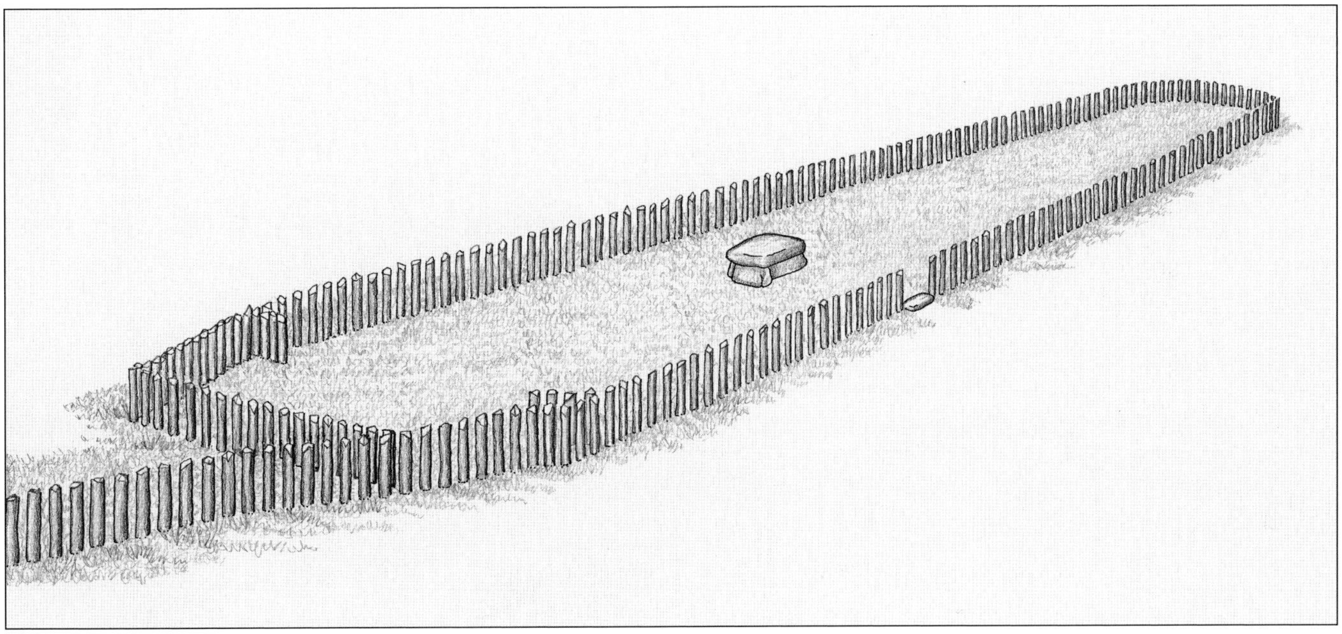

inhumation grave (A1) was established here, and slightly south of this, perhaps at the same time, a trapezoid enclosure (A4) was built. A small dolmen cist (A3) was erected within the latter. From approximately the same time there is a causewayed enclosure with system-ditches (A33), one of which has a small dolmen at its base.[12] Next, two solitary dolmen chambers were built, without earthen mounds, one of which (A2) appears typologically earlier than the other (A34). Finally, two small passage-grave chambers (B) were erected and covered and framed by an earthen long barrow with kerbstones; a monument usually referred to as a long dolmen. This latter monument must be presumed to have been constructed during the Klintebakke phase.

Over the course of three centuries – from c. 3500 to 3200 BC – people revisited this locality five, perhaps six times, and constructed a monument. This suggests that there must have been a special affiliation with the place, which prompted the local inhabitants, at intervals of perhaps 50 years, to return to it, even though there was plenty of space in the area and the monuments could easily have been built much further apart.

Strandby Skovgrave

Just less than 2 km southeast of the Sarup site, a several hundred-metre-long promontory extends out between some extensive wetland areas that lie close to the shore of Helnæs Bugt (fig. 20.2). This promontory is only a couple of hundred metres wide, but there are indications in several places of its use in prehistory. One of these, located on a slight elevation in the middle of the promontory, will be described here.

The locality was discovered by field survey and was the first major megalithic complex investigated in connection with the Sarup project.[13] Shortly before the excavation began, the trees of a shelter belt were removed, leading to the destruction of parts of long barrow D II.

The excavation exposed an area of 46 x 60 m, corresponding to 2760 m^2, within which were traces of four monuments containing megalithic graves, two of which had several construction phases (fig. 20.7). Based on analyses of the excavation plans and finds, the following course of events can presently be outlined:

The earliest monument on the site appears to have been a small, rectangular dolmen chamber, D II N, which later became framed by long dolmen D II (fig. 20.7). This small dolmen was surrounded by a low, circular, 7 m diameter elevation on top of which lay some head-sized stones. There were no traces of kerbstones around the elevation. The chamber was found to contain sherds of a funnel beaker, of a type corresponding to those at Sarup I.[14]

Coeval, or virtually coeval, with the dolmen is a rectangular post-built enclosure, monument D III (figs. 20.7 and 20.8), which had enclosed an area of c. 8.5 x 25 m. Running along the middle of the structure was a row of head-sized stones, a number of which had been removed when a dolmen chamber was constructed. Two pottery vessels, a funnel beaker and a lugged beaker ornamented in Fuchsberg style had been placed immediately west of the post-built fence (fig. 20.9 A and B). The post-built

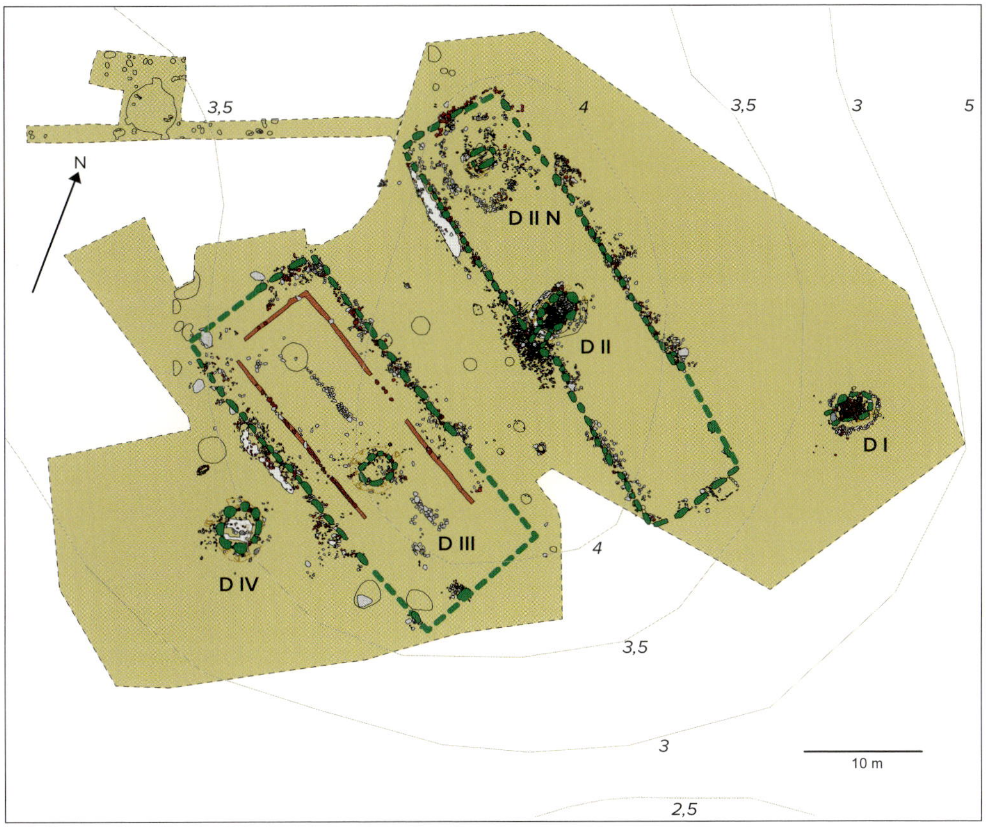

Fig. 20.7. *On a sandy promontory, surrounded by wetlands and close to Helnæs Bugt, remains of a number of Neolithic structures, known collectively as Strandby Skovgrave, have been discovered and excavated. The former positions of large stones are marked in green. – Structures: D I: Dolmen chamber with passage, set of a couple of stones. D II: Long barrow with earthen fill, surrounded by kerbstones. In the middle of the structure is a small passage grave with a passage towards the southwest. D II N: Small, body-length stone cist, originally only surrounded by a slight earthen elevation with head-sized stones and framed by the northern end of D II. D III: Rectangular structure framed by kerbstones and dry-walling but with no earthen mound. A polygonal dolmen chamber in the middle. Also within the structure is a rectangular foundation ditch with post traces and stones. Running along this structure is a row of head-sized stones. D IV: Solitary, free-standing, polygonal dolmen chamber.*

enclosure here corresponds to the trapezoid structure at Sarup Gamle Skole (see fig. 20.5 A4) and must be considered to be a Barkaer-structure. However, no traces were found of a burial within it, so if this had been present, and it lay in the middle of the structure, it must have been removed in connection with the construction of the dolmen chamber.

The next building activity on the site was probably the framing of the aforementioned post-built enclosure with kerbstones and the erection of the polygonal dolmen chamber D III in the middle of the structure. As a consequence, the monument now had the form of a 31 m long and 12.5 m wide long dolmen. Remains of stacks of dry-walling slabs were found, collapsed in a fan-shape inwards or outwards from the gaps between the kerbstones.

After the complex monument D III had been built, the next structure was probably the free-standing dolmen chamber D IV. This was very large, with a floor surface measuring 2.7 x 2.8 m, and appears to have had an opening to the west, over a narrow threshold stone. Around the chamber orthostats was a low clay packing, but apart from this there were no traces of either mound or kerbstones.

After this, dolmen D I was built furthest to the east. This had a polygonal chamber with a passage facing towards the southwest (see fig. 20.7). Numerous potsherds from the Klintebakken phase were found in front of the passage.

Fig. 20.8. *Structure D III at Strandby Skovgrave consisted of a rectangular, post-built enclosure, marked in brown, in the middle of which was a row of large stones. A polygonal dolmen chamber had been built on top of this stone row. The rectangular, post-built enclosure was framed by a rectangle of stones, the gaps between which were filled with dry-walling slabs. The former positions of large stones are marked in green, and the black crosses show the locations of finds. There were clearly also many finds within the row of large stones here. Conversely, long dolmen D II, part of which can be seen in the upper right corner, has had a mound, and the finds here are seen located outside the mound and the kerbstones, or inside the chamber.*

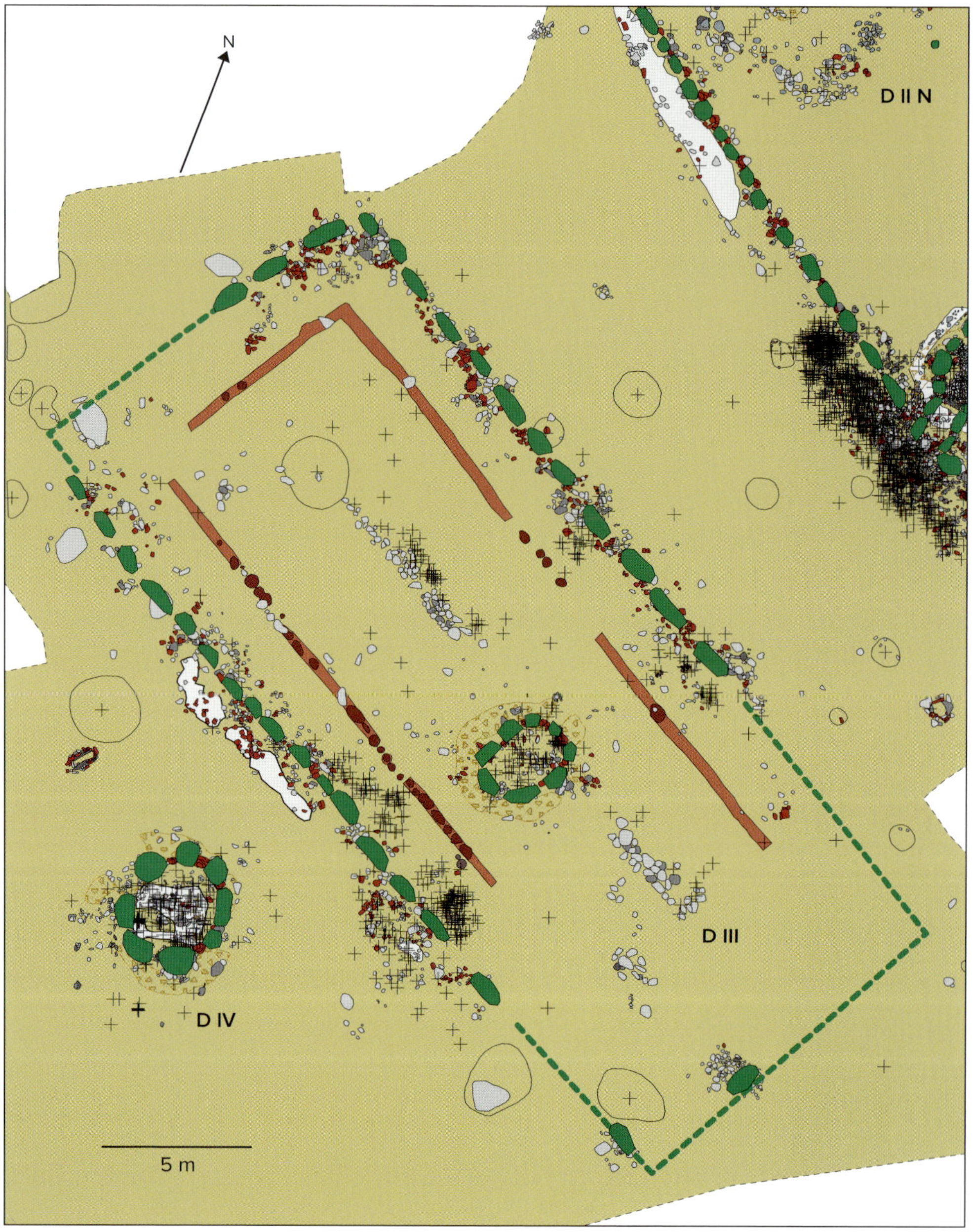

The last structure built here appears to have been long dolmen D II, in the middle of which had stood a small, rounded passage grave with a passage to the southwest, extending out to the framing kerbstones (fig. 20.7). The latter enclosed an area of 9 x 37 m, resulting in the early dolmen D II N also becoming enclosed within the mound. The long dolmen with mound fill was the only monument of this kind built here. A large number of potsherds from the Klintebakke phase were found deposited in front of the entrance to the passage-grave chamber. Sherds from the same period had also been deposited on the east side of the long barrow.

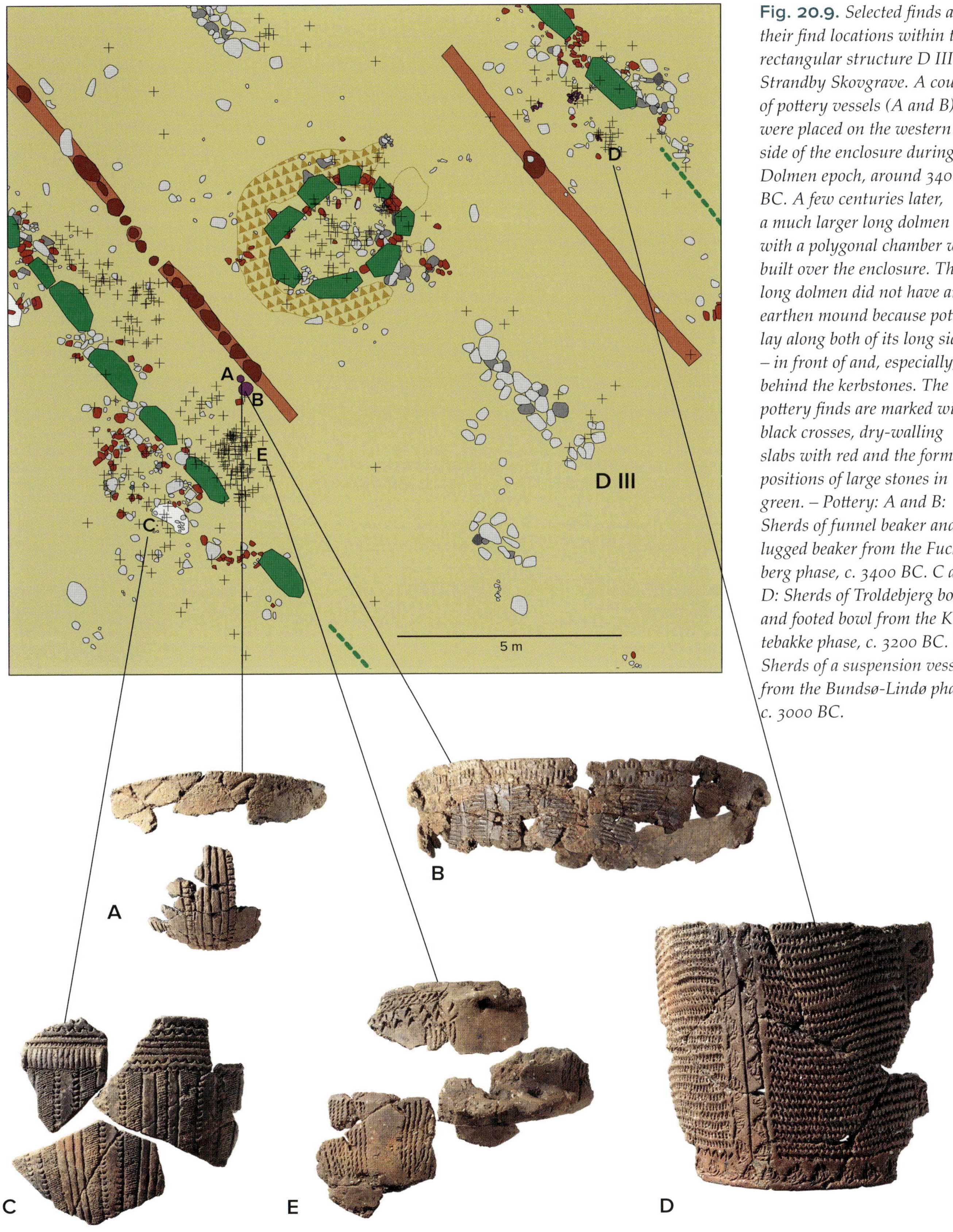

Fig. 20.9. *Selected finds and their find locations within the rectangular structure D III at Strandby Skovgrave. A couple of pottery vessels (A and B) were placed on the western side of the enclosure during the Dolmen epoch, around 3400 BC. A few centuries later, a much larger long dolmen with a polygonal chamber was built over the enclosure. The long dolmen did not have an earthen mound because pottery lay along both of its long sides – in front of and, especially, behind the kerbstones. The pottery finds are marked with black crosses, dry-walling slabs with red and the former positions of large stones in green. – Pottery: A and B: Sherds of funnel beaker and lugged beaker from the Fuchsberg phase, c. 3400 BC. C and D: Sherds of Troldebjerg bowl and footed bowl from the Klintebakke phase, c. 3200 BC. E: Sherds of a suspension vessel from the Bundsø-Lindø phase, c. 3000 BC.*

Relative to the question of dolmens with or without mounds, it is remarkable that there has been no earthen fill around polygonal dolmen chamber D III. The fact that an earthen mound was preserved at long dolmen D II, which only lies 10 m further east, shows that the missing mound in D III cannot be due to the effects of cultivation or ordinary soil erosion.[15]

The absence of a mound in association with D III is further confirmed by the discovery of very large quantities of pottery also *within* the kerbstones (fig. 20.9 D-E). This dates primarily from the Klintebakken phase (fig. 20.9 D), but pottery from much later phases, around 3000 BC, is represented, too (fig. 20.9 E). The deposition of pottery over the course of several centuries further confirms that there was no earthen mound here. Moreover, some of the sherds were weathered, indicating that they had lain exposed for quite a long period of time.

It is difficult to explain why dry-walling was originally stacked up between the kerbstones around long dolmen D II. There does not appear to be enough slabs for the stacks to have closed the gaps completely. As the dry-walling had collapsed both inwards and outwards, and was found on the same level as the potsherds, we must presume that there had been no earthen fill on the inside to stabilise the stacked slabs. The kerbstones and the dry-walling possibly simply constituted a relatively low barrier, intended to mark the boundary to the enclosed area, exactly as we saw with the trapezoid enclosure at Sarup Gamle Skole, which had a fence or barrier made of relatively short wooden posts.

Strandby Skovgrave provides a picture of a megalithic complex that was extremely complex! The sequence of events may have unfolded as follows (fig. 20.10):

The first structure at the site was a small dolmen cist (D II N), surrounded by a low earthen elevation. Perhaps coeval with this, possibly even earlier, a rectangular post-built enclosure (D III) was constructed, and a couple of pottery vessels were deposited on the outside of the fence. Structure D III was then framed by a row of large stones set 2 m outside the post-built enclosure. These stones, together with dry-walling, constituted a stone barrier around an open area without an earthen mound. A dolmen chamber was then erected in the middle of this area. Later, in the western part of the area, a large free-standing polygonal dolmen chamber (D IV) was built, followed, in the eastern part, by a further solitary dolmen chamber (D I), furnished with a passage. There are no indications that these two dolmens (D IV and D I) have ever had a mound or been framed by a fence or kerbstones. Finally, a large long barrow (D II) with kerbstones was built, incorporating the earliest dolmen cist (D II N) at the site. The monument enclosed a small, newly-built, rounded passage grave with a passage to the west, extending out to the kerbstones. At the time of construction, a quantity of fine pottery in Klintebakke style was deposited in front of dolmen D I and along both sides of both long barrow D II and "long barrow" D III, in the latter case also by the inside of the kerbstones.

It is also worth noting that all the stone chambers at this locality had their entrance facing towards the southwest or west. Entrances are usually oriented towards the southeast, especially in the case of passage graves.

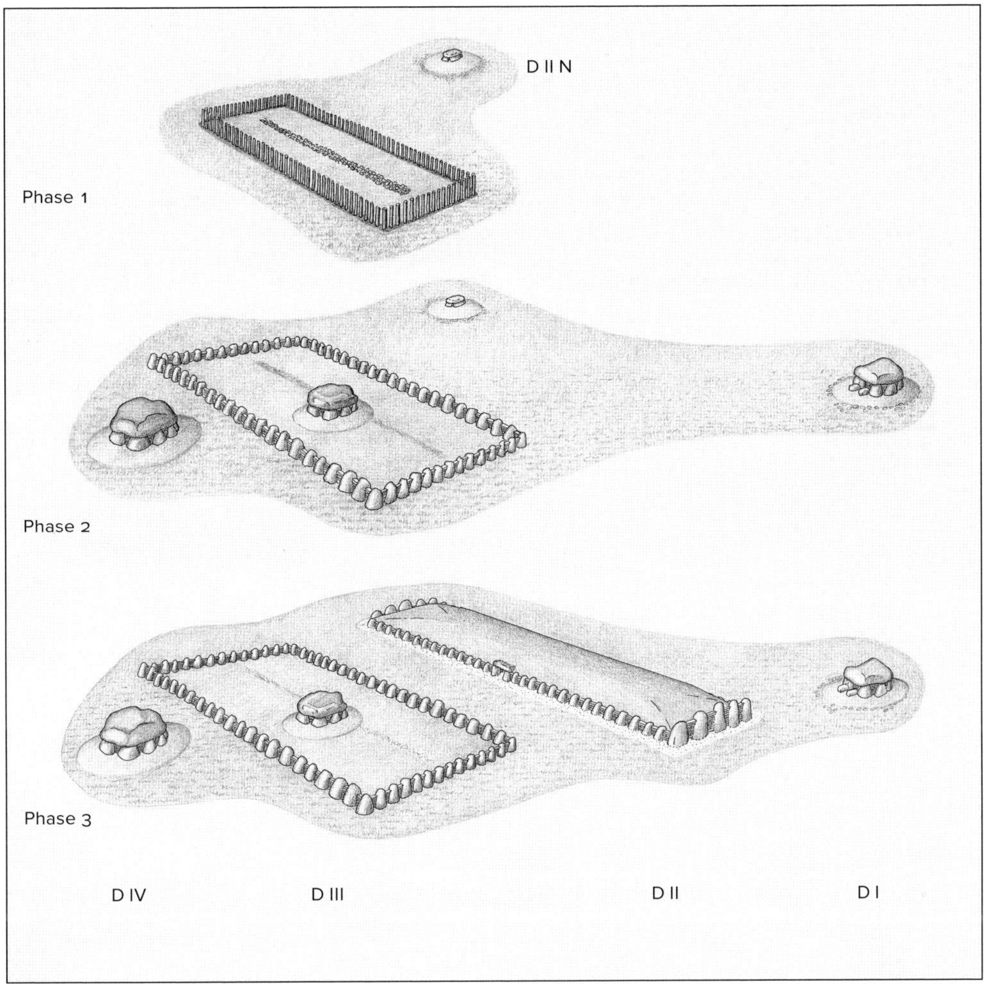

Fig. 20.10. *Reconstruction of the three construction phases we believe we can identify at Strandby Skovgrave. – Phases: A: A small dolmen cist (D II N) was constructed, surrounded by a low earthen elevation, as well as a Barkaer-structure (D III) about 10 m to the west. B: The Barkaer-structure was framed by large stones (D III) and the gaps between them filled with dry-walling. A dolmen chamber was built within this frame, and a further dolmen chamber (D IV) was built to the west, as well as a small dolmen (D I) with a passage directly to the east. C: A round passage grave was built in continuation of the dolmen cist constructed in the first phase. These two stone chambers were then covered by a long earthen mound, framed by the kerbstones.*

Damsbo

In 2003-08, a private donation enabled the investigation of an area of 1.5 ha, measuring 170 m north-south and 90 m east-west, on a field sloping west towards Helnæs Bugt, c. 2.5 km southeast of Sarup (figs. 20.2 and 20.11). This area had been known to us for many years, as it contains a scheduled stone cist; one of the two aforementioned scheduled megalithic monuments within the study area for the Sarup project. On a site visit to the field where the stone cist stood, we observed remains of five ploughed-down megalithic monuments, three of which had human bone visible on the field surface. Aerial photography of the area in June 1992 further confirmed that two of the structures were located in round barrows.

On excavation, it became evident that the structures varied significantly in their state of preservation. This was due in particular to the fact that they were situated on sloping ground. This had led to the western part of the monuments often having been completely ploughed away, while the eastern part was generally rather better preserved. Despite these limitations, the investigation yielded a large number of finds – 47,800 in total – and many interesting structures.

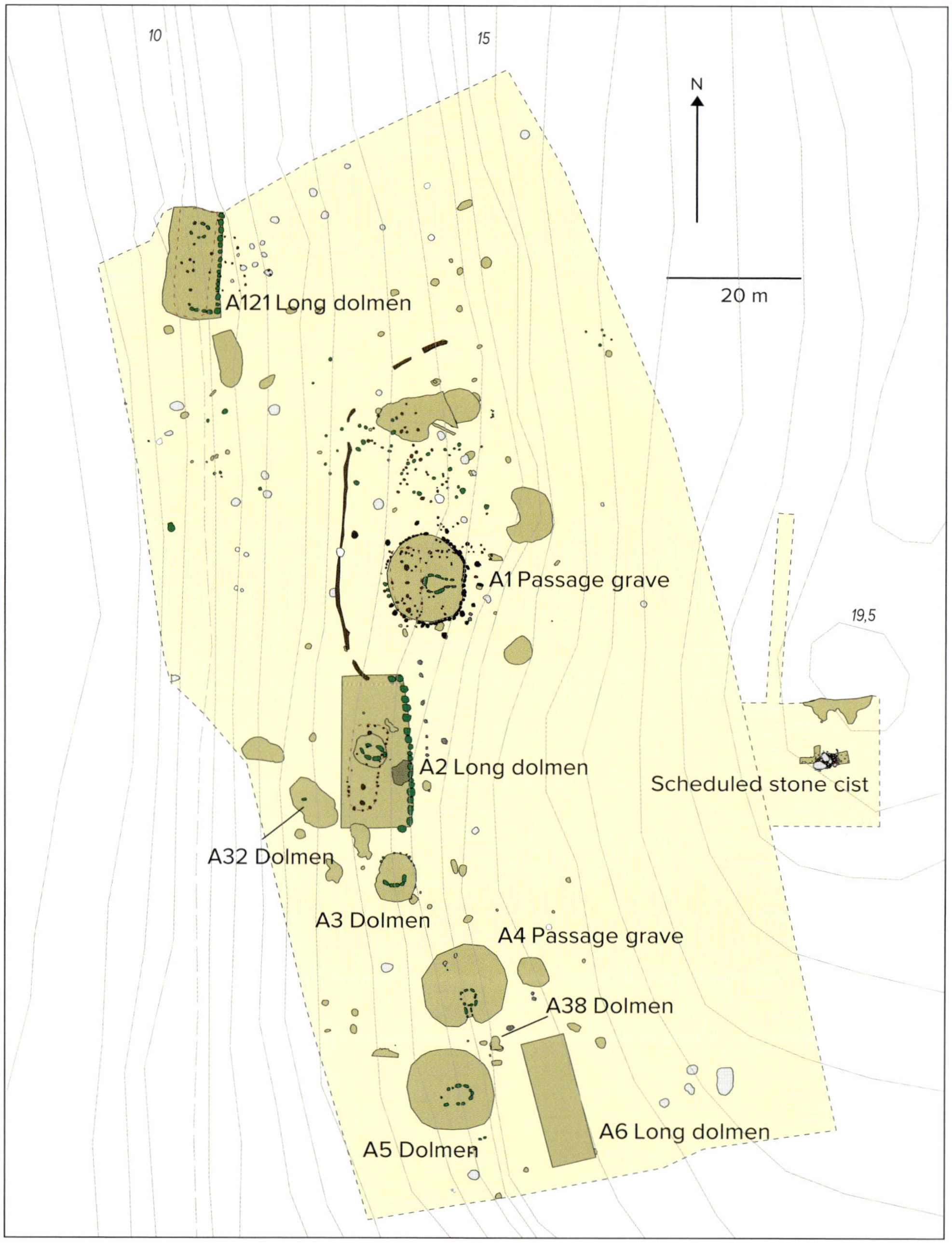

Fig. 20.11. *The 1.5 ha area at Damsbo, showing the most important structures. To the south, a group comprising a long dolmen (A6), two dolmen chambers (A5 and A38) and a small passage grave (A4). In the centre, a group comprising a long dolmen (A2), two solitary dolmen chambers (A3 and A32) and a passage grave (A1). To the north, a long dolmen (A121), part of which was excavated. The other half extends below a field bank and continues into the neighbouring field. The three northernmost structures – A1, A2 and A121 – are located on the sites of two-aisled houses.*

In addition to the five megalithic monuments that we located on the surface of the field, on removal of the topsoil we discovered traces of a further four megalithic structures, giving a total of nine excavated monuments: seven dolmens and two passage graves (fig. 20.11). Eight of these lay together in two groups. To the south was a group consisting of an almost completely destroyed long dolmen (A6), two free-standing dolmen chambers (A5 and A38) and a small passage grave in a round barrow (A4). To the north of these were a long dolmen (A2), two free-standing dolmen chambers (A3 and A32) and a small passage grave in a round barrow (A1). Further to these, part of a long dolmen (A121) was uncovered on the northern edge of the excavation.

Long dolmen A2 was originally 25 m long, north-south, and 11 m wide, east-west (fig. 20.12). Only at its eastern side could we see where the kerbstones had stood. In the middle of the structure were traces of a polygonal stone chamber, set of six orthostats and with an opening to the northwest, which was surrounded and supported by clay packing. The chamber was built on top of part of a burnt house site dated, by way of finds recovered from postholes, a thin cultural layer east of the house site and a pit, to the Fuchsberg phase. This long dolmen must not have had any earthen fill because dry-walling slabs and pottery from the Klintebakke phase, c. 3200 BC, were found not only between, but also inside and outside the imprints left by its kerbstones. Furthermore, on both sides of the kerbstones was pottery from the Store Valby phase, c. 2800 BC, i.e. c. 400 years later (fig. 20.12).

In the far north of the excavated area at Damsbo lay the remains of a third long dolmen (A121) (see fig. 20.11). Here too, the eastern side was best preserved. In the middle of the structure were the remains of a polygonal dolmen chamber with surrounding clay packing. This chamber was also built over the remains of a burnt-down house, with finds dating the building to the Fuchsberg phase. It should be noted that the dry-walling of A121 lay in situ between the kerbstones and also outside them, but not, as seen in the other structures, inside the kerbstones. Later pottery, deposited in front of the chamber, was also only found outside the kerbstones. No unequivocal traces of a mound were recorded, but given the location of the collapsed dry-walling and the later pottery, which were only found outside the kerbstones, this could suggest that the enclosed area had some kind of earthen fill.

There were four free-standing dolmens at Damsbo, of which one (A32) was so badly damaged only part of an orthostat and part of the floor were preserved. This monument was located on sharply sloping terrain to the west of long dolmen A2, and given its situation, A32 seems very unlikely to have had any form of mound material associated with it. The second free-standing dolmen (A38) was a very small structure with a chamber floor measuring c. 1.3 x 1 m. It stood very close to the two structures A4 and A5 and there was therefore no space for a mound around its chamber.

The two other free-standing dolmens, both with polygonal chambers were, however, framed by kerbstones. By one of them (A3) there were traces of an oval frame that, to the north, had consisted of stones up to 50 cm in size. The other (A5) had a large chamber which covered an area of 4.5 x 2.6 m, but no passage (fig. 20.13). Around the chamber there had been a 50 cm wide clay packing, followed by a 80 cm wide stone-free belt and then a finely-laid, almost 2 m wide, stone pavement, which was however only preserved in its eastern part. It is not possible to determine whether these two chambers (A3 and A5) had an earthen mound that extended some way up the chamber orthostats.

The excavated area also included traces of two small, round passage graves (A1 and A4) dating from the Klintebakke phase. The chambers were located in round barrows (fig. 20.11). Only A1 had a kerbstone circle and, like structures A2 and A121, this passage grave was built on the site of a house.[16]

Fig. 20.12. *Traces of kerbstones were only found on the eastern side of long dolmen A2 at Damsbo. In the middle of the monument there had been a polygonal dolmen chamber with an opening to the northwest. The dolmen chamber was built over the remains of a burnt-down house, the outline of which is marked with a broken, red line. Finds of pottery belonging to the house can be dated to the Fuchsberg phase, c. 3400 BC; these are marked in yellow on the plan. Both inside and outside the kerbstones of the later long dolmen there was pottery – the red dots on the plan – dating from the Klintebakke phase, c. 3200 BC. In addition, there was later pottery – the blue dots on the plan – dating from the Store Valby phase, c. 2800 BC.*

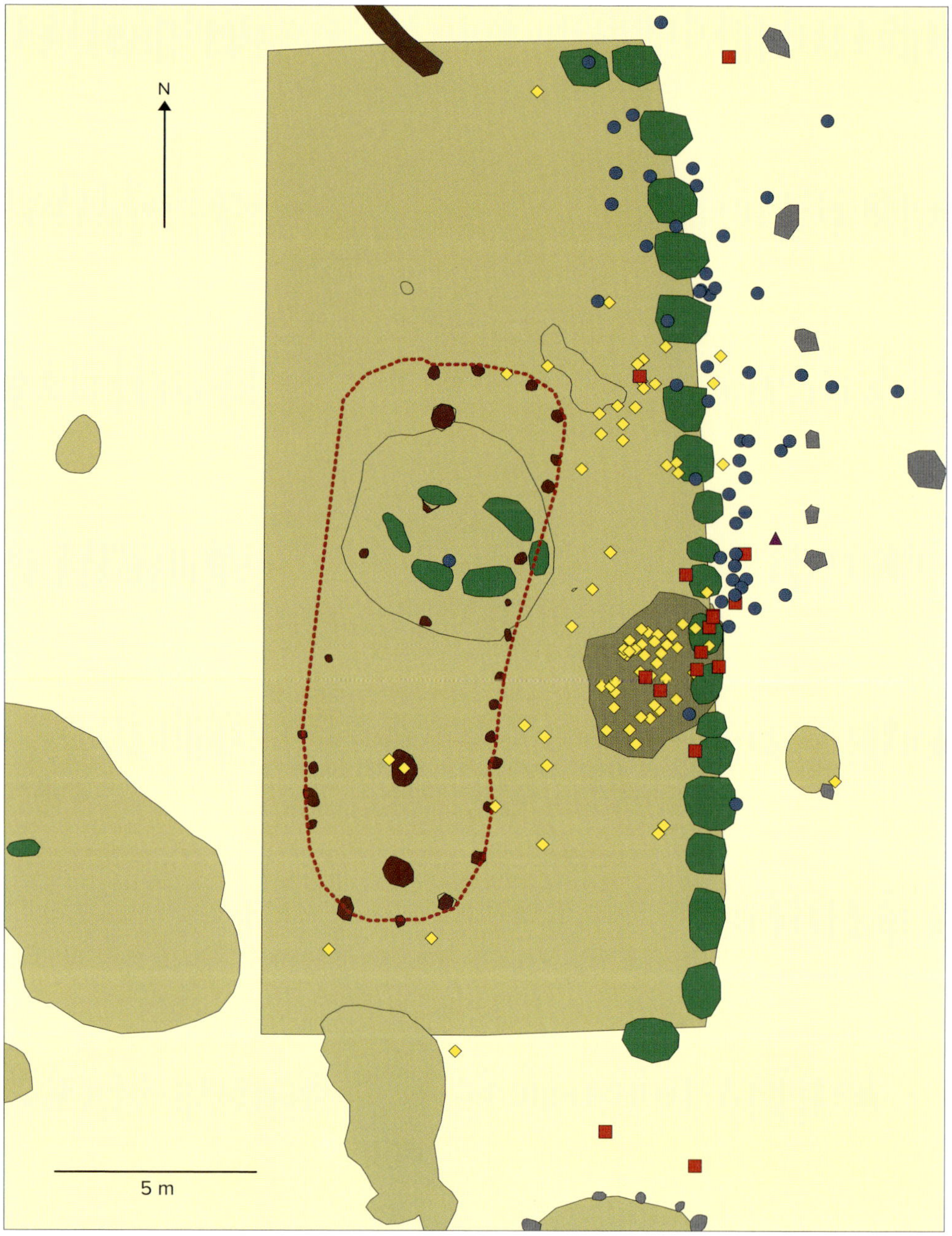

As is apparent from the above, many different types of megalithic tombs have been demonstrated at Damsbo. Of these, one of the long dolmens (A2) had no mound material, while the other long dolmen (A121) may have had a mound though this was perhaps not very conspicuous. In addition, there were a couple of free-standing dolmens (A32 and A38), which clearly did not have a surrounding or enclosing mound. A couple of other dolmens (A3 and A5) were marked by a kind of terrace or pavement, or a tablet, as Märtha Strömberg termed it at Trollasten (see chapter 15). Here at Damsbo, we also see a development from long barrows to free-standing dolmen chambers and then, ultimately, a couple of small passage graves. What we do not encounter are post-built enclosures of Barkær type. On the other hand, Neolithic people built at least three houses here, on the sites of which they later constructed megalithic monuments. It appears to be no coincidence that these megalithic monuments were built directly on top of the remains of the houses.

The dolmens of the Sarup area

Presented above are three areas containing excavated megalithic monuments which, despite the fact that they lie, at most, 2 km apart, appear very different, though with some shared features. Common to all three areas is their association with water, in the form of either watercourses, wetlands or the coast. At two of the localities, at least some of the monuments were built on sloping terrain, as if they were intended to offer a view over, or be seen from, the wetland areas.

Moreover, all three areas have a construction period that extends over a couple of centuries. At two of them – Sarup Gamle Skole and Strandby Skovgrave – enclosures without any earthen fill were built during the Fuchsberg phase (figs. 20.5 A4 and 20.7 D III). At Sarup Gamle Skole, a small dolmen was built in the middle of one of these enclosures (fig. 20.5 A3). Somewhat later, a similar structure was built at Strandby Skovgrave, which was then framed by a row of large kerbstones interspersed with dry-walling. A kind of stone barrier, though with no fill material behind, i.e. a long dolmen without a mound (fig. 20.7).

The earliest structure at Damsbo was also a long dolmen without a mound (figs. 20.11 A2 and 20.12), while another long dolmen at this locality (fig. 20.11 A121) must have had some kind of earthen fill that extended partly up the kerbstones and the sides of the chamber.

There were free-standing dolmens at all three localities; eight monuments in total. At none of these was there evidence giving reason to believe there had been an earthen mound around the chamber. However, in the case of two dolmens at Damsbo (A3 and A5) (see fig. 20.11) there are indications that these were surrounded by a horizontal platform – or tablet – made of earth and stone.

At all three localities, the building activity concluded with the construction of small passage graves and – in contrast to the situation with the dolmens – it is demonstrable that these later monuments were always enclosed within an earthen mound. At Damsbo, there were two round barrows (A1 and A4) (fig. 20.11), while the passage graves at Strandby Skovgrave (fig. 20.7 D II) and Sarup Gamle Skole (fig. 20.5 B) stood in long barrows, which are normally referred to as long dolmens. This must be said to be an unfortunate term, which can give the wrong impression, because long barrows were not originally built around dolmen chambers, but around passage graves. The finds show, furthermore, that these long barrows date from the Klintebakke phase, i.e. couple of centuries later than the time when dolmens were constructed.[17]

It is interesting that there are two instances at Damsbo (A2 and A121) where "long dolmens" were built directly on the sites of longhouses, with the chambers being placed directly between the postholes for two of the central posts that carried the

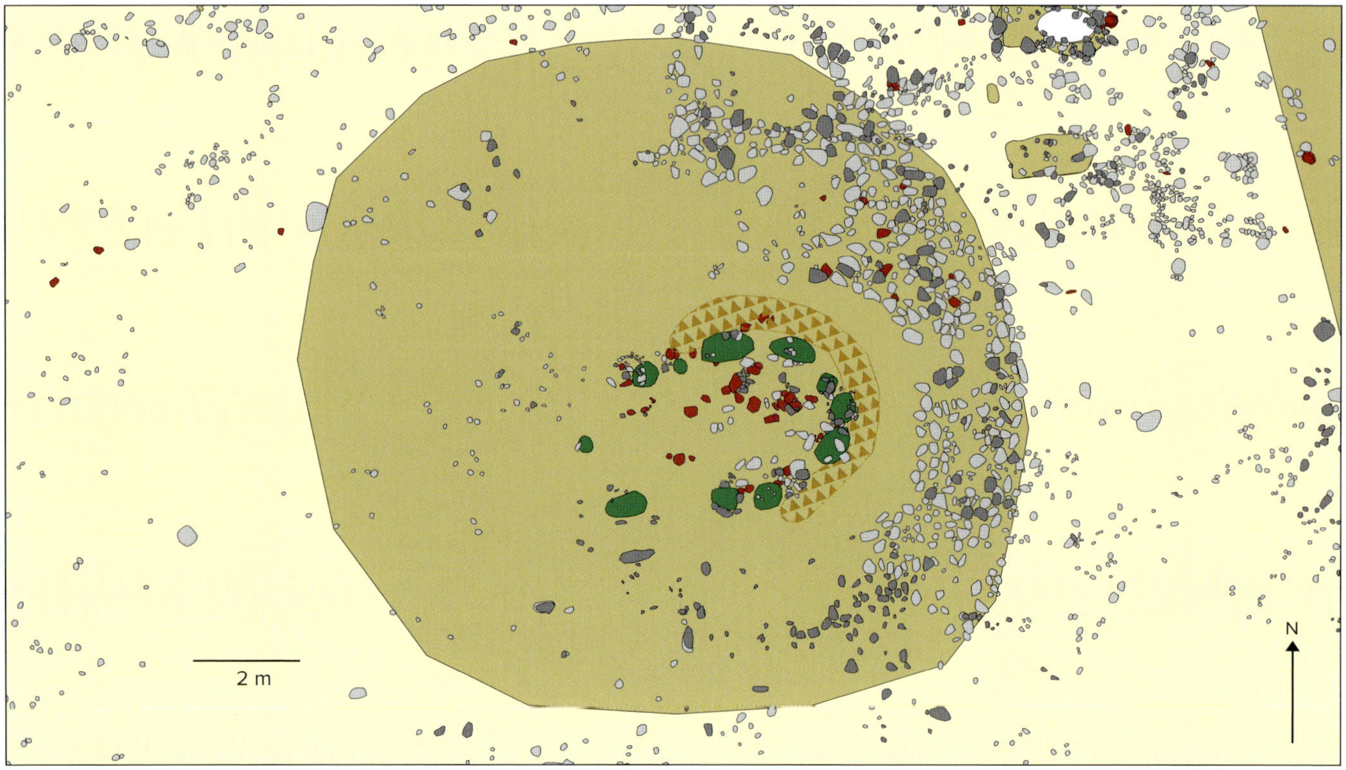

Fig. 20.13. *A free-standing dolmen chamber (A5) was excavated southernmost in the the area investigated at Damsbo. Shown in green on the plan are the traces left by the large stones of the chamber. With dimensions of 4.5 x 2.6 m, the chamber was impressive. The finds found inside it included well-preserved human bones dating from a later part of the Funnel Beaker culture, i.e. c. 3000 BC. There had been a clay packing around the chamber, followed by a stone-free zone and then a fine, 2 m wide stone pavement – a kind of terrace or tablet. Due to modern cultivation, only the eastern part of the monument was reasonably well preserved.*

roof (fig. 20.11). The placing of a burial monument on a former house site is also seen at another archaeological locality in the area, Frydenlund. Here, a richly-furnished burial in a plank-built coffin, dating from c. 3550 BC, was sited in a similar way (see fig. 9.4). On the site of a third house at Damsbo, a couple of centuries after the house was built, a passage grave was carefully constructed, with a surrounding mound that precisely covered the footprint of the former longhouse (fig. 20.11 A1).[18]

The house remains at Damsbo and Frydenlund were only discovered because we took time and great pains to study the soil layers under different conditions. The traces were clearest in early spring, when the very pale postholes stood out by retaining the moisture in the soil. During our previous excavations we have probably overlooked a number of house sites, and the same is presumably true of many other excavations. The finds from the house sites beneath the burial monuments show that there may have been a connection between those who occupied these buildings and those who constructed the burial monuments.

All three of the areas at Sarup described above were, over a period of about 200 years, visited and revisited by people through numerous generations. These people, who must have known and been related to each other, were prompted, driven even, to return to a specific delimited area that must have been significant to them. Here, they then followed a more or less uniform pattern of monument construction, first by establishing mound-free structures of Barkær type, followed by the construction of free-standing dolmen chambers and culminating with the building of small passage graves covered by round or long barrows.[19]

Of the 18 megalithic chambers investigated, only five – i.e. the passage graves – showed definite traces of having been enclosed within an earthen mound. The dolmen chamber in long barrow A121 at Damsbo was possibly also surrounded by a little earthen fill, though this does not appear to have fully occupied the area framed by the kerbstones.

The investigations of ploughed-down megalithic monuments in the Sarup area have, despite the fact that many of these structures had suffered heavy damage from cultivation, provided a diverse and informative picture of the form and function of these monuments. A picture – it should be noted – that has not been obtained to date from better-preserved, scheduled monuments. It is therefore desirable for further, similar investigations to be carried out of ploughed-down megalithic monuments, because it is to be presumed that the picture may well be different in other areas – just look at the degree of variation apparent within the very limited area at Sarup!

21. The living and the dead

In 1843, at the age of only 22, J.J.A. Worsaae published his book *Danmarks Oldtid oplyst ved Oldsager og Gravhøie*, and six years later it appeared in English: *The Primeval Antiquities of Denmark*. In this work, the first academic book on Danish prehistory, Worsaae states that dolmens had up until that time been perceived as heathen thingsteads or altars. Long dolmens in particular were seen as the former, a place where people had gathered to hold council on common affairs, resolve disagreements and so on. The judges and elders sat on the surrounding kerbstones and offerings were made to the gods on the stone chambers or altars. The sacrificial animal was laid on the dolmen chamber's capstone and when it was killed, its blood, on the basis of which the sacrificial priest predicted future events, flowed down into the chamber.

Worsaae rejected this interpretation on the purely practical grounds that the kerbstones were uncomfortable to sit on and the capstones had their flat surface facing down towards the chamber. If a sacrificial animal was to be placed on a capstone, it would have been appropriate for the flat side of the stone to be uppermost. Moreover, these "thingsteads" were very unevenly distributed across the country. Some parishes had more than a hundred, while others had none. But Worsaae attached particular weight to the fact that human bones and artefacts were found within the chambers, which must mean that they represented burial places.[1]

Worsaae's interpretation of dolmens as tombs has prevailed to the present day. They have even been interpreted as the tombs of chieftains, because some people believe that dolmens – and causewayed enclosures too, for that matter – could only have been the product of a stratified, hierarchical society led by such figures.[2] It is possible that this is true, and it would also be a plausible explanation for the function of these monumental structures. But in archaeology, we should confine ourselves to the available finds, features, structures and observations – the so-called *hardcore evidence* – and not let wishful thinking guide our interpretations. That only results in a confused and confusing picture.

In 2011, Danish megalithic tombs were subjected to an excellent analysis and presentation by Klaus Ebbesen. In his major work *Danmarks Megalitgrave*, Ebbesen also addresses the burial practices associated with dolmens,[3] and records 29 Danish dolmens containing human skeletal remains. These remains can, however, only in a few cases be presumed to date from the time when the monuments were built. Further to these, 123 dolmens were excavated that contained grave goods, but no preserved human remains. It is also remarkable that one third of the undisturbed chambers that were investigated apparently contained no trace whatsoever of corpses

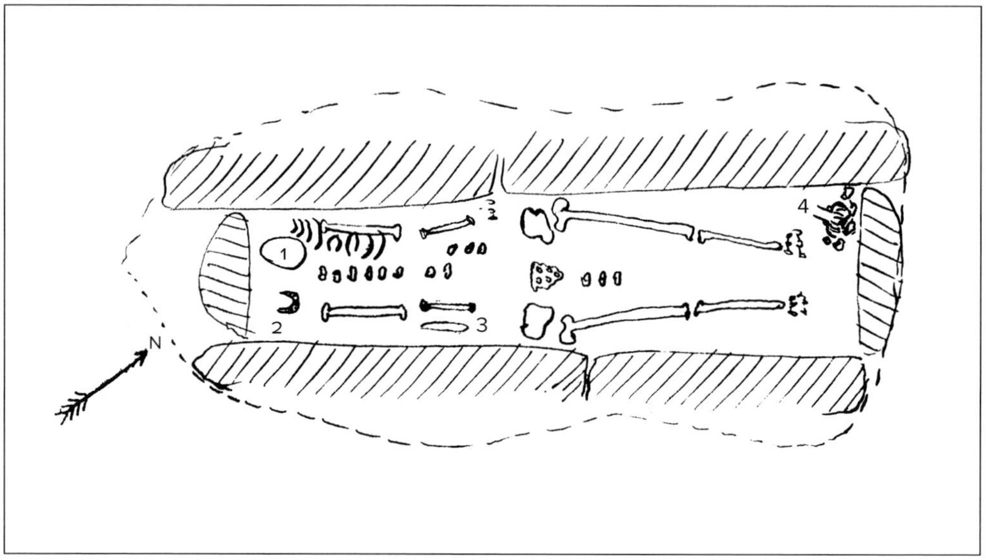

Fig. 21.1. *In 1933, some boys found a skeleton in the dolmen cist in the Kellerød long dolmen. The corpse had been laid on its back with its head to the south. The cist also contained a pottery vessel and a flint blade. Knud Thorvildsen of the Danish National Museum drew this sketch of the site, based on information from the excavators. – 1: Skull. 2: Lower jaw. 3: Flint blade. 4: Pottery vessel.*

or so-called grave goods.[4] It was apparently still common practice at that time not to place grave goods in a grave. The grave goods found in the 123 chambers comprise pottery, flint axes and ornaments, but often only one of these items was present in any one chamber. These "grave finds" show that burials may indeed be involved, but their number is not at all impressive given the total number of dolmens there are, or once were. Let us now take a look at some of the dolmens containing traces of human remains.

Skeletons from dolmen cists and chambers

In 1984, Poul Otto Nielsen of the Danish National Museum published an account of the few Danish dolmens that have been found to contain human bones, and from where there also are radiocarbon dates.[5] His article mentions two cases where these dates were obtained for the actual bones.

Kellerød

The Kellerød long dolmen was excavated in 1933 by some young school boys (see chapter 10). They investigated the rectangular dolmen cist, which was 2.5 m long and, at its base, 60 cm wide to the south and 75 cm wide to the north. The internal height of the cist was 60 cm. The capstone was a large, 35-50 cm thick flagstone, which was 3 m long and up to 1.6 m wide. The excavation of the cist was undertaken by entering from the northern end, after the boys had removed the end stone here. The fill of the cist was carefully investigated using teaspoons and knives. In it they found the somewhat disturbed skeleton of an older man, whose lower jaw was separated from his skull, but lay parallel to the latter (fig. 21.1). The cist was also found to contain a flint blade and a broken pottery vessel, the sherds of which lay scattered. In 1981, a radiocarbon date of 3365-2936 BC was obtained.[6] However, we believe this date to

150-200 years later than would be expected, if the skeleton represents the first burial in the dolmen cist. A new date is therefore desirable, now that the radiocarbon-dating method has been refined to give smaller error margins. At present, we must consider the age of "Kellerød Man" to be in some doubt, given that his remains were deposited as one of the first activities in the cist. Moreover, it is worth noting that the skeleton was perhaps not buried as a complete corpse – another good reason for undertaking a new dating analysis of the human remains.

Klokkehøj

Another dolmen possibly containing a preserved human skeleton is the extended dolmen chamber Klokkehøj at Horneland in southern Funen, excavated in 1977 by Sven Thorsen.[7] In the chamber lay parts of a skeleton in extended supine position, which was considered to represent a primary burial (fig. 21.2). The bones were well preserved, but the skull and the upper four neck vertebrae were missing and the lower jaw lay in two halves on either side of the remaining neck vertebrae. Contrary to the excavator, we believe the skull and the four upper vertebrae were removed from the corpse in the Neolithic, when they were still held together by sinews. The placing of the two halves of the corpse's lower jaw on either side of the remaining neck vertebrae must be seen as being a deliberate act.

It must be presumed that the body buried here was not in a fresh state, but a more or less disintegrated corpse. The skeleton is that of a 20-35-year-old man, and high carbon 13 values show that he had obtained some of his food from the sea. Radiocarbon dating of the skeleton gave a result of 3501-3026 BC. The chamber was also found

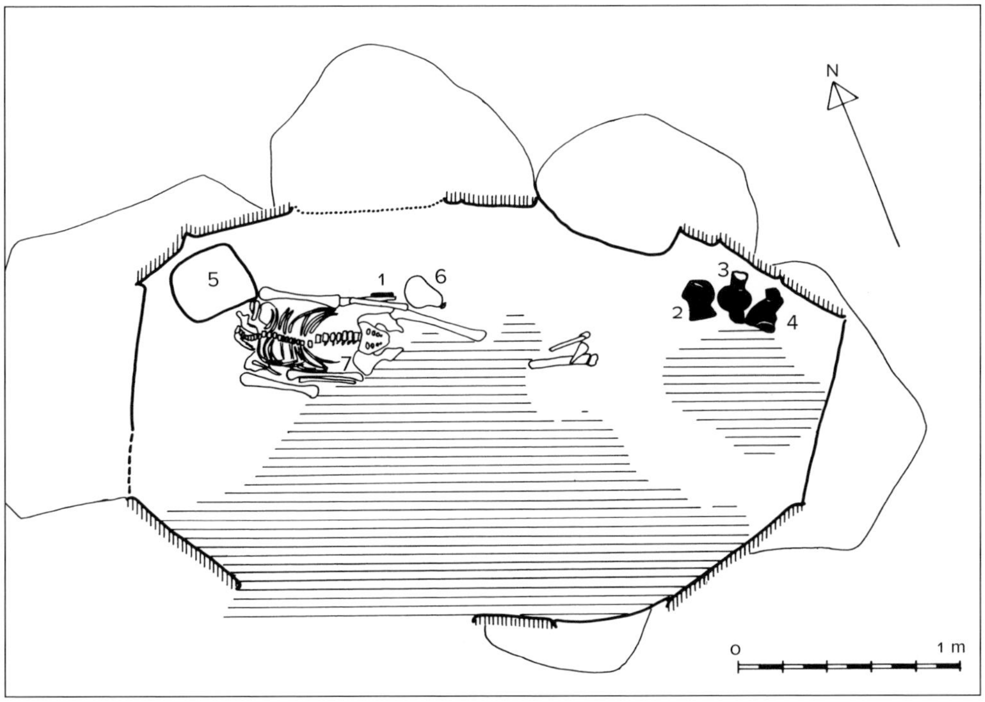

Fig. 21.2. *The primary burial layer in the dolmen chamber in Klokkehøj, investigated in 1977, consisted of the major part of a skeleton, as well as the bones from two other individuals. Half of the chamber floor was disturbed. – 1: Elongate bone plate. 2-4: Three pottery vessels. 5: Stone. 6: Child's skull. 7: Upper and lower arm bones*

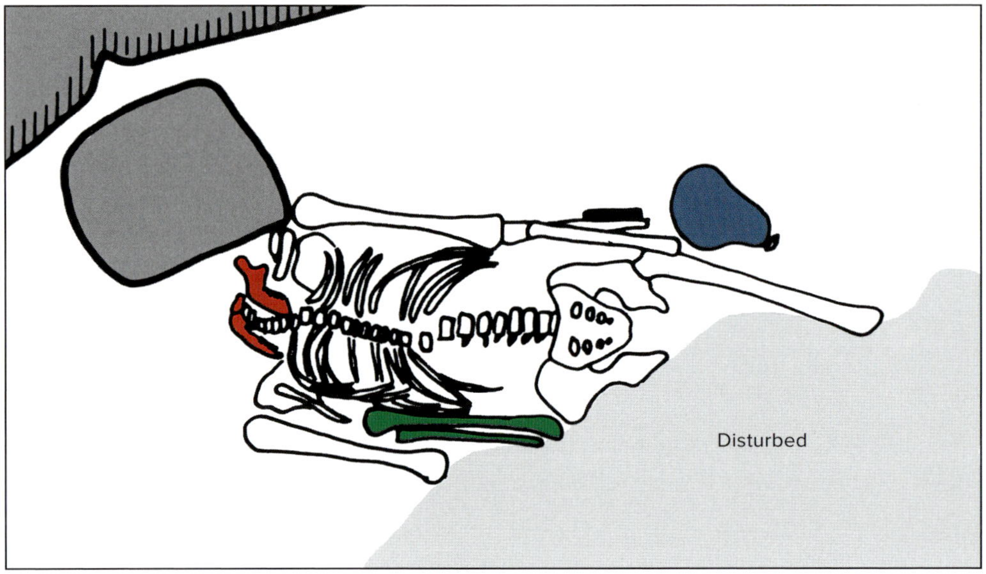

Fig. 21.3. *The skeletal parts in the primary burial layer in the Klokkehøj dolmen, marked by individual. The almost complete skeleton of a male adult lacks the skull and associated upper neck vertebrae, which were probably removed in the Neolithic. But the man's lower jaw – shown in red – was in two halves, which lay on either side of the remaining upper vertebrae. Bones of another adult are marked in green, while the skull of a child is marked in blue.*

to contain parts of two funnel beakers and a dolmen flask that corresponds typologically to those from the Fuchsberg phase, the time frame of which is very consistent with the date for the skeleton.[8] The dolmen flask contained 232 small pieces of burnt and crushed flint.[9] The almost complete male skeleton partially overlay bones from at least one other "burial", whereby only a few bones of the deceased had been placed in the chamber. In addition, human bones that must be from another earlier "burial" were also found beneath one shoulder of the male skeleton, and close to its left femur lay a child's skull (fig. 21.3). There is therefore evidence here of the deposition of a small number bones from more than one individual, in addition to an almost complete corpse, from which the skull and part of the neck had, however, been removed.

Ølstykke

In his article, Poul Otto Nielsen also mentions a skeleton from Ølstykke in northeast Zealand.[10] The investigation of the dolmen chamber, in which this was found, was undertaken in February 1890 by Sophus Müller. The narrow, rectangular chamber – of type I – was 1.9 m long, 40-50 cm wide and around 1.5 m high. The base was covered by a 30 cm thick layer of crushed flint which, in turn, was covered by a layer of charcoal, on which the skeleton rested (fig. 21.4).

In his report, Sophus Müller mentions that under a couple of inches of earth at the southern end was a heavily decomposed human skull and that the bones continued through the entire grave, being best preserved at the northern end, where there was virtually no earthen cover. This description matches his drawing, and his conclusion was that there was a single skeleton. The bone material was, however, analysed in greater detail and published a couple of decades later by H.A. Nielsen, who discovered that the chamber contained bones from three individuals: an adult male and

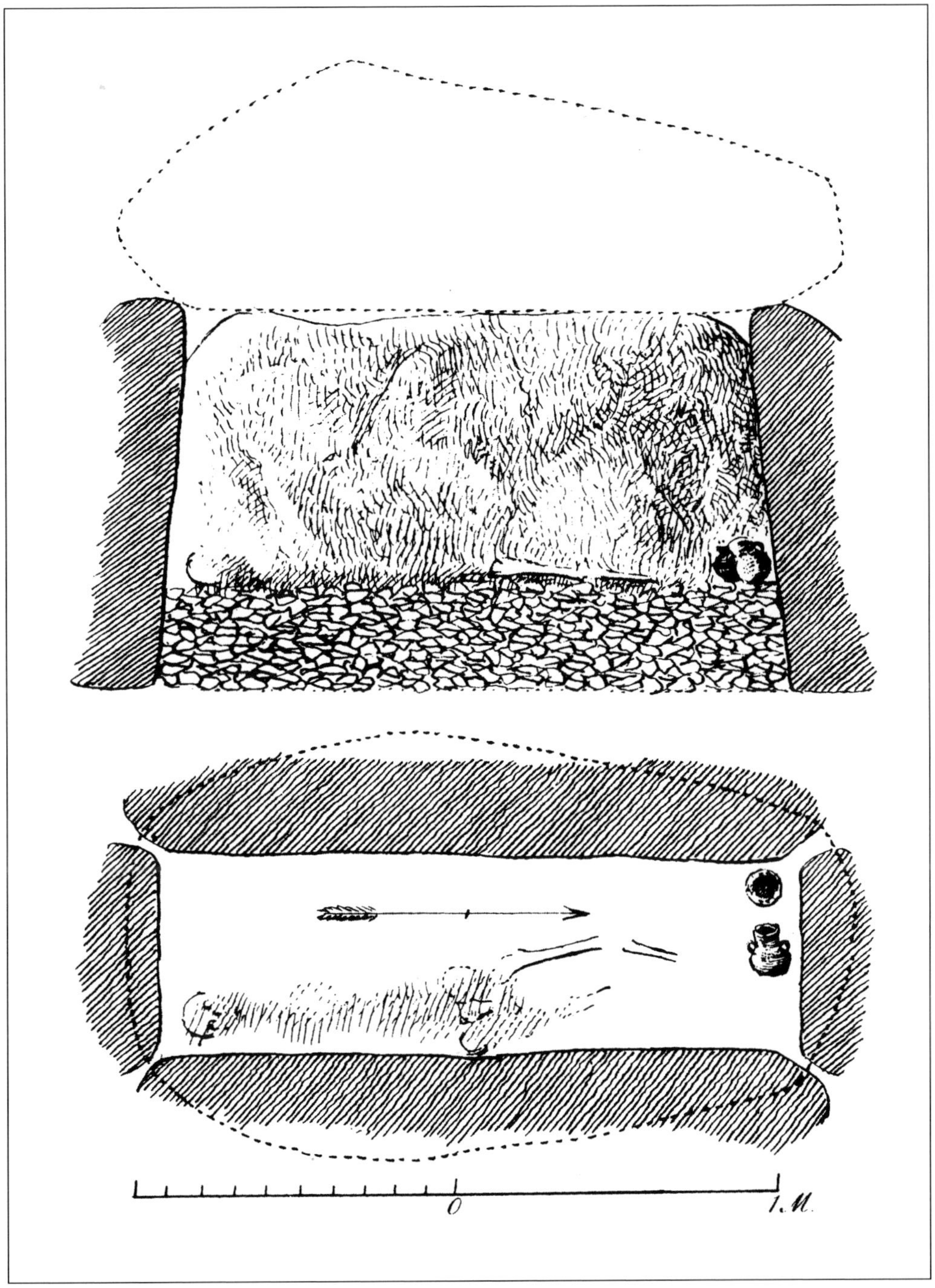

Fig. 21.4. *In the Ølstykke dolmen, investigated in 1890, lay a partially preserved skeleton. But later analyses showed that there were skeletal remains of at least a further two individuals. The bones had been placed on a layer of charcoal, which in turn lay over a 30 cm thick layer of crushed flint. At one end of the chamber stood two pottery vessels – a collared flask and a dolmen flask. The latter contained small pieces of human bone.*

an adult female, together with a child of 8-10 years of age.[11] At the northern end of the chamber were also two pottery vessels: a collared flask and a dolmen flask. The dolmen flask contained small fragments of human bone, including parts of a pelvis. This convinced Sophus Müller that the bones were already excarnated and brittle before they were placed in the vessel.[12]

The radiocarbon date, which was undertaken in 1974 on a sample of the charcoal on which the presumed skeleton lay, gave a result of 3704-3116 BC. Today, we would be very cautious about dating charcoal, because the sample could come from the inner part of a tree trunk that was already old before the tree was felled and burnt. If, for example, the wood is oak, it is very important to know if the sample comes from the inner heartwood or the outer sapwood, as there can be an age difference of several hundred years between the two. The date suggests that the finds may represent the deposition of bones from several bodies, but these remains could also be associated with activities that took place several hundred years later than the construction date for the dolmen.

In the case of Ølstykke, we now know that this was not a case of a single skeleton in a dolmen chamber, but involved bones from at least three individuals. It is not possible, on the basis of the preserved material, to determine whether three whole skeletons were originally interred, or whether only parts of them were placed in the dolmen chamber. The presence of only a single skull does, however, suggest that only skeletal parts were deposited here. It is also interesting that excarnated and brittle bones were put in a pottery vessel which was placed at the northern end of the chamber.

Taking everything into consideration, the conclusion reached here is that all three of the above-mentioned dolmens containing skeletal remains are deserving of a new analysis and further radiocarbon dates. Only a very small bone sample is now required for a radiocarbon date, and this would, furthermore, have only a modest statistical error. Interestingly, the evidence already shows that "burials" were undertaken in all three dolmen chambers, which it seems could not have involved whole corpses and that, furthermore, the body parts had been manipulated prior to deposition.

Grøfte

In 1990, a further two dolmen chambers containing skeletons – this time at Grøfte – were published by Klaus Ebbesen.[13] The two chambers stand within the same long dolmen (see chapter 6). They were investigated in 1946-47 by Harald Andersen for the Danish National Museum. Although coeval, the two chambers are not quite identical. One, chamber A, is a dolmen cist, while the other, chamber B, is a dolmen chamber. Well-preserved human bones were found in both of them.[14]

In the dolmen cist (A) lay 23 bones from at least two individuals, identified as two men, one a mature adult, the other younger – 15-25 years of age (fig. 21.5). It was in particular the larger bones that were represented.[15] It is interesting that the bones were sorted and arranged so they lay parallel. Klaus Ebbesen believes that the bones had been moved around by animals that had entered the chamber, even though the latter was hermetically closed and sealed by stacked stones. Ebbesen is convinced that originally the bodies lay in extended supine position in both stone chambers in the Grøfte long dolmen.[16] Numerous gnaw marks on the bones, made by mice, are taken as evidence that there have been small animals inside the dolmen cist, and as an explanation for the lack of, for example, finger and toe bones.[17] To us, however, it seems remarkable that animals would behave in such a systematic way, and that they had sorted and arranged the bones. Gnawing mice could, of course, have disposed

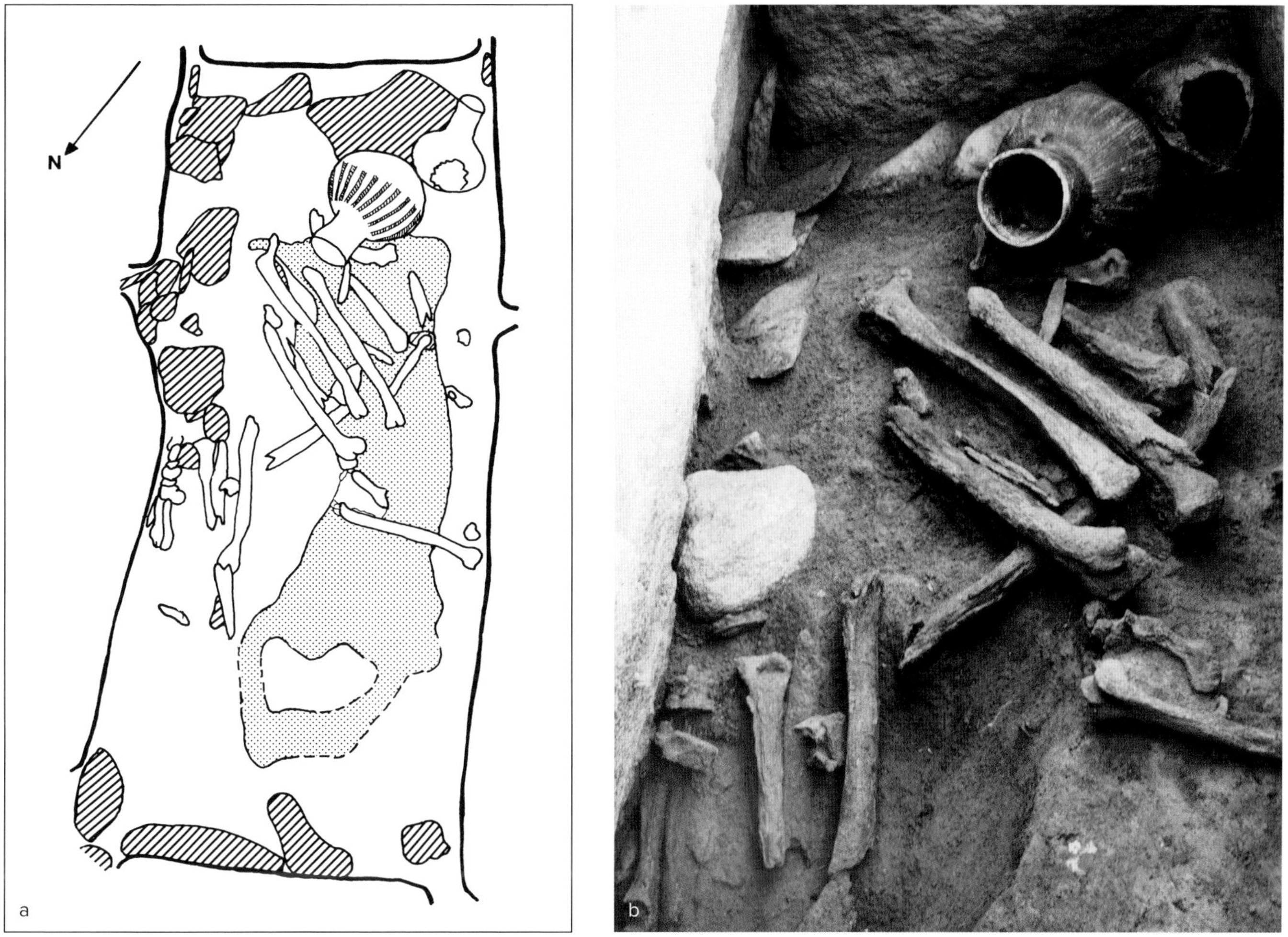

of some of the bones, but this must be presumed to have taken place at an early stage while there was still fat and protein in and on them.[18] An explanation more consistent with the finds circumstances is that the bodies of the two men were defleshed outside the chamber and then some of the bones, especially the larger ones, were gathered together and deposited in the dolmen cist.

Buried in the dolmen chamber (B) at Grøfte were the remains of a woman, between 35 and 55 years of age (fig. 21.6). About 20 of her bones were deposited there, including both her thigh bones, her right arm and her skull.[19] The woman's bones appear to be randomly placed on the floor of the chamber, and here too, the body must have been excarnated before the bones entered the chamber. The fact that they have lain exposed outside is shown by a lower jaw having gnaw marks made by the canine teeth of a fox.[20]

In the case of all three Neolithic individuals buried at Grøfte, much less than half of their bones are represented, and their bodies must have been excarnated before the bones were placed in the dolmen cist and the dolmen chamber.

Fig. 21.5. *On the base of dolmen cist A at Grøfte lay 23 bones from two men, a mature adult and younger man of between 15 and 25 years of age. It was, in particular, the men's large limb bones that had been deposited in the cist. At one end of the cist were also two dolmen flasks. The investigation took place in 1946-47.*

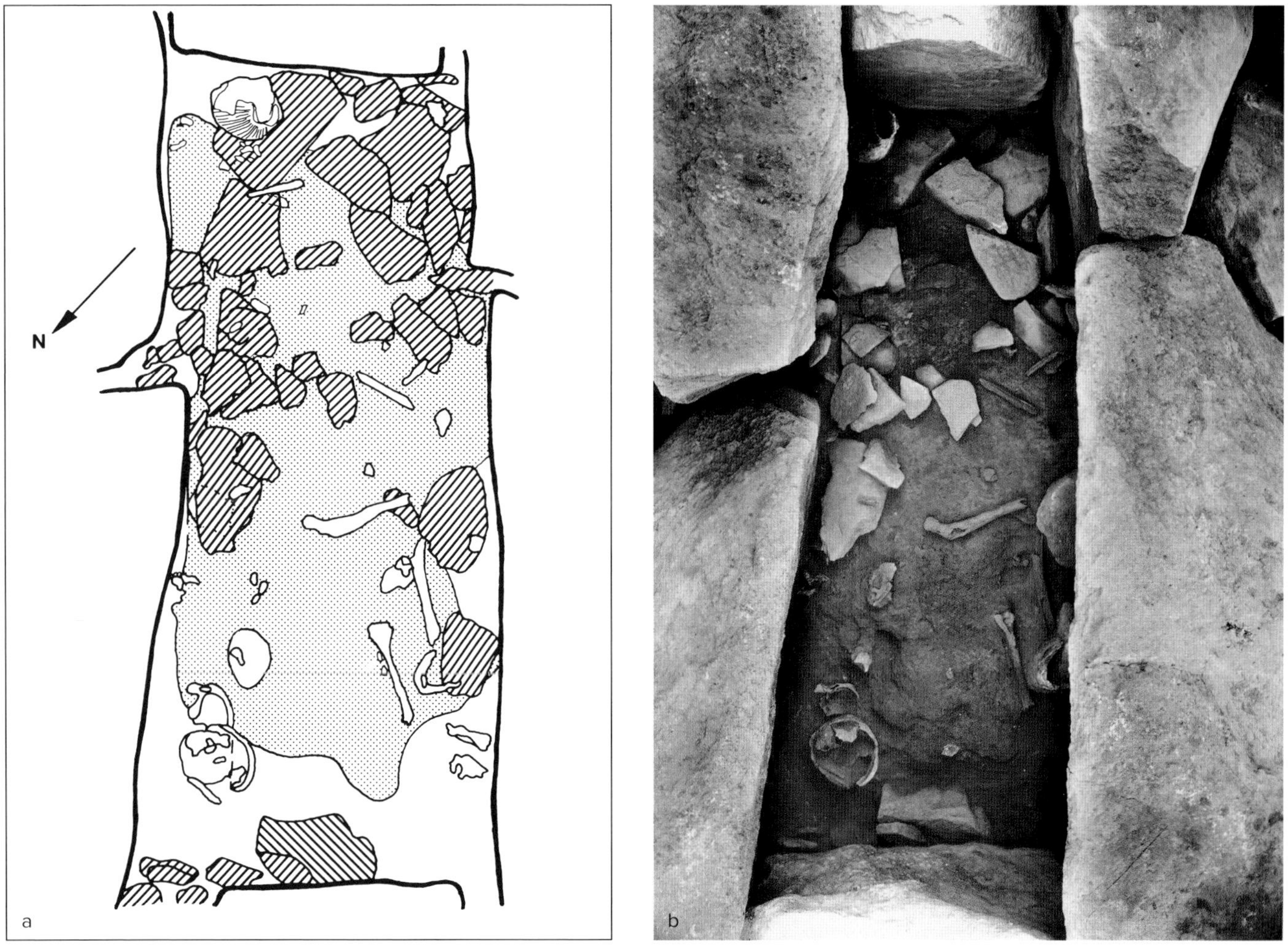

Fig. 21.6. *On the base of dolmen chamber B at Grøfte were 20 bones of a woman of 35-55 years of age. The bones appear to have been placed randomly on the chamber floor. In the upper left corner of the chamber stood a dolmen flask.*

Mouse gnaw marks and fox bite marks show that the bodies of the two men and the woman were defleshed in places accessible to these animals, so they must have lain temporally exposed or only covered by a little earth.

Havnbjerg Skov and Bogø

In 1926, Jens Raben of Sønderborg Museum investigated a dolmen cist in Havnbjerg Skov on the island of Als, in which he found a partially disarticulated human skeleton (fig. 21.7). By the skeleton's left lower arm lay an ornamented bone plate, a so-called archer's wrist guard. In a Danish prehistoric context, this artefact type is normally characteristic of the Bell Beaker culture, a Late Neolithic culture dated to c. 2300 BC, which was widespread across most of Europe. However, based on its position next to a skeleton in a dolmen cist, the wrist guard has been dated to the time of the construction of the earliest dolmens, making this artefact type 1000-2000 years older than previously assumed. The find was analysed and published by Professor C.J. Becker of the University of Copenhagen, who mentions other, similar bone plates found in dolmens.[21] The dating of these finds to the Early Neolithic is, however, doubtful as it is the grave type, i.e. the dolmen, that is used to date both the artefact and the skeleton. A number of Danish megalithic tombs contain finds from the Bell Beaker culture, and we should therefore be sceptical of the suggested date for the wrist guard found in the dolmen cist in Havnbjerg Skov.[22]

A good example of how cautious one should be in interpreting skeletons found in dolmen chambers as being coeval with the construction of these monuments is provided by a long dolmen on the island of Bogø, between Falster and Møn (fig. 21.8).[23] This has, quite extraordinarily, two dolmen chambers lying parallel to each other. In one of these, in 1881, a human skeleton was found in extended supine position, and at the northern end stood a collared flask that could be coeval with the construction of the chamber. However, it also contained several thick-butted flint axes of so-called B-type from the middle of the 3rd millennium BC, i.e. these are around a 1000 years later than the collared flask and the construction of the chamber.

Northern Germany

Dolmens containing parts of human skeletons have also been excavated in the north German areas of Mecklenburg and Lower Saxony. The human remains are found together with Early Neolithic pottery, but it is not possible to determine whether the

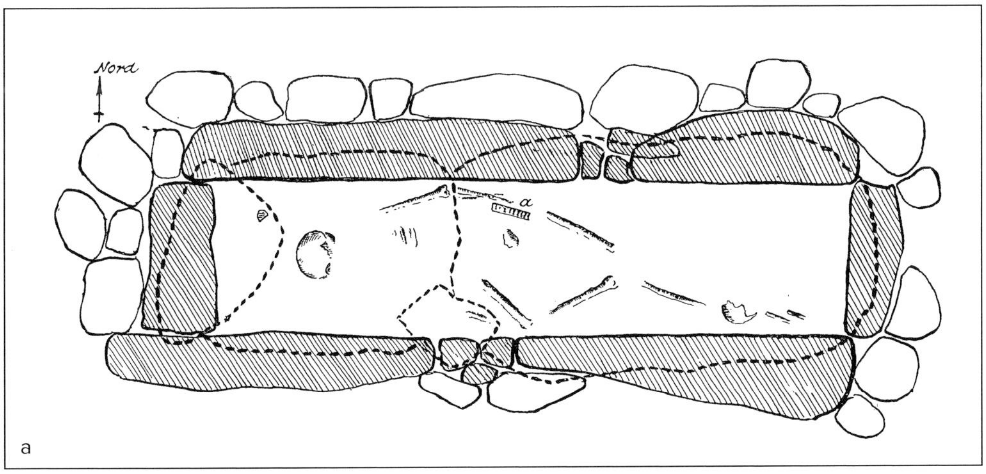

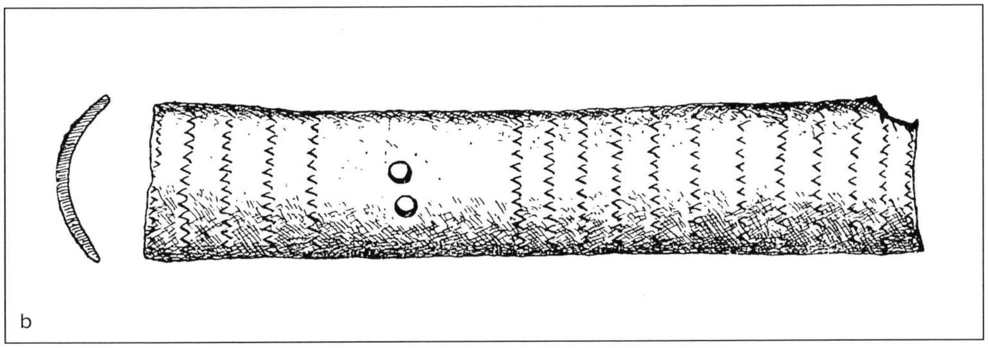

Fig. 21.7. *In Havnbjerg Skov on the island of Als stands a long dolmen with a dolmen cist. An investigation in 1926 revealed the presence of a human skeleton in the cist. Under the lower left arm lay an ornamented, 14 cm long archer's wrist guard of bone.*

Fig. 21.8. *A dolmen chamber in a long dolmen on Bogø, investigated in 1881, was found to contain a human skeleton accompanied by a pottery vessel, a couple of blades, a transverse arrowhead and no fewer than nine polished flint axes. The vessel – a collared flask – could be coeval with the construction of the monument, but the flint axes are around 1000 years later!*

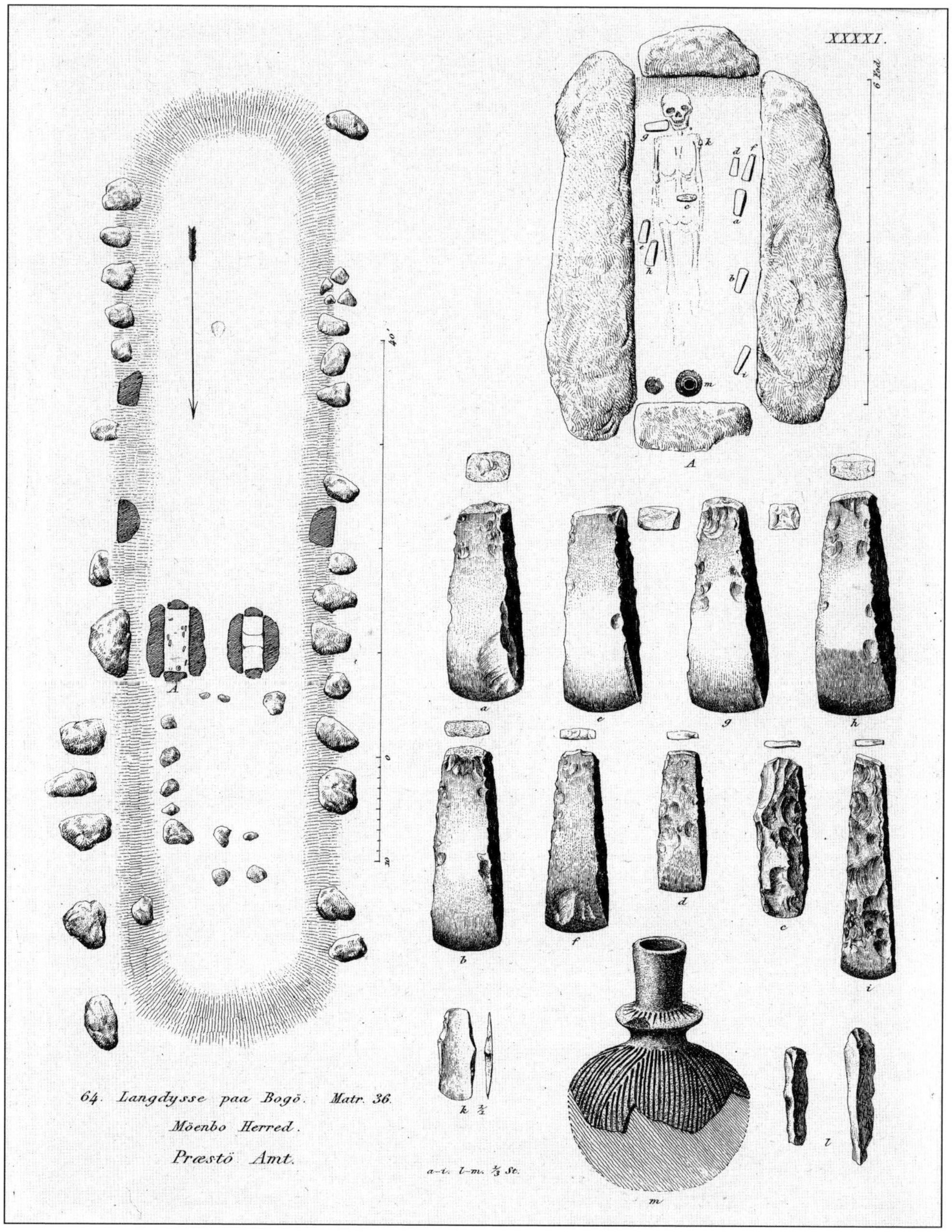

skeletal parts and the pots are of the same age. It is, however, worth noting that the human remains were deposited in a defleshed state and that large parts of the skeletons are missing.[24]

At Flintbek, north of Kiel, the archaeological institutions in Schleswig-Holstein excavated 80 localities between 1976 and 1996, in particular burial mounds dating from the Neolithic and Bronze Age. These monuments had been almost completely destroyed by cultivation. Nevertheless, as in the case of the ploughed-down monuments in the Sarup area (chapter 20), they have provided much important information. One of the better known localities is LA 3, which comprises two conjoined long dolmens (fig. 21.9). One of these covered six, possibly seven, decayed plank-built cists, laid in a line, as well as having three dolmen chambers. The other long dolmen had contained a single dolmen chamber, running up to which were tracks left by a cart; the earliest wheel tracks yet found in Europe.[25]

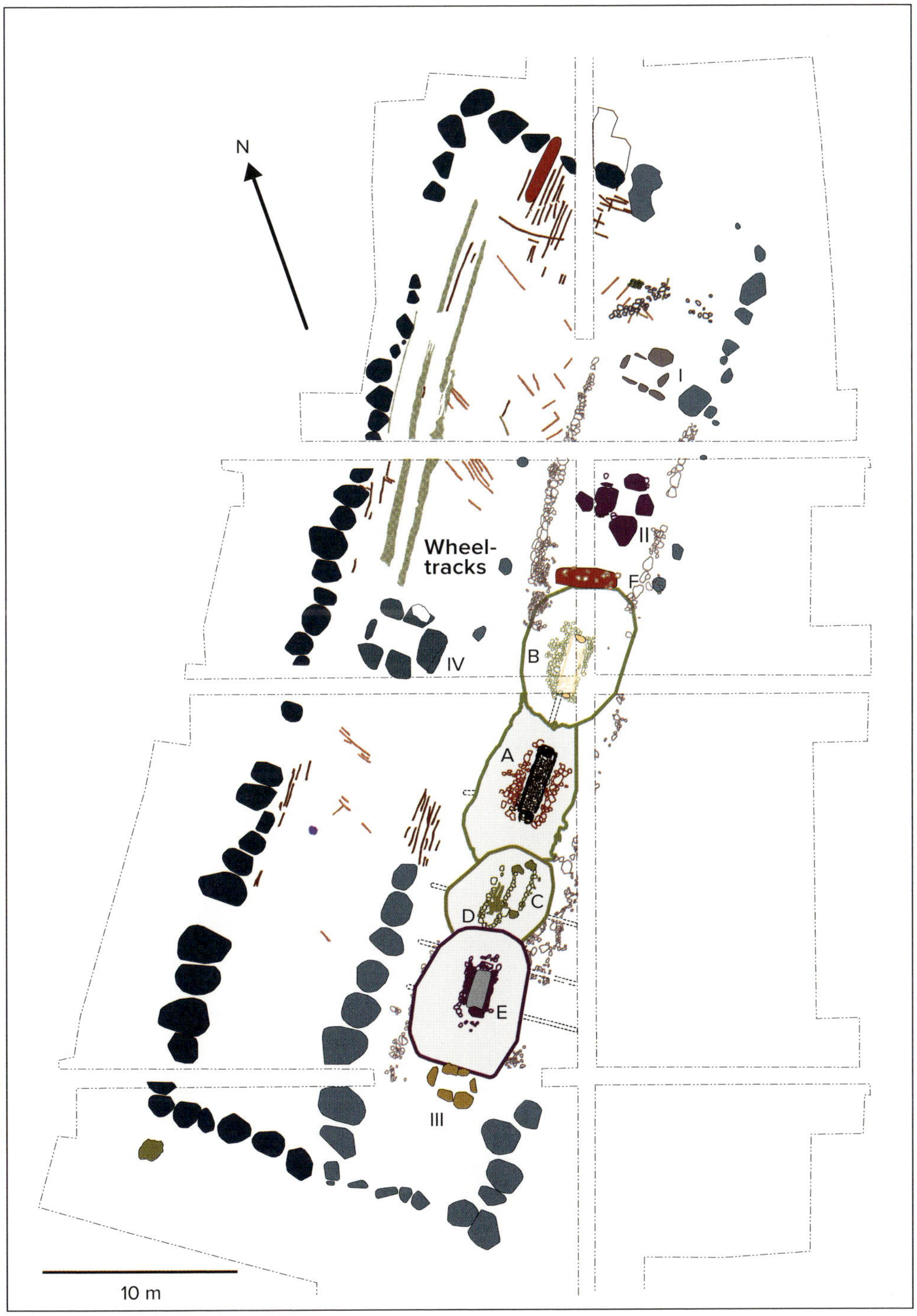

Fig. 21.9. *The site of the double long dolmen LA 3 at Flintbek near Kiel was investigated in 1988-89. In the southern long dolmen were six plank-built cists (A-F) in a line and three dolmen chambers (I-III). The northern long dolmen contained dolmen chamber IV, running up to which were the earliest wheel tracks found in Europe to date.*

Of particular interest here is dolmen chamber II in the southern long dolmen. Here there were traces of a rectangular chamber of type II with a floor measuring 2.15 x 1.43 m. Soon after construction, one of the chamber's orthostats had toppled into the chamber and, as a consequence, it had covered half of the floor before earth sifting into the chamber became deposited upon it. This provided a unique opportunity to investigate what had originally stood on the chamber floor. Beneath the fallen orthostat, on the floor, lay a small point-butted greenstone axe, which is dated somewhat earlier than the time when the dolmen was built. Scattered across the preserved part of the chamber floor, sealed by the fallen orthostat, were also numerous human bones, representing at least four individuals: two adults and two children. The bones were heavily fragmented and a third of them showed the effects of fire.[26] The chamber had been built in a shallow pit in which a fire had burnt, leaving a great amount of charcoal. During excavation of dolmen chamber II, more than 30 samples of this charcoal were taken for radiocarbon dating. The dates show that the chamber could have, at the latest, been built between 3515 and 3373 BC, more probably between 3475 and 3430 BC. The charcoal is of oak, which can of course have a certain "wood age", so the construction of the dolmen could even be later than indicated by the radiocarbon dates. However, four radiocarbon dates for human bones show that these are at least a century *older* than the time frame given by the charcoal for construction of the chamber![27] If these dates are correct, this means we have a situation where century-old human bones were deposited in a newly-constructed dolmen chamber. It must be presumed that the human bones had been kept in one or more other places for many years before their final deposition in the chamber. The fact that some of the bones also display the effects of fire shows that parts of the skeletons had been subjected to various forms of treatment prior to their final deposition in the dolmen chamber. These circumstances confirm what we have seen elsewhere, i.e. that only individual bones, and not entire skeletons, were placed in the chamber. We must therefore presume that the bones have undertaken a "long journey" before finally being laid to rest in the dolmen.

It would be very convenient if we could say that dolmens were originally built in order to accommodate the burials of entire corpses, which were brought to the chamber shortly after death. However, no evidence has been forthcoming to date in support of such a conclusion, even though this has been commonly and generally accepted. On the contrary, we see evidence of complex burial rituals whereby parts of bodies and/or skeletons were placed in the chambers. The bones that have been found appear to have passed through various stages and processes, possibly over many years, before their final deposition in dolmens. It would be interesting to discover the detailed history of the bones prior to deposition, but for the moment we must content ourselves with the fact that the activities and course of events were rather more complex than a simple burial in a dolmen chamber.

It is remarkable that what we would refer to as grave goods, including intact pottery vessels, have been placed in several of the chambers. One vessel even contained human bones and another pieces of burnt and crushed flint. These grave goods could of course have been placed at the same time as the disarticulated human remains were laid in the chamber. The pots always seem to have been placed at one end of the dolmen chamber and are, as a rule, intact and finely ornamented vessels. Vessels found placed by the interred remains are usually perceived as grave goods, possibly containing food for the deceased. But we prefer to see these vessels as independent "individuals" with their own lives.[28] This would also provide a good explanation for why several dolmen chambers have been found to contain vessels and other artefacts but no human skeletal remains.

Skeletons outside dolmen chambers

As our interest extends to the entire dolmen monument, mention will be made of a couple of other discoveries.

One of these is from the locality of Fakkemose on the island of Langeland, where Jørgen Skaarup investigated the remains of a ploughed-down and almost completely erased round dolmen in the mid-1970s, as part of Langelands Museum's major megalith project. About 6 m from the dolmen chamber, very close to the inner edge of the traces of the kerbstone circle, an east-west-oriented pit grave was uncovered that measured 1.3 x 0.7 m. In the pit lay two skeletons in extreme hocker position, back to back with their heads to the west (fig. 21.10). The corpses must have been excarnated prior to burial, as they would otherwise have been unable to fit into such a narrow pit. This is also evident from the fact that one of the femurs lay turned through 180 degrees, so that the ball which fits into the pelvic socket lay by the knee joint. One of the skeletons was of an adult, the other of an individual of about 20 years of age; neither could be identified to gender. There were no artefacts in the pit grave and the skeletons were too degraded to permit radiocarbon dating. However, the position of the grave within the kerbstones of the round dolmen indicates that it could have been established in connection with the activities that took place in and at the monument.[29]

A very similar example involving reorganisation of the bones was evident in another pit grave, which was excavated in 2001-02 as part of a major archaeological project in advance of the construction of the City Tunnel in Malmö, southern Sweden. At the locality of Almhov, remains were found of a ploughed-down east-west-oriented pit grave, now only measuring 1.3 x 0.6 m and 10 cm in depth. In the pit lay the poorly-preserved bones of an individual of 15-30 years of age, possibly a woman (fig. 21.11). The bones were clearly disarticulated, as the thighbones lay furthest to the west, followed by the bones of the lower and upper arms; furthest to the east lay the skull and the teeth. A radiocarbon date of 3650-3100 BC was obtained for bone tissue from the skull. A high carbon 13 content means that the date is actually even earlier than this, though still within the time frame of interest here.[30] It is interesting that the pit grave lay without any contact to other graves, let alone a dolmen. Pits like this will therefore often only be discovered by careful and extensive surface excavation.

Fig. 21.10. *At Fakkemose, on the island of Langeland, a pit grave containing two skeletons was discovered during the excavation of a demolished round dolmen in 1974. The skeletons were placed back to back in a pit measuring 1.3 x 0.7 m. They had been defleshed prior to burial, as shown by a femur having been turned through 180 degrees before it was placed in the grave.*

The two pit graves, at Fakkemose and Almhov, containing preserved skeletal remains, show that the bodies had been subjected to more complicated treatment than simple, ordinary inhumation.

Other relevant discoveries have been made at two dolmens in Scania, where burnt human bones were found in the areas immediately outside the chambers. One of these dolmens is Trollasten, excavated by Märta Strömberg in the mid-1960s (see chapter 15). The burnt human bones here lay in 11 small heaps on a semicircular stone pavement in front of the entrance to the dolmen (see figs. 15.5 and 15.6).[31] In several cases, the burnt bones were accompanied by very small fragments of burnt flint axes. Most appear to date from the time of construction of the dolmen, while others, such as those in heap 4, must be later.[32] It is stated that the bone present in several of the heaps is cranial tissue.

In 1970-71, Göran Burenhult investigated a ploughed-down long dolmen, Hindby Mosse, near Malmö. It once had a polygonal chamber, but this had been removed long ago. Outside the demolished kerbstones, opposite the opening to the chamber, 71 concentrations of burnt bone were located (fig. 21.12).[33] Each concentration lay under a stone, which had been deliberately placed there. In all, 1636 bone fragments were found, of which no less than 97% were human, and 94% were from the skulls of adults. The bones had been systematically fragmented.[34]

The evidence from these two Scanian dolmens tells us that numerous depositions of burnt human bone, in particular cranial tissue, took place by the dolmen chambers. The locations of these depositions indicate that they must have been involved in the activities undertaken by the dolmens, and that these monuments served other purposes and functions than simply as burial places for entire corpses, as has otherwise been assumed to date. At the Tustrup passage dolmen (see chapter 16), burnt bones were also found in a couple of features outside the stone pavement and in front of the passage, but these have not yet been analysed. During the excavations in the Sarup area, when sieving soil samples, we saw small lumps of white powder that simply "disappeared" before our eyes. We cannot be sure that these are human bone, only that they represent bones that have been burnt at such a high temperature that they are easily pulverised.

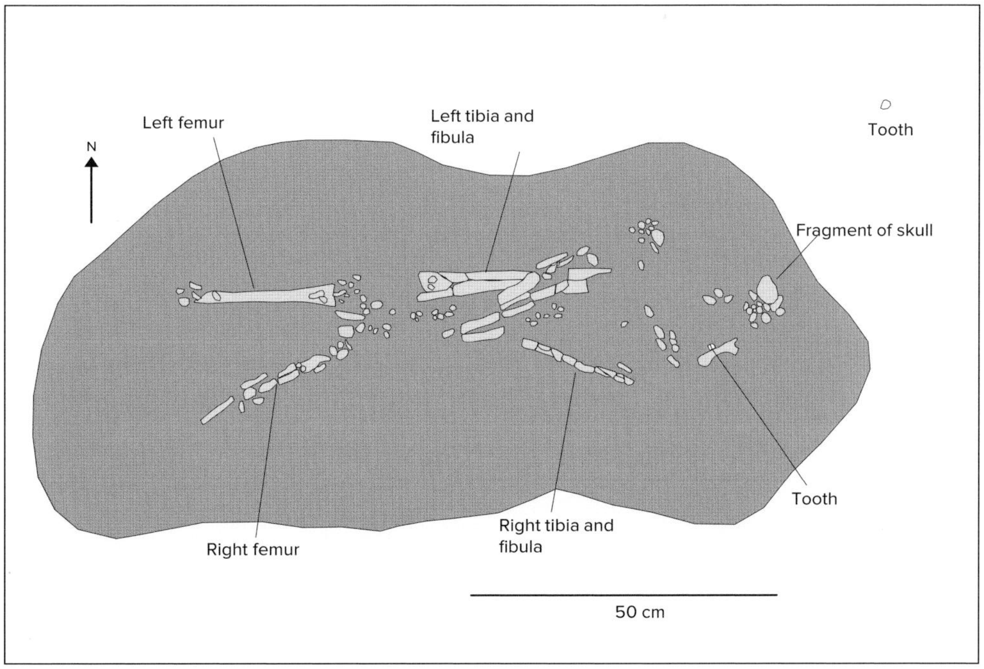

Fig. 21.11. *In 2001, a pit grave containing a disarticulated skeleton was excavated at Almhov near Malmö in Scania. The corpse had clearly been excarnated prior to burial in the 1.3 x 0.6 m pit. The poorly-preserved skeleton – the remaining part of the pit was only 10 cm deep – has been radiocarbon dated to 3650-3100 BC, so the "burial" could well have taken place during the Dolmen epoch.*

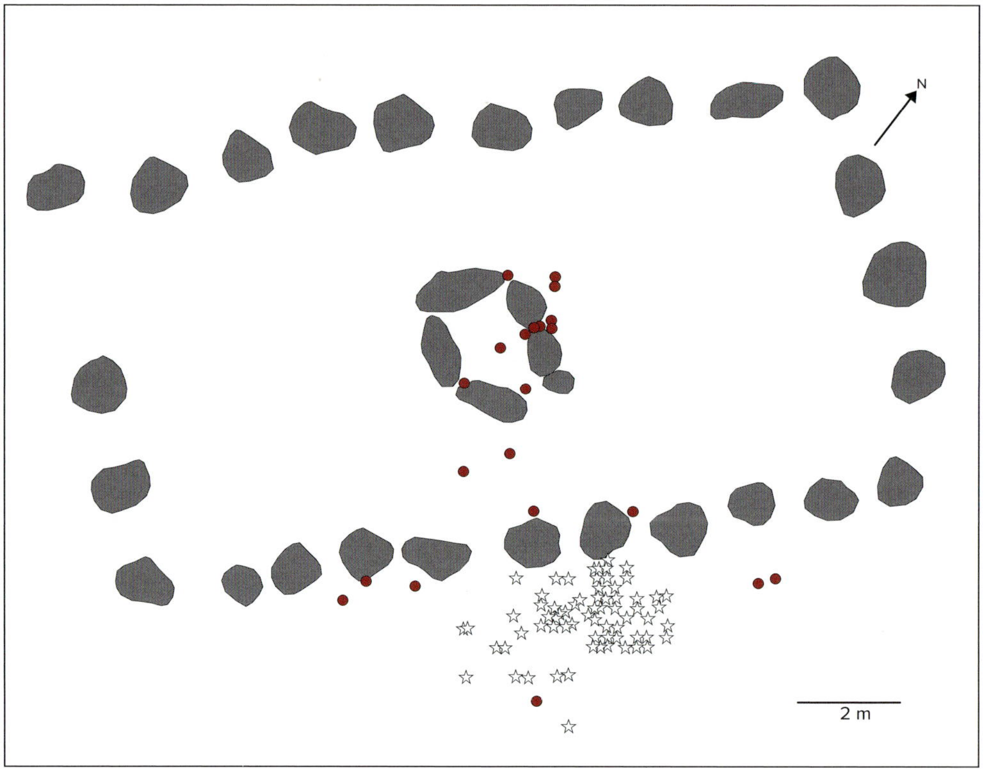

Fig. 21.12. *The demolished long dolmen Hindby Mosse near Malmö in Scania was investigated in 1970-71. In the area directly outside the kerbstones and in front of the entrance there was a dense concentration of small depositions of burnt human bones. Their positions are marked with white stars on the plan, while the red dots mark finds spots for amber. The traces of removed stones are shown in grey*

Human bones at Sarup I and II

Parts of human corpses were also found in the features and structures at Sarup, which date, of course, from the time when megalithic tombs were constructed.[35]

At Sarup I, from the Dolmen epoch around 3400 BC, parts of human jawbones were found in the system-ditches, and burnt bones lay by the palisade ditch. The latter remains are heavily fragmented and many pieces are no larger than a grain of rice; only one bone could be identified – a human finger bone.[36]

At Sarup II, which is from the Passage-grave epoch, burnt human bones were found in three features on the inner, enclosed surface of the site; two of these features were large postholes. The bones are of a young woman, but only about one-tenth of the expected number of bones are present. The woman's bones had first been burnt after her body had been excarnated and the bones had fully dried out – a process that can take 10-15 years.[37]

Skeletons from bogs

In addition to the skeletons, or skeletal parts, that have been found on "dry land", human skeletons dating from the Dolmen and Passage-grave epochs have also been encountered in bogs. In some instances, these have been found during peat cutting, as at Sigersdal in northern Zealand. In 1949, two skeletons, probably of young women of 16 and 18 years of age, were excavated here (fig. 21.13). They have been radiocarbon dated to c. 3500 BC, the time of the Funnel Beaker culture. A cord around the neck of the 18-year-old suggests that she had been strangled.[38]

Skeletons have been found in other bogs, too.[39] A review of the bones from bogs on Zealand led Eva Koch to the conclusion that human bones were present in 53 of the 100 bogs investigated. Seventeen of these have been radiocarbon dated: four predate the Dolmen epoch, eight are from the Dolmen and Passage-grave epochs and five are from the Late Neolithic or Late Bronze Age/Early Iron Age. The Neolithic skeletons comprise six women and three men, and three are so young that their gender could not be determined. There appears to have been a tendency for women in particular to have been sacrificed in bogs.[40]

Analyses of well-dated bog bodies from the entire country show a tendency towards the sacrificing of 16-20-year-olds in bogs during the Neolithic, while in the Bronze Age it was individuals of more than 20 years of age.[41] This apparent selection, and the fact that one of the young women from Sigersdal had a cord or noose around

Fig. 21.13. *In 1949, the skeletons of two young women, of 16 and 18 years of age, were discovered in a bog at Sigersdal in northern Zealand. They had possibly been killed and sacrificed, as one of the skeletons had a cord around the neck, suggesting the girl had been strangled.*

her neck, could suggest that what we perceive as "interment" in the bog was more probably an act of sacrifice in connection with a fertility cult or similar religious practice. This is elegantly expressed in Stravinsky's ballet *Le Sacre du Printemps*, which is based on stories of offerings of young women in Russia in former times, as part of an agricultural fertility cult.[42]

A different view of the human bones found in dolmen chambers

This review demonstrates that many activities involving dead people took place in the Dolmen epoch. It seems that these activities involved the dead being included in various forms of events and ceremonies that culminated in the skeletons, or just parts of them, being deposited in lakes and bogs, and in causewayed enclosures, pit graves and dolmens.

During the time when dolmens and causewayed enclosures were built and had their primary function, great transformations must have taken place in society. If we look at the period prior to the Dolmen epoch, i.e. the era of the Barkaer-structure, this was also a time of major monument construction, but these monuments were of earth and wood, not of stone. They were structures with tall façade posts at one end and earth graves in the middle. The graves within them were most often plank-built wooden cists (see chapter 9). There were also more simple earth graves, pit graves almost. It is interesting that we find entire corpses buried in these graves, sometimes accompanied by extensive furnishings in the form of pottery vessels, axes, transverse arrowheads, amber beads etc.[43] In some cases, several people appear to have been buried at the same time, and sometimes their remains are slightly charred.[44]

At the time when dolmens were constructed, great transformations took place in Neolithic society. We know from pollen studies that the landscape was opened up by clearance of the forest and that agriculture now made a major impact. A new cultivation tool, the ard – a primitive plough drawn by a pair of oxen – was also introduced. This made it possible to take larger areas into cultivation. And, of course, we also see the construction of great monuments like dolmens and causewayed enclosures. The building of such monumental structures required detailed planning and the coordinated efforts of a large number of people. Associated with these monuments we have evidence suggesting that strange ceremonies were acted out involving the deposition of various items and materials, which had in advance been subjected to fragmentation – this applies to human bones, flint axes, grinding stones and quernstones. It is worth noting that human bones, some of which had been burnt at a high temperature, were deposited both by and in dolmens and causewayed enclosures.

Given the finds and evidence presently at our disposal, we cannot possibly interpret dolmen chambers as places where entire human corpses were buried. Judging from the available evidence, dolmens were where special activities took place involving the deposition of, among other things, human remains in a more or less excarnated state. In advance of their deposition in dolmens many of these human remains appear to have been kept in various other places.

The role of dolmens in Neolithic society

The construction and primary use of dolmens took place in a time when very major changes occurred in the landscape and the way in which this was used and exploited. Around 4000 BC, we see the first faint indications in Denmark that the hunter-gatherer people of the Ertebølle culture had become aware of agriculture and animal husbandry. This radical innovation in the subsistence economy is accompanied by the introduction of the well-fired pottery that is characteristic of the Funnel Beaker culture, and we also see the appearance of large, impressive, polished stone axes. Pollen analysis provides faint indications of the cultivation of cereals and the growth of ribwort plantain, a plant that thrives in places grazed by domesticated animals. But it is first around 3700 BC that we can see evidence of extensive burning of the forest and opening up of the landscape.[45] This takes place at the same time as the introduction of the large Barkaer-structures, as exemplified by the sites of Barkær, Bygholm Nørremark and Frydenlund (see chapter 9). These monuments often contained earth graves, usually wooden, plank-built cists, somewhat similar in form to the early dolmen cists. It is remarkable, relative to the situation evident in dolmens, that these wooden cists contain unequivocal evidence of the burial of entire corpses, and sometimes several of them together. Some of the single burials in the plank-built cists are accompanied by abundant grave goods that have no parallel in the dolmens.[46]

At the time of the Barkaer-structures, the Neolithic people appear to have lived on very large settlements with quite a number of houses, as seen at Frydenlund, near Sarup (see chapter 9). In the Dolmen epoch, this settlement pattern changed, at least in the Sarup area, where it is characterised by the activities becoming less concentrated, i.e. more dispersed (see fig. 20.2). We have found the remains of solitary two-aisled houses in the area, with only very few finds in the near vicinity. But we also find areas with cultural layers containing abundant settlement waste, but no traces of houses.[47] Furthermore, there are also records from this period of hunting stations and flint-knapping sites at various locations around the country.[48] About 40 settlements from the Dolmen and Passage-grave epochs have been discovered in the Sarup area. These settlements are very small, but around 3100 BC, during the Blandebjerg phase, i.e. the time following construction of passage graves, people again began to occupy large settlements, for example on the actual Sarup site itself.[49]

Based on the evidence presently available, there are no indications of a hierarchical society headed by for example chieftains. There are no finds from burials to confirm the presence of people of high status. Similarly, there are no records of special buildings that could be interpreted as chieftain's residences. It is difficult to say whether this was a society controlled by priests or by masters of ceremonies, because we have

Fig. 21.14. *Several of the Funnel Beaker culture's so-called battle axes are made of exquisite types of stone, such as this example from the Passage-grave epoch, found at the Sarup site. There is, however, no evidence that axes such as these, which often have a very small handle hole, were actually used as combat weapons (see fig. 21.15).*

no evidence, i.e. finds, in support of such an interpretation. The only thing that could point in this direction are some special artefact types, for example the beautiful, but massively over-dimensioned and probably also completely impractical flint axes and, not least, the so-called battle axes of the time (fig. 21.14). With regard to the latter, we have no clear evidence of any serious conflicts at this time. But if we, in line with the situation in Switzerland where these kinds of axes are found mounted on long poles, refer to them instead as ceremonial axes, we suddenly have a group of artefacts that could have played a prominent role in religious ceremonies (fig. 21.15)! In addition to the various exquisite stone artefacts, the Dolmen and Passage-grave epochs have also yielded some of the most beautiful pottery vessels ever seen in European prehistory. These were often involved in special ceremonies that included their systematic fragmentation, whereby the potsherds from the individual broken pots were widely scattered, and we find them deposited in various features and structures and perhaps also at different localities. The same treatment also appears to have been applied to human bones.

The construction of dolmens, passage graves and causewayed enclosures required extensive and detailed planning and the participation of a large number of people. In the case of the Sarup I site, it has been calculated that almost 2000 m^3, or 3350 tonnes, of earth was dug up and almost 3400 wooden posts, or 600 tonnes of wood, were transported to the site.[50] Whereas in the case of the passage grave at Maglehøj on Stevns, Lars Holten has calculated that 77 tonnes of large stones, 80.6 tonnes of other stones for the dry-walling, flint packing and so on, and 832 tonnes of earth were moved and used.[51] All of this material was deliberately selected and processed by the Neolithic people: Straight tree trunks had to be found, felled, cloven, shaped and transported, dry-walling slabs had to be split and shaped, flint had to be mined and burnt at very high temperatures, with the use of great quantities of wood for the fires, and so on. The figures show that many hundreds of people must have participated in these huge construction projects.

It is still a mystery how these great building works were organised, and we do not know the extent of the area from which the participants came. There are suggestions that these projects were undertaken on the basis of a common perception and understanding of what was required and necessary. Today, we always perceive projects such as these from an economic, cost-benefit perspective and from the point of view of what we now consider to be common sense. But "common sense" back then need not necessarily have been the same common sense as today.[52] In a transitional period from a hunter-gatherer to an agricultural society, the very fact that people jointly undertook and executed major construction projects could have constituted the "glue" that held communities together and taught them how to work together and get along with each other in a new way. An agricultural society would have required a completely new form of planning and "land ownership" than was the case previously in a hunter-gatherer society. Only through collective efforts and acceptance could such a huge transformation in peoples' subsistence economy and way of life, and their way of interacting with each other, have been successfully accomplished. There is no way in which all of this could have been achieved simply through the efforts, actions and decisions of a few individual chieftains. The actual end result of the construction project – whether this was a dolmen, a passage grave or a causewayed enclosure – was perhaps not the most important. The pivotal aspect was the actual process of getting so many people from such a large area to work together, get to know each other and, collectively, accept a Neolithic way of life. Well into the 20th century – for example in southeast Asia – structures were built that are very reminiscent of our Danish dolmens. In some areas, the deceased were exhumed to be involved in important, elaborate and costly rituals, whereby their bones were cleaned and placed in dolmen-like mausoleums that often took their form from the houses of the living. These rituals were performed to secure the goodwill of the deceased, as it was believed that they had the power to ensure their descendants a good and bountiful life. Furthermore, no distinction was made between life and death, they were simply seen as stages in a perpetual, cyclical course of events. With the moving of the bones, the deceased lost their individuality and became part of a group. In some

Fig. 21.15. *In Switzerland, in a wetland area at Cham-Eslen, an axe like the one from Sarup (fig. 21.14) was found mounted on a long, thin shaft that was also ornamented with strips of birch bark. As the shaft is 1.2 m long, it could not have been a battle axe, and it seems much more likely that its function was purely ceremonial.*

Fig. 21.16. *On the island of Nias, as in other parts of Indonesia, dolmen-like stone monuments were built by mobilising hundreds, even thousands of participants for major communal construction projects. In 1914, 500 men hauled this stone, weighing 8 tonnes, up a slope in order to use it as a capstone on a dolmen.*

areas, for example in Indonesia, organisation of, and participation in, the construction of dolmens, involving the mobilisation of hundreds of participants, was associated with great prestige (fig. 21.16).[53]

In our part of the world, it seems that complex activities took place in and by the dolmen chambers, the character of which we have little information on and which we, therefore, can only imagine. In some ways we have not advanced very far in our conclusions since J.J.A. Worsaae's time, and our interpretations are almost reverting the early perception of these monuments as heathen "altars". Or more precisely, as perhaps places where many ceremonies and events took place that encompassed the partial burial or rather deposition of human bones and many other items. It is remarkable that, after almost 200 years of study of that Danish national symbol – the dolmen, we actually do not know the original function of these monuments. We are, however, convinced that further investigations in the future will bring us closer to a better understanding of dolmens and their significance.[54]

22. Conclusion and perspectives

On the basis of the findings from many different kinds of excavations, both large and small, old and new, results of literature and archival studies and our own site visits, excavations and surveys as well as, not least, a range of new analyses, we have outlined in the above how Denmark's earliest architecture in stone – the dolmen – emerged in the Neolithic, around the middle of the 4th millennium BC, and then developed until the appearance of first passage graves around 3200 BC.

To date, no traces of cists or structures have been found associated with Mesolithic burials in northern Europe. The graves recorded so far are simple inhumations – pit graves – in the earth. This uncomplicated burial practice continued for a couple of centuries after 3950 BC, when the first indications of agriculture and animal husbandry appear in Denmark. Here, on the threshold to the Neolithic, new subsistence patterns and social structures had to have time to assimilate and replace former patterns of behaviour. But after only a couple of centuries – around 3700 BC – the first evidence of "the new age" appears: proper houses and elongate, fenced enclosures – Barkaer-structures – built for the religious activities of the time, which included a death cult.

The long, rectangular or slightly trapezoid Barkaer-structures – some as much as 100 m in length – were impressive monuments, constructed in recently opened up areas of the primeval forest, after the clearances had first been used to accommodate settlements and fields. Apart from their length, these structures, some of which were surrounded by ditches or wooden fences, were rendered conspicuous by often having a high, robust façade at one narrow end. This was constructed of sturdy timbers that – judging from the depth of the foundation ditches – could easily have had a height of at least 5-6 m. Barkaer-structures may contain one or more man-sized plank-built cists. In some cases, we can see how these cists have been deliberately sited over demolished and levelled house sites, positioned on the central axis of the building, with a back-filled posthole from the earlier house located precisely beneath each end.

Dolmen cists – stone cists made of thin flagstones with a plank-like capstone – were in use at the same time as the wooden plank-built cists. Investigations show that Barkaer-structures were very dynamic monuments that were often altered and extended. From originally not having a mound enclosing the free-standing dolmen cists, smaller and larger amounts of earth were sometimes added and the resulting long dolmens framed by a row of small kerbstones.

Dolmen cists were the forerunners of dolmen chambers, which were built of massive boulders. The earliest dolmen chambers, referred to as type I, were constructed around 3400 BC, and they resemble the dolmen cists in form. They were the length of a man, had sides of equal height and, when the capstone was in place, they were completely sealed chambers. Dolmen chambers, also the later types, were either free-standing and solitary or were surrounded by standing kerbstones in long or round dolmens. The gaps between the framing kerbstones were usually closed with stacked stone slabs – dry-walling. This could extend all the way up to the tops of the kerbstones, so the combination of kerbstones and dry-walling took on the character of a solid, free-standing wall which can, in a way, be equated with the walls built around churchyards. A small, low mound – a packing – often encircled the chamber to stabilise the orthostats so they did not slip outwards. The surface around the dolmen chamber was sometimes covered with stones of varying size.

Some long dolmens, which contained dolmen cists and/or the related dolmen chambers of type I, have so much mound fill that cists and chambers, including their capstones, would not have been visible. The flat capstones made it easier to seal and conceal the chambers entirely. Further investigations of these long dolmens with abundant mound fill are required before anything definite can be said about precisely when in the construction process this material was added. But if there is a passage grave in a mound of this kind, the fill could have been added when this structure was built. A more intriguing theory, when no passage graves are present, is that the mounds were added shortly after construction of the cists and/or the chambers in order to seal them off completely, corresponding to the situation observed in the c. 1000 year earlier long barrows in Brittany.

Many dolmen chambers of types I and II – the latter type resembles the former, but has an opening for access – stand today in long or round barrows with so much mound material that only the chamber's capstone is visible. In the cases where investigations have been undertaken of the mound fill, these reveal that it consists of two or more layers that were added in a corresponding number of operations. These dolmens are, therefore, like Barkaer-structures, "multi-period mounds".

Later and, as a rule, larger dolmen chambers of types III and IV were almost always exposed and free-standing, with or without surrounding kerbstones. The latest dolmen chambers – the polygonal chambers of type IV – are possibly coeval with the earliest passage graves, dating from around 3200 BC.

Dolmens clearly differ from the passage graves in their symbolic marking of the entrance to the chamber with passage stones. Where these stones occur in dolmens, they are never conjoined with the kerbstones or extend out to the foot of the mound. This difference is due to fact that passage graves were, from the outset, always intended to be covered by a mound, with continued access to the chamber via their covered passages.

The sequential development of the chambers can be roughly outlined as follows: plank-built cists – dolmen cists – dolmen chamber of types I and II – dolmen chambers of types III and IV – passage graves. As for the "mounds", the development proceeds from: Barkaer-structures – long dolmens – long and round dolmens – passage graves in long and round barrows surrounded by kerbstones.

Through the five centuries between 3700 and 3200 BC, when the development from Barkaer-structures to passage graves unfolded, numerous changes took place in the form and layout of these monumental structures.

The plank-built cists often contained burials in the usual sense, with entire corpses bring interred. But the closely-related dolmen cists have so far only yielded incomplete skeletal parts, and an individual is often only represented by a limited number of bones. This treatment of the dead continues throughout the Dolmen epoch and into the beginning of the Passage-grave epoch. Consequently, the dolmens and passage graves are not to be perceived as traditional burial places, but rather as defined spaces that appear to enter into a symbiosis with the system-ditches at the causewayed enclosures, where there was also deposition of parts of deceased individuals. The rituals associated with the dead were not immutable, and people did not stubbornly hang on to their traditions. Consequently, there appear to have been major transformations in their perception of the dead.

The many changes in the layout and organisation of the "defined spaces" – plank-built cists, dolmen cists, early dolmens, later dolmens and passage graves – reflect these ritual shifts. The architectural form was dictated by the cult. One of the most significant shifts is the transition from open dolmens, where it was possible to follow and participate in the rituals, to the mound-encapsulated passage graves, where only a very few people could participate in the activities.

Based on these studies of the architecture, we have some suggestions with respect to tasks and themes it would be useful to address in future research into dolmens:

First and foremost, research into Danish dolmens has urgent need of a database containing updated information, thorough and detailed archive references, accurate survey data, records of new site visits and descriptions undertaken by archaeologists with a special knowledge of megaliths.

There is also a lack of modern, all-round investigations of selected, well-preserved, scheduled dolmens, of free-standing chambers and round and long dolmens, including long dolmens with particularly abundant mound fill and chambers of the earliest type.

Demolished dolmen sites contain a wealth of information and are still able to provide significant new insights. In this respect it is important – as has been done in the Sarup area – to investigate coherent, related complexes. Many dolmen sites are only investigated because they lie in areas affected by road construction, building developments, aggregate extraction and the like. However, when excavated by archaeologists with a good prior grasp of the subject, these sites represent an obvious opportunity to obtain new information, not least because there is the possibility of locating finds resulting from the primary activities in the chambers, because these have usually not been disturbed, as is normally the case in better preserved monuments.

In Denmark, a country with an unusually high concentration of dolmens, there is a serious lack of studies of the location of these monuments in the landscape, their visibility in the Neolithic and their relations to coeval settlements. As a dolmen is not a one-man undertaking, an investigation should be undertaken of the size of the area served by these monuments. Similarly, their relations to the coevally constructed causewayed enclosures should be studied and clarified. A clear conclusion from our studies and, consequently, of this book, is that we still know remarkably little about dolmens, even though they have been the subject of antiquarian interest for a couple of centuries.

Many scheduled dolmens have suffered severe damage but are, nevertheless, still of scientific value. Their destruction is not just a result of the various activities and actions of smallholders, farmers, stonemasons, road menders and contractors, but also of the antiquarians and archaeologists who, in their professional zeal, interfered with ancient monuments before they were given protection.

Scheduled ancient monuments, such as dolmens, passage graves and barrows, are currently legally protected by a 2 m wide zone around the monument. This zone is based on a realisation that, around the ancient monument, there are not only traces of the deposition of pottery vessels and axes, but also the stone pavements, hearths and other associated structures and features. In the case of dolmens and passage graves, this 2 m zone is far from adequate. Excavations have demonstrated that important traces of structures and features and a whole range of finds may lie several metres

Fig. 22.1. *The future appears rather insecure and problematic for many dolmens, as we see here at Bårse in southern Zealand. Ploughing close to the dolmen and vibrations caused by the large machines have rendered the stone construction unstable. Small pieces of burnt flint, originating from destroyed parts of the dolmen's essential structures, can be seen on the soil surface. This otherwise handsome dolmen is further defaced by the close proximity of a dense Christmas-tree plantation and intensive ongoing aggregate extraction.*

from the current margin of the monument (see fig. 20.11). The protected zone should be expanded and, in cases where this is not possible, funds should be allocated to permit investigation of the areas outside the 2 m zone (fig. 22.1).

The neat and, in many people's eyes, rather dull appearance of many dolmens today is largely due to heavy-handed, cosmetic restoration works, often undertaken in the 1930s and 1940s – without prior archaeological investigations. Similar, radical and cosmetic restorations should, under no circumstances, be undertaken today. The great and almost unanswerable question is: What should we actually show? Is it the first, second, third or fourth phase of a particular dolmen's construction history? And how can we be completely sure this is how it appeared? An overlooked phase or event can easily and unexpectedly turn up and exert a major influence on the understanding of the monument in question. The best solution is to maintain a dolmen as is appeared when it was scheduled. In this way, the visible evidence of the *entire* cultural history of an individual dolmen is preserved – including the holes in its surface and its split and damaged stones.

Dolmens represent our earliest architecture in stone. In the future, we should take very good care of these more than 5000-year-old elements of our cultural heritage while, at the same time, being delighted, astonished, dismayed and continuously curious about these fascinating and intriguing monuments and their European background, as well as the form they attained in northern Europe, and their significance for our earliest farming cultures.

Notes

1. The Danish dolmen

1. Fergusson 1872; Joussaume 1985, 1988; Mohen 1989a-b; Kaul 1998.
2. Grundtvig 1808b, 1809, 1811.
3. Nørregård-Nielsen 2004, 2013; Brøndsted 1958; J. Jensen 1994.
4. The painting is on display in the National Gallery of Denmark, Copenhagen. The monument that inspired J.C. Dahl can still be seen today. It is known as the Bakkebølle or Ørnehøj dolmen. Claus Dam, Danish Agency for Culture and Palaces, is thanked for drawing our attention to this fact.
5. Vejlager 1939; Eriksen 1990, pp. 122-125 (Brundby); Eriksen & Olesen 1991 (Ringkøbing and Vejrum). The Ringkøbing monument was demolished in 1960.
6. Adriansen 2010, pp. 116-117.
7. Adriansen 2010, p. 187; Bjørnvad 1999.
8. The little dolmen is known as Klokkestenen, and it stands directly in front of the large stone mound, cf. Eriksen 1990, p. 166.
9. Wivel & Engelhart 1995; Wivel 2002.

2. With or without a mound

1. Eriksen 1999.
2. The weight of the capstone was previously estimated at 11.5 tonnes (Eriksen 1999, p. 58), but a new calculation, based on a scan undertaken by Jens Vedel, gives a figure of 16.3 tonnes, cf. box 6, pp. 246-247.
3. Eriksen 1999, pp. 58-64, 2010.
4. Eriksen 1990.

3. Research history

1. S. Hansen 1993.
2. Nordman 1918, pp. 87-91; Brøndsted 1957, p. 228.
3. Bakker 2001.
4. Mathiassen 1936.
5. Voss 1963; E. Jørgensen 2000, pp. 76-77.
6. Worsaae 1843, p. 64.
7. Ebbesen 1985; P.O. Nielsen 1981b.
8. Müller 1897, p. 56.
9. Kjær 1925, p. 40, p. 43.
10. Brøndsted 1938, pp. 198-201.
11. Glob 1942, pp. 22-24.
12. Mathiassen 1957; Ebbesen 1985; Eriksen 1987; I. Nielsen (ed.) 1987.
13. M.A. Hansen 1952, pp. 44-45.
14. Thorsen 1984, p. 38.
15. P.O. Nielsen 1981a, p. 76; J. Jensen 1988, p. 153; Ebbesen 2007, p. 11.
16. J. Jensen 1988 p. 153.
17. In the exhibition building in the car park for the Tustrup monuments it was still possible to read the following in 2010: "The excavations showed that many stones had been removed from the graves over time. In order to give visitors an impression of an intact round dolmen, the Forest and Nature Agency decided in 1994 to restore the earthen mound and the degraded dry-walling in the eastern round dolmen, as a contrast to the ruined dolmen chamber."
18. Eriksen 1999, pp. 72-77; J. Jensen 2001, pp. 362-363; N. Nielsen 2003.
19. N.H. Andersen 2008, p. 341; Eriksen 2009; Eriksen & Andersen 2010.
20. S.I. Hansen 2009a-b, 2010; Dehn 2013; Dehn et al. 2013.

4. Dolmens and the people of the Neolithic

1. Vedbæk: Albrethsen & Petersen 1975, 1976. Nivå: O.L. Jensen 2006. Skateholm: Larsson 1986. For further references to works by Lars Larsson on Skateholm, see J. Jensen 2001, which also contains further information on and references to Danish Mesolithic graves.

5. Typology and chronology

1. Adamsen & Jensen 1995-2003, 1995.
2. Length 0.8-3 m; width 0.4-1.6 m; height 0.5-1.6 m, cf. Ebbesen 2011, p. 176.
3. Eriksen 1980, pp. 36-37.
4. The division of the dolmen chambers into types I-IV corresponds largely to Klaus Ebbesen's classification (Ebbesen 2007, 2011). Ebbesen also gives the number, size, occurrence, finds, dating etc. for the individual types, as well as references to many dolmens belonging to one or other of these types.
5. Mathiassen 1942; E. Jørgensen 2006.
6. In 1957, the number of scheduled megalithic tombs was given as 2067 (Mathiassen 1957, p. 10). This figure includes a small number of stone cists from the Late Neolithic. In the 5th edition of *Trap Danmark*, 1954-1972, Therkel Mathiassen lists the number and type of scheduled ancient monuments for each parish and county, and summing these figures, county by county, gives a total of 2031 megalithic monuments, comprising 1584 dolmens, 382 passage graves and 65 indeterminable megalithic tombs plus 56 stone cists. In 1985, a new calculation showed that there were now 2364 scheduled megalithic tombs, including stone cists (Ebbesen 1985, pp. 138-142). In 2013, the number of scheduled megalithic tombs was given as c. 3000 (Dehn et al. 2013, p. 695). In which case there must have been an increase of more than 600 megalithic tombs in just less than 30 years, which seem very surprising. Remarkably, there are no recent totals and statistics for scheduled megalithic tombs.
7. Danish megalithic monuments with rows or circles of kerbstones or standing stones include the following: The long dolmen Brudager, north of Svendborg (Sehested 1878, p. 11); the long dolmen Skedysse at Kyndby, northern Zealand (Kaul 1987, p. 20; Ebbesen 2007, p. 56); the long dolmen Troldhøj in Nørreskoven on Als (Raben 1982, p. 47); one of dolmens – the passage dolmen – at Tustrup (cf. chap. 16) and Bygholm Nørremark at Horsens, with a passage grave in the converted Early Neolithic long barrow (Rønne 1979); the demolished round barrow Damsbo A1 on southwest Funen, also with a passage grave, investigated in 2006-08 by Niels H. Andersen, FHM archive no. 4401, OBM archive no. 3527 (N.H. Andersen 2011, p. 151 fig. 5).
8. Low stone walls: Barkær: Liversage 1992, p. 19 fig. 6; The northernmost of two parallel long dolmens at Ibjerg near Årslev, southeast of Odense, investigated by Odense City Museums in 2008-09, cf. Juel et al. 2016. Horizontal timber: Lindebjerg, cf. Liversage 1983. Stakes and posts: Southwest Funen, cf. chap. 20; Mosegården, cf. Madsen & Petersen 1984.
9. Kjær 1925, p. 48.
10. Ebbesen 2011, p. 158.
11. The other scheduled five-chambered long dolmen, in which all the chambers had already been blown up and destroyed in 1847, is at Abkær near Vedsted, southwest of Haderslev. We do not know whether all the chambers were dolmen chambers.
12. When the Fuchsberg pottery was published, it was perceived as reflecting "a transitional phase between the Early and Middle Neolithic. Ostensibly, however, it would be preferable to see it as the earliest Middle Neolithic phase …" (Andersen & Madsen 1978, p. 144). Other researchers have not accepted this and have placed the Fuchsberg phase at the end of the Early Neolithic (cf. for example Ebbesen 2011, p. 42). This is now widely accepted, even though we believe that the Fuchsberg phase contains such innovation that it points forwards rather than back in time.
13. Nordman 1935.
14. N.H. Andersen 2000, p. 43.

6. Dolmens with mounds

1. Dehn et al. 2013, p. 699.
2. Ebbesen 1990.
3. Ebbesen 1990, p. 62 fig. 20. The stone pavement, which lies directly on the Neolithic topsoil, could very well be associated with an unrecognised inhumation in the uninvestigated part of the long barrow.
4. Ebbesen 1990, pp. 63-64.
5. Berg 1956; Skaarup 1985, pp. 111-112, cat. no. 65.
6. Berg 1958; Skaarup 1985, pp. 176-179, cat. no. 229.
7. Two other good examples are the passage grave mound of Damsbo A1 on southwestern Funen, cf. note 7 in chapter 5, and the long barrow Frellesvig on the island of Langeland, with two small passage grave chambers, cf. Berg 1974; Skaarup 1985, pp. 114-115, cat. no. 73.
8. Eriksen 1980; Skaarup 1985, pp. 315-318, cat. no. 544; Eriksen & Thorsen 1979.
9. Gebauer 1990.
10. Ethelberg 1994; AUD 1991: no. 380, pp. 1991-200; E. Jørgensen 2000, pp. 75-78; Andersen & Rasmussen 1993, pp. 13-15.
11. Andersen & Rasmussen 1993, pp. 13-15; E. Jørgensen 2000, pp. 75-78.
12. Holst 2006.
13. Holst 2006, p. 8; Thorsen 1981.
14. S.I. Hansen 2010, pp. 12-13; Dehn 2013, p. 98.
15. Eriksen 1980, p. 35 fig. 5.

7. Tricky open dolmens

1. Thorvildsen 1985.
2. Perhaps A.P. Madsen only included the larger stones in his drawing, omitting kerbstones marked by smaller stones or stone fragments.
3. Declaration of 24th November 1890. Declaration archive, Danish Agency for Culture and Palaces.
4. Adamsen & Jensen 1998, p. 306. The investigation was carried out by customs officer Machesen, probably in the second half of the 18th century, as in 1809 he is referred to as "an old honourable Norwegian".
5. The southern orthostat has a flat surface that does not appear natural, but no cleavage marks are evident.
6. Adamsen & Jensen 1998, p. 290.
7. Poulsen 2001.
8. Sites and Monuments (*F&F*) no. 141101-116: Research history, 1894.
9. Sites and Monuments (*F&F*) no. 141101-116: Research history, 1946.
10. Letter dated 19/9 1936 from Mogens Mackeprang to the Danish National Museum, archive no. NM I 198/36.

8. The selection process

1. For example, the text at the foot of the ground plan for Kjallesten was not included: "(Only slightly elevated above the surrounding soil.)". This important piece of information is not evident from Conrad Engelhardt's very brief text.
2. For example, the report archive containing information on earlier excavations and restorations of dolmens as well as the records and excavation logs of a number of amateur archaeologists, including that of Ludvig Zinck containing a detailed section through the fill layers in a megalithic grave, drawn in 1865, cf. Dehn et al. 1995, p. 41 fig. 38.
3. Reviewed in *Kuml* 2007, cf. Eriksen 2007.
4. *Danmarks megalitgrave* comprises three books: two of text and maps (volumes 1.1 and 1.2) published in 2011, and a catalogue (volume 2) published in 2008. *Danske jættestuer*, 2009, consists of 46 chapters on the Danish National Museum's earlier investigations

of dolmens (including Kellerød and Grønsalen) and passage graves, and associated descriptions and analyses. The books are reviewed in *Kuml* 2012, cf. Gebauer 2012.

5. Ebbesen 2008, p. 7.
6. Clerical reports from the 17th century: F. Jørgensen 1970, 1974. Clerical reports from the 19th century: Adamsen & Jensen 1995-2003.
7. Zealand is covered by four map booklets, the rest of the country by a further 63 booklets, numbered 1-66, as 1-2, 4-5 and 7-8 have been each combined in a single booklet. Some map booklets were published in up to four editions.
8. Introductory text to *Vore Fortidsminder.*
9. Becker 1969, p. 6.
10. J.V. Jensen 1931, p. 47.
11. Therkel Mathiassen also wrote all the sections on scheduled ancient monuments, parish by parish in the 5th edition of *Trap Danmark*, which was published in the period 1953-72, cf. note 6 in chapter 5.
12. Mathiassen 1957.
13. The island of Møn is not included under Zealand.
14. Of the 1584 scheduled dolmens that are listed the 5th edition of *Trap Danmark*, 851 are long dolmens, 228 round dolmens and 505 dolmen chambers. Also see note 6 in chapter 5.
15. The description of the first 29 numbered monuments in the list of potential open dolmens is from *Vore Fortidsminder.* The emphasis in *italics* is ours. It is worth noting that they are all located on Zealand and Lolland. The list includes their number in *Vore Fortidsminder* (VF), while their number in the Sites and Monuments (*F&F*) database is given in the site register at the back of this book. – 1: Long dolmen in Avnede Skov, Lolland. VF 61 Maribo no. 26: "Beautiful long dolmen *without earth mounding;* many kerbstones and chamber with capstone". – 2-4: Long dolmens in Hildesvig Skov, Lolland. VF 62 Nykøbing Falster no. 9: "Three long dolmens, *almost without earth mounding*, with many kerbstones; the two to the east have a chamber and rolled-off capstone." – 5: Long dolmen in Hamborg Skov, Lolland. VF 62 Nykøbing Falster no. 85: "Long dolmen, *almost without earth mounding;* many kerbstones and chamber without capstone." – 6: Round dolmen in Hamborg Skov, Lolland. VF 62 Nykøbing Falster no. 86: "... a round dolmen *without earth mounding* and with a partially collapsed chamber." – 7: Long dolmen in Hamborg Skov, Lolland. VF 62 Nykøbing Falster no. 87: "Long dolmen *without earth mounding;* a number of kerbstones and chamber with capstone. Restored." – 8: Round dolmen in Hamborg Skov, Lolland. VF 62 Nykøbing Falster no. 113: "Round dolmen *without earth mounding* with capstone over chamber. Restored." – 9: Long dolmen in Flintinge Byskov, Lolland. VF 62 Nykøbing Falster no. 89: "... a long dolmen *without earth mounding* with chamber of 8 orthostats, no capstone." – 10: Long dolmen at Priorskov, Lolland. VF 62 Nykøbing Falster no. 122: "Long dolmen, *almost without earth mounding;* chamber has capstone." – 11: Long dolmen in Keldskov, Lolland. VF 65 Gedser no. 14: "Long dolmen *without earth mounding* and chamber." – 12: Round dolmen in the forest Store Møsten. VF NV-Sjælland no. 161: "Round dolmen *without mound*, but with many kerbstones and chamber of 5 orthostats and capstone." – 13: Long dolmen in Vinskoven. VF NV-Sjælland no. 169: "Exceptionally beautiful and impressive long dolmen, somewhat restored by the owner; there is *no earth mounding*, but a large chamber of 3 orthostats, threshold stone and 1 large capstone; the kerbstones are large and handsome." – 14: Long dolmen west of Ugerløse. VF NV-Sjælland no. 199: "Long dolmen with *only modest earth mounding*, with two chambers, one rectangular, no capstone, the other hexagonal, with capstone." – 15: Long dolmen east of Ugerløse. VF NV-Sjælland no. 200: "Impressive long dolmen in a small grove; *virtually no mound;* many impressive kerbstones and rectangular chamber without capstone." – 16-17: Two long dolmens in Grønholt Hegn. VF NØ-Sjælland no. 173: "Two long dolmens, *both without earthen mound* and chamber, but with impressive kerbstones. The southern one had a circle of smaller stones within the kerbstones" – 18: Long dolmen at Birkede. VF NØ-Sjælland no. 283: "Videdysse, *long dolmen without earthen mound*, 26 large kerbstones

and 2 transverse stone rows, rectangular chamber with capstone." – 19: Long dolmen at Valbygård, northwest of Slagelse. VF SV-Sjælland no. 42: "Long dolmen *without enclosing mound*, with 2 somewhat disturbed chambers, framed by handsome kerbstones." – 20: Long dolmen in Valbygård Skov, Sønder Overdrev, Nykobbel Skov, east of Slagelse. VF SV-Sjælland no. 75: "Long dolmen *without earth mounding*, consisting of 2 chambers with capstone and threshold stone, surrounded by kerbstones." – 21: Long dolmen in Broby Vesterskov. VF SV-Sjælland no. 108: "Long dolmen surrounded by kerbstones; but *no earth mounding*. In the middle a grave chamber formed of 3 side stones [orthostats] and 1 capstone, which bears cupmarks." – 22: Long dolmen in Korsør Skov. VF SV-Sjælland no. 129: "Long dolmen *without earth mounding*. Chamber of 3 orthostats and 1 capstone and surrounded by kerbstones." – 23: Long dolmen in Syllinge Skov. VF SV-Sjælland no. 172: Long dolmen *without earth mounding*, but surrounded by a double row of kerbstones. Grave chamber of 6 side stones [orthostats], but without capstone." – 24: Long dolmen in Gunderslevholm Skov. VF SV-Sjælland no. 201: "Impressive and handsome long dolmen, surrounded by tall, closely-spaced kerbstones. *Free-standing chamber* of 4 orthostats and 1 capstone. Mentioned in N.F.S. Grundtvig's poem: *Gunderslev Skov*." – 25: Dolmen chamber in unidentified mound, north of Herlufmagle. VF SV-Sjælland no. 228: "Dolmen chamber comprised of 3 side stones [orthostats], 1 threshold stone and 1 capstone. Enclosed by a *low earthen mound* and a few kerbstones." – 26: The round dolmen Tinghøj at Vejlø, south of Næstved. VF SV-Sjælland no. 238: "Round dolmen, surrounded by kerbstones and with a *free-standing dolmen chamber* of 2 side stones [orthostats] and 1 capstone." – 27: Long dolmen in Magleby Skov. VF SØ-Sjælland no. 27: "... one long dolmen, *almost without earth mounding*, with many kerbstones, ..." – 28: Strandegårds Dyrehave south of Fakse Ladeplads. VF SØ-Sjælland no. 58: "... a small long dolmen *without earthen mound* with a chamber without a capstone and many kerbstones." – 29: Long dolmen in Vintersbølle Skov, east of Vordingborg. VF SØ-Sjælland no. 105: "Long dolmen Valdemars Plads; there is *no earth mounding*, but a number of kerbstones and remains of two chambers."

9. From wood to stone – from fence to mound

1. E.B. Petersen 1974; Petersen & Egeberg 2007.
2. Johansen 1917; Thorvildsen 1941.
3. T. Madsen 1993. For overviews of Barkaer-structures, long barrows and earth structures, see T. Madsen 1979; Kristensen 1991; Ebbesen 1994; Rudebeck 2002 (incl. the Swedish examples); Ebbesen2007; Kossian 2005; Rzepecki 2011.
4. Stürup 1966.
5. A further account and overview plan can be found in T. Madsen 1972, pp. 127-128.
6. Stürup 1966, pp. 15-16.
7. Liversage 1970, 1981, 1983.
8. Liversage 1983, pp. 5-7 with figs. 1-2.
9. Liversage 1983, pp. 8-10 with figs. 3-4.
10. Liversage 1983, pp. 12-13.
11. Rønne 1979.
12. Preben Rønne is thanked for this information.
13. Kaul 1988, p. 61.
14. Noble 2006, pp. 86-92.
15. Investigated by Niels H. Andersen. The results and finds are undergoing examination and analysis. Joint excavation between Odense City Museums (archive no. 6973) and Moesgaard Museum (archive no. 5025).
16. Studies of the transverse section over the grave revealed only faint and indistinct traces of the side planks. This could be due to the collapse of the cist.
17. Glob 1949.
18. Glob 1975.
19. Glob 1949, p. 14.

20. Liversage 1992, pp. 22-23.
21. Glob 1949, p. 6; Liversage 1992, p. 9 and pp. 22-23.
22. Liversage 1983, p. 12.
23. Ebbesen 1994, p. 69 and p. 86.
24. Kjærum 1971.
25. Müller 1911, pp. 280-281.
26. Liversage 1992, p. 23.
27. Kellerød (H. Andersen 1998; Ebbesen 2009, pp. 358-360). Rude (T. Madsen 1980). Havnbjerg Skov (Becker 1960). Skelde (Ethelberg 1994). Mention can also be made of the following dolmen cists: chamber 1 at Harreby (E. Jørgensen 2006, p. 62), Tindbæk, between Viborg and Randers, and Løjt Skovby, east of Åbenrå (Liversage 1992, p. 23).
28. Aner 1963, p. 13.
29. C.H. Hansen 2010.
30. Ebbesen 2011, p. 294.
31. Rønne 1979.
32. Kjærum 1977.
33. Madsen & Petersen 1984.
34. Rzepecki 2011.
35. Long dolmens are defined here as long barrows framed by kerbstones. In addition to framing ordinary dolmens from the Dolmen epoch, these long dolmens were also constructed in the Passage-grave epoch, as several of them are seen only to contain passage graves. Examples of this are evident in the final phase of the monument at Bygholm Nørremark, cf. illustration on the cover of *Skalk* 1979, no. 5. The Sarup area also has long dolmens only containing passage graves, including Sarup Gamle Skole XII structure B (fig. 20.5) and Strandby Skovgrave structure D II (fig. 20.7). A very well-known and impressive example is Kongehøjen, which stands west of Mariager.

10. Long dolmens with abundant mound fill

1. For example, the internal height of the Gunderslevholm dolmen chamber is 1.7 m, and a similar height was recorded in a dolmen chamber in the forest Pipstorn, east of Faaborg, that had been damaged by a tree toppled in a storm (windthrow) and was subsequently restored in 2000 by Torben Dehn and Svend Illum Hansen (report Odense City Museums archive no. 8790).
2. Pontoppidan 1764, p. 329.
3. H. Andersen 1998; Ebbesen 2009, pp. 358-360.
4. Eriksen 1990, pp. 35-37 and pp. 136-137.

11. The Gunderslevholm dolmen

1. Grundtvig 1808a.
2. Molbech 1808. Same description in Molbech 1811.
3. Adamsen & Jensen 1998, p. 519.
4. Christian Adamsen is thanked for providing this information.
5. *Antikvariske Annaler* 1812 no. 1, pp. 142-143.
6. Dehn & Nielsen 1987.
7. Letter dated 4th May 1809 from landowner Neergaard to Stemann, the prefect of Sorø county. Declaration archive, Danish Agency for Culture and Palaces.
8. A.P. Madsen 1868, p. 10.
9. Scheduling declaration of 1st September 1886. Declaration archive, Danish Agency for Culture and Palaces.
10. Sites and Monuments (*F&F*) no. 040505-1: Research history, 1904.
11. Sites and Monuments (*F&F*) no. 040505-1: Research history, 1940. The abbreviation "v." stands for *væltet* = "toppled".
12. Description of kerbstones undertaken on 28th March 2008 by Palle Eriksen: 1-2: Toppled outwards, split at top. 3: Leaning outwards. 4-5: Toppled outwards. 6:

Toppled outwards, top shot at. 7: Toppled outwards. 8: Toppled outwards, top split, piece missing. 9: Leaning slightly inwards. 10: Stands vertically. 11: Leaning heavily inwards, base possibly slipped outwards. 12: Completely split, only a stub protruding. Added to drawing in 2008. 13: Toppled completely outwards, small corner of top broken off. 14: Toppled completely outwards. 15: Leaning slightly inwards. 16-17: Leaning heavily inwards. 18: Toppled completely outwards. 19: Leaning slightly to the west. 20-22: Toppled completely outwards. 23: Leaning slightly outwards. 24: Toppled completely outwards. 25-26: Leaning slightly outwards, top of no. 26 is split off and a piece lies inside the long dolmen. 27: In situ but leaning slightly inwards. 28: Leaning slightly outwards. 29: Toppled completely outwards, top overgrown by tree root. 30: Leaning slightly inwards, stands OK. 31: Leaning heavily inwards. 32: Completely toppled inwards and fallen over, and base (possibly) slipped outwards. 33: Toppled slightly inwards. 34: Probably toppled to the east. 35: Toppled completely outwards and pressed out, possibly by a large tree. 36: (Possibly) split. Must have stood – and stands – at the gable, possibly leaning towards the north. 37: Toppled completely, 2.6 m long. 38: Toppled completely, at least 2.5 m long. 39 A-B: Stone split into two pieces, the one to the west (A) stands in situ and has a 65 cm long cleavage furrow; the other part (B) lies 3-4 m east of A. 40: Toppled completely and split into two parts, 60 cm long cleavage furrow. 41: Toppled completely, direction NNE. 42: In situ. 43: In situ, stands OK. 44: As no. 43, but transverse crack in the western third. 45: Leaning (slightly) inwards and the base has slipped outwards. 46: Stands apparently in situ. 47: Top split off and lies inwards. 48: Possibly intact. 49: Toppled almost completely outwards. 50: Intact, possibly leans too far inwards. 51: OK, included in section in eastern wall of trench 1, 1 m long. 52: Slipped outwards, base therefore leans heavily inwards. 53-54: OK, stand OK and close together. 55: Toppled inwards and base possible slipped outwards. 56: Almost completely toppled over and outwards. 57: "Pressed" outwards, transverse crack. 58: Toppled completely over, included in section in east wall of trench 2, 1.3 m long. 59: Toppled almost completely over and outwards. 60-62: Toppled completely over and outwards. 63-64: OK, in situ. 65: Toppled outwards. 66-68: Toppled completely over and outwards. 69: Top split off, stands (apparently) in situ. 70: Leaning somewhat inwards, base slipped outwards. 71: Split top, otherwise OK. 72: Leaning inwards. 73: Stand almost in situ, though with vertical front, and leans slightly to the east, towards the gap left by no. 72. 74: In situ. 75: Toppled completely outwards and split into two pieces, clear cleavage marks; one is a 10 cm long and 7 cm deep cleavage hole. 76: Lies almost completely toppled outwards. 77: Stands in situ, but leans slightly outwards. 78: OK, in situ. 79: Toppled completely outwards. 80: The entire side (facing out) to the north is split off. 81: Toppled outwards and turned towards the west. 82: Toppled completely outwards and "displaced towards the north"; must have stood between nos. 81 and 83. 83: Long narrow stone that leans inwards. 84: Toppled completely outwards, the northernmost stone in the west gable. 85: Leaning slightly inwards, but otherwise almost in situ. 86: Toppled completely outwards and split into three pieces. 87: Toppled completely outwards. 88: Possible kerbstone that has been split and moved. Lies to the south of kerbstone no. 1. 89: Two pieces of split stone that could well be a kerbstone. One piece lies inside the long dolmen, opposite the gap from nos. 11-12, the other (not shown on plan) lies outside the monument. 90: Around 6-7 m beyond the southeast corner of the long dolmen lies a large stone that could be a displaced kerbstone. The terrain slopes sharply outwards from here. 91-92: Stones with split-off fragments, could be kerbstones, lie opposite nos. 40-41.

13. Kaul & Krogh 1990, p. 237.
14. The capstone is 3.6 m long, 2.7 m wide and up to 90 cm thick. If we assume that it is rectangular and has an average thickness of 50 cm, its volume is 4.9 m^3. As 1 m^3 of granite weighs 2.75 tonnes, the weight of the capstone is 13.5 tonnes, i.e. about 15 tonnes.
15. Steensberg 1983, p. 29 and pp. 40-41.
16. Participants in the investigation: Torben Dehn, Lars Bjarke Christensen and Jørgen

Westphal, all of the Danish Agency for Culture, and Palle Eriksen, Ringkøbing-Skjern Museum. The report "Undersøgelsesrapport, Grundtvigsdyssen (Sandbæks-dyssen – Gunderslevholmdyssen), Danish National Museum archive no. 8333/03-33", dated February 2009, was written by Lars Bjarke Christensen. The investigation has to date (2014) been mentioned in three papers, all of which make a strong argument for the Gunderslevholm dolmen originally having had a mound: S.I. Hansen 2009a-b and Dehn 2013, cf. also Dehn et al. 2013, p. 16.

17. S.I. Hansen 2009a, p. 7.
18. Dehn 2013, p. 100.
19. Excavation report p. 4, cf. note 16.
20. With regard to several layers in dolmen mounds, see chapter 6.

12. Kjallesten and other dolmens with internal stone circles

1. J.M. Petersen 1909, pp. 152-163.
2. Sites and Monuments (*F&F*) 070619-15: Research history, 1879. An early description by Rosenørn-Lehn could not be located in the archives of the National Museum of Denmark.
3. Declaration archive, Danish Agency for Culture and Palaces.
4. Eriksen 1999, pp. 99-101.
5. Sites and Monuments (*F&F*) 070619-15: 1954: "Round dolmen, "Kjallesten", 1 x 10 m. Chamber, 5-sided, of 4 orthostats and 1 large capstone. 18 kerbstones, very small". On the list in the notebook "2 circles of kerbstones" is crossed out (The scheduling surveys, Danish Agency for Culture and Palaces).
6. On an earlier site visit in 1984 it was also noted that there was an animal burrow in the chamber, cf. Sites and Monuments (*F&F*) 070619-15: Research history, 1984.
7. The best known subterranean dolmen chambers and cists are the Harreby dolmens in South Jutland, cf. E. Jørgensen 2006.
8. Sites and Monuments (*F&F*) 070615-10: Research history, 1879.
9. Eriksen 1990, p. 98.
10. Sites and Monuments (*F&F*) 070615-10: Research history, 1926.
11. Museum Lolland-Falster (previously Lolland-Falsters Stiftsmuseum) archive no. 700-1987-24. Report by Karen Løkkegaard Poulsen 9. September 1987.
12. Sites and Monuments (*F&F*) 070608-171: Research history, 1879. The longitudinal profile is reproduced in Eriksen 1999, p. 25 no. 3.
13. Sites and Monuments (*F&F*) 070608-171: Research history, 1954.
14. Sites and Monuments (*F&F*) 070608-181: Research history, 1879. Magnus Petersen's drawing is reproduced in Eriksen 1999, p. 24 no. 2.
15. Sites and Monuments (*F&F*) 040419-4: Research history, 1937.
16. The National Museum of Denmark, Prehistoric department, archive no. 456/70.
17. Dehn et al. 1995.
18. Pontoppidan 1768, p. 311.
19. Søren Abildgaard's notebooks are kept at the Danish National Museum, cf. Grinder-Hansen 2010.
20. Eriksen 1999, pp. 27-29.

13. Videdysse – a long dolmen with stone circles and two mounds

1. Randsborg 1994.
2. Further long dolmens with transverse stone rows are depicted in A.P. Madsen 1896. The most convincing of these is Priorskov II, referred to by Madsen as Prierskovgård, plate L no. 79. Like the Priorskov mentioned in chapter 8, it stands by the manor of the same name in eastern Lolland.
3. Dehn 2009, p. 34.
4. Adamsen & Jensen 1998, p. 82.
5. Thorlacius 1809, p. 13.

6. *Antikvariske Annaler* 1812.
7. Sites and Monuments (*F&F*) 020102-6: Research history, 1901.
8. I.e. scheduled by title registration, but scheduled since 1809 according to a letter from the Danish Royal Commission for the Collection and Preservation of Antiquities to the Danish Chancery in 1809. The following quote is from the declaration that was registered on 3. September 1937.
9. Though perceived by some as a mound (Ebbesen 2011, p. 241).
10. Skaarup 1985, pp. 276-277, cat. no. 353.
11. Skaarup 1985, p. 277, including a reference in this to Hübertz 1834, p. 17.

14. Stenhus – a dolmen on a mound

1. Kjær 1925, p. 49; Glob 1942, p. 26; Service & Bradbery 1993, p. 33.
2. This can be seen on the Original I / first cadastral map of 1792.
3. Sites and Monuments (*F&F*) 140510-59: Research history, 1877.
4. Eriksen 1999, p. 37.
5. Eriksen 1999, p. 42. In 1963, according to the 5th edition of *Trap Danmark*, there were 31 scheduled dolmens in Mols district.
6. Ritzau 1987. The distributed beakers were copies of a small footed beaker (small vessel with a tall narrow base) from the Roman Iron Age, like the one depicted in Ritzau's article, p. 146.
7. Scheduling declaration registered on 28 July 1925. Hans Kjær's text dated 19 July 1925. The declaration archive, Danish Agency for Culture and Palaces.
8. The difference – a mere 9 cm – can be attributed to the fact that Sophus Müller endeavoured to "rounded" number: 4 feet, 4½ feet, 5 feet etc. 1 foot corresponds to 31.4 cm.
9. On splitting of stones in the Stone Age, see Noe-Nygaard 1984 and Eriksen 1990, pp. 65-67.
10. This could very well be the original Neolithic packing/dry-walling.
11. The precise weight of the capstone can first be calculated after its volume has been determined by scanning, see box 6: "Volume and weight of a capstone", pp. 246-247.
12. The decreasing height of the passage stones outwards is a commonly occurring feature. Also in passage graves, where the outer set at the kerbstones often does not have a capstone.
13. Solhøj is the name of a marked hill located 0.5 km to the northwest. It lies in the same post-enclosure field as Solhøj, and the farm in Strands to which it belongs is also known as Solhøjgård. Place-name researcher Peder Gammeltoft, Department of Nordic Research at the University of Copenhagen, has kindly informed that the two localities – Stenhus and Solhøj – are separate as far back as they can be followed on maps, village land registers etc. In 1683, a field, Stennis Agre, is mentioned, which is very probably the field on which Stenhus stands.

15. Trollasten and other free-standing dolmen chambers

1. Cf. note 14 in chapter 8 for a comparison with the distribution of dolmen chambers and round and long dolmens.
2. Ebbesen 2009, pp. 65-71.
3. Strömberg 1971.
4. Strömberg 1968, pp. 162.
5. Tablet comes from the French *tablette*, which means for example a thin wooden board or stone slab.
6. See also Bagge & Kaelas 1952, pp. 101-102.
7. During the investigation of Trollasten, the excavators were apparently unaware of features in plan, cf. the rather indistinct surfaces on the otherwise sharp photos reproduced in the publication. With regard to postholes, it is also possible that these could belong to one or more building that were earlier, or slightly earlier, than the time of construction of the dolmen.

8. Strömberg 1968, pp. 183-189.
9. Strömberg 1968, pp. 190-191, our translation.
10. T. Madsen 1982.
11. N. Nielsen 2003, p. 142.
12. Skaarup 1985, p. 214, cat. no. 268.

16. The passage dolmen at Tustrup

1. Kjærum 1955, 1957 and 1967.
2. The excavation report "FHM 359b. Beretning for undersøgelsen og restaureringen i 1955-56 af den fredede gangdysse i Tustrup" was completed by Palle Eriksen in 2011.
3. In both the scheduling declaration of 1887 and the district survey of 1891 mention is made of a solitary, prostrate 10-11 feet long stone being a possible capstone for the passage dolmen. Even very large dolmen chambers, such as Hylledysse and Troldkirken, have only one, albeit very large, capstone. It is very rare to see a single dolmen chamber with more than one capstone.
4. Kaul & Krogh 1990, p. 228.
5. Excavation report pp. 10-11, cf. note 2.
6. Cf. note 7 in chapter 5.
7. Damsbo A1, cf. note 7 in chapter 5.
8. O'Kelly, M.J. 1982; Eriksen 2008. The Scottish passage grave mound Balnuaran at Clava is also surrounded by a stone circle, which is dated to the Late Neolithic/Early Bronze Age, cf. Bradley 2007, pp. 173-174. Passage graves and stone circles: see Bradley 1998.
9. In addition to the stone circles at Newgrange and Clava, mentioned in the previous note, a similar date, later than the period when megalithic tombs were constructed, for Danish stone circles or rows of standing stones is supported by the finds circumstances encountered during the investigations at Damsbo. In the case of both of the demolished passage grave mound Damsbo A1 and the demolished long dolmen Damsbo A4, the standing stones had stood on an earlier cultural layer. The investigations at Damsbo are described in chapter 20.

17. The round dolmen at Tustrup

1. Kjærum 1957, pp. 17-18 and figs. 7 and 8.
2. The excavation report "FHM 359c. Beretning for undersøgelsen og restaureringen i 1956 af den fredede runddysse i Tustrup" was completed by Palle Eriksen in 2011.
3. From the section "Tolkning" (Interpretation) in the excavation report p. 17, cf. note 2.
4. From the section "Opførelsen" (Construction) in the excavation report p. 22, cf. note 2.
5. Kjærum 1986, p. 14.
6. Ebbesen 2011, p. 260.
7. From the section "Restaurering" (Restoration) in the excavation report pp. 13-14, cf. note 2.
8. Lunden, which was fully excavated, is not a round dolmen, but a free-standing dolmen chamber on a scutiform elevation, cf. description at the end of chapter 15.
9. Ebbesen 2011, p. 198. For a general account of polygonal dolmens, see same publication pp. 192-198.
10. Ebbesen 2011, p. 196.
11. S. Hansen 1993; Dehn et al. 1995, 2007 and 2013.
12. N. Nielsen 2003, pp. 143-144.
13. Eriksen 1999, pp. 72-74, 2009; N.H. Andersen 2008, p. 341.
14. S.I. Hansen 2010.
15. Eriksen 2006.
16. Dehn 2013.
17. Kjærum 1957, p. 20.

18. Dolmens without mounds in Britain, France and Ireland

1. Longueville-Jones 1865.
2. Fergusson 1872.
3. Fergusson 1872, p. 169.
4. Lukis 1864, p. 146.
5. Lukis 1864, p. 150.
6. Lukis 1864, p. 150.
7. Mahé 1825, pp. 17-37.
8. De Fréminville 1834, pp. 23ff.
9. Bonstetten 1865, p. 8.
10. Fouquet 1853, p. 6.
11. Cartailhac 1889, p. 162.
12. Cartailhac 1889, p. 157.
13. Montelius 1899, p. 9.
14. Lubbock 1913, p. 113.
15. Lubbock 1913, p. 141.
16. Childe 1957, p. 218.
17. Tilley 1994; Cummings & Whittle 2004.
18. Tilley 1994, p. 105.
19. Fergusson 1872, pp. 169-170.
20. Barnwell 1874, p. 62.
21. Grimes 1948, p. 15.
22. Kinnes 1975, p. 25.
23. Lynch 1972.
24. Barker 1992, pp. 23-26.
25. Turner 1992, fig. 8.
26. Whittle 2004.
27. Lynch 1975; Richards 2004.
28. Berry 1929, 1930.
29. Corcoran 1969, p. 78; Darvill 2004, p. 123.
30. Saville 1990; Benson & Whittle 2007.
31. Hemp 1930.
32. O'Kelly, C. 1969.
33. Eogan 1983; Bradley 1998; Burrow 2010.
34. Rowlands 1723, plate VII fig. 3; Daniel 1958, fig. 4.
35. Hemp 1930, p. 221.
36. Burrow 2010.
37. Burrow 2010, p. 261.
38. Kytmannow 2008, pp. 42-43.
39. Kytmannow 2010, p. 212.
40. O'Kelly, M.J. 1958, 1960.
41. Jones 2007, pp. 234-237.
42. O'Brien 1999, p. 86.
43. O'Brien 1999.
44. Kytmannow 2008, p. 42.
45. Bergh 1995, pp. 62-71.
46. Burenhult 1980, p. 55, 1984.
47. Bergh 1995, pp. 79-81.
48. Holst 2006, p. 9.
49. Burenhult 2003, pp. 67-68.
50. O'Sullivan 2005.
51. Eriksen 2008.
52. Arnal 1956, p. 518.
53. Le Rouzic 1914.

54. Giot 1987, pp. 31-32.
55. Masset 1997, pp. 147-148.
56. Masset 1997, p. 152.
57. For example *Liscuis II og III*: Le Roux 1984; *Kernic*: Lecerf 1985; *Prajou-Menhir*: L'Helgouach 1966.
58. L'Helgouach 1965, p. 261.
59. Gruet & Passini 1986, p. 43.
60. Galles 1862, 1865; Le Rouzic 1932.
61. Le Rouzic 1932.
62. Galles 1864.
63. Evans & Hodder 2006.

19. Capstones

1. 8.5 m² – actually calculated as 8.7 m² – is the original floor area. The present floor area of the filled-in chamber is 6.4 m². The floor area of Hylledysse is 6 m², while the demolished dolmen chamber Vartov has had a floor area of 7.8 m², cf. fig. 5.5.
2. The capstone on Grønsalen has one flat side that differs from the rest of the stone (granite?) by having a thin layer of whitish, quartz-like type of rock. The same phenomenon is seen on a couple fragments of stones in the passage of the Bakkebølle dolmen, east of Vordingborg. Lis Helles Olesen is thanked for these observations. The flat side of the Grønsalen capstone is due to a fracture along an existing plane of weakness in the original stone, cf. Noe-Nygaard 1984; Eriksen 1999, p. 58.
3. Eriksen 1999, pp. 58-64; Eriksen 2010.
4. S. Hansen 1995; Dehn et al. 1995, pp. 55-59; Dehn & Hansen 2000.
5. Jørgen Westphal is thanked for drawing our attention to the large capstone on the Ristinge dolmen.
6. Eriksen 1999, p. 58.
7. Burenhult 1992; Eriksen 2002.
8. Fergusson 1872, p. 169.
9. Müller 1897, p. 56.
10. Glob 1942, pp. 23-24.
11. Juhl 1949, p. 56.
12. Journalist Louise Fogh Hansen wrote the following in the newspaper *Weekendavisen* in 2013, after taking part in a megalith tour led by one of the Danish Agency for Culture's archaeologists who had been involved in restoring many megalithic tombs: "… when they were built, the dolmens were covered with earth so that only the upper part of the capstone was visible." L.F. Hansen 2013, p. 7.
13. Eriksen 1999, pp. 88-89.
14. For example: Capeshøj, Skelde and Tårup, all mentioned in chapter 6.

20. Dolmens without mounds in the Sarup area

1. N.H. Andersen 2001.
2. Skaarup 1985.
3. N.H. Andersen 1997, 1999.
4. T. Madsen 1988; N.H. Andersen 1997, pp. 185, 282; P.O. Nielsen 2004; Geschwinde & Raetzel-Fabian 2009, p. 26 Abb. 10; Klatt 2009.
5. Thrane 1989.
6. N.H. Andersen 2009, p. 32 fig. 9.
7. Value at two standard deviations (σ). AAR-9208.
8. AAR-9211.
9. Liversage 1992, pp. 22-23, and chapter 9 in this book.
10. N.H. Andersen 1999, p. 278 fig. 6.5.
11. Rzepecki 2011.
12. N.H. Andersen 2009, p. 32 figs. 9 and 10.

13. N.H. Andersen 1997, pp. 94-96.
14. N.H. Andersen 1997, p. 96 fig. 125a.
15. Similar to the two long dolmens in Valbygård Skov, though there are clear differences. At Strandby Skovgrave, two long dolmens lie parallel and close together; one has a mound and the other doesn't. The Valbygård Skov monuments have different type of graves and mounds: a long dolmen with a very large amount of mound material and a long dolmen without a mound and two early dolmen chambers, see box 3: "Valbygård Skov" see box 3, p. 125.
16. N.H. Andersen 2011, p. 151 fig. 5.
17. In a short presentation of a long barrow excavated in the area between Strandby Skovgrave and Damsbo, a long barrow containing a passage grave chamber was erroneously referred to as a long dolmen, see N.H. Andersen 1988, pp. 56-57.
18. N.H. Andersen 2011, p. 151 fig. 5.
19. An important task is to find out, for example through analyses of the pottery, whether Neolithic people only came to the area in connection with the construction of new monuments, or whether they engaged in various other activities there between the construction phases. They could, of course, have visited the areas without necessarily leaving any trace whatsoever.

21. The living and the dead

1. Worsaae 1843, p. 67.
2. Skaarup 1985, p. 372; Ebbesen 2011, pp. 545-548.
3. Ebbesen 2011, pp. 289-292.
4. Ebbesen 2011, pp. 283 and 293.
5. P.O. Nielsen 1984.
6. P.O. Nielsen 1984, p. 379. The date is given in radiocarbon years BC. Calibration of this value today, at two standard deviations (σ), i.e. with a statistical probability of 95.4% that the correct date lies within the given range, means the skeleton is dated to 3365-2936 BC.
7. Thorsen 1981; P.O. Nielsen 1984, pp. 379-380.
8. N.H. Andersen 1999, p. 33 fig. 3.4 with dates for Sarup I.
9. Thorsen 1981, p. 124 fig. 10.
10. P.O. Nielsen 1984, pp. 376-377.
11. H.A. Nielsen 1906, p. 264, and 1911, pp. 114-115. Part-time lecturer Pia Bennike PhD is thanked for helping us to understand the bone material from Ølstykke.
12. According to Sophus Müller's report at the Danish National Museum, archive no. A 9680-9681. Senior Curator Poul Otto Nielsen is thanked for assistance in procuring a copy of the report.
13. Ebbesen 1990.
14. Bennike 1990.
15. Bennike 1990, pp. 70-71 fig. 1A.
16. Ebbesen 1990, p. 66.
17. Bennike 1990, pp. 73-74.
18. Wahl 2008, p. 730.
19. Bennike 1990, pp. 70-72.
20. Bennike 1990, pp. 73-74 fig. 3.
21. Becker 1960.
22. Glob 1952, p. 61 nos. 480-485. It would also be interesting to obtain radiocarbon dates for the skeleton and the wrist guard from the dolmen cist in Havnbjerg Skov.
23. A.P. Madsen 1896, p. 33 Pl. XXXXI.
24. Schuldt 1972, p. 71; Raddatz 1979.
25. Mischka 2011.
26. Mischka 2011, p. 76 figs. 21 and 22; Mischka & Fuchs in press.
27. Mischka 2011, p. 87 fig. 44 and p. 89; Mischka & Fuchs in press. Professor, Dr. Doris

Mischka, Friedrich-Alexander-Universität Erlangen-Nürnberg, is thanked for permission to refer to the unpublished material from Flintbek.

28. We know from ethnographic studies that the human body and pottery vessels can be associated metaphorically. In some societies the form and decoration of a pottery vessel are linked to societal and cosmological messages. Interesting studies in this respect are presented in the book *Smashing Pots* by Nigel Barley.
29. Skaarup 1985, pp. 206-207.
30. Gidlöf et al. 2006, pp. 51-53.
31. Strömberg 1968, pp. 119-136.
32. Strömberg 1968, p. 126 Abb. 79.
33. Burenhult 1973, pp. 43-44.
34. Gejvall 1973, pp. 45-46.
35. At sites with more favourable conditions for the preservation of bone than the Danish causewayed enclosures, which most commonly lie on sand, numerous human bones are found in the primary layers, though never whole skeletons. These human bones show that they have been subjected to complex treatment, often over an extended period, before they were finally deposited in the system-ditches, cf. N.H. Andersen in press.
36. N.H. Andersen 1999, p. 279.
37. Wahl 2008, p. 730; N.H. Andersen 1999, p. 289.
38. Bennike & Ebbesen 1987.
39. Ebbesen 1993.
40. Koch 1998, pp. 155-156.
41. Bennike et al. 1986, p. 203.
42. Taruskin 1996.
43. T. Madsen 1993; Larsson 2002; Kossian 2005.
44. T. Madsen 1993, p. 97 (Skibhøj) and p. 99 (Bygholm Nørremark).
45. Rasmussen et al. 2002.
46. Kossian 2005, pp. 90-113.
47. N.H. Andersen 2009.
48. Skaarup 1973; Rasmussen 2012.
49. N.H. Andersen 1999, pp. 303-313.
50. N.H. Andersen in press.
51. Holten 2009, p. 167.
52. Pearson 2012, pp. 272-273.
53. Waterson 2009, pp. 199-228.
54. In Denmark at the present time, ploughed-down megalithic monuments are suffering serious destruction as cultivation with new agricultural implements gradually, year by year, removes the last remnants of these sites. This means that the plough is now approaching the last few remains of these monuments. Ploughed-down dolmen sites have proved to be well-suited to studies of the original use of dolmens, as these monuments were not excavated in the 19th century. See for example chapter 20 and the account of Flintbek in chapter 21. Often, when plundering these monuments of stones, the lower parts were left untouched, as only the stones were removed from them.

References

Adams, R.L. 2007: *The Megalithic Tradition of West Sumba, Indonesia: An Ethnoarchaeological Investigation of Megalithic Construction*. Simon Fraser University, Canada. (Pdf, Internet).

Adams, R.L. 2010: Megalithic Tombs, Power, and Social Relations in West Sumba, Indonesia. In: D. Calado, M. Baldia & M. Boulanger (eds.): *Monumental Questions: Prehistoric Megaliths, Mounds and Enclosures*. Oxford, pp. 279-284.

Adamsen, C. & V. Jensen 1995: Om hedenske altre, runesten, helgenbilleder og deslige. *Skalk* 1995 nr. 5, pp. 20-29.

Adamsen, C. & V. Jensen (eds.) 1995-2003: *Danske præsters indberetninger til Oldsagskommissionen af 1807*. 1995: Vest- og Sydjylland; 1996: Nord- og Østjylland; 1997: Bornholm, Lolland-Falster og Fyn; 1998: Sjælland, Samsø og Møn; 2003: Tillæg og registre. Højbjerg.

Adriansen, I. 2010: *Erindringssteder i Danmark. Monumenter, mindesmærker og mødesteder.* Copenhagen.

Albrethsen, S.E. & E.B. Petersen 1975: Jægerfolkets grave. *Skalk* 1975 nr. 5, pp. 3-10.

Albrethsen, S.E. & E.B. Petersen 1976: Excavation of a Mesolithic Cemetery at Vedbæk, Denmark. *Acta Archaeologica* 47, pp. 1-28.

Andersen, H. 1998: Asernes altre. *Nytårsgave til Borupris' Venner 1999*, pp. 9-15.

Andersen, N.H. 1988: *Sarup. Befæstede kultpladser fra bondestenalderen*. Højbjerg.

Andersen, N.H. 1997: *The Sarup Enclosures. The Funnel Beaker Culture of the Sarup site including two causewayed camps compared to the contemporary settlements in the area and other European enclosures*. Højbjerg.

Andersen, N.H. 1999: *Saruppladsen. Tekst* (vol. 2), *Katalog* (vol. 3). Højbjerg.

Andersen, N.H. 2000: Kult og ritualer i den ældre bondestenalder. *Kuml* 2000, pp. 13-57.

Andersen, N.H. 2001: Status over storstensgrave. In: A.N. Jørgensen & J. Pind (eds.): *Før landskabets erindring slukkes – Status og fremtid for dansk arkæologi*. Copenhagen, pp. 53-64.

Andersen, N.H. 2008: Anmeldelse af Midgley 2008. *Kuml* 2008, pp. 339-343.

Andersen, N.H. 2009: Sarupområdet på Sydvestfyn i slutningen af 4. årtusinde f.Kr. In: A. Schülke (ed.): *Plads og rum i tragtbægerkulturen*. Copenhagen, pp. 25-44.

Andersen, N.H. 2011: Causewayed enclosures and megalithic monuments as media for shaping Neolithic identities. In: M. Furholt, F. Lüth & J. Müller (eds.): *Megaliths and Identities. Early Monuments and Neolithic Societies from the Atlantic to the Baltic*. Bonn, pp. 143-154.

Andersen, N.H. In press: Causewayed enclosures of Northern and Western Europe – an overview seen from Denmark. In: H. Mellar et al. (eds.): *Salzmünde – Regel oder Ausnahme?* Halle.

Andersen, N.H. & T. Madsen 1978: Skåle og bægre med storvinkelbånd fra yngre stenalder. Overgangen mellem tidlig- og mellemneolitikum. *Kuml* 1977, pp. 131-160.

Andersen, N.H. & P. Eriksen 1996: Dysser uden høje. *Skalk* 1996 nr. 2, pp. 5-9.

Andersen, S.T. & P. Rasmussen 1993: *Pollenanalyser fra gravhøje og søer 1992. Geobotaniske undersøgelser af kulturlandskabets historie*. DGU Kunderapport nr. 16.

Aner, E. 1963: Die Stellung der Dolmen Schleswig-Holsteins in der nordischen Megalithkultur. *Offa* 20, pp. 9-38.

Arnal, J. 1956: Petit lexique du mégalithisme. *Bulletin de la Société Préhistorique Française* 53, pp. 518-531.

AUD: *Arkæologiske udgravninger i Danmark*. Copenhagen.

Bagge, A. & L. Kaelas 1952: *Die Funde aus Dolmen und Ganggräbern in Schonen, Schweden*. II. Stockholm.

Bakker, J.A. 2001: Childe, Van Giffen, and Dutch archaeology until 1970. In: W.H. Metz, B.L. Van Beek & H. Steegstra (eds.): *Patina. Essays presented to Jay Jordan Butler on the occasion of his 80th birthday*. Groningen og Amsterdam, pp. 48-74.

Barker, C.T. 1992: *The Chambered Tombs of South-West Wales*. Oxford.

Barley, N. 1994: *Smashing Pots*. London.

Barnwell, E.L. 1874: South Wales cromlechs. *Archaeologia Cambrensis* 5, pp. 59-73.

Becker, C.J. 1960: Bueskytten fra Havnbjerg Skov. Et stenalder-problem. In: *Jens Raben. 14. marts 1880 – 18. februar 1960. Et mindeskrift*. Sønderborg, pp. 28-37.

Becker, C.J. 1969: Therkel Mathiassen og dansk arkæologi. *Aarbøger for Nordisk Oldkyndighed og Historie* 1968, pp. 3-25.

Bennike, P. 1990: Human Remains from the Grøfte Dolmen. *Journal of Danish Archaeology* 7, pp. 70-76.

Bennike, P., K. Ebbesen & L.B. Jørgensen 1986: Two Early Neolithic Skeletons from Boelkilde bog, Denmark. *Antiquity* 60, pp. 199-209.

Bennike, P. & K. Ebbesen 1987: The Bog Find from Sigerdal. Human Sacrifice in the Early Neolithic. *Journal of Danish Archaeology* 5, pp. 85-115.

Benson, D. & A. Whittle (eds.) 2007: *Building Memories. The Neolithic Cotswold Long Barrow at Ascott-Under-Wychwood, Oxfordshire*. Oxford.

Berg, H. 1956: Langdolmen bei Pæregaard, Langeland. *Acta Archaeologica* 27, pp. 108-127.

Berg, H. 1958: En stenhob på marken. *Skalk* 1958 nr. 2, pp. 9-13.

Berg, H. 1974: En mellemneolitisk gravhøj med to pæreformede dyssekamre. En præliminær redegørelse. *Fynske Minder* 1974, pp. 49-70.

Bergh, S. 1995: *Landscape of the Monuments. A study of the passage tombs in the Cúil Irra region*. Stockholm.

Berry, J. 1929: Belas Knap long barrow, Gloucestershire: report of the excavations of 1929. *Transactions of the Bristol and Gloucestershire Archaeological Society* 51, pp. 273-303.

Berry, J. 1930: Belas Knap long barrow, Gloucestershire. Second report: the excavations of 1930. *Transactions of the Bristol and Gloucestershire Archaeological Society* 52, pp. 123-50.

Bjørnvad, A. 1999: *Krigens monumenter 1940-1945*. Odense.

de Bonstetten, Baron A. 1865: *Essai sur les dolmens*. Genève.

Bradley, R. 1998: Stone circles and passage graves – a contested relationship. In: A. Gibson & D. Simpson (eds.): *Prehistoric Ritual and Religion*. Stroud, pp. 2-13.

Bradley, R. 2007: *The prehistory of Britain and Ireland*. Cambridge.

Brøndsted, J. 1938: *Danmarks Oldtid* I. *Stenalderen*. Copenhagen.

Brøndsted, J. 1957: *Danmarks Oldtid* I. *Stenalderen*. Copenhagen.

Brøndsted, J. 1958: Oldtidsminderne i Kunsten. *Nationalmuseets Arbejdsmark* 1958, pp. 5-16.

Burenhult, G. 1973: *En långdös vid Hindby Mosse, Malmö*. Malmø.

Burenhult, G. 1980: *The Archaeological Excavation at Carrowmore, Co. Sligo, Ireland. Excavation seasons 1977-79*. Stockholm.

Burenhult, G. (ed.) 1984: *The Archaeology of Carrowmore: environmental archaeology and the megalithic tradition at Carrowmore, Co. Sligo, Ireland*. Stockholm.

Burenhult, G. 1992: *StenMännen. Megalitbyggare och människoätare*. Höganäs.

Burenhult, G. 2003: The chronology of Carrowmore. In: G. Burenhult (ed.): *Stones and Bones. Formal disposal of the dead in Atlantic Europe during the Mesolithic-Neolithic interface 6000-3000 BC*. Oxford, pp. 66-69.

Burrow, S. 2010: Bryn Celli Ddu passage tomb, Anglesey: alignment, construction, date, and ritual. *Proceedings of the Prehistoric Society* 76, pp. 249-270.

Cartailhac, É. 1886: *Les âges préhistoriques de l'Espagne et du Portugal*. Paris.
Cartailhac, É. 1889: *La France Préhistorique d'après les sépultures et les monuments.* Paris.
Childe, V.G. 1957: *The Dawn of European Civilization.* London.
Corcoran, J.X.W.P. 1969: The Cotswold-Severn Group: 2. Discussion. In: *Megalithic Enquiries in the West of Britain.* Liverpool, pp. 73-104.
Cummings, V. & A. Whittle 2004: *Places of Special Virtue: megaliths in the Neolithic landscapes of Wales.* Oxford.
Darvill, T. 2004: *Long Barrows of the Cotswolds and surrounding areas.* Stroud.
Dehn, T. 2009: The *Videdys* long Dolmen 1643-2006. In: M.S. Midgley (ed.): *Antiquarians at the Megaliths.* Oxford, pp. 31-35.
Dehn, T. 2013: "Open dolmens" – a Matter of Decay? In: J.A. Bakker, S.B.C. Bloo & M.K. Dütting (eds.): *From Funeral Monuments to Household Pottery – Current advances in Funnel Beaker Culture (TRB/TBK) research.* Oxford, pp. 95-109.
Dehn, T. & I. Nielsen 1987: Kancellifredningerne. In: I. Nielsen (ed.): *Bevar din arv. 1937-Danmarks fortidsminder-1987.* Copenhagen, pp. 86-92.
Dehn, T., S.I. Hansen & F. Kaul 1995: *Kong Svends høj. Restaureringer og undersøgelser på Lolland 1991.* Copenhagen.
Dehn, T. & S.I. Hansen 2000: Doubleness in the Construction of Danish Passage Graves. In: A. Ritchie (eds.): *Neolithic Orkney in its European context.* Cambridge, pp. 215-221.
Dehn, T., N. Engberg, V. Etting, J. Frandsen, S.I. Hansen, K.B. Vesth & J. Westhal 2007: Bevaring og restaurering af fortidsminder. *Nationalmuseets Arbejdsmark* 2007, pp. 273-290.
Dehn, T., S.I. Hansen & J. Westphal 2013: Restoration of Megalithic Tombs in Denmark. In: Bergerbrant, S. & S. Sabatini (eds.): *Counterpoint: Essays in Archaeology and Heritage Studies in Honour of Professor Kristian Kristiansen.* Oxford, pp. 695-702.
Ebbesen, K. 1985: *Fortidsminderegistrering i Danmark.* Copenhagen.
Ebbesen, K. 1990: The Long Dolmen at Grøfte, South-West Zealand. *Journal of Danish Archaeology* 7, pp. 53-69.
Ebbesen, K. 1993: Offer til naturens magter. In: S. Hvass & B. Storgaard (eds.): *Da klinger i Muld … 25 års dansk arkæologi.* Aarhus, pp. 122-125.
Ebbesen, K. 1994: Simple, tidligneolitiske grave. *Aarbøger for Nordisk Oldkyndighed og Historie* 1992, pp. 47-102.
Ebbesen, K. 2007: *Danske dysser. Danish Dolmens.* Copenhagen.
Ebbesen, K. 2008: *Danmarks megalitgrave. Katalog.* Copenhagen.
Ebbesen, K. 2009: *Danske jættestuer.* Copenhagen.
Ebbesen, K. 2011: *Danmarks megalitgrave.* Copenhagen.
Engelhardt, M.L. & H. Wivel 1995: *Tumulus. New Paintings and Gouaches.* New York.
Eogan, G. 1983: Bryn Celli Ddu. *Antiquity* 57, pp. 135-136.
Eriksen, P. 1980: Capeshøj på Tåsinge. En langdysse dækket af en bronzealderhøj. *Antikvariske studier* 4, pp. 31-48.
Eriksen, P. 1987: Kampen for gravhøjene. *Skalk* 1987 nr. 6, pp. 18-27.
Eriksen, P. 1990: *Samsøs store stengrave.* Ebeltoft.
Eriksen, P. 1999: *Poskær Stenhus. Myter og virkelighed.* Højbjerg.
Eriksen, P. 2002: Ramper og stilladser. Løft af store sten i oldtiden. *Kuml* 2002, pp. 65-107.
Eriksen, P. 2006: The rolling stones of Newgrange. *Antiquity* 80, pp. 709-710.
Eriksen, P. 2007: Anmeldelse af Ebbesen 2007, *Kuml* 2007, pp. 290-294.
Eriksen, P. 2008: The great mound of Newgrange: an Irish multi-period mound spanning from the megalithic tomb period to the Early Bronze Age. *Acta Archaeologica* 79, pp. 250-273.
Eriksen, P. 2009: Med eller uden fyld. *Weekendavisen* nr. 27, *Ideer* pp. 12-13.

Eriksen, P. 2010: Poskær Stenhus. *Skalk* 2010 nr. 5, pp. 16-17.
Eriksen, P. & S. Thorsen 1979: Restaureringen af Capeshøj-langdyssen. *Antikvariske studier* 3, pp. 217-218.
Eriksen, P. & L.H. Olesen 1991: Nye Dysser. *FRAM* 1991, pp. 71-80.
Eriksen, P. & N.H. Andersen 2010: Nybyggede fortidsminder. *Kuml* 2010, pp. 257-263.
Ethelberg, P. 1994: Høj over høj. *Broagerland* 8, pp. 52-69.
Evans, C. & I. Hodder 2006: *A Woodland Archaeology: Neolithic sites at Haddenham.* Cambridge.
Fergusson, J. 1872: *Rude Stone Monuments in All Countries; their Ages and Uses.* London.
Fouquet, A. 1853: *Des monuments celtiques et des ruines romaines dans le Morbihan.* Vannes.
de Fréminville, C.P. 1834: *Antiquités de la Bretagne. Monuments du Morbihan.* Brest.
Frederik VII 1857: *Om Bygningsmaaden af Oldtidens Jættestuer.* Copenhagen.
Frederik VII 1862: On the Construction of "Giants' Houses," or "Cromlechs". *Archaeologica Cambrensis* 4, pp. 1-13.
Galles, R. 1862: Rapport à M. le Préfet du Morbihan sur les fouilles du Mont Saint-Michel en Carnac faites en septembre 1862. *Bulletin de la Société Polymathique du Morbihan* 1862, pp. 7-17.
Galles, R. 1864: Fouilles du tumulus du Moustoir-Carnac. *Bulletin de la Société Polymathique du Morbihan* 1864, pp. 117-125.
Galles, R. 1865: Rapport à M. le Préfet du Morbihan sur l'emploi des fonds accordés, par le Conseil général, pour les fouilles archéologiques du Mont-Saint-Michel de Carnac. *Bulletin de la Société Polymathique du Morbihan* 1865, pp. 53-55.
Gebauer, A.B. 1990: The Long Dolmen at Asnæs Forskov, West Zealand. *Journal of Danish Archaeology* 7, pp. 40-52.
Gebauer, A.B. 2012: Danske stenalderhøvdinge? En anmeldelse af K. Ebbesens "Danmarks megalitgrave". *Kuml* 2012, pp. 205-215.
Gejvall, N-G. 1973: Den osteologiska undersökningen. In: G. Burenhult: *En långdös vid Hindby Mosse, Malmö.* Malmø, pp. 45-48.
Geschwinde, M. & D. Raetzel-Fabian 2009: *EWBSL. Eine Fallstudie zu den jungneolithischen Erdwerken am Nordrand der Mittelgebirge.* Rahden.
Gidlöf, K., K.H. Dehman & T. Johansson 2006: *Citytunnelprojektet. Almhov – delområde 1.* Malmø.
Giot, P.-R. 1987: *Barnenez, Carn, Guennoc.* Rennes.
Glob, P.V. 1942: *Danske Oldtidsminder.* Copenhagen.
Glob, P.V. 1949: Barkær. Danmarks ældste landsby. *Fra Nationalmuseets Arbejdsmark* 1949, pp. 5-16.
Glob, P.V. 1952: *Danske Oldsager II.* Copenhagen.
Glob, P.V. 1975: De dødes lange huse. *Skalk* 1975 nr. 6, pp. 10-14.
Grimes, W.F. 1948: Pentre Ifan burial chamber, Pembrokeshire. *Archaeologia Cambrensis* 100, pp. 3-23.
Grinder-Hansen, P. 2010: *Søren Abildgaard (1718-1791) – Fortiden på tegnebrættet.* Copenhagen.
Gruet, M. & B. Passini 1986: La Bajoulière en St Rémy-la-Varenne (Maine-et-Loire). Fouille et restauration d'un grand "Dolmen Angevin". *Revue Archéologique de l'Ouest* 3, pp. 29-46.
Grundtvig, N.F.S. 1808a: Gunderslev Skov. *Nyeste Skilderie af Kjøbenhavn.* No. 101. Copenhagen.
Grundtvig, N.F.S. 1808b: *Nordens Mytologi eller Udblik over Eddalæren for dannede Mænd, der ei selv ere Mytologer.* Copenhagen.
Grundtvig, N.F.S. 1809: *Optrin af Kæmpelivets Undergang i Nord.* Copenhagen.

Grundtvig, N.F.S. 1811: *Optrin af Norners og Asers Kamp*. Copenhagen.
Hansen, C.H. 2010: Tidligneolitiske gravanlæg i Danmark – udefra, oppefra og indefra. In: H. Lyngholm & B. Storgaard (eds.): *Brudstykker af en helhed. Specialer i forhistorisk arkæologi 2008 og 2009 fra Copenhagens Universitet*. Copenhagen, pp. 9-27.
Hansen, L.F. 2013: 5.000 års urokkelighed. *Weekendavisen* nr. 13, *Faktisk*, pp. 6-7.
Hansen, M.A. 1952: *Orm og Tyr*. Copenhagen.
Hansen, S. 1993: *Jættestuer i Danmark. Konstruktion og restaurering*. Copenhagen.
Hansen, S. 1995: Tvillingsten. *Skalk* 1995 nr. 5, pp. 16-17.
Hansen, S.I. 2009a: Dysser i høj – Grundtvigs offersted. *Fund & Fortid. Arkæologi for alle* 2009 nr. 4, pp. 4-7.
Hansen, S.I. 2009b: Dyssen i Gunderslevholm Skov. *Årsskrift. Fuglebjergegnens Lokalhistoriske Forening – Borupris' Venner*, pp. 4-9.
Hansen, S.I. 2010: Dysserne ved Strids Mølle. Dysser i høj, del 2. *Fund & Fortid. Arkæologi for alle* 2010 nr. 1, pp. 12-15.
L'Helgouach, J. 1965: *Les Sépultures Mégalithiques en Armorique*. Rennes.
L'Helgouach, J. 1966: Fouilles de l'allée couverte de Prajou-Menhir en Trébeurden (Côtes-du-Nord). *Bulletin de la Société Préhistorique Française* 63, pp. 311-342.
Hemp, W. J. 1930: The chambered cairn of Bryn Celli Ddu. *Archaeologia* 80, pp. 179-214.
Holst, M.K. 2006: Tårup. A round dolmen and its secondary burials. *Journal of Danish Archaeology* 14, pp. 7-21.
Holten, L. 2009: Åbninger til en anden virkelighed. Megalitanlæg som mediatorer mellem her og hisset. In: A. Schülke (ed.): *Plads og rum i tragtbægerkulturen*. Copenhagen, pp. 159-177.
Hübertz, J.R. 1834: *Beskrivelse over Ærø*. Copenhagen.
Jensen, J. 1988: *I begyndelsen. Fra de ældste tider til ca. år 200 f.Kr.* Gyldendals og Politikens Danmarkshistorie, bind 1. Copenhagen.
Jensen, J. 1994: Historiens spejl. Da historiemaleriet blev til landskabsmaleri. In: B. Scavenius (ed.): *Guldalderhistorier. 20 nærbilleder af perioden 1800-1850*. Copenhagen, pp. 30-37.
Jensen, J. 2001: *Danmarks Oldtid. Stenalder. 13.000-2.000 f.Kr.* Copenhagen.
Jensen, J.V. 1931: *Paa danske Veje*. Copenhagen.
Jensen, O.L. 2006: Stenalderjægernes hytter og grave ved Nivå. *Hørsholm Egns Museum, Årbog* 2005-06, pp. 6-31.
Johansen, K.F. 1917: Jordgrave fra Dyssetid. *Aarbøger for Nordisk Oldkyndighed og Historie* 1917, pp. 5-70.
Jones, C. 2007: *Temples of Stone. Exploring the megalithic tombs of Ireland*. Cork.
Joussaume, R. 1985: *Les dolmens pour les morts. Les mégalithismes à travers le monde*. Paris.
Joussaume, R. 1988: *Dolmens for the Dead. Megalith-Building throughout the World*. London.
Juel, C., J. Hansen & A.B. Andersen 2016: Grave i lange baner – et højkompleks fra tragtbægerkulturen ved Ibjerg, sydøst for Odense. *Aarbøger for Nordisk Oldkyndighed og Historie* 2015, pp. 7-57.
Juhl, F. 1949: FORTID nutid fremtid. *Dansk Kunsthaandværk* Nr. 4, pp. 56-60.
Jørgensen, E. 2000: Yngre stenalder. In: P. Ethelberg, E. Jørgensen, D. Meier & D. Robinson: *Det Sønderjyske Landbrugs Historie. Sten- og bronzealder*. Haderslev, pp. 63-133.
Jørgensen, E. 2006: Fra underjordiske dysser til synlige trapezformede anlæg. Om stenaldergravene ved Harreby i Sønderjylland. *Kuml* 2006, pp. 59-100.
Jørgensen, F. 1970: *Præsteindberetninger til Ole Worm. Indberetninger fra Ålborg og Ribe stifter 1625-42*. Copenhagen.
Jørgensen, F. 1974: *Præsteindberetninger til Ole Worm. Indberetninger fra Århus, Fyns og Lunde stifter 1625-42*. Copenhagen.
Kaul, F. 1987: *Dysser og jættestuer i Horns Herred*. Jægerspris.

Kaul, F. 1988: Neolitiske gravanlæg på Onsved Mark, Horns Herred, Sjælland. *Aarbøger for Nordisk Oldkyndighed og Historie* 1987, pp. 27-83.

Kaul, F. 1998: *Europas dysser og jættestuer.* Copenhagen.

Kaul, F. & K. Krogh 1990: En lidet påagtet stenkløvningsteknik – og om oldtidsminder som stenbrud. *Aarbøger for Nordisk Oldkyndighed og Historie* 1990, pp. 225-260.

Kinnes, I. 1975: Monumental function in British Neolithic burial practices. *World Archaeology* 7, pp. 16-29.

Kjær, H. 1925: *Vor Oldtids Mindesmærker.* Copenhagen.

Kjærum, P. 1955: Tempelhus fra stenalder. *Kuml* 1955, pp. 7-35.

Kjærum, P. 1957: Storstensgrave ved Tustrup. *Kuml* 1957, pp. 9-23.

Kjærum, P. 1967: Mortuary Houses and Funeral Rites in Denmark. *Antiquity* 41, pp. 190-196.

Kjærum, P. 1971: Skavangedyssen. In: C. Nørrelykke (ed.): *Brudstykker. Holger Friis tilegnet på firsårsdagen 15. oktober 1971.* Hjørring, pp. 63-71.

Kjærum, P. 1977: En langhøjs tilblivelse. *Antikvariske studier,* pp. 19-26.

Kjærum, P. 1986: Stenaldergrave og helligdom ved Tustrup. *Turistmagasinet* 1986 nr. 2, pp. 14-15.

Klatt, S. 2009: Die neolithischen Einhegungen im westlichen Ostseeraum. Forschungstand und Forschungsperspektiven. In: T. Terberger (ed.): *Neue Forschungen zum Neolithikum im Ostseeraum.* Rahden, pp. 7-134.

Koch, E. 1998: *Neolithic Bog Pots from Zealand, Møn, Lolland and Falster.* Copenhagen.

Kossian, R. 2005: *Nichtmegalithische Grabanlagen der Trichterbecherkultur in Deutschland und den Niederlanden.* Halle.

Kristensen, I.K. 1991: Storgård IV. An Early Neolithic Long Barrow near Fjelsø, North Jutland. *Journal of Danish Archaeology* 8, pp. 72-87.

Kytmannow, T. 2008: *Portal Tombs in the Landscape. The chronology, morphology and landscape setting of the portal tombs of Ireland, Wales and Scotland.* Oxford.

Kytmannow, T. 2010: Round mounds containing portal tombs. In: J. Leary, T. Darvill & D. Field (eds.): *Round Mounds and Monumentality in the British Neolithic and Beyond.* Oxford, pp. 211-218.

Larsson, L. 1986: Skateholm. *Skalk* 1986 nr. 4, pp. 21-31.

Larsson, L. 2002: Långhögar i samhällsperspektiv. In: L. Larsson (ed.): *Monumentala gravformer i det äldsta bondesamhället.* Lund, pp. 147-171.

Lecerf, Y. 1985: L'allée couverte de Kernic à Plouescat (Finistère). *Bulletin de la Société Archéologique du Finistère* 114, pp. 17-34.

Liversage, D. 1970: Stendyssens forløber. *Skalk* 1970 nr. 1, pp. 5-11.

Liversage, D. 1981: Neolithic Monuments at Lindebjerg, Northwest Zeeland. *Acta Archaeologica* 51, pp. 85-152.

Liversage, D. 1983: Træbyggede grave fra den ældste bondestenalder. Udgravninger ved Lindebjerg. *Nationalmuseets Arbejdsmark* 1983, pp. 5-16.

Liversage, D. 1992: *Barkær. Long Barrows and Settlements.* Copenhagen.

Longueville Jones, H. 1865: Pembrokeshire antiquities. Cromlechs – Newton, Manorbier, St. David's Head, Pentre Ifan. *Archaeologia Cambrensis* 11, pp. 281-285.

Lubbock, J. 1913: *Prehistoric Times as illustrated by ancient remains and the manners and customs of modern savages.* London.

Lukis, W.C. 1864: Danish cromlechs and burial customs compared with those of Brittany, the Channel Islands, and Great Britain. *Wiltshire Archaeological and Natural History Magazine* 8, pp. 145-169.

Lynch, F. 1972: Portal Dolmens in the Nevern Valley, Pembrokeshire. In: F. Lynch & C. Burgess (eds.): *Prehistoric Man in Wales and the West.* Bath, pp. 67-84.

Lynch, F. 1975: Excavations at Carreg Samson megalithic tomb, Mathry, Pembrokeshire. *Archaeologia Cambrensis* 124, pp. 15-35.

Madsen, A.P. 1868: *Afbildninger af Danske Oldsager og Mindesmærker. Steenalderen.* Copenhagen.

Madsen, A.P. 1896: *Gravhøje og Gravfund fra Stenalderen i Danmark. I – Det østlige Danmark.* Copenhagen.

Madsen, A.P. 1900: *Gravhøje og Gravfund fra Stenalderen i Danmark. II – Fyen og Jylland.* Copenhagen.

Madsen, T. 1972: Grave med teltformet overbygning fra tidlig-neolitisk tid. *Kuml* 1971, pp. 127-149.

Madsen, T. 1979: Earthen Long Barrows and Timber Structures: Aspects of the Early Neolithic Mortuary Practice in Denmark. *Proceedings of the Prehistoric Society* 45, pp. 301-320.

Madsen, T. 1980: En tidligneolitisk langhøj ved Rude i Østjylland. *Kuml* 1979, pp. 79-108.

Madsen, T. 1982: Settlement Systems of Early Agricultural Societies in East Jutland, Denmark: A Regional Study of Change. *Journal of Anthropological Archaeology* 1, pp. 197-236.

Madsen, T. 1988: Causewayed Enclosures in South Scandinavia. In: C. Burgess, P. Topping, C. Mordant & M. Maddison (eds.): *Enclosures and Defences in the Neolithic of Western Europe.* Oxford, pp. 301-337.

Madsen, T. 1993: Høje med træbyggede grave. In: S. Hvass & B. Storgaard (eds.): *Da klinger i muld ... 25 års dansk arkæologi.* Aarhus, pp. 96-99.

Madsen, T. & J.E. Petersen 1984: Tidligneolitiske anlæg ved Mosegården. Regionale og kronologiske forskelle i tidligneolitikum. *Kuml* 1982-83, pp. 61-120.

Mahé, J. 1825: *Essai sur les Antiquités de Département du Morbihan.* Vannes.

Masset, C. 1997: *Les Dolmens. Sociétés néolithiques et pratiques funéraires.* Paris.

Mathiassen, T. 1936: En vestjydsk Megalitbygd. *Aarbøger for Nordisk Oldkyndighed og Historie* 1936, pp. 1-17.

Mathiassen, T. 1942: En Stenalders Gravplads ved Harreby. *Sønderjyske Aarbøger* 1942, pp. 1-16.

Mathiassen, T. 1957: Oldtidsminderne og fredningsloven. *Fra Nationalmuseets Arbejdsmark* 1957, pp. 5-14.

Midgley, M.S. 2008: *The Megaliths of Northern Europe.* London og New York.

Mischka, D. 2011: Flintbek LA 3, biography of a monument. in M. Furholt, F. Lüth & J. Müller (eds.): *Megaliths and Identities. Early Monuments and Neolithic Societies from the Atlantic to the Baltic.* Bonn, pp. 67-94.

Mischka, D. & K. Fuchs. In press: Sekundäre Deponierung von Menschenresten in einem Megalitgrav des Langbetts Flintbek LA3. In: H. Mellar et al. (eds.): *Salzmünde – Regel oder Ausnahme?* Halle.

Mohen, J.-P. 1989a: *Le Monde des Megalithes.* Tournai.

Mohen, J.-P. 1989b: *The World of Megaliths.* London.

Molbech, C. 1808: Postscriptum til brevet fra Sorøe. *Nyeste Skilderie af Kjøbenhavn.* No. 100. Copenhagen.

Molbech, C. 1811: *Ungdomsvandringer i mit Fædreland.* Copenhagen.

Montelius, O. 1899: *Der Orient und Europa. Einfluss der orientalischen Cultur auf Europa bis zur Mitte des letzten Jahrtausends v. Chr.* Stockholm.

Müller, S. 1897: *Vor Oldtid.* Copenhagen.

Müller, S. 1911: Vendsyssel-Studier II. Sten- og Bronzealderens Mindesmærker og Fund. *Aarbøger for Nordisk Oldkyndighed og Historie* 1911, pp. 276-320.

Münter, F. 1805: Lejre i Sjelland, i Begyndelsen af det Nittende Aarhundrede. *Det Skandinaviske Litteraturselskabs Skrifter*, Andet Bind, pp. 265-324.

Nielsen, H.A. 1906: Bidrag til Danmarks forhistoriske Befolknings – særligt Stenalderfolkets – Anthropologi. *Aarbøger for Nordisk Oldkyndighed og Historie* 1906, pp. 237-318.

Nielsen, H.A. 1911: Yderligere Bidrag til Danmarks Stenalderfolks Anthropologi. *Aarbøger for Nordisk Oldkyndighed og Historie* 1911, pp. 81-205.

Nielsen, I. (ed.) 1987: *Bevar din arv. 1937-Danmarks Fortidsminder-1987*. Copenhagen.

Nielsen, N. 2003: Ormslev-dyssen – en dysse uden høj? Fritstående dysser i tragtbægerkulturen. *Kuml* 2003, pp. 125-156.

Nielsen, P.O. 1981a: *Bondestenalderen*. Sesams Danmarkshistorie, Stenalderen 2. Copenhagen.

Nielsen, P.O. 1981b: Hundredtusind fortidsminder. Om den arkæologiske kortlægning i Danmark siden 1807. *Nationalmuseets Arbejdsmark* 1981, pp. 61-69.

Nielsen, P.O. 1984: Flint axes and megaliths – the time and context of the early dolmens in Denmark. In: G. Burenhult (ed.): *The Archaeology of Carrowmore. Theses and Papers in North-European Archaeology* 14. Stockholm, pp. 376-387.

Nielsen, P.O. 2004: Causewayed camps, palisade enclosures and central settlements of the Middle Neolithic in Denmark. *Journal of Nordic Archaeological Science* 14. Stockholm, pp. 19-33.

Noble, G. 2006: *Neolithic Scotland. Timber, Stone, Earth and Fire*. Edinburgh.

Noe-Nygaard, A. 1984: nr. De "kløvede" sten i megalitanlæggene. *Naturens Verden* 1984, 5/6, pp. 187-190.

Nordman, C.A. 1918: *Jættestuer i Danmark. Nya Fynd*. Copenhagen.

Nordman, C.A. 1935. *The megalithic Culture of Northern Europe*. Helsinki.

Nørregård-Nielsen, H.E. 2004: *Undervejs med J. Th. Lundbye*. Copenhagen.

Nørregård-Nielsen, H.E. 2013: Grundende på den resignation. In: B. Bramming & E. Rocca (eds.): *Længsel Lundbye og Kierkegaard*. Copenhagen, pp. 21-96.

O'Brien, W. 1999: *Sacred Ground. Megalithic tombs in coastal South-West Ireland*. Galway.

O'Kelly, C. 1969: Bryn Celli Ddu, Anglesey. *Archaeologia Cambrensis* 118, pp. 17-48.

O'Kelly, M.J. 1958: A wedge-shaped gallery-grave at Island, Co. Cork. *Journal of the Royal Society of Antiquaries of Ireland* 88, pp. 1-23.

O'Kelly, M.J. 1960: A wedge-shaped gallery grave at Baurnadomeeny, Co. Tipperary. *Journal of the Cork Historical and Archaeological Society* 65, pp. 85-115.

O'Kelly, M.J. 1982: *Newgrange. Archaeology, Art and Legend*. London.

O'Sullivan, M. 2005: *Duma na nGiall. The Mound of the Hostages, Tara*. Bray, Co Wicklow.

Pearson, M.P. 2012: *Stonehenge. Exploring the greatest stone age mystery*. London.

Petersen, E.B. 1974: Gravene ved Dragsholm. Fra jægere til bønder for 6000 år siden. *Nationalmuseets Arbejdsmark* 1974, pp. 112-120.

Petersen, E.B. & T. Egeberg 2007: Between Dragsholm I and II. In: L. Larsson, F. Lüth & T. Terberger (eds.): *Innovation and Continuity – Non-Megalithic Mortuary Practices in the Baltic*. Mainz, pp. 447-467.

Petersen, J.M. 1909: *Minder fra min Virksomhed paa Arkæologiens Omraade fra 1845 til 1908*. Copenhagen.

Pontoppidan, E. 1764 (1968): *Den Danske Atlas*. Tomus II. Copenhagen.

Pontoppidan, E. 1768 (1968): *Den Danske Atlas*. Tomus IV. Copenhagen.

Poulsen, K.L. 2001: Oldsagssamlinger på danske herregårde. *Kuml* 2001, pp. 71-110.

Raben, J. 1982: *Oldtidsminder på Als og Sundeved*. Sønderborg.

Raddatz, K. 1979: Zur Funktion der Grosssteingräber. In: H. Schirnig (ed.): *Grosssteingräber in Niedersachsen*. Hildesheim, pp. 127-141.

Randsborg, K. 1994: Ole Worm: An Essay of the Modernization of Antiquity. *Acta Archaeologica* 65, pp. 135-169.

Rasmussen, P., E. Bradshaw & N.H. Andersen 2002: Et nyt forskningsprojekt og et overraskende fund af laminerede søsedimenter. *Geologi – Nyt fra GEUS* 2, pp. 2-6.

Rasmussen, U. 2012: Lystrup Østergård. En værkstedsplads fra yngre stenalder. *Kuml* 2012, pp. 9-73.

Richards, C. 2004: Labouring with monuments: constructing the dolmen at Carreg Samson, south-west Wales. In: V. Cummings & C. Fowler (eds.): *The Neolithic of the Irish Sea. Materiality and traditions of practice*. Oxford, pp. 72-80.

Ritzau, M. 1987: Erkjendtlighedstegn. In: I. Nielsen (ed.): *Bevar din arv. 1937-Danmarks fortidsminder-1987*. Copenhagen, pp. 147-149.

le Roux, C.-T. 1984: L'implantation néolithique en Bretagne centrale. *Revue Archéologique de l'Ouest* 1, pp. 33-54.

le Rouzic, Z. 1914: Carnac. Restaurations faites dans la région. Dolmen à coupole et à galerie de l'Ile Longue. *Bulletin de la Société Polymathique du Morbihan* 1914, pp. 114-116.

le Rouzic, Z. 1932: *Carnac. Fouilles faites dans la Région. Tumulus du Mont Saint-Michel 1900, 1901, 1902, 1903, 1904, 1905 & 1906*. Vannes.

Rowlands, H. 1723: *Mona Antiqua Restaurata. An archaeological discourse on the antiquities, natural and historical, of the Isle of Anglesey, the ancient seat of the British Druids*. Dublin.

Rudebeck, E. 2002: Likt og olikt i de sydskandinaviska långhögarna. In: L. Larsson (ed.): *Monumentala gravformer i det äldsta bondesamhället*. Lund, pp. 119-146.

Rzepecki, S. 2011: *The roots of megalithism in the TRB Culture*. Lodz.

Rønne, P. 1979: Høj over høj. *Skalk* 1979 nr. 5, pp. 3-8.

Saville, A. 1990: *Hazleton North. The excavation of a Neolithic long cairn of the Cotswold-Severn group*, London.

Scarre, C. 2007: *The Megalithic Monuments of Britain and Ireland*. London.

Schröder, E.E.W.G. 1917: *Nias. Etnographische, Geographische en Historische Aanteekningen en Studien*. Leiden.

Schuldt, E. 1972: *Die mecklenburgischen Megalithgräber*. Berlin.

Sehested, F. 1878: *Fortidsminder og Oldsager fra Egnen om Broholm*. Copenhagen.

Service, A. & J. Bradbery 1993: *The standing stones of Europe. A guide to the great megalithic monuments*. London.

Skaarup, J. 1973: *Hesselø – Sølager. Jagdstationen der südskandinavischen Trichterbecherkultur*. Copenhagen.

Skaarup, J. 1985: *Yngre stenalder på øerne syd for Fyn*. Rudkøbing.

Steensberg, A. 1983: *Borups bønder*. Højbjerg.

Strömberg, M. 1968: *Der Dolmen Trollasten in St. Köpinge, Schonen*. Lund.

Strömberg, M. 1971: *Die Megalithgräber von Hagestad. Zur Problematik von Grabbauten und Grabriten*. Lund.

Stürup, B. 1966: En ny jordgrav fra tidlig-neolitisk tid. *Kuml* 1965, pp. 13-22.

Taruskin, R. 1996: *Stravinsky and the Russian Traditions*. Los Angeles.

Thorlacius, B. 1809: *Bemærkninger over de i Danmark endnu tilværende Hedenolds-Høie og Steensætninger*. Copenhagen.

Thorsen, S. 1981: "Klokkehøj" ved Bøjden. Et sydvestfynsk dyssekammer med velbevaret primærgrav. *Kuml* 1980, pp. 105-146.

Thorsen, S. 1984: Dysserne. Kæmpers værk. Nedrige altre. Oldheltenes grave. Arkæologiens smertensbørn. Eller de dødes huse? In: A. Bolvig & D. Mahler (eds.): *Fortid og Nutid*. Søllerød, pp. 29-38.

Thorvildsen, K. 1941: Dyssetidens Gravfund i Danmark. *Aarbøger for Nordisk Oldkyndighed og Historie* 1941, pp. 22-87.

Thorvildsen, K. 1985: Restaurering af megalitgrave. Gustav Rosenberg og Julius Raklev. *Fortidsminder. Antikvariske studier* 7, pp. 36-47.
Thrane, H. 1989: Siedlungsarchäologische Untersuchungen in Dänemark. *Praehistorische Zeitschrift* 64, pp. 5-47.
Tilley, C. 1994: *A Phenomenology of Landscape. Places, paths and monuments.* Oxford.
Turner, R.C. 1992: Pentre Ifan burial chamber, Pembrokeshire. The story of the first ancient monument in Wales. *Transactions of the Ancient Monuments Society* 36, pp. 99-118.
Vejlager, J. 1939: *Genforeningsmindesmærkernes historie.* Kolding.
Voss, O. 1963: Steneng. *Skalk* 1963 nr. 1, pp. 18-19.
Wahl, J., 2008: Profan oder kultisch – bestattet oder entsorgt? *Materialhefte zur Archäologie in Baden-Württemberg,* Heft 81/3, pp. 703-848.
Waterson, R. 2009: *The Living House. An Anthropology of Architecture in South-East Asia*. Singapore.
Whittle, A. 2004: Stones that float to the sky: portal dolmens and their landscapes of memory and myth. In: V. Cummings & C. Fowler (eds.): *The Neolithic of the Irish Sea. Materiality and traditions of practice.* Oxford, pp. 81-90.
Wivel, H. 2002: *Maja Lisa Engelhardt. En monografi*. Copenhagen.
Worm, O. 1643: *Danicorum Monumentorum libri sex*. Hafnia (Copenhagen).
Worm, O.: Præsteindberetninger, se F. Jørgensen 1970 og 1974.
Worsaae, J.J.A. 1843: *Danmarks Oldtid oplyst ved Oldsager og Gravhøie.* Copenhagen.

Image credits

Abbreviations:
MM: Moesgaard Museum
NHA: Niels H. Andersen
NM: Danish National Museum
PE: Palle Eriksen

Cover photo: Thomas Nykrog (Poskær Stenhus)

Title page: J.Th. Lundbye

Preface: P.V. Glob (Poskær Stenhus)

1.0: Excerpt from figure 1.3 – 1.1: Ole Woldbye, Thorvaldsen Museum. Oil on canvas, 67 x 89 cm – 1.2: Galerie Neue Meister, Albertinum, Dresden. Oil on canvas, 61 x 80 cm – 1.3: National Gallery of Denmark. Oil on canvas, 173 x 205.5 cm – 1.4: Peter Helles Eriksen – 1.5: PE – 1.6: Unknown – 1.7: Christiansborg, Social Democrat committee rooms. Acrylic on canvas, 230 x 244 cm.

2.0: Thomas Nykrog (Poskær Stenhus) – 2.1: PE – 2.2: John Jedbo – 2.3: After information board at Poskær Stenhus – 2.4: After Thorsen 1984.

3.0: MM (Passage dolmen at Tustrup) – 3.1: NM – 3.2: After M.A. Hansen 1952 – 3.3: John Jedbo –3.4: PE.

4.0: PE (Torup dolmen).

5.0: Peter Helles Eriksen (Vielsted dolmen) – 5.1: NM – 5.2: After Adamsen & Jensen 1998 – 5.3: NM – 5.4: After A.P. Madsen 1868 – 5.5: PE; Gustav Rosenberg; NHA – 5.6a: C.L. Vebæk – 5.6b: Hakon Berg, After S. Hansen 1993 – 5.7: Bo Lavindsgaard, Photo/Medialab, Moesgaard – 5.8a-b: NM – 5.8c: After A.P. Madsen 1868 – 5.9: PE – 5.10: After Sehested 1878 – 5.11: Lis Helles Olesen and Esben Schlosser Mauritsen – 5.12: NM – 5.13: After J. Jensen 2001, red line and Bornholm added – Box 2: After Schröder 1917.

6.0: PE (Ormstrup dolmen) – 6.1: NM – 6.2: NHA, coloured after Ebbesen 1990 – 6.3: After Berg 1956 – 6.4: Hakon Berg – 6.5: Hakon Berg, after Skaarup 1985 – 6.6: Jørgen Holm – 6.7: PE – 6.8: Lis Helles Olesen, after Eriksen 1980 – 6.9: Christian Aabo Jørgensen, after Eriksen 1980 – 6.10-11: After Gebauer 1990, red line added – 6.12: Air Base Karup – 6.13: PE – 6.14: NHA, redrawn after Holst 2006.

7.0: PE (Rønde dolmen) – 7.1-4: PE – 7.5: Jyderup local archive – 7.6: NM – 7.7-8: PE – 7.9: NM, secondarily coloured.

8.0: PE (Dolmen in Glumsø Østerskov) – 8.1 and 8.3: NM – 8.4: PE – 8.5 and 8.6a-b: NM – 8.6c: NHA.

9.0: PE (Lindeskov dolmen) – 9.1: After Stürup 1966 – 9.2: Lars Jørgensen, after Liversage 1983 – 9.3: Jørgen Kraglund and NHA – 9.4-5: NHA – 9.6: After J. Jensen 2001 – 9.7-8: David Liversage – 9.9: NM – 9.10a: Henning Nielsen, after Kjærum 1971 – 9.10b: Lone Andersen – 9.11: NHA, redrawn after Müller 1911 – 9.12: After Liversage 1992, P.O. Nielsen 1984, Becker 1960, Ethelberg 1994 and T. Madsen 1980 – 9.13: After P.O. Nielsen 1984 – 9.14: After Kjærum 1977.

10.0: PE (Langben Rises Høj) – 10.1: NHA – 10.2-4: PE – Boks 3: NM.

11.0: PE (Gunderslevholm dolmen) – 11.1: PE – 11.2-3: NM – 11.4: After A.P. Madsen 1868 – 11.5-6: NHA – 11.7: PE – 11.8-9: NHA – 11.10: After S.I. Hansen 2009a – 11.11: Tim Grønnegaard, after S.I. Hansen 2009a – 11.12: Jørgen Kraglund.

12.0: Birgitte Fløe Jensen (Kjallesten) – 12.1: NM – 12.2: NHA – 12.3-4: NM – 12.5: PE – 12.6: NM – 12.7: NHA – 12.8: NM – 12.9: NHA – 12.10: NM – 12.11: Jørgen Kraglund – 12.12: After Sehested 1878.

13.0: Tom Christensen (Videdysse) – 13.1: PE – 13.2: After Worm 1643 – 13.3: After Pontoppidan 1764 – 13.4: NM – 13.5: PE – 13.6: NM – 13.7: After Münter 1805.

14.0-1: PE – 14.2: NM – 14.3: NHA – 14.4: PE – 14.5: NM – 14.6: NHA – 14.7: Jørgen Kraglund.

15.0: PE (Ormslev dolmen) – 15.1: Private ownership – 15.2: Eigil Nikolajsen – 15.3: NM – 15.4: Historical Museum at Lund University – 15.5: After Strömberg 1968 – 15.6: Historical Museum at Lund University – 15.7: PE – 15.8: After N. Nielsen 2003 – 15.9: Torsten Madsen – 15.10: Jørgen Skaarup – 15.11: Jørgen Holm and Jørgen Skaarup, after Skaarup 1985 – 15.12: PE.

16.0: Børge Venge – 16.1: Lis Helles Olesen – 16.2: PE – 16.3: NHA, redrawn after plan by Poul Kjærum – 16.4-6: Poul Kjærum.

17.0: Poul Kjærum – 17.1: NHA, redrawn after plan and section by Poul Kjærum – 17.2-5: Poul Kjærum – 17.6: Hans Berg – 17.7: Poul Kjærum – 17.8: NHA, redrawn after section by Poul Kjærum – 17.9: Jørgen Kraglund.

18.0: Chris Scarre (Pentre Ifan) – 18.1: After Archaeologia Cambrensis 1865 – 18.2: After Grimes 1948 – 18.3: After Archaeologia Cambrensis 1847 – 18.4: Chris Scarre – 18.5: After Burenhult 1980 – 18.6: After O'Sullivan 2005 – 18.7: Chris Scarre – 18.8: After information fra Galles 1864 – 18.9: Kate Sharpe.

19.0: PE (Carrickglass, Irland) – 19.1: John Jedbo – 19.2: PE – 19.3: Unknown – 19.4: Torben Dehn – 19.5: NM – 19.6: After Antikvariske Annaler 1842-43 – 19.7: NM – Box 5: Ron Adams – Box 6: NHA (the first photo) and Jens Vedel.

20.0: NHA (Sarup Gamle Skole I) – 20.1-2: NHA – 20.4: Louise Hilmar – 20.5: NHA – 20.6: Jørgen Kraglund – 20.7-8: NHA – 20.9 (drawing): NHA – 20.9 (photos): Bo Lavindsgaard, Photo/Medialab, Moesgaard – 20.10: Jørgen Kraglund – 20.11-13: NHA.

21.0 NM (Grøfte) – 21.1: NM – 21.2-3: After Thorsen 1980, though with later colouring – 21.4: NM, after Kaul 1998 – 21.5-6: NM – 21.7: After Becker 1960 – 21.8: After A.P. Madsen 1896 – 21.9: After Mischka 2011 – 21.10: Jørgen Skaarup – 21.11: After Gidlöf et al. 2006 – 21.12: After Burenhult 1973, though with later colouring – 21.13: NM – 21.14: Preben Dehlholm – 21.15: Res Eichenberger, Museum für Urgeschichte, Amt für Kultur des Kantons Zug – 21.16: After Schröder 1917.

22.0: PE (Troldkirken) – 22.1: Benny Staal.

Site index

The 7-9 digit number given after many of the names below is the respective monument's unique Danish scheduled ancient monument number, its *F&F* number, in the Danish Sites and Monuments database, see box 1 "Guide to dolmens" on page 25.